MIDNIGHT MARQUEE ACTORS SERIES

VINCENT PRICE

MIDNIGHT MARQUEE ACTORS SERIES
VINCENT PRICE

Edited by Gary J. Svehla
and Susan Svehla

Midnight Marquee Press, Inc.
Baltimore, Maryland

ISBN 1-887664-21-1
Library of Congress Catalog Card Number 98-65676
Manufactured in the United States of America
Printed by Kirby Lithographic Company, Arlington, VA
First Printing by Midnight Marquee Press, Inc., October 1998

Acknowledgments: John Antosiewicz Photo Archives, Betty Cavanaugh, Lawrence French, Jerry Ohlingers Movie Material, Eric Hoffman, Don Leifert, Photofest, Michael H. Price, Linda J. Walter, Tom Weaver

I really find the revelation of people's personal life, unless it has to do with their art, to be boring.   When they [biographies] have to do with people's art, then they're interesting.

—Vincent Price

For Vincent Price

TABLE OF CONTENTS

TABLE OF CONTENTS

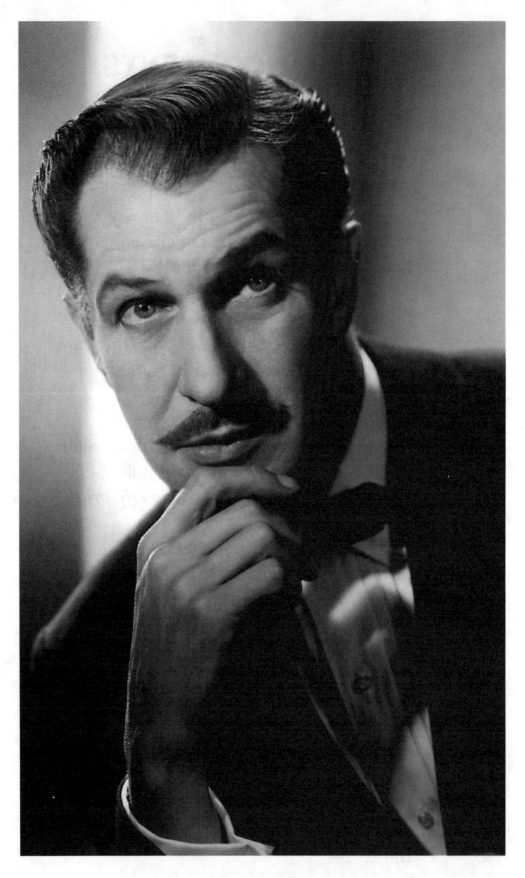

INTRODUCTION

For the fourth installment in the Midnight Marquee Actors Series, we have decided to profile Vincent Price, the actor considered to be the horror film icon for the baby boomer generation. Mr. Price produced his most significant work during the decades of the 1950s and the 1960s—seminal films such as *House of Wax, House on Haunted Hill, The Tingler, The Fall of the House of Usher, Pit and the Pendulum, The Masque of the Red Death* and *The Tomb of Ligeia*.

Interestingly enough, Vincent Price began his film career in the late 1930s by starring or co-starring in several films at Universal, the preeminent studio of golden age horror. Although most of Price's Universal movies were not true horror movies (*Tower of London* and *The House of the Seven Gables*), there was one exception: *The Invisible Man Returns*. It would be the American-International Pictures/Edgar Allan Poe connection two decades later that would establish Price's contributions to the horror genre. There he would star portraying morally disintegrating characters who were both obsessed and haunted by their ancestral past. Vincent Price was a star before the AIP pictures, but these movies forever cemented his fame.

Unlike Bela Lugosi who died in 1956 or Boris Karloff who died in 1969, Vincent Price was in his prime during the 1960s and 1970s and he frequently appeared on television and in the theater. After theatrical performances he always allowed time to meet and greet his fans in his dressing room. It was after watching a production of *Charley's Aunt* in Delaware during the 1970s that I first met Vincent Price and had him autograph my color photograph from *Theater of Blood* (his co-star, the late Roddy McDowall, also graciously signed autographs). A few years later in Baltimore, after seeing Price perform his one-man production as Oscar Wilde in *Diversions and Delights* at the Morris Mechanic Theater, I was one of a handful of fans who, afterward, scurried up the stairs to Price's dressing room to spend about 10 minutes with the legend who appeared wearing his bath robe, having just removed his makeup. Even though Vincent Price appeared to be casually dropping by to chat with fans, in all reality he was still performing, running off one-liners and making hilarious comments to those assembled about stealing people's pens and making the right selection in toupees. Attentive and friendly to each person assembled, Price made every one of us feel as though we were bantering about in each other's den or living room. Even two decades later, the glow has not yet faded from this experience.

It is interesting to note that Vincent Price, very outgoing and accommodating to his fans, nonetheless was still an immensely private man and little of his life outside the movies was ever revealed. *Midnight Marquee Actors Series: Vincent Price* focuses on the man as actor, both within films and beyond, and our purpose is to illuminate his professional and public life, not pry into his private life.

By rounding up the usual suspects—our writing staff extraordinaire—to cover all the important Vincent Price performances, the intent of this work is to create a chronological profile of Vincent Price, actor and cinematic icon. Chapters have been augmented by sections from two lengthy interviews that writer Lawrence French conducted with Price during the 1970s and 1980s (excerpts from which appeared in truncated format in a few genre magazines), so the volume contains writers' subjective views of Price's performances alongside Price's own reflections of what it was like making the movies being discussed. As with the entries in the first three published Actors Series, we do not try to be definitive by covering every movie made, but by selecting the most influential ones from every era, we hope to offer the most complete and balanced portrait yet of Vincent Price the performer and the professional.

Gary J. Svehla
October, 1998

ALL THE WORLD'S A STAGE

The following is from interviews conducted by author/historian Lawrence French with Vincent Price in Westport, Connecticut in 1979 and in San Francisco, California in 1985.

VINCENT PRICE: I went to Yale University, in New Haven, Connecticut and after I graduated from Yale, I taught school for a year. Then, I had that extraordinary experience of finding out that I knew nothing. Those little kids that I was teaching knew a lot more than I did. So I went to get my master's degree at the University of London, and there I fell in love with the theater, which was very easy to do in England, particularly at that time (1934), because it was very cheap. You could go and see any play, or any concert for 50 cents. I started in a little theater, called the Gate Theater. It was a private experimental theater and there I first did *Victoria Regina*, which was a great success, but in a tiny little theater, that only held 100 people. Then, when (producer) Gilbert Miller brought *Victoria Regina*, to do in New York with Helen Hayes, I came along with the sets (laughter). I played in it for three years, starting the day after Christmas in 1935. It was a very exciting experience, to be the leading man to the number one actress in America, at the time.

LAWRENCE FRENCH: Helen Hayes was a very important person in your early career, wasn't she?

VINCENT PRICE: Yes, I really owe so much to Helen. I had a wonderful experience with her. When we did *Victoria Regina*, she was 35 years old, and I was 23. She really could have made it very tough for me. You know, as a young man coming in and doing his first play on Broadway, with the top star of the day. But she was so marvelous to me! I don't think she is America's greatest actress, but I do think she is one of the kindest people I've ever met in my life. Really, *Victoria Regina* was the very peak of her career. She was wonderful in it, just wonderful. At the time, Helen had already been on the stage for 25 years, since the age of 10! It was the first play ever reviewed in *Life* magazine. Somebody gave me that review the other day, and I was so amazed to find out that this production cost $75,000! To produce the whole play. You couldn't buy the costumes today for $75,000! It had 11 scenes, and I mean scenes. There was Balmoral Castle, Buckingham Palace, Windsor Castle. It was a great production, really unbelievable.

Following is Vincent Price's biography, as it appeared in the original 1936 program for *Victoria Regina*:

Vincent Price's appearance as leading man to Helen Hayes marks his professional as well as his American debut on the stage. This extraordinary circumstance is due to the fact that although Mr. Price has had stage aspirations since he was ten years old, he was forced to earn his living as a schoolmaster until mere chance decreed otherwise. He was studying the history of German art at the Courtauld Institute in London when a friend took him to London's Gate Theater, where casting of Maurine Watkins' *Chicago* was in process. American accents being at a premium, Mr. Price was thrust into the production and found himself doubling as a burly policeman and a venerable judge. His remarkable resemblance to Prince Albert led to his being offered the important role of the Price Consort in the ensuing production of *Victoria Regina*. He received glowing notices and was subsequently signed by Gilbert Miller for the American production.

Helen Hayes and Vincent Price starred in *Victoria Regina*. (Photofest)

LAWRENCE FRENCH: When you started out in the 1930s, did you ever take any acting lessons?

VINCENT PRICE: I don't think you can teach acting, really. The only thing you can do is act. But during the '30s, Stanislavsky and the Moscow art theater were really a big influence, especially on the Group Theater, so one time I started to take some lessons and one night I started to play my part in *Victoria Regina* in a more emotional way. After the first act Helen Hayes stopped me in my dressing room and said, "What's come over you? Who do you think you're playing, the Russian Czar?" So that was the end of my 'method' acting. You know, you read so much about 'method actors' and how they live their parts. My God, if I ever lived some of the parts that I've played! (laughter) It's really a lot of nonsense. I remember doing a comedy show on TV with Dennis Hopper. He was a method actor, but he had the kookiest method I've ever known. The director was waiting to rehearse a scene with Dennis and myself. Well, Dennis was out around the set spinning around, like a top, and he came up to me, and he could hardly stand up, so I said, "Dennis what are you doing?" He said, "I'm playing a drunk," and I said, "Yes, but drunks try to stand up straight! They don't want to fall over." So every actor has his own way of preparing for a part. On *Victoria Regina*, when I played Prince Albert, I discovered that Albert, who was a German Prince, never really learned to think in English. He didn't like the English very much, and they didn't like him. He always thought in German, so I translated the whole part, and learned it in German, then learned it in English, but I thought in German. That was a method of preparation, a kind of reality I could give myself. You need every crutch you can get, and all actors have them. A very famous character actor, Edward Arnold, laughed after every line he said. He had one of these great laughs, and people adored it, but the truth of the matter was that he couldn't remember his lines! (laughter).

LAWRENCE FRENCH: What do you think motivates people into becoming actors?

VINCENT PRICE: That's a good question, and it's something that I think should be written about. I've come to the conclusion that an awful lot of actors are hiding from a self that they want to go away, basically. If you think about it, almost everybody I've ever talked to in my life, has thought about becoming an actor, but they don't do it, because of family, or friends, or many other reasons. But basically the actors I've known, and I've known almost every actor in the business, one way or another, they are people who feel that in acting they are getting away from a self that is maybe boring to them, or somebody they don't want, or else someone they'd like to forget, by playing someone else. I don't mean that they're escaping. It's just a chance at having a double personality. It's really great fun.

LAWRENCE FRENCH: Let's talk about your long friendship with Boris Karloff. You worked with him quite a few times, didn't you?

VINCENT PRICE: Yes, I worked with him right from the beginning of my career, up through both of our careers. I think one of the extraordinary things about Boris was his gratitude for *Frankenstein*. It was something that plagued him all his life, as a good part plagues every actor, but he was so grateful for it, because it gave him enormous fame. He knew he had gotten stuck on something, but he had a great pride in it.

LAWRENCE FRENCH: John Carradine said Boris bitterly regretted being typecast as a horror star, even though he never admitted it.

VINCENT PRICE: But he wasn't! He didn't just play Frankenstein's monster. I saw him play the inquisitor in Jean Anouilh's *The Lark* on Broadway, and he was wonderful. Then he did that whole series on TV, *Colonel March of Scotland Yard*, where he played a detective. He had a lot of variety. He was playing macabre things, but Boris was a very peculiar looking man. He had that funny voice, and a strange complexion, you know, green skin. Of course in Hollywood everyone is typecast. Look at Robert De Niro and poor Al Pacino. Robert Redford is just typecast as himself all the time. Everybody is because Hollywood has no imagination. If you make money at one thing, they don't want you to do anything else. I've been very lucky, because I had a big career in television doing very different kinds of things. I worked with all of the great comics: Carol Burnett, Lucille Ball, Milton Berle, Jack Benny. I did 25 shows with Red Skelton. I made fun of myself by doing send-ups of the kinds of films I was making, and those shows were all very funny.

Margaret Lindsay and Vincent Price star in *The House of the Seven Gables*. (Photofest)

THE HOUSE OF
THE SEVEN GABLES (1940)
by Gary J. Svehla

The House of the Seven Gables features Vincent Price billed third, listed in the credits behind George Sanders and Margaret Lindsay, but his role is definitely a starring one, his appearances becoming scant only during the middle third of the film when he is sentenced to life in prison. This 1940 Gothic melodrama is a different sort of Universal Picture, darkly moody with hints of ghosts and family curses, but a Universal production that seems mainstream and star-studded. It's an A production, appealing to an adult audience, that takes its literary (Nathaniel Hawthorne) roots very seriously. While Vincent Price was near the beginning of his cinematic acting career, his virtual dual role (as both the young, enthusiastic puppy Clifford and, when released from prison 20 years later, as the older, lower-energy and more resolute hound Clifford) allowed the young thespian the latitude to portray two different extremes of the same human being, a challenge for any actor. And Vincent Price, even though he hadn't developed all the idiosyncratic flourishes with which we associate him, creates a memorable performance of depth and resonance, one that belies his lack of experience.

The film begins by recounting the Pyncheon family curse, founded in the middle of the 17th century, whereby a Colonel Pyncheon, a leader of the Colonial Government, stole a valuable piece of land from its owner Matthew Maule by accusing him of practicing witchcraft. Maule, condemned and sentenced to hang, cries from the scaffold, "God hath given him blood to drink," and with these words the Curse is born. Pyncheon defiantly builds his mansion—Seven Gables—on the dead man's ground, but on the very day of the house's completion, Pyncheon is found dead in his library, blood trickling from his mouth. "Maule's Curse" still dwells with the Pyncheon family 160 years later, in September of 1828, when the movie begins.

The early sequences of the film, contrasting the flamboyant and animated composer Clifford (Vincent Price) against brooding brother Jaffrey (George Sanders), the more sedate and aristocratically stuffy of the two, becomes the dramatic high point of the movie. Price, who was to culture a low-octave resonating voice, here in these scenes of youthful exuberance relies more on high tones and shrill declarations. Later, in the sequences where Clifford is released from prison, his enthusiasm and energy tamed, his voice speaks as a quiet whisper, and while its timber does not quite resonate with those deep, bellowing tones, his voice is slower, more fragile, and deeper nonetheless. Quite an interesting performance all way round, but his sibling rivalry with Sanders creates real tension. Career minded brother Jaffrey, a lawyer, is called home to Seven Gables by his father and seems more than a little annoyed. "I was in the midst of my first important case. Young lawyers don't find cases growing on trees in Boston these days, even if they have made excellent reputations for themselves," the arrogant brother tells cousin Hepzibah Pyncheon (Margaret Lindsay). Jaffrey hears the tones of the family harpsichord and brother Clifford singing at the keyboard. Excitedly Hepzibah announces Jaffrey will be proud of his brother, but he simply groans, "I'll forgo the pride if only I'm spared the noise!" Clifford smiles and excitedly declares, "Why, if it isn't the pride of the Pyncheons! Welcome home." Jaffrey, maintaining complete composure, barely acknowledges the brother he hasn't seen in years. "Same old Jaff—been away two years and all you can manage is 'good evening'," Clifford honestly declares.

For the recent past Jaffrey has been the focus of the family, because of his escalating law career, but Clifford declares with pride to his brother, "You know, Jaff, you're no longer the only success in the family. I've sold a composition, quite a remarkable piece of music... shall I play it for you?" Jaff sputters, caught off guard, and tries to come up with any reason *not* to hear his enthusiastic brother perform. "Yes, my legal colleagues will be most impressed. My brother, a musician, a Gypsy," Jaffrey replies. Clifford classifies Boston, where Jaffrey lives, as provincial, literally becoming a symbol of the old-world culture and aristocracy that the brother represents. But Clifford declares, "It's New York for me, old fellow," the evolving haven for artists and a city alive with vitality and energy, a description that equally describes Clifford himself.

When father Gerald Pyncheon (Gilbert Emery) returns, he asks to see Jaffrey privately in his study, but in the midst of a somber conversation, the effervescent Clifford dashes in and announces, "...decision has been made... we are selling the house tomorrow!" Jaffrey's jaw drops as he bellows, "Selling Seven Gables, that's impossible... it can't be done without my consent!" Then brother Clifford offers his side: "Why not, for the past two years you and father have been investing the family fortune, without my consent! You succeeded in bankrupting us. That money was mine, as well as yours, but nobody bothered to get my consent!" Clifford, delivering what normally might have been a an angry speech, still remains quite pleasant and smiling, yet he stands erect and speaks forcefully. Clifford goes on to state the obvious, that the creditors will take the house whether it is sold or not. Jaffrey then speaks of family tradition, but Clifford counters with, "As a student of law, Jaffrey, you must know the bankruptcy court does not accept family tradition as legal tender!" "Do you not have any respect for the name you bear," Jaffrey shouts, but Clifford recounts the ugly family traditions, every one a skeleton in the closet, beginning with their great, great grandfather who had Matthew Maule executed in order to steal his land. "Hail to thee, guiding spirit," Clifford deadpans to his brother. Soon, in ironic intensity, Clifford relates the history of all their ancestors, pointing at their formal hanging portraits before him, raising his voice but his face framed by a bitter smile: "I fairly burst with pride!" Relating the story of one scoundrel after another, Clifford's voice is almost hysterical as he rants, "By all means, let us sacrifice ourselves to such traditions!" Finally, Jaffrey interrupts by declaring, "You go too far, Sir," to which Clifford states, "I'm going as far as the sale price of this mausoleum will carry me, away from its rotting walls and decaying memories!" In a rage Jaffrey declares, "This house will never be sacrificed. I'll take the matter to court... The world will know of this father!" To which Gerald replies, "The world already knows too much." Distressed by the bickering occurring between two brothers arguing over property and reputation, the father has to literally hold the two boys apart. "What a pity men must inherit their ancestors' ignorance instead of their wisdom," Clifford barks the parting words, still a smile on his face. This sequence, ablaze with frustration, bitterness and family history, brims over with Vincent Price's passion and pleas. Here the young Price catches the audience's attention with his staccato delivery, overwhelming the more subdued George Sanders performance.

Hepzibah, in love with Clifford, is saddened by the rift between the brothers, and mentions that Clifford's father asked her to speak to him. "A clean wound heals much more quickly," referring to the simple fact that he had to speak the truth. "He shan't use petticoats as weapons," he says, but soon, melting to Hepzibah's charms, he apologizes; however, Hepzibah responds that she loves Clifford because of his courage and sense of justice. She agrees it is best that the house be sold. Clifford looks forward to moving with Hepzibah to New York City: "People there have vitality, they look ahead, not backward. We'll leave the dirges behind us... there's music in those people!"

The reason Jaffrey does not wish to sell Seven Gables is made clear later that night as he, borrowing a key, opens and shuffles through the contents of a trunk at two a.m., looking for the fabled Pyncheon Land Grant that deems one million acres of the state of Maine belongs to the Pyncheons. He declares that finding such a grant, most likely buried and hidden in the walls of the house, "will mean millions for us... help me, work with me—we'll tear the house down, board by board, until we find it." But Clifford does not believe in those rumors: "You fool, there's nothing to find." Clifford does not believe in Maule's Curse either. Instead he describes the Pyncheon Curse as comprising "greed, willful inhuman selfishness, the combination of high blood pressure and thin-veined aristocracy... They're haunted by conscience, not by the calcified bones of old Matthew Maule." Clifford disregards the past, all curses, all traditions, all

Hepzibah tries to break up the battling brothers, Jaffrey (George Sanders) and Clifford. (Photofest)

blighted ancestry, all rumors; instead, he thinks of the future, a new home in a new city, people who live in the present and do not dwell exclusively in the past.

However, by the next morning Jaffrey has already managed to change his father's mind about the sale of the house. By suggesting that the few bonds remaining could be invested in less secure but more profitable avenues, Gerald Pyncheon now agrees that it is "unthinkable that the Pyncheon birthright should be put upon the auction block." Clifford solemnly reminds his father of the promise he made to him. But father, now working himself up to a rage, declares, "As long as I am alive, I am the head of this house and it shall not be sold!" Then continuing his angry and emotional outburst, he screams, "...your conduct has brought us nothing but shame, disgraceful scenes in public... you have humiliated me beyond all existence. Now I command you to leave this house at once. You're no longer my son!" To which Clifford calmly replies, "That's the easiest way to get out of a promise!" However, the father soon clutches his throat, stumbles and falls to the floor cracking open his head, and dies with a trickle of blood dripping from his mouth. Immediately Jaffrey enters, and knowing differently, accuses his brother of murdering his father, realizing this is the only way he can have the house for himself.

Manipulating the jury, Jaffrey has them convinced of Clifford's guilt so completely that they do not even have to deliberate but agree to the guilty verdict immediately. Before he is taken away, Clifford gives an impassioned speech, one of Price's best moments during the entire film. Starting out calm and controlled, by the speech's end, Price has worked himself up to a hysterical rave which ends with the laughter of a madman. "More than any living soul, he knows that I am innocent. It is because your lie is so great, so infamous, that decent human beings cannot believe it is a lie. You sacrificed everything that is decent... honorable. You've used the most degenerate means to achieve your ends. You have the house. With it, you have

Clifford returns home to Hepzibah after 20 years in prison. (Photofest)

inherited the Pyncheon traditions... may you also inherit Maule's Curse. God has given you blood to drink!"

However, as Clifford is sentenced to life in prison for his crimes, in an ironic twist it is revealed that Gerald Pyncheon's will leaves the house solely to Hepzibah, that insurance covers all the household debt, and that she will inherit $400 per year for life. As it is now her time to crow, she throws Jaffrey out of the house declaring: "No crime has been as nakedly shameless as yours! You destroyed your brother for it, a joyous, loving human being. You exchanged him for rotting timbers, depraved dreams of gold... I'll pray for a long life... You'll never get it!" In the days to come, the bitter but vital young woman closes the windows and shutters to the world for the next 20 years, becoming transformed into a spinsterish and sexless recluse who lives alone, angry that the great joy in her life has been taken away forever!

But everything changes in the next 20 years as Clifford Pyncheon solemnly serves his time in prison, for a few brief days sharing his jail cell with an impassioned young man, very much like he used to be— Matthew Holgrave (Dick Foran)—an abolitionist who fights to politically free the slaves by any means possible and grant them their freedom. Holgrave claims he has been sentenced to 10 days in prison because the judge and jury made up their minds about his guilt even before hearing his case (similar to Pyncheon's own legal woes). Clifford introduces himself, but Matthew Holgrave declares that his real name is Maule, that he is the direct descendant of the man who started the Maule Curse. But Pyncheon only laughs and extends his hand in friendship.

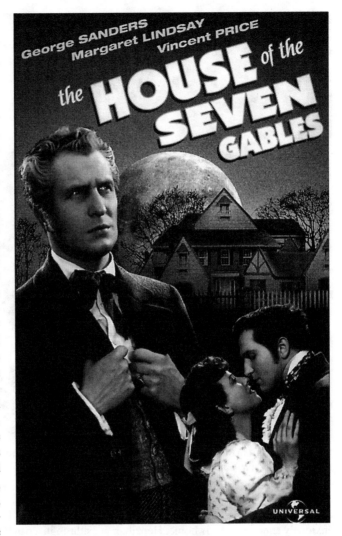

Meanwhile back at the house, Hepzibah receives news that a distant relative has died and that her young daughter, Phoebe Pyncheon (Nan Grey), having no place to go, is coming to live with her. In a sense Hepzibah has grown so secure in her insulated, private world that the entrance of another human being must be at least disconcerting, if not downright terrifying. But it is a way for Hepzibah to reach out one more time to humankind and to become part of human society again. In order to make ends meet, Hepzibah has taken in a boarder, none other than Matthew Holgrave himself, and with the arrival of Phoebe, she converts her front parlor into a Cent Shop that Phoebe is delighted to be able to help run, to earn her keep. However, the still nasty Jaffrey, now a judge, is insulted by what Hepzibah has done to the ancestral home. "First you allow this house to deteriorate into a village slum, then you turn it into a lodging house, and now this... a huckster's enterprise. I'll not permit such a blot on our name... this shop will be closed... I'll request the courts to issue a restraining order!" However, after much work with family friend (perhaps her only friend during her period of isolation) and lawyer Mr. Barton (Cecil Kellaway), the new governor has commuted Clifford's sentence and he too will be coming home shortly.

Hepzibah, instead of registering great joy with the announcement of the return of Clifford, instead remains indifferent declaring even though his room has always been ready for his return, she will not meet him at the prison doors, instead she will act as though Clifford is returning from a brief journey. Meanwhile, as Phoebe and Matthew are falling in love, Hepzibah seems to dread the return of her beloved.

The night of his return, Clifford slowly walks toward Seven Gables, and finding the front door unlocked (purposely left open by Hepzibah), he goes inside. Clifford's face is now tired

In *The House of the Seven Gables*, Vincent Price, a young man and a young talent, only hints at the rich, fulfilling characterizations yet to come.

and worn, filled with concern, lacking the old energy as he looks around his home. As Phoebe anxiously announces he is home, Hepzibah goes through a trunk and holds up her old dress that Clifford loved so much, but she stuffs it back into the trunk, sadness in her face. In a parallel sequence, Clifford looks through his old clothes, finding them tattered and filled with holes, and looking in a mirror, for the first time he sees the ravages of 20 years of harsh prison life on his face. Strangely, Hepzibah does not approach Clifford the entire evening of his return.

The next morning, preparing breakfast, Hepzibah tells Phoebe that Clifford must see her youthful beauty first, that the vision of her will please him—"the golden sunlight of your hair will warm his heart." But the smiling Phoebe declares, "He'll find you as lovely as ever." With these words Clifford enters, stiffly and awkwardly, but within seconds of seeing the love of his life, the old youthful radiance and charm returns. Hepzibah, fearfully thinking 20 years apart may have dimmed their magnetism toward one another, is concerned that they will not be able to pick up where they left off. But Clifford's words melt her heart. "I want to look at you... let my eyes be your mirror... in them your beauty will never fade... time only makes more beautiful a heart such as yours... how can I ever make known to you, my gratitude, my humility before such a loyalty and a courage... smile!" She cries and runs to Clifford's outstretched arms: "It's not too late for us... the past will be yet a shadowy memory."

By the movie's end, Clifford offers to hand over the house if Jaffrey signs a paper admitting he was in error, that he made a mistake in accusing his brother of the murder of their father. After signing the paper, Jaffrey's throat tightens and he falls to the floor dead, blood trickling from the corners of his mouth. Then in a double marriage ceremony, both Phoebe and Matthew and Clifford and Hepzibah are married and ride off in their carriage to enjoy their honeymoon and new life, a "For Sale" sign hanging over Seven Gables.

Vincent Price shines as the romantic lead, playing both youthful exuberance and maturing commitment. His portrayal of Clifford Pyncheon is multi-layered, becoming a symbol of the future living amidst rotting timbers of the past. His only wish is to sell his ancestral home, constructed on the soiled ground of the unfairly executed, living in the shadows of ancestors vile and evil, occupying a cursed house of hidden skeletons and shame. His vision is to become a music composer and move to a youthful, vital, growing urban center, New York City, and then carve out a new life for himself, not a life depending upon his family fortune nor name, but a life created anew out of his passion and talent for creating music today. He is a man unfairly condemned and sentenced to rot away in prison, much like Seven Gables has rotted away from the sins of its past, but Clifford's pure heart and love for a special woman persevere and energize him, allowing their relationship to immediately restore the passion and love within Hepzibah whose soul and feelings have lain dormant for 20 odd years, awaiting either her own death or the seemingly impossible return of her lover (but she must live long enough to deny Jaffrey ownership of Seven Gables).

Surprisingly, after such a strong performance, Vincent Price was mostly relegated to supporting roles during the bulk of the 1940s, after an impressive starring performance here in 1940. However, after fine-tuning his talents and honing his skills, by the 1950s Price was once again ready to demand and win starring billing and characters worth his considerable talent. But here in *The House of the Seven Gables*, Vincent Price, a young man and a young talent, only hints at the rich, fulfilling characterizations yet to come. If Price here hasn't yet mastered his easily recognized style, he has certainly tapped into a well of energy and vivacity and made his character one well worth remembering.

CREDITS: Associate Producer: Burt Kelly; Director: Joe May; Screenplay: Lester Cole; Adaptation: Harold Greene (Based on the Novel by Nathaniel Hawthorne); Cinematography: Milton Krasner; Art Director: Jack Otterson: Set Decorator: R.A. Gausman; Musical Score: Frank Skinner; Musical Director: Charles Previn; Editor: Frank Gross; Gowns: Vera West; Running Time: 89 minutes; released 1940 by Universal

CAST: George Sanders (Jaffrey Pyncheon); Margaret Lindsay (Hepzibah Pyncheon); Vincent Price (Clifford Pyncheon); Dick Foran (Matthew Holgrave); Nan Grey (Phoebe Pyncheon); Cecil Kellaway (Philip Barton); Alan Napier (Mr. Fuller); Gilbert Emery (Gerald Pyncheon); Miles Mander (Deacon Arnold Foster); Charles Trowbridge (Judge); Edgar Norton (Phineas Weed); Harry Woods (Wainwright); Harry Cording (Blacksmith Hawkins); Michael Mark (Man)

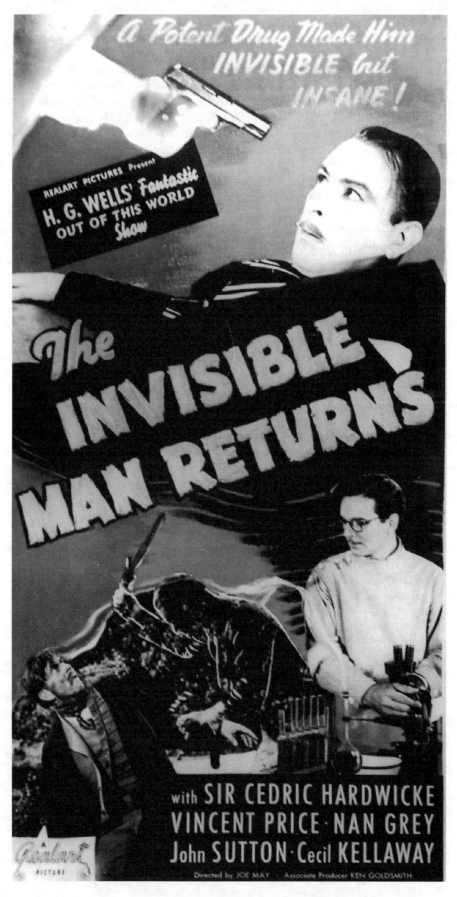

THE INVISIBLE MAN RETURNS (1940)

by Gary J. Svehla

Universal's 1940 release, *The Invisible Man Returns*, features most of the same cast (Vincent Price, Nan Grey, Cecil Kellaway, Alan Napier) and same director (Joe May) as Universal's same year release, *The House of the Seven Gables*. However, *The Invisible Man Returns* is mediocre, showcasing a simplistic (and predictable) plot that only reminds viewers just how much better James Whale's original 1933 movie was. However, the B programmer does feature Vincent Price in an early performance, one that is not as memorable nor as demanding as his performance as Clifford Pyncheon in *The House of the Seven Gables*, but a role that showcased Price's voice (not having yet acquired the deep, resonant timber with which we associate the actor) for he is either invisible or partially visible/bandaged for the duration of the movie. Only in the final sequence of the film do we finally see Vincent Price's face.

As the camera approaches Radcliffe Manor, shrouded in dense fog at night, the household is quietly awaiting word that the life of young Geoffrey Radcliffe can still be saved (he is awaiting his execution in prison for murdering his brother Michael). Helen Manson (Nan Grey), Geoffrey's fiancée, wearing black, sits alone on the couch, looking sad, only moving to glance out the huge living room windows. Richard Cobb (Sir Cedric Hardwicke) wants her to have tea, but she'd rather just await any good news. Dr. Griffin enters (brother of the late, original Invisible Man) to offer support to Helen. Cobb apologetically announces he's spoken to dozens of old friends, influential people, but nothing can be done.

However, Griffin does make one last frantic visit to the prison, and at one last request of Geoffrey, the doctor is allowed a 10-minute visit with the prisoner before the execution. After a half hour passes, one prison guard comes running out of the cell yelling "he's gone," telling his strange story to prison authorities. The prison guard states he never took his eyes off Radcliffe for even one second, as they were all playing cards and talking about the weather. Radcliffe went to use the sink, but while he was drying his hands, he seemingly vanished, a pile of his clothes left behind in the far corner of the cell. The guard proclaims, "He vanished into thin air!" However, in the foggy moors, branches of trees and bushes are disrupted, pulled aside, indicating the obvious presence of you know who.

Richard Cobb approaches the taciturn Frank Griffin, informing the good doctor that Geoffrey has escaped from prison, "the noose practically around his neck!" Strangely, Helen also disappeared this morning and hasn't been seen since. Cobb puts two and two together and realizes that Helen is with Geoffrey, but he is worried that with the police in hot pursuit, both of them may be injured or killed. "You wouldn't be working here as calmly as you are unless you knew where they were," Cobb comments, but Griffin reveals nothing. "It's obvious you know where they are," and since neither has money, Cobb wants to offer whatever assistance he can, if only Griffin would reveal their whereabouts. "I'm sorry," the faithful doctor utters.

The Radcliffes own and operate the coal mining operation which employs the majority of the local citizens, and Mr. Spears (Alan Napier), former watchman now superintendent, tries to get the men to return to work, their concern going out for the safe return of beloved Geoffrey. Inspector Sampson (Cecil Kellaway) from Scotland Yard visits Griffin, having done his homework and realizing the doctor might be involved with the convicted man's escape from jail. "What can you do for me, doctor," Sampson requests, and Griffin answers, "Very little, I'm afraid." Sampson presents Griffin with a file, now nine years old, detailing the case history of Frank's brother (a photo of Claude Rains is flashed), the so-called Invisible Man. Calling the departed Griffin's work "very ingenious," Frank matter-of-factly comments, "I can remember it pretty well." The wily inspector comments, "Of course, you would never make a man invisible unless you had the means of bringing him back in time," referring to the insanity which results if the subject is allowed to remain invisible too long. Sampson mentions in nine years the doctor may have found a way to avoid the insanity problem, but Frank calmly states, "I was never interested in my brother's activity." However, Sampson fearing the worst warns, "You must realize, that in the monster murders, the scientist hangs... have a cigar." Sampson leaves but orders his men to keep tabs on the area.

Helen is waiting inside the quaint cabin of mine worker Ben Jenkins (Forrester Harvey), a man she can trust to keep his mouth shut. Jenkins lives alone, with his perpetually barking dog, in the middle of nowhere, in an isolated boggy region of woods and mist. Stating that Radcliffe will be appearing momentarily, she warns Ben that he had a very serious accident and doesn't want anyone to know he's here. In the moodiest sequence of the film, off in the distance, a man wearing a tweed suit, his hand completely covered in white bandages, his eyes covered by large goggles, slowly makes his way toward the cabin, the misty fog swirling around him. Calling out Helen's name, his arms outstretched, he is warmly welcomed to the cabin, as Helen apologizes it's not Buckingham Palace. But Geoffrey corrects her, "You're wrong... it is!" Helen is happy that she can "touch" her love, calling him "the best phantom I know."

Going inside, Geoffrey is happy to be out of prison, but not happy that his brother's murderer is still free. "I'm lucky, I can see you. Afterall, I'm not much to look at anyway," Geoffrey says as they hug. "We're together... soon it will be as it always was. All this is just a dream." However, Geoffrey mentions just how cold it is outside, so much colder *before* he found the clothes that Griffin left for him. "I'm beginning to understand why ghosts moan so in this sort of weather," Geoffrey explains. Trying to put a positive spin on everything, Geoffrey states, "If the worst comes to the worst, I can always get a job haunting a house." But even though he is tired, Geoffrey is anxious to find his brother's murderer. Helen tells him that Griffin is sure he will have the antidote in the next few days. However, his voice growing serious, he says, "Helen, promise me something. Frank gave me his word, if my mind should begin to go, before he found a way back for me, he'd prevent me from doing any harm... help him keep that promise." He then falls asleep.

In a marvelous special effects sequence (all such effects created and supervised by John P. Fulton), Griffin has invisible guinea pigs wearing leather harnesses scampering around their metal cages. When he takes one such animal out of its cage and straps it to his observation table, injecting it with an antidote, the guinea pig does regain visibility, but within seconds, the animal dies, a fate Griffin is trying to avoid with humans.

A policeman on bicycle, finding Ben Jenkins' dog barking and chained far from home (by Geoffrey's request), decides to return the dog personally to Ben at his cabin. But first, Geoffrey tells Helen not to pity him: "Helen, don't look at me like this. I should have let them hang me. Who was ever faced with a choice like that? To be hanged by the neck until I was dead, or to take life on the terms of this fantastic drug—invisibility at the price of almost certain madness, today, tomorrow!" Helen tells Geoffrey to be patient, and he calms down bemoaning, "I'm a worm to treat you like this after all that you've been through... I'll try to act like a normal man." But by this time the policeman arrives to find Geoffrey and Helen hiding out in Ben's cabin, forcing Geoffrey to promptly disrobe and escape. The shock of seeing half a man causes Helen to faint dead away on the bed. The policeman enters the bedroom to find Helen passed out on the bed, a pile of man's clothes on the floor before her, and states, "No wonder she fainted!"

Richard Cobb assumes more and more power at the mines, promoting Willie Spears from watchman to supervisor of mining operations. In a drunken show of power, Spears visits Frank Griffin and criticizes him for telling the workers not to work in #3 tunnel. "My duty's the men's health," Griffin explains. Spears states that Cobb is giving Griffin a long vacation. Griffin

exclaims, "As long as Geoffrey's alive, he [Cobb] has nothing to say!" The arrogant Spears leaves, but the invisible presence of Geoffrey angrily notes, "What's come over this place? An imbecile like Spears talking to you in that manner! A night watchman! He never did that job well!" Griffin tells Geoffrey the major job Spears has as superintendent is to ignore every one of the safety rules Geoffrey established. Then, for the first time, a hysterical giggle overcomes the Invisible Man who yells, "It's surprising how invisibility heightens one's sense of smell... I think I smell something dead, up a creek."

Geoffrey toys with Willie Spears who is driving his car down the road when the side hood suddenly flips up, and soon wires are being pulled out of place. Stopping the car to investigate, while Spears is examining the engine under the hood, the hood suddenly smashes down on his hands. "You can't repair it, Mr. Spears," a disembodied voice announces. Thinking his two glasses of whisky are the cause of such hallucinations, Spears panics and runs off into the woods, being stopped dead in his tracks when Geoffrey grabs the man's scarf. "You can't escape either, Mr. Spears." Spears runs hither and fro, as the voice instructs, "Now, over there, over here." The drunken Spears runs all over, quickly exhausting himself and collapsing. "I told you there's no escape!" When Spears screams he can't see anybody, the voice then pretends to be a spirit: "I'm a ghost... it's cold in the other world, so cold! I escaped the noose... I can't find peace in the other world." Then Geoffrey quickly gets to the point, by first tightening the tie around Spears' neck, almost choking him. "Did you have any pity on me? Had you one thought for me, laying down day after day in that prison of despair, feeling the rope around my throat choking the very breath of life out of me... what was it to you—nothing!" Spears confesses everything, that Cobb made him lie, promised to reward him with promotions, that Cobb was with Sir Michael when he was killed. "Mr. Cobb told me he'd kill me if I told on him!"

Geoffrey pays a visit to Cobb—"I've come for a little chat," ironically adding, "Friends like you are a great comfort!" Slapping the started man on the cheek to remind Cobb just where his "friend" is hiding, Geoffrey pushes paper and pen before him and demands he write his own

murder confession. Helen, also present, is told by Geoffrey, "it was his charming way of getting rid of both of us—killing Michael, implicating me!" Cobb throws a desk paper weight at the rocking chair in which Geoffrey is seated and then pulls out a pistol, firing all around the room.

Sampson arrives with his army of policeman, and forcing Cobb and Helen to remain, they begin to set off smoke bombs and then they spray smoke throughout the household, hoping to trap Geoffrey. Cleverly, Geoffrey knocks an officer

Nan Grey and Vincent Price in *The Invisible Man Returns*.

unconscious and puts on his clothes, including gas mask and helmet, making the Invisible Man the visible cop. Having Helen pretend to faint, Geoffrey simply walks her out of the house, the police finally finding the missing policeman knocked cold on the floor upstairs wearing nothing but his underwear.

However, in the next sequence (after Griffin reveals to Helen he has been a fool, thinking he could concoct a safe antidote in days when in reality it might take years), Griffin, Helen and the again nattily-suited and bandaged Geoffrey reveal the extent to which further mental deterioration has occurred in Geoffrey. Again, unable to use his face, his eyes, Vincent Price only has his body language and voice to convey his changing mental state. "You should have seen them searching for me, Frank—smoke bombs, gas masks and fish nets. They must have thought I was a herring... and I marched straight through them with Helen, took her politely to the car." Now the insanity and delusions of grandeur not so subtly peek through. "I am beginning to get a new perspective on this *crawling*, little animal known as man. A dog or a cat or a bird is cleverer than any human... they sense me immediately. Take away one of man's senses and you render him helpless." Even though Geoffrey states he possesses absolute proof that Cobb murdered brother Michael, he refuses to give this information to Sampson. But Griffin and Helen are shocked, stating such information will make Geoffrey once again free. But the Invisible Man begins to rant and rave: "Free, I am free! I've never been more free in all my life! You know being invisible has distinct advantages. It gives one a sense of power that is exciting. Power for good if you are so inclined, or, should you feel perverse, for evil. You hold the balance and decide which way life should go—no one can stop you, no one can touch you. You don't need any infantile little Sampsons to carry out your will... more wine, Frank!" Sensing the invisibility potion has produced insanity, Griffin mixes a powder in Geoffrey's wine, but the man will not drink. Changing into his robe without wearing any head bandages, Geoffrey finally drinks to a toast: "Drink to my invisible power... with me as its guiding genius!" Passing out, Geoffrey is secured in a side room.

Interestingly, once Geoffrey awakens, now chained to his chair in the study, his voice changes back to its calmer, peaceful state, now telling Griffin, "I'm glad you did it" and "I feel safer." However, requesting water for a dry throat, Griffin gets the water splashed into his face as Geoffrey subdues the doctor and effects his escape. By being able to again say the right things in the right way, Geoffrey realizes he can get the upper hand on all those who attempt to contain him.

The climax upon us, Geoffrey forces Richard Cobb to accompany him to find Spears, but first they must get past the police guards who are protecting Cobb. In one marvelous scene, as Cobb is walking down the stairs of his house, going toward the front door, he momentarily stumbles, as though Geoffrey had just pushed him slightly. In another eerie sequence, Spears, a noose around his throat, is standing on a wooden stool. Spears confesses to everything, but Cobb simply trips the stool over, thus actually hanging and killing the only witness, as Geoffrey looks on helplessly. But a few minutes later, Geoffrey drops Cobb from a coal car as he falls helplessly downward, mortally injured. With his dying breath, Cobb confesses to the murder of Michael. Meanwhile, Geoffrey steals the clothes of a scarecrow and marches straight down main street to Griffin's laboratory, desperately in need of blood transfusions (the miners immediately offer their own blood). Griffin states he must operate to prevent internal bleeding, but that he cannot operate on an invisible subject. However, because of all the newly transfused blood, Geoffrey turns visible again, and without mention of any further operation, the end credits pop up as Geoffrey smiles calmly and says, "Helen, darling."

Even though many people incorrectly assume that only Vincent Price's voice appears in this movie, what they really mean is that a body without a face is almost the same as acting without a body. We must remember that Vincent Price does use his body, his gestures, his motion, body language and, most importantly, his voice to create his invisible man persona. While the special effects (eyes that see inside of a bandaged head, a body without a head, a pair of trousers slipping off to nothingness, etc.) dominate and impress, Price's voice creates and maintains the sensitivity of the role. Too bad that the script was listless and the direction pedestrian, for Vincent Price does as much as any actor could do with the part, as written. Again, it is fascinating to think of Price's voice around the time of his William Castle epics and then listen to the voice in *The Invisible Man Returns*—it's almost an entirely different voice, with just enough of the hint of the mature Price voice apparent that was waiting to be nurtured and developed. *The Invisible Man Returns* is neither a great film nor does it feature a great Price performance, but for an upstart movie actor, it was a movie that drew attention and garnered better film work further down the line. Sometimes seeing a great actor paying dues is reason enough to watch.

CREDITS: Producer: Ken Goldmsith; Director: Joe May; Writers: Curt Siodmak, Lester Cole (Based on a Story by Curt Siodmak and Joe May); Cinematography: Milton Krasner; Editor: Frank Gross; Music: Frank Skinner and Hans J. Salter; Special Effects: John P. Fulton; Universal; 1940; 81 minutes

CAST: Cedric Hardwicke (Richard Cobb); Vincent Price (Geoffrey Radcliffe); Nan Grey (Helen Manson); John Sutton (Dr. Frank Griffin); Cecil Kellaway (Inspector Sampson); Alan Napier (Willie Spears); Forrester Harvey (Ben Jenkins); Harry Stubbs (Constable Dukesbury); Harry Cording (Shopworker)

Vincent Price in *The Song of Bernadette* **(Photofest)**

THE SONG OF BERNADETTE (1943)

by Susan Svehla

Vincent Price has often made audiences laugh and just as often sent shivers down our spines. But this is perhaps his only film role that can make us cry.

The Song of Bernadette was filmed by 20th Century-Fox in 1943 and released to the general public in early January of 1944. In the opening credits Vincent Price is third billed after William Eythe and Charles Bickford (Jennifer Jones was listed as "Introducing Jennifer Jones" after the main cast) in the four-star film. A title card displays the following:

> This is the story of Bernadette Soubirous who lived in Lourdes, a village in southern France close to the Spanish border.
> For those who believe in God, no explanation is necessary.
> For those who do not believe in God, no explanation is possible.

February 11, 1858. Bernadette (Jennifer Jones in her first starring role) goes with her sister and friend to gather wood. She has asthma and the other girls leave her behind when they cross a stream. She remains in a grotto and sees a vision of a beautiful lady in a white veil and blue girdle with gold roses on her feet. Nobody believes her, but her aunt convinces her mother (Anne Revere) to go with her to the grotto. The family's show of support leads others to the grotto to pray. Bernadette says the lady told her to come to the grotto every day for 15 days.

The town authorities consider this a dangerous nuisance and try to convince each other to take control of the situation. The village Priest, Peyremaie (Charles Bickford), refuses to take a stand. The church prefers to ignore the whole incident. Vincent Price portrays Imperial Prosecutor Dutour, a man who thinks the villagers are ignorant peasants and Bernadette is a fraud. He gives an impassioned speech to the town authorities:

> What can you expect from a peasantry fed on religious dogmas and nurtured on superstitious nonsense? I firmly believe that this girl and what she stands for is a menace to civilization... She's a religious fanatic and every time religious fanaticism steps forward, mankind moves backward and that is why I will fight this vigorously and I'll resort to any measures to defeat it.

The people continue to follow Bernadette to the grotto. Peyremaie tells Bernadette to have the lady perform a miracle and make the wild rose bush in the grotto bloom (since this is February he does not expect anything to happen). The lady tells Bernadette to eat plants and drink and wash from the spring. But there is no spring, so Bernadette digs into the ground and brushes her arms and face with the dirt. The crowd thinks she has gone mad and the police order them to leave. Antoine (William Eythe), who loves Bernadette, and another man remain behind. Antoine feels water running beneath his hand and finds that a spring has appeared. He runs to tell the departing crowd while the man with him splashes the water over his face. His injured eye is cured. Neighbors of the Soubirous family are told by the doctor that their baby son has no chance of survival. A priest begins to administer last rites. The mother (Edith Barrett, Price's wife at the time) grabs the baby and takes him to the grotto. She places the child into the water

Dutour (Vincent Price) threatens Bernadette (Jennifer Jones).

and he immediately begins to cry. The doctors are amazed. The child has been completely cured. Word spreads and soon people from across the countryside are visiting the grotto.

Dutour finds an out-of-date law stating it is forbidden to drink from wells or springs unless they have been tested. He has the mayor order the grotto boarded up. Peyremaie is finally convinced that Bernadette may be telling the truth and goes to the church to ask for an investigation. They refuse unless the Emperor orders the grotto be opened once again. Peyremaie is told by the disbelieving church spokesman it is a test for the lady. But the Emperor does order the grotto opened when Empress Eugenie (Patricia Morison) sends someone to fetch some of the water for her ill son and the boy soon recovers.

The church begins a lengthy investigation that goes on for years. Dutour receives a letter telling him to remain at his duties in Lourdes. His voice is hoarse and he remarks about having another bout of influenza. Bernadette goes to Peyremaie to tell him she is accepting a job as housemaid and is so happy because she cares for Antoine. Peyremaie tells her she was chosen by the Virgin Mary and she should enter a convent. Bernadette agrees and departs from her family. Eventually she is diagnosed with tuberculosis of the bones and there is no hope. She tells the other sisters the water of Lourdes is not for her.

Dutour, who has been gone from Lourdes for five years, returns to visit. The argument of whether or not Bernadette saw something is still going on among the doctors, priests and officials. Peyremaie is called to Bernadette.

The line of the sick and injured leading toward the grotto is filled with despair and suffering, but also hope and faith. Dutour walks with the crowd toward the grotto. He thinks to himself how alone he is and how he will soon die of cancer of the throat, never having loved or believed in anyone. It is dark and he walks through the candle-holding worshipers toward the bars in front of a statue of the Virgin Mary in the grotto. This is Price's shining moment as he grips the bars and looks at the statue. Dutour is a man who believes in science and in his own superiority. But he now knows everyone is alike, he no better than the rest. He falls to his knees and finally acknowledges the truth, "Pray for me Bernadette."

The Song of Bernadette, released during WWII, brought the story of the faith of a simple country girl to thousands of war-weary Americans who

Price and wife Edith Barrett on the set of *The Song of Bernadette*. **(Photofest)**

sorely needed some faith and hope during those dark times.

The film received multiple Academy Award nominations and took home several awards including one for Jennifer Jones. The film was nominated for Best Picture, Actress, Supporting Actor (Charles Bickford), Supporting Actress (Gladys Cooper, as a nun who refuses to believe Bernadette), Director, Screenplay, Cinematography, Editing, Score, Art Direction and Sound. Along with Jones, Oscar would go home with cinematographer Arthur Miller, composer Alfred Newman, art directors James Basevi, William Darling and Thomas Little and soundman E.H. Hansen.

A dying Dutour approaches the shrine of Lourdes. (Photofest)

William Eythe appeared with Vincent Price in four films including *The Song of Bernadette, A Royal Scandal, Wilson* and *The Eve of St. Mark*. Eythe died at the age of 38 in 1957. Director Henry King began as a leading man in silent films before graduating to directing. His resume includes titles such as *Alexander's Ragtime Band, In Old Chicago, Jesse James, Love is a Many Splendored Thing* and *Twelve O'Clock High*. King would direct Price once again in *Wilson* (1944).

Variety's review read, "[*The*] *Song of Bernadette* is an absorbing, emotional and dramatic picturization of Franz Werfel's novel. It's big in every respect; will rate fine critical attention; great in prestige for the industry; and due for top boxoffice reaction.

"...It's a strong and inspirational religious theme, particularly strengthening in these troublous times when people are turning to God.

"Cast, extensively running through 39 credits, is one of the most expertly-selected in several years, and even the one-shot bits click solidly in fleeting footage... Support is studded with numerous brilliant portrayals, including Charles Bickford, William Eythe, Vincent Price, Lee J. Cobb, Gladys Cooper..."

Vincent Price gives one of his finest performances as Dutour. He plays Dutour as neither villain nor saint, only a man sure of his ideas and not willing to allow what he considers ignorance to destroy gains society has made. His final scene at the grotto is heart-wrenching and a tour de force performance and, of all his roles, this is one that should have earned him an Academy Award nomination.

CREDITS: Producer: William Perlberg; Director: Henry King; Writer: George Seaton (Based on the Novel by Franz Werfel); Cinematography: Arthur Miller; Music: Alfred Newman; Costumes: Rene Hubert; Set Designers: Thomas Little and Frank E. Hughes; Art Designers: James Basevi and William Darling; Sound: E.H. Hansen; 20th Century-Fox; 1943; 156 minutes

CAST: Jennifer Jones (Bernadette Soubirous); William Eythe (Antoine); Charles Bickford (Peyremaie); Vincent Price (Dutour); Lee J. Cobb (Dr. Dozous); Gladys Cooper (Sister Vauzous); Anne Revere (Louise Soubirous); Roman Bohnen (Francois Soubirous); Patricia Morison (Empress Eugenie); Edith Barrett (Croisine); Sig Rumann (Louis Bouriette)

Gene Tierney and Vincent Price in *Laura*. (Photofest)

LAURA (1944)
by Gary J. Svehla

"I shall never forget the weekend Laura died. A silver sun burned through the sky like a huge magnifying glass. It was the hottest Sunday in my recollection. I—Walter Lydecker—was the only one who knew her."

In 1944 Vincent Price was a rising star, a supporting player fourth or fifth billed, someone who might either be destined for stardom or relegated to character roles for the remainder of his career. Fortunately for Price, his mid-to-late 1940s film roles generally placed him in films noir and mysteries, mostly in major secondary roles. A decade later, his career would once again radically change, thus avoiding typecasting and allowing Price's career to prosper, expand and develop in new directions.

However, *Laura*, director Otto Preminger's 1944 Academy Award-winning picture, was destined for classic movie status, and Vincent Price, fourth billed, was given the despicable yet unforgettable role of a Southern gigolo, a spineless coward who uncharacteristically attracted both the matronly rich and the sexually charged young to his lair. Price's character Shelby Carpenter was an oily, smooth-talking lizard of a man, but his screen presence, alternating between lounge-lizard lover and pathetic weakling, commanded the audience's attention, making Vincent Price an acting talent to notice.

Laura, a three-star movie always given four-star status, is a noirish mystery that teeters upon the interactions between four quirky personalities, all of the performances delivered with enthusiasm: newspaper and radio personality Waldo Lydecker (Clifton Webb), a man whose self-promotion becomes the classic illustration of style over substance; hot and sizzling 22-year-old Laura Hunt (Gene Tierney), rising young star of the advertising world, a young girl who becomes the mistress of Lydecker after he takes her under his wing, introducing her to all the right clients in polite society; the aforementioned Shelby Carpenter (Vincent Price), a Southern "gentleman" who avoids work whenever possible, but a man always able to flash beautiful or rich women on his arm; and uncharismatic police lieutenant Mark McPherson (Dana Andrews), the quietly intense policeman, who always occupies himself with a child's handheld game while questioning witnesses and who becomes increasingly more and more obsessed with the letters, personal affairs and portrait of the late Laura Hunt. With a few peripheral characters thrown into the mix to round out the plot, *Laura* is basically a four-person character study that throws one hell of a surprise into the mix in the middle—Laura Hunt is not dead; the gorgeous corpse, whose face was disfigured by two shotgun blasts to the face, is in reality a fashion model who was carrying on an affair with Shelby Carpenter at the same time he was romantically linked to both Laura Hunt and Anne Treadwell (Judith Anderson). Thus, all the major characters possess a motive for murder.

When viewed as a character study, *Laura* shines when it features pithy and intelligent dialogue, the type that rolled off characters' tongues every other syllable in the cynical film noir Hollywood era. First confronting Waldo Lydecker soaking in his marble bathtub, a typewriter on a swinging shelf before him, Mark McPherson begins his round of questioning allowing the hyperbolic Lydecker to create a caustic character that somehow is cultured and entertaining at the same time. The deadpan McPherson, pulling a clipping out of his pocket, reminds Lydecker that two years ago, in his October 17 column, he started out to write a book review, but by the bottom of the column he switched over to the Harrington murder case. Matter-of-factly, the policeman reads that Harrington was "rubbed out with a shotgun loaded with buckshot..." but then adds, "...the way Laura Hunt was murdered, the night before last... but he was really killed with a sash weight!" The non-shakable Lydecker responds coolly: "How ordinary. My version was obviously superior. I never bother with details!" to which McPherson replies, "I do!" Lydecker asks if he can accompany McPherson as he questions suspects—"I want to study their reactions." McPherson reminds Lydecker that he himself is a suspect too. "To overlook me would have been a pointed insult... how singularly innocent I look this morning. Have you ever seen such candid eyes?"

But what McPherson wishes to know about is Lydecker's relationship with Laura Hunt. With a glint in his eye, Lydecker babbles, "Laura considered me the wisest, the wittiest, the most interesting man she ever met. I was in complete accord with her on that point. She felt me the kindest, the gentlest, the most sympathetic man in the world... I tried to become these things." Interestingly, in the more innocent 1940s, Waldo Lydecker becomes the Larry King or Geraldo Rivera of his era, a personality of the press whose own identity (he is proud of his walking stick and white carnation trademarked image) always threatens to upstage the news to be told. But such a personality is quickly established as a direct contrast against the equally self-serving Shelby Carpenter, a man that Lydecker hates with a passion.

Journeying to Anne Treadwell's apartment, McPherson takes little time to establish the fact that Anne has been giving Shelby Carpenter a great deal of money, having traced bank account statements to show how Treadwell withdraws money a day or so before Carpenter deposits a similar amount. McPherson both embarrasses and angers Treadwell when he asks her if she loves Mr. Carpenter. At this point, from the back room, Shelby Carpenter enters, obviously sleeping and feeling quite at home in Treadwell's apartment. "I was just lying down here. My hotel room was so hot and then all the people and reporters... you know how it is... I hardly slept a wink since it happened," Carpenter explains. Getting closer to the point, Carpenter politely offers: "I'm at your disposal, Lieutenant... I'm as eager to find the murderer as you are. But what possible motive could I have for killing Laura? Miss Hunt and I were to be married this week, you know!" Waldo, incensed, erupts with, "No, he doesn't know," adding his first-hand knowledge that Laura had not definitely made up her mind whether to marry Shelby or not. "As a matter of fact, she was going to the country to think it over... She was extremely kind but I was always sure she wouldn't throw her life away on a male beauty in distress!" Vincent Price, literally called a male bimbo by Lydecker, pulls all his inner strength and focuses it all on his face, a face that erupts into a sneer: "I suppose you've heard losers whine before," referring to the fact that Laura was supposed to marry *him*, not Lydecker.

Soon, the trio of men are off to Laura's apartment, still surrounded and protected by police guards. Waldo, upset by the police photos taken of Laura's body, prompts McPherson to calmly

A jealous Lydecker (Clifton Webb) looks on as Laura and Shelby Carpenter embrace. (Photofest)

state, "When a dame gets killed, she doesn't worry about her looks." And Lydecker is immediately insulted by the policeman's juxtaposing the word "dame" and Laura. Looking at the huge portrait of Laura hanging in her apartment, Lydecker states, "He never captured her vibrance, her warmth." Almost immediately McPherson catches Carpenter in another lie, this time about the musical program played at a concert that Shelby attended with Laura. After Shelby announces the musical program, McPherson states that the program was changed at the last moment. "You see, I've been working on that advertising campaign with Laura, and we've been working so hard. I couldn't keep my eyes open—I didn't hear a note at the concert. I fell asleep!" Carpenter explains. To which Lydecker adds his snide aside, "Next he'll produce photographic evidence of his dreams." Immediately, Carpenter snaps back with, "I know it sounds suspicious but I'm resigned to that by now. I'm a natural born suspect just because I'm not the conventional type." Such verbal sparring becomes the heart of the movie, with Vincent Price's oozing and swarthy charming personality suddenly recoiling inward, hardening itself, and then striking outward toward those who threaten him. Price is seldom likable in the role, but his performance is always surprising and filled with energy.

Carpenter pretends to find a key to Laura's getaway cottage in her bedroom drawer, when actually the key was in his possession all the time and he is simply trying to protect her character. But this soon leads to an explosive sequence between Carpenter and Lydecker. Carpenter says, "Waldo, for your own good, I'm warning you to stop implying I had anything to do with Laura's death." But Lydecker holds his ground, pulls in his chin, and erupts with, "Very well, I will stop implying; I'll make a direct statement!" Incensed, Carpenter announces "All right, you asked for it" as he charges the elder media darling. McPherson breaks them apart. Even though Price's character appears to depend entirely on verbal fisticuffs, in several sequences his bulk

McPherson (Dana Andrews) confronts Shelby and Laura.

and size seem to materialize into a character who is not afraid to get his clothes dirty from a rolling-around-the-floor fight.

Lydecker tells McPherson the story of how he met Laura five years earlier. Lydecker's eyes sparkle as he becomes, in his retelling, Svengali to the lovely Trilby as he relates how he introduced Laura to the right people, told her what clothes to wear and what hairdo to display to the public. "Through me she met everyone. She captivated them all—she had warmth and magnetism. She became as well known as my walking stick and white carnation." He further explains that on Tuesday and Friday evenings they stayed home. "I read my articles to her... these were the best nights!" But soon, Laura begins to cancel such regular engagements. She becomes involved with an artist, Jacoby, who painted her portrait which hangs on the living room wall. Lydecker takes pride in the fact that he literally destroyed the artist's reputation in his regular column, forcing the impressionable girl to return to him. However, everything changes the night Laura meets Shelby Carpenter at one of Anne's parties. The dazzling Carpenter, asking the equally beautiful Laura for a dance, is gently rebuked by the simple fact that she is not alone. Carpenter looks at Lydecker, smiles and dismisses the haughty reporter: "Oh him, I bet he's still doing the polka." This is one of the best lines of the movie.

As Laura and Shelby's relationship matures, she asks the playboy why he doesn't work, since the sheriff took over his estate inheritance 10 years earlier. With a twinkle in his eye and a smile on his lips, Carpenter demonstrates his smooth style in recounting the story: "Believe it or not, I asked one of my many friends for a job once, executive of a big company, 2,500 employees. He could have pushed a button and done it. But he laughed; he thought I was joking!" Accepting a job at the advertising agency that Laura offers him, Carpenter is soon involved with one of the fashion models at the agency (the actual murder victim Diane). Even though Waldo tries to poison the image of Carpenter to Laura ("he almost went to jail for passing rubber checks"; "he was suspected of stealing his hostess' jewels when he was a house guest in Virginia"), he realizes he has lost her when she declares, "A man can change, can't he... I'm helping Shelby" and then Laura announces she will marry Shelby next week.

McPherson, who spends many nights sitting in Laura's apartment reading her mail and staring at her portrait, is also frequently visited by Lydecker who asks if he can have his grandfather clock and other personal articles back, but McPherson makes clear that nothing is leaving the apartment. One night, to everyone's surprise, Laura returns from the country, having gone there to reconsider her marriage to Carpenter. She answers McPherson directly that she has decided not to marry him, that he no longer means anything to her. When McPherson reminds Laura that disfigured model Diane was discovered wearing Laura's dressing gown and slippers, found in the intimate company of Shelby Carpenter, the cop further reminds her this isn't the "regulation costume" for an "impersonal chat between a man and a woman who mean nothing to each other," quoting Laura's own words.

LAWRENCE FRENCH: How do you feel about the musical scores of your movies? Boris Karloff felt that music sometimes got in the way of an actor's performance.

VINCENT PRICE: It all depends on how well it's done. *Laura* has one of the most famous scores ever written (by composer David Raksin), and I never felt it got in the way at all. When we all went to see *Laura* on opening night, Gene Tierney, Clifton Webb, Judith Anderson, Dana Andrews and myself, we had never heard the score! That was written long after the film was finished. So we sat there and thought, "Isn't that marvelous." We also watched ourselves, as well (laughter). Sometimes the score does get in the way. I must say, with some of those Alfred Newman scores, you often felt that the orchestra was swelling behind you, but nothing was swelling on the screen. For the most part, I think the scores have fit very well. David Raksin, who did *Laura,* was really a very good composer.

As Laura becomes attracted to McPherson, Anne puts in her claim for Shelby, stating he is better for her than anyone else because "I can afford and understand him." Elaborating, Anne continues, "He's no good but he's what I want. I'm not a nice person and neither is he. He knows I know he is just what he is—he also knows I don't care. We belong together because we're both weak and can't seem to help it." With her resolute passion and intense, honest delivery, Anne describes two flawed people who seem the perfect match, one, if not made in heaven but hell, that suits both parties equally well. Amazingly, for such a heel, and one that people literally see for just what he is, Shelby Carpenter seems to be a man always in demand. Later, under interrogation at the police station, Laura confesses that she had meant to break up with Shelby, but that he convinced her that if she dumped him now, everyone would think he was guilty of the murder. As Laura dutifully reports, "He got himself into a position people would always believe the worst about... he's that sort of man." A bastard, a gigolo and a ladies' man faithful only to what he can get out of the relationship, yet everyone in this movie, except Lydecker, seems to have a soft spot for the despicable Carpenter.

In Vincent Price's final scene of the movie he appears at Anne's party given in Laura's honor. After Anne professes her love for Shelby, the phone rings and it's a police call for McPherson who announces, for everyone to hear, that he is ready to make the arrest for the case. At that instant Shelby's face turns as guilty as sin, his countenance resembling the cat that ate the canary. But McPherson strolls past him and the sleazy playboy sighs in relief. The officer approaches Laura and tells her to go with him to headquarters. The cowardly Shelby, himself seemingly off the hook, momentarily grows strong and defiant stating to Laura: "Laura, I told

you to look out for this fellow. I warned you!" To which the generally passive lieutenant barks back, venom in his eyes, "It's too bad you didn't open that door Friday night, Carpenter," referring to the fact that Carpenter allowed Diane to open the door during their romantic rendezvous. "Wait a minute," Carpenter retorts, quickly assembling a margin of pride and dignity, and once again, ready to physically fight for his honor (or the semblance of honor remaining). McPherson quickly punches Carpenter in the stomach, doubling him up in pain. Carpenter is immediately comforted by Anne.

In the movie's climax, the murderer, who is again trying to kill Laura, is identified as Waldo Lydecker, who tells Laura: "The best part of myself, that's who you are," claiming he intended to murder her rather than have her pawed by a vulgar second-rate detective. What it all boils down to is in his deluded sense of importance, Waldo would rather see Laura dead than with another man. Once again sneaking into Laura's apartment armed with his shotgun (which was hidden in the base of the grandfather clock which he gave to Laura and so desperately wanted back from McPherson), Lydecker is quickly cut down by a hail of police bullets.

But in a certain sense, the real climax of Laura is the sucker-punch delivered to Shelby Carpenter's mid-section, doubling up the Southern rubbage, demonstrating a clear moral ending to such immoral affairs, society gatherings and sexually motivated murders. The least flashy and most evenly balanced character, the impartial McPherson, suddenly takes a stand not only speaking out his moral outrage in words but demonstrating moral disgust with his fists. Lydecker—self-serving, cruel and totally obnoxious—is revealed as the film's psychopathic murderer. Carpenter—oily, cowardly and also totally obnoxious—is revealed to be a gutless user, with few redeeming characteristics. Laura—sensuous, erotic and totally conniving—is revealed to be a woman who uses men to get what she wants. This leaves McPherson—annoying, vague and totally, obsessively dedicated to doing the best job he can. He is bland yet honorable, moral yet unexciting. But he's the only major character worth a damn.

This is why Vincent Price, as Shelby Carpenter, is so memorable and effective in this movie. Price's performance makes being an oily, sleazy snake in the grass interesting. He plays the bully when he knows he can win; he plays the receding coward when he knows he will win sympathy; and he plays the lover tenderly, sympathetically, knowing his relationships with women will benefit him economically. Unlike McPherson, Carpenter is a man adrift without a moral center, not actually a villain but a man who disgraces both his sex and the human species. However, his performance shines like spit and shoe polish, never subtle but—as in the best Price tradition—never too broad or over the top to lose its effectiveness. Price's creation of Shelby Carpenter, himself a stereotype larger than life, points to performances two decades down the road, in the AIP Poe series, where an older, wiser and craftier Vincent Price weaves the same magic by creating characters who are also larger than life and interesting as hell to watch! But isn't that the gift and craft of Vincent Price—making the overblown and hyperbolic totally believable and yet fun to watch?

CREDITS: Producer/Director: Otto Preminger; Screenplay: Jay Dratler, Samuel Hoffenstein, Betty Reinhardt (Based on the Novel by Vera Caspary); Cinematography: Joseph La Shelle; Art Directors: Lyle Wheeler, Leland Fuller; Set Decorator: Thomas Little; Music: David Raksin; Musical Director: Emil Newman; Editor: Louis Loeffler; Costumes: Bonnie Cashin; Makeup: Guy Pearce; Released 1944 by 20th Century-Fox; Running Time: 88 minutes

CAST: Gene Tierney (Laura Hunt); Dana Andrews (Lt. Mark McPherson); Clifton Webb (Waldo Lydecker); Vincent Price (Shelby Carpenter); Judith Anderson (Anne Treadwell); Dorothy Adams (Bessie Clary); James Flavin (Sergeant McAvity); Clyde Fillmore (Bullitt); Ralph Dunn (Fred Callahan); Kathleen Howard (Louise the Cook); Lee Tung Foo (Servant)

Ben Ames Williams'
Leave Her To Heaven
IN TECHNICOLOR
Starring
GENE TIERNEY
CORNEL WILDE
JEANNE CRAIN
20th CENTURY-FOX
VINCENT PRICE
MARY PHILIPS
RAY COLLINS
GENE LOCKHART
REED HADLEY
DARRYL HICKMAN
CHILL WILLS
DIRECTED BY JOHN M. STAHL
PRODUCED BY WILLIAM A. BACHER

LEAVE HER TO HEAVEN (1945)
by Nathalie Yafet

Leave Her to Heaven is told in flashback as Ellen Berent and Richard Harland "meet cute" on a train in New Mexico while she is reading a novel he wrote. They eventually discover that they are both invited to the Robie ranch, along with Ellen's mother and adopted sister, Ruth. The Berent family is there to ceremonially scatter the deceased Mr. Berent's ashes in his beloved Southwest. Ellen and Richard are strongly attracted to each other and fall in love. Ellen calls off her engagement to a young, ambitious lawyer—Russell Quinton—who is a very sore loser. After the couple marries, Ellen tries to keep Richard entirely to herself. However, Danny (Richard's crippled younger brother) joins them at their remote Maine lodge, Back of the Moon. Richard, trying to concentrate on his writing and sensing Ellen's unhappiness, invites Mrs. Berent and Ruth as company for Ellen. Naturally, this exacerbates the situation even further. One day, Ellen takes Danny out in the boat, encourages him to swim beyond his strength, and lets him drown. Ellen then becomes pregnant, but soon resents the baby as well and she miscarries after she deliberately falls down the stairs. Richard, having fallen in love with Ruth and knowing that Ellen murdered both Danny and her baby, announces that he is leaving her. Ellen reacts by deliberately poisoning herself with arsenic-tainted sugar, leaving enough evidence to incriminate Ruth in her death. Ellen's discarded fiancé Russell Quinton (who is now the district attorney) interrogates Richard and Ruth relentlessly until Richard confesses that he knew of Ellen's crimes. Ruth goes free, but Richard gets two years for being an accessory to murder. After serving his time, Richard returns to Back of the Moon, where Ruth is waiting.

Only Vincent Price could portray someone with an outlandish name like Russell Quinton with such flair. Although fourth-billed behind Tierney, Wilde, and Crain, he matches Tierney's Oscar-nominated performance in every way. His two scenes are unforgettable.

Russell Quinton is an ambitious politician/lawyer who has his sights set on becoming district attorney and, eventually, governor. He is engaged to wealthy, beautiful and exceedingly strange Ellen Berent, who has been postponing their marriage for a long time. However, Ellen meets Richard, who bears a startling resemblance to her adored father, and breaks her engagement with Russell (after knowing Richard for just a few days). Ellen sends her fiancé a Dear John telegram and he joins her at the ranch soon afterwards. As he walks in the door, he sees Ellen laughing and holding hands with a total stranger. Ever the practiced politician, he forces away the pain that flashes across his face and derisively tells her, "I wanted to be among the first to congratulate you on your forthcoming marriage." He ignores Richard, tersely greets Mrs. Berent and Ruth and asks to speak to Ellen alone. His former fiancée informs him that she plans to be married "...as soon as possible." Quinton asks, "Would it be convenient for you to postpone it until the fall..." and suggests that it wouldn't be good for his campaign if the news got out that he "...had been jilted and thrown aside like an old shoe." Ellen mockingly assures him that people won't hold it against him because she changed her mind and tells him, "Don't look so downcast. I'll still be able to vote for you." At this point, the jilted lover has had enough and exclaims, "Perhaps you don't think I'm good enough for you, or romantic enough. I know people thought I was marrying into the Berent family for reasons, but that's not true. I want you to know that I had only one reason. I want you to know that I was in love with you. I'm not a man who loves more than once." Ellen breaks in with, "Thank you, Russ, that's quite a concession." Ignoring her obvious sarcasm, he continues, "I loved you and I'm still in love with you." Untouched by all this emotion, she says, "That's a tribute." Desperate for her to understand him, Russell finishes by stating, "And I always will be; remember that!" Ellen faces him down and asks, "Russ, is that a threat?" He responds with a stonily intense look, then abruptly leaves without speaking to anyone else. Price and Tierney move through their lines almost as if they are singing a duet. Neither one upstages the other and their timing is razor sharp. Price crescendos gradually as he first tries the political gambit to delay the marriage. When that fails, he has no other recourse but to tell the truth. A truth that he may not have even admitted to himself. His monologue is sincerely spoken with an undercurrent of bitterness lurking in his voice. The politician's mask crumbles with the slow realization that, without any effort at all, another man has won his elusive love. Price emphasizes his repeated phrases carefully, giving each one a slightly different spin. Ellen seems to hold all the cards at the end, but we admire Russell more with his disturbing farewell, "...and I always will be; remember that." Using every resource he has—voice, face, eyes and body—the actor reaches far beyond Russell Quinton's glossy veneer and presents us with a wounded, jilted man unable to forget his love for an impossible woman.

Nevertheless, *Leave Her to Heaven* is Gene Tierney's picture. We discover almost at once that all is not right with Ellen. Her unblinking stare at Richard on the train—neither friendly nor seductive—is distinctly unbalanced. She's not sitting with her mother or adopted sister, though they have the same destination, and seems to remain apart even when she is with them. Ellen tells Richard that she and her father were "inseparable." Richard, who is basically clueless until late in the film, ignores this red flag and falls in love with her anyway. He also disregards her mother's odd little statement, "Nothing ever happens to Ellen," and Glen Robie's caustic comment, "Ellen always wins." One of the more telling moments is when Ellen, Mrs. Berent and Ruth gather at dawn for Mr. Berent's "funeral." Her mother and her adopted sister watch from a distance while Ellen clutches the funerary urn to herself, wildly flinging the ashes as she rides her horse. She refuses to share even the final remnants of her father's memory with the other two women who loved him. When the ritual is completed, Ellen buries her face in her hands and breaks down completely.

Deciding that she wants Richard, Ellen removes her engagement ring and tells Russell Quinton that she is getting married before she has bothered to discuss it with the prospective bridegroom. She silences Richard's feeble protests by proposing to him and avowing, "I'll never let you go—never, never, never!" After they marry, she refuses to have household help, in spite of her wealth, and tells her new husband, "I don't want anybody else but me to do anything for you... I don't want anybody else in the house but us... ever!" Hoping to help Danny recover enough so that he won't need to live with them, Ellen is startled to learn that the boy's doctor is impressed with his remarkable recovery and recommends that Danny accompany them to Richard's lodge, Back of the Moon. She tries to manipulate the physician into telling her husband that his brother should not go with them, but he will not. Angry that things are not going her way, Ellen venomously exclaims, "But after all—he's a cripple!" Tierney is downright scary in this scene as she dissembles—trying all her proven tricks—to bend Dr. Mason to her will. Richard enters suddenly and Ellen, realizing that she has to switch gears, is all sweetness as she enthuses that the doctor is allowing Danny to go with them and she wants to be the first to tell him. The actress' flawless face betrays Sybil-like emotions as her madness and evil whirl inside of her.

Richard throws another log on Ellen's fire when he invites Mrs. Berent and Ruth to join them at Back of the Moon. She says she would like it at the lodge if it "...weren't so crowded," and spits out that they should rename the lodge, Goldfish Manor. She shamelessly eavesdrops on her mother and Ruth through the wall, and insults Leick Thorne (the hired man who is Richard's friend). After Richard confronts her with her shrewishness, she declares, "I love you so; I can't bear to share you with anybody!"

Tierney's nastiest moment comes when she takes Danny out on the lake and encourages him to swim to the shore to surprise his brother. Danny weakens, she urges him on, he cramps up and begins to go down. Ignoring his frantic cries for help, Ellen sits calmly in the boat and watches her brother-in-law drown. Only after she hears her husband approaching and is sure Danny has drowned does she dive in and try to "save" him. The sight of this lovely woman, her soulless eyes behind dark glasses, sitting absolutely still and allowing a helpless boy's death is

Ellen (Gene Tierney) dumps Russell Quinton (Vincent Price) for Richard Harlan (Cornel Wilde). (Photofest)

unnerving. After this, Richard avoids Ellen more and more. Desperate to regain his affection, she becomes pregnant. But this supreme egoist cannot abide her changing body or confinement to her room. She says that, "The baby's making a prisoner out of me... I hate the little beast. I wish he would die." Ellen forces her wish to come true. Gene Tierney again excels as she prepares for her planned miscarriage by selecting one of her most glamorous gowns and then peeks in the mirror for one more satisfying look before she falls down the stairs.

Richard can no longer stay with her after the death of their son and pressures her to acknowledge that she not only caused Danny's death but the baby's as well. Ellen accuses him of leaving her for Ruth, which he denies. As a last resort, Ellen writes to Russell Quinton, replaces Ruth's bath salts with arsenic, takes the poison herself with her sugar, extracts a last promise from Richard that he will mingle her cremated remains with those of her father, and dies—still gripping her husband's hand tightly. Tierney chooses to depict Ellen's increasing mania with deadly calm and a clear sense of purpose. No deathbed confessions here; she's a liar to the end with the face of an angel and the heart of a devil.

Cut to a tight close-up of Richard's hand loosening Ellen's grasp with difficulty; then a startling transition to Russell Quinton in the courtroom declaiming, "Murder—cold, brutal, premeditated murder." The juxtaposition is unexpectedly jarring; a brilliant editing decision. Vincent Price takes center stage here and does it masterfully. He uses a repeated phrase, in this case,

Quinton asks Ruth (Jeanne Crain), "When did you fall in love with Richard Harland?" (Photofest)

"The State will prove...," like a mantra, hypnotizing the courtroom with the power of his voice. The district attorney swings into action, first cross-examining the state chemist who testifies that he found arsenic mixed with the sugar that Ellen used in her coffee. Second, the mortuary manager states that Ruth Berent made arrangements to cremate Ellen's body. Then the bank manager, who is the trustee for Ellen's estate, testifies that his client's will specified burial in the family vault. Following all this, Richard's low-key lawyer, Glen Robie, tells him that Quinton will "have his brass knuckles on" when he interrogates Richard. This is true. The district attorney begins innocuously enough by asking Richard to read Ellen's letter to him (Quinton) out loud. The letter talks about Richard and Ruth falling in love and accuses Ruth of threatening to kill Ellen. She ends by saying, "I am writing this letter to you because we once meant a great deal to each other." Price starts to move in for the kill at this point, "You knew when you met her that she was engaged to another man. Were you reluctant?" The actor's incisive drawl on "engaged to another man" is right on target and he lets his face darken as if remembering Ellen and Richard holding hands. In addition, a significant pause before "reluctant" makes Richard (and us) squirm.

Harland uneasily provides the details of his courtship to which Quinton responds, "I don't say this critically nor in mockery nor to suggest that you are conceited, but simply to be sure that I understand you correctly. You suggest that a beautiful young woman falls in love with you, wins you, and persuades you into a quick marriage against your better judgment. Is that a fair statement of the facts?" A weak assent from Harland, and then Quinton, "How soon after this did you begin to regret your surrender? Were you happy the first month, the second, the third, the fourth?" The gloves are now completely off as Quinton pounds away; he gains speed as he asks about their trip to Back of the Moon. "In June were you still happy with your wife? How about July; you loved her in July—how about August?" Vincent Price fires off the months like bullets as he questions his prey. His back against the wall, Harland admits that he saw Ruth nearly every day while Ellen was confined to her room with a difficult pregnancy. Jeering, Quinton asks, "Perhaps you didn't understand me. I shall repeat it for you. Are you in love with Ruth? Are you in love with Ruth? Are you in love with Ruth? Are you in love with Ruth?" With each sentence, Price leans in farther and more insistently as his vocal volume rises.

Now it's Ruth's turn. Asked about the dedication in Richard's latest book, Ruth explains that she is fond of gardening and admits that she would have access to toxic chemicals and insecticides. I love the actor's contemptuous line reading of the book's dedication, "to the gal with the hoe." Quinton goes on to say that an envelope containing sugar mixed with arsenic was found in Ruth's jacket and forces Ruth to confess that she served the coffee and gave the sugar to Ellen. In reference to the arsenic that was found in her (Ruth's) bottle of bath salts, Quinton says, "By what chemical process do you suppose that bath salts turn into poison?" Bingo! With his foot hard on the gas pedal, Vincent Price zooms in on the frightened witness with, "...and that day she was dead and the very next day her body was cremated... so that no autopsy could be possible." Ruth says her sister asked to be cremated. Quinton insists, "Then why did she take the trouble to have a clause inserted in her will that she be buried in Mount Auburn?" Ruth says she "can't explain." Now comes the race to the finish line, as Price roars past all objections with spectacular eloquence. "There are a great many things you can't explain. You can't explain how the poison got into the bottle of bath salts. You can't explain how it got in the sugar. You can't explain why Ellen's body was cremated so as to make an autopsy impossible. You can't explain why you made plans to leave this country shortly before your sister was poisoned. Well, perhaps you can explain this. When did you fall in love with Richard Harland? When did you first fall in love with him? Did you ever tell him that you loved him? When did you fall in love with him? You've dodged long enough; you can answer a simple question and I demand that you do so. Just when did you fall in love with Richard Harland? Did you love him after his brother, Danny, was drowned? Did you love him after the death of his stillborn child? Did you love him after his wife died? Did you love him last week; a month before; a year before..." (and shouting) "Are you in love with him today?" Ruth says she's always loved him, steps down from the witness stand and faints. Like a fencer, Price parries and thrusts with the word "love" each time and hits home with, "Are you in love with him today?"

No bleeding heart, Quinton wastes no time in recalling Richard to the stand after Ruth faints. "And now I want the truth out of you... and now I ask you as I have asked you over and over and over time and time again. Are you in love with her? Are you in love with the woman who killed your wife?" Forcefully (for the first time) Richard Harland says that Ellen killed herself. Quinton cannot imagine this and asks, "Knowing her as you did and I did; you honestly think her capable of not only committing suicide but falsely accusing her own sister of her death... you actually want the jury to believe that she was that sort of monster?" Harland replies that his late wife "loved only for what it could bring her;" that her love estranged her own father and mother; and that she confessed to killing Danny and her unborn child. "And who is now reaching from the grave to destroy her innocent sister. Yes, she was that sort of monster!" Quinton heads for the judge's bench and the courtroom goes wild. The jury finds Ruth not guilty but Richard gets two years for withholding evidence.

Leave Her to Heaven ends with the wordless reunion of Ruth and Richard (after his prison term) as the music swells and unseen choirs sing. Nauseating!

Performances vary widely in this movie. Price and Tierney command top honors. Although it is clearly Tierney's picture, Price's achievement is more impressive because of his severely limited screen time. Mary Phillips, playing Mrs. Berent, draws a careful character

Quinton wastes no time in recalling Richard to the stand after Ruth faints. (Photofest)

sketch of a woman who loses her husband to her daughter, finally making the horrific discovery that her daughter was a murderer and a madwoman. Reed Hadley, as Dr. Mason, makes the most of his brief scene with Ellen as he sees through her false concern for Danny. Chill Wills (Leick Thorne) is hard not to like and we identify with his unease around Ellen. However, his "hootenanny" scene at Back of the Moon with everyone but Ellen sitting around and singing is a bit much. This is one time that Ellen is justifiably annoyed! Darryl Hickman as the crippled brother, Danny, is sweet but his character is cloying so there is not much he could have done. A similar situation exists with Jeanne Crain playing Ruth Berent. She is a fine actress, but has little opportunity to get past her girl-next-door persona. Ms. Crain rises above this twice. Pushed beyond endurance by Ellen, she yells, "With your love, you've made a shadow of Dick... you're the most pitiful creature I've ever known!" Vincent Price helps her in the courtroom action by goading and jabbing and goading again. Her responses are appropriately tentative, but she spoils it when she pours on the syrup and tells of her love for Dick. Speaking of Dick, most leading men from the 1940s were cardboard cutouts of each other and Cornel Wilde is no exception. He uses two or three interchangeable expressions throughout. Ellen is not only wicked but stupid as well to prefer this curly headed dimwit to the fascinating, clever Quinton.

Direction is tight, although Cornel Wilde has too much screen time for my taste. The luscious cinematography earned a well-deserved Oscar. It is a visually beautiful movie—from the strangely breathtaking New Mexico desert to the secluded lake in Maine. Costumes are ravishing, especially Tierney's silks and satins that undulate with her every move. Alfred Newman provides a solid, although somewhat generic, score. I like his "big bad Ellen" theme with ominous descending tritones.

Reviews, although generally positive, were mixed. *The Los Angeles Times*, December, 1945 said, "The picture runs heavily to theatricalism, in fact, too much so in the courtroom scenes, notwithstanding these are brilliantly sustained by Vincent Price whose portrayal merits attention as contending for the Academy supporting honors." *Hollywood Citizen News*, December, 1945 noted, "Thereafter, the story spins to a rousing climax centering on a murder trial, in which Vincent Price, as the prosecuting attorney, rises to new dramatic heights. His performance—brief as it is—shines like a beacon." *Variety*, December, 1945 enthused, "Sumptuous Technicolor mounting and a highly exploitable story lend considerable importance...." *The New York Times* accused Price, and some of the other actors, of playing their parts too "mechanically." And *The New York Post* said that Vincent's presence added the "luxury of the bravura."

Leave Her to Heaven is worth a look for a monumental Price, a rotten-to-the-core Tierney and some of the most glorious 1940s Technicolor going. It is not a film that can bear watching over and over without the fast forward on the remote handy. Cornel Wilde comes close to spoiling every scene he's in with his posed acting and canned facial expressions. Regrettably, he appears in 90 percent of the footage so this is a problem. Fortunately, Vincent Price, Gene Tierney, Mary Phillips and, to a lesser extent, Jeanne Crain are in most of his scenes (running damage control and acting up a storm). To enjoy this movie, it is necessary to ignore him but listen to his dialogue so that you don't miss out on the plot.

CREDITS: Producer: William A. Bacher; Director: John M. Stahl; Screenplay: Jo Swerling from the Novel by Ben Ames Williams; Cinematography: Leon Shamroy; Art Directors: Lyle Wheeler, Maurice Ransford; Set Decorator: Thomas Little; Music: Alfred Newman; Orchestrations: Edward B. Powell; Editor: James B. Clark; Costumes: Kay Nelson; Makeup: Ben Nye; Running Time: 110 minutes, Technicolor; Released: December 19, 1945, by Twentieth Century-Fox

CAST: Gene Tierney (Ellen Berent); Cornel Wilde (Richard Harland); Jeanne Crain (Ruth Berent); Vincent Price (Russell Quinton); Mary Philips (Mrs. Berent); Ray Collins (Glen Robie); Gene Lockhart (Dr. Saunders); Reed Hadley (Dr. Mason); Chill Wills (Leick Thorne); Darryl Hickman (Danny Harland); Paul Everton (Judge); Olive Blakeney (Mrs. Robie); Addison Richards (Bedford); Harry Depp (Catterson); Grant Mitchell (Carlson/Bank President); Milton Parsons (Medcraft/Mortician)

Gene Tierney and Vincent Price in *Dragonwyck*. (Photofest)

DRAGONWYCK (1946)
by Nathalie Yafet

Beautiful Miranda Wells lives on a farm in Connecticut with her religiously stern father, Ephraim, hardworking mother, Abigail, and assorted siblings. When Nicholas Van Ryn, the "patroon" (or lord) of a magnificent Hudson River estate and a distant relation of Abigail's, proposes that they send one of the daughters on an "extended visit," Miranda manages to convince skeptical Ephraim that she should be the one to go. Father accompanies daughter to New York where they connect with Van Ryn (who is younger and handsomer than Ephraim would like). Arriving at Dragonwyck, the Van Ryn ancestral home, the awed Miranda meets Nicholas' neglected wife, Johanna, and ignored daughter, Katrine. Magda, the housekeeper, tells her about Nicholas' great-grandmother Azilde who committed suicide in the house and apparently never left because anyone with Van Ryn blood can hear her playing the harpsichord, singing and laughing whenever misfortune is about to occur. Katrine introduces Miranda to Dr. Jeff Turner, who sympathizes with the rebellious tenant farmers at Dragonwyck. Gathered together to pay rent and "tribute," Klaas Bleecker, one of the farmers, makes an attempt on Nicholas' life but is stopped by Dr. Turner. Later that evening at a party on the estate, Miranda embarrasses herself by admitting that her father is a farmer, but Nicholas soothes her wounded pride by asking her to dance. Soon afterwards, Johanna gets a cold, takes to her bed, and Nicholas sends her his favorite oleander (a poisonous evergreen shrub) as a gift. Dr. Turner, who is at Dragonwyck pleading a fair trial for Bleecker, prescribes a light diet and some medicinal drops. Johanna dies that evening, ostensibly from acute gastritis. Nicholas later informs Miranda that she must surely know that "they were inevitable." Miranda returns to Greenwich the next day. Some months later, Nicholas appears at the farm and he and Miranda are married. In short order, the new bride is pregnant. Dr. Turner is called in to assist the doctor in residence and tries to tell Nicholas that his son has a malformed heart and cannot survive, which Nicholas refuses to believe. After a hasty baptism, the baby dies and Nicholas begins spending weeks at a time alone in the tower room. Miranda forces him to admit that he has become a drug addict and offers to help, which he refuses. Nicholas then gives her an oleander also and she becomes steadily weaker. Dr. Turner, by now, has made a connection between the plant and Johanna's death and accuses Nicholas of murdering her and of trying to do the same to Miranda. They fight. Nicholas escapes to the Van Ryn ancestral "tribute" throne and Dr. Turner returns with the mayor and some of the farmers. Nicholas aims at Miranda, but Jeff shoots him. Miranda returns to her parents' farm and invites Dr. Turner to visit soon.

Unlike the Manderley of Daphne du Maurier's *Rebecca* and Shirley Jackson's *The Haunting of Hill House*, Dragonwyck itself is not the central character in the Anya Seton novel or the film. Seton's novel focuses on Miranda Wells and how characters, events and circumstances affect her. The film attempts to do the same. Gene Tierney is top billed and we certainly sympathize with her, but dominating everyone and everything else is Vincent Price's Nicholas Van Ryn. We are drawn to him almost against our will.

It is nearly impossible to imagine anyone replacing Vincent Price as Nicholas Van Ryn. Handsome, elegant and polite yet at the same time arrogant, insane and murderous—Van Ryn seems to be a composite of past and future "honey on the bullet" villains that the actor specialized in portraying. Lucy Chase Williams in her engaging book, *The Complete Films of Vincent Price*, says of the actor, "Cast again as expertly as in *Laura*, Vincent Price was the physical incarnation of the glamorous patroon of author Anya Seton's imagination: 'He was tall, over six feet and of a slender build... His hair, nearly as black as his boots, was abundant and slightly waving... As for his face, it was so nearly the embodiment of the descriptions of heroes in Miranda's favorite books that she was awed. Here were the full flexible mouth, the aquiline nose with slightly flaring nostrils, the high and noble forehead accented by stern black brows...'" Mr. Wells' description is somewhat insulting, but just as accurate, "This fellow had the kind of looks that might turn a silly girl's head..." He charms us effortlessly, just as he does Miranda, pulling back from any real warmth or involvement when it suits him. Price's early scenes with Gene Tierney are appealing and I admit that it is always fun (for a limited time) to see our "monsters" as romantic leads. One example is when Nicholas and Miranda aboard the *Swallow* are approaching Dragonwyck together for the first time. She asks if he minds that she is not wearing her bonnet because "the breeze feels so wonderful against (her) face." His tender response, "The breeze must feel wonderful indeed with a face as beautiful as yours against it," coupled with a well-chiseled profile indicate that he could easily have taken the leading-man route. Fortunately for us, he chose the more twisted path.

Our first glimpse of Nicholas Van Ryn is reminiscent of Hjalmar Poelzig's in *The Black Cat*: Each man makes a majestically unexpected entrance and sizes up the situation immediately. Miranda stares as if one of her fictional heroes had come to life and Nicholas seems to return her interest. Ephraim, however, is not so easily won over. Discussing politics, Nicholas mentions his tenant farmers and Mr. Wells remarks that he's never heard of such an arrangement and asks if they own their own land. Nicholas replies, "No, it belongs to me. It belonged to my father and his father back to the first patroon who took title in 1630." Totally amazed, Ephraim wants to know if they are able to buy the land. Again, the answer, "No... because it belongs to me." I can think of any number of actors who would have delivered these lines with arrogance, anger or an emotional outburst. Mr. Price, to his credit, keeps it simple and merely states the facts. The effect is unsettling and vaguely hints at the man's puzzling personality. Another skillfully underplayed moment occurs after Nicholas' and Miranda's arrival at Dragonwyck. Johanna is already dining and anxiously asks if her husband remembered to get all the pastries she requested. As Nicholas lovingly assures her that he brought them, an infinitesimal whisper of disdain darts across his face and then disappears. After dinner, they retire to the "haunted" Red Room where Nicholas recounts the story of Azilde and his great-grandfather to a bored Johanna and a rapt Miranda, who asks if they fell "in love at first sight." Nicholas' deadpan counter, "No Van Ryn does anything at first sight," is perfect.

Later on after the annual rent ceremony turns ugly, Nicholas makes a speech that reveals one of the governing forces of his life. Speaking of Dr. Turner's efforts to incite an anti-rent rebellion, the patroon vehemently declares, "...just what is it he wants you to want so passionately? It has an assortment of highly romantic names; the rights of man, life, liberty and the pursuit of happiness. But my rents and tributes and my responsibility are hereditary—the symbols of a way of life to which I have been born and in which I shall continue to live. I shall never relinquish my position." The actor stands tall and ramrod straight as he delivers these stirring, yet condescending, lines with absolute certainty and resolve. That same evening at the party after Miranda's humiliating encounter with some of the Hudson River "royalty," Nicholas fol-

Nicholas Van Ryn seduces Miranda Wells (Gene Tierney) in *Dragonwyck*. (Photofest)

lows her, saying, "Dance with me, Miranda," repeating it twice not as an invitation but rather a hypnotic suggestion. He dismisses her misgivings with a creepily seductive, "You must never be afraid of anything with me, Miranda." Price and Tierney have incredible chemistry which works to their advantage throughout the film, especially during their waltz together at the Dragonwyck ball. Nicholas expertly whirls Miranda around the floor as they stare at each other, trance-like. Encouraging her to express her feelings about the party, she exclaims, "Golly Moses!" as he throws back his head, laughing.

The mood changes drastically in the next scene, as Nicholas stands at the window in Johanna's room watching the violent thunderstorm. Johanna complains about the storm, her cold and the Catskills until Magda enters with an oleander, a gift from the patroon to his wife. She's touched that he would send her one of his favorite plants and Nicholas remarks, "How alive it is—as if it had thoughts of its own and desires of its own." Vincent Price instills these lines with a deadly grace, evoking Hawthorne's *Rappacini's Daughter*. As the scene continues, Johanna testily asks what he does during all the time spent in the Tower Room. His humorously macabre retort, "...Anything from pinning butterflies to hiding an insane twin brother..." prefigures his delightful Trumbull from *The Comedy of Terrors*. Adroitly slipping back into the role of the concerned and loving spouse, Nicholas promises Johanna that they will go away together when she is "well again." Shortly afterwards, Johanna dies. Talking with Miranda late into the night, he tells her about his wedding to Johanna and that they were never happy, especially after she gave birth to a daughter rather than a son. Miranda tries to comfort him and Nicholas tells her, "Miranda, you've known as well as I that this was inevitable; that we were inevitable... you couldn't help yourself any more than I... but I had to say it, there was no way for me not to and no one but you to hear it..." On paper, this scene has more than a whiff of Harlequin Romances about it, but Price's line reading is so ardent and heartfelt that we forget the purple prose and revel in the moment.

LAWRENCE FRENCH: *Dragonwyck* was also the first picture to be directed by Joseph L. Mankiewicz. How did you like working with him?

VINCENT PRICE: Joe was a very good director. He had been a producer at Fox and he produced *The Keys to the Kingdom*, so I already knew him. *Dragonwyck* turned out to be a really marvelous film, even though we had to change a lot of things from the book. Those were the days when censorship meant that the villain had to be caught or else die at the end, even though, in the book, he reforms and goes scot free. Joe gave me a marvelous piece of direction for the scene where I proposed to Gene Tierney. I had lost a lot of weight for the part, because the character I was playing (Nicholas Van Ryn, the Patroon), was a drug addict. Joe told me he wanted me to stand very straight and erect, so I'd look as tall and thin as possible. Then, as we started to shoot the scene, Joe yelled at me, "Remember Vincent, nice erection." (laughter). It took us quite a few takes to finish that scene, because everybody on the set was so convulsed with laughter.

LAWRENCE FRENCH: The house in *Dragonwyck*, like in most Gothic films, is an important part of the story. Your character lives in a manor house that was very impressive.

VINCENT PRICE: Yes, that was a beautiful set built by (Art Director) Lyle Wheeler, right on the stage at Fox. It was a wonderful house, you could have moved right in, except they tore it down a week after we finished shooting. The exterior of the house was a glass shot, but the interior was a complete house. The only other picture I did which had as complete an interior setting was *Wilson*, which was about President Wilson. They reproduced the White House, but it was hysterical, because the famous blue room was reproduced exactly, but it didn't photograph blue. It was in the early days of Technicolor, so they had re-paint it, and start all over.

Naturally, their newly married happiness is short lived. Nicholas returns after a three day absence and they have a blissful reunion. Meanwhile, Miranda has acquired a new maid, Peggy O'Malley, who happens to be crippled. Nicholas cannot control his distaste, refers to the girl as an "untidy little cripple" and "it"; telling his new wife that, "Deformed bodies depress me." Miranda doesn't stop with one transgression, but goes on to speak about the night Johanna died and her guilt over their being married so soon afterwards. Nicholas sarcastically responds, "Do you believe there is a God who spends eternity snooping on human behavior and punishing all violators of the pastor's latest sermon?" Asked if he believes in God, Van Ryn answers, "I believe in myself and I am answerable to myself. I will not live according to printed mottoes like the directions on a medicine bottle." Vincent Price's emotional range in this scene is impressive. He enters like an impassioned newly-wed husband and exits like an agnostic philosopher. His lines referring to Peggy are particularly skillful as he disdainfully emphasizes the double "p" in cripple and accents the initial "d" consonants in "deformed" and "depress." As the scene continues, Miranda is visibly shaken, but Nicholas is prepared to dress their salads as if nothing had happened. A weeping Miranda runs off to her room, her husband hesitating slightly before he follows her. Needless to say, after she announces her pregnancy, he is mollified. Again, Price is right on the mark as he begins to mix the salad dressing, obviously annoyed but determined not to let it disturb his composure. Finally, he realizes that his wife has done this in front of the servants and he goes to her room, demanding, "What possible excuse can you have for humiliating me like that...," with icy hauteur—which he loses the instant he understands that she might at that moment be carrying his long desired heir.

All of Nicholas Van Ryn's entrances in this film are memorable and the next one is no exception. He silences a noisy celebration at the local tavern as he asks Dr. Turner to return with him to Dragonwyck because he does not trust the physician he has on the premises to attend the birth of his child. Vincent Price's incredulous expression as Jeff Turner worriedly inquires after Miranda is perfectly done, as is his instantaneous change of expression as he says, "...nothing must happen to my son!" Following the baby's birth, Van Ryn stands absolutely motionless, looking into the crib and holding onto it with both hands as if to defy anyone to take his heir from him. Turner tells him that the child cannot live and he replies, "My son is entirely well...," as if to say the matter is closed and no more discussion. The next scene has the Dominie baptizing Adriaen Pieter Van Ryn and the barest flicker of relief shades his father's face, proving that he is perhaps not so indifferent to God as he thinks he is. Yet again, Price succeeds in confusing our sensibilities with his marvelous subtleties. Should we loathe Van Ryn or pity him? We vacillate continually while he keeps us guessing.

After the baby's death, Nicholas becomes more remote than ever and spends most of his time in the Tower Room. Miranda decides to join him there. Nicholas, robed and unshaven, greets her with, "...frankly, I almost succeeded in forgetting you." When asked what he does there, he jabs at her with, "What do I do; I live... brace yourself; prepare to have your God-fearing, prayer fattened, farmbred morality shaken to its core..." Seconds after this wildly startling statement, he reveals his drug addiction. When asked why, he feverishly blurts out, "It is because I have set free something within me—something that ever since I can remember has been like a rock caught in my heart, in my brain; pushing at me—choking me!" Van Ryn then continues in one of the film's most eloquent speeches, "...Don't be offended; by ordinary standards, you're quite intelligent. But I will not live by ordinary standards. I will not run with the pack. I will not be chained into a routine of living which is the same for others. I will not look to the ground and move on the ground with the rest, not so long as there are those mountaintops and clouds and limitless space!" This man cannot even admit that the dead baby belonged equally to both of them and simply walks away in response to Miranda's moving appeal, "...Let me love you and love me, too." Vincent Price is astonishing in this Tower Room scene, using his sonorous baritone, expressively sensitive features, and long, lean body to perfection. So vivid is his image of the rock caught in his heart—as he accents the "p" in pushing and the "ch" in choking—that we gasp for air along with him. He doesn't stop there, but continues with a monologue that is as close as we ever come to understanding the enigma that is Nicholas Van Ryn. Price takes full advantage, spouting this elitist philosophy with panache.

Peggy goes to Dr. Turner to tell him that Nicholas has recently sent an oleander to his second wife as well. Cut to Miranda reading the Bible that was a present from Ephraim when Nicholas joins her, commenting derisively on her "joy" in seeing him. Ever conciliatory, Miranda apologizes and says she is "so tired." With his entire face curled in a sneer, the patroon informs her that, "...strangely enough your tribulations seem to have become you. I cannot remember you more beautiful than you are now; and your beauty amazes me as much now as always... your strength, the earthiness of your peasant stock—and more—your grace, your unexpected look of quality. It would be a pity if we were not to have another—if you were barren." As soon as the exhausted woman declares the baby's death to be God's will; her husband demands, "...why did He take my son's life... it could not have been without purpose. No one gives life and takes it without purpose." Then, he grandly states that, "...what you are is the reflection of what I wanted you to be." Suddenly, the unhinged man panics as he hears Azilde singing and playing, masking his terror by calling the sound, "...the wind through the trees." I particularly enjoy the actor's entrance in this scene as he walks in, slowly closing the door, still retaining his dignity in spite of his 10 o'clock shadow and disheveled state. Delightful also is his rendering of the words, "beautiful" and "beauty"; twisting them around until they might as well be "ugly" and "ugliness" and simultaneously transforming his handsome countenance so that it projects his double meaning. (A heartwarming touch for AIP fans is Van Ryn's horror at hearing Azilde's ghost foreshadowing his string of haunted Poe heroes, with a special nod to Roderick Usher.)

Nicholas bolts to the Red Room where Azilde's portrait smiles mockingly as her singing ends abruptly. Jeff Turner shows up with Peggy and confronts Van Ryn with the toxic qualities of his beloved oleander which he is fond of giving to wives who no longer please him. (Price hastily metamorphoses haughty Van Ryn into a trapped criminal and then just as quickly recovers sufficiently to attack Dr. Turner.) They struggle and Nicholas goes to the Van Ryn ancestral chair, holding forth to an invisible audience that, "...No babbling idiot of a governor will make laws that have to do with my manor; with the manor that my son, *that my son* will inherit." Finally, Jeff, Miranda, the mayor and assorted farmers with guns materialize in order to arrest the patroon for Johanna's murder. He refuses to go peacefully, takes aim at his wife and is shot. The farmers respectfully remove their hats and he declares, "That's right. Take off your hats in the presence of the patroon!" Vincent Price does not disappoint us in the denouement. He impresses with his undiminished spirit in spite of exposure and humiliation. Interestingly enough, Nicholas' demise in the book is much more complicated. Jeff bests him in their fight, ties him up, and flees with Miranda—whom he places aboard the *Mary Clinton*, a steamboat which Van Ryn partially owns—to take her back to Connecticut. Nicholas boards later on. The captain races with another vessel in order to impress the patroon and the *Mary Clinton* catches fire. Nicholas saves his wife and two other people; telling her, "You shall see that I can save life as well as destroy it!"

Fortunately, Mr. Price is not the only reason for *Dragonwyck*'s appeal; his characterization is further strengthened by outstanding production values as well as talented co-stars and supporting players. Gene Tierney is excellent, expertly evolving from the daydreaming, countrified farm girl into the fabulously wealthy, stylish patroon's wife. Yet in spite of her elevated status, she never completely forgets her basic upbringing or her faith in God. The actress seems a bit too gorgeous for a Connecticut country girl, but except for her dark hair, the physical match is faithful to the Seton novel. Abigail, Miranda's mother, "...thought her remarkably like one of those exquisite creatures in *Godey's Lady's Book*, the same graceful height, small nose, and full, pouting lips." And Nicholas muses to himself about her "...delicate face with its unrealized potentialities for real beauty..." The look on her face when she sees Nicholas for the first time is, again, in perfect sync with the novel when the girl is attracted to his physical beauty and tries "...rather frantically to rearrange her ideas" (that Van Ryn must be an elderly gentleman). We sympathize with her yearnings, are touched by her love for Nicholas, pity her when her dreams turn into nightmares, and sincerely hope that she will be happy with Jeff Turner after the final reel (although he is a bore).

Second billed Walter Houston as Ephraim Wells delivers a focused, finely etched performance. His annoyance at the elaborate dinner ordered for them at the Astor House is priceless, "...there's something peculiar about a man who orders supper someplace when he's someplace else. How did he know what I wanted to eat?" Not missing a beat, he answers Miranda's, "But there's everything here you could possibly want," with a strangely prophetic and tersely final, "Everything is what no man should ever want." Yet another of his rejoinders to Miranda is worth repeating, "A woman oughta get a man first and then want him." His character is skillfully drawn and the actor succeeds in making the unbending Ephraim much more likable than the novel does. We see an inflexible Yankee farmer with unshakable religious faith and strenuously populist viewpoints, who is, nonetheless, devoted to his family. Anne Revere as his wife, Abigail, is a solid match for him. She is the perfect New England matron but remembers when her longings were like Miranda's, is proud of her Van Ryn connections and generally has more balanced viewpoints than her spouse. Her hurt when Nicholas fails to introduce himself to her when he comes for Miranda is palpable and we readily forgive her this small vanity. She neatly conveys her own doubts when she ends the declarative statement, "I'm sure he has fine manners," with a question mark. Ms. Revere's finest moment is when she questions Miranda's feelings, "But you can't marry a dream, Miranda. What about him? Do you love *him*?"

Vivienne Osborne is a triumph as Johanna Van Ryn. We first see her digging away at her dinner with exuberant, abandoned gusto. Yet when her husband enters the room we sense her

mingled love and dread. The woman can barely control herself when she asks Nicholas if he remembered to get all of her pastries from New York and resumes her meal a heartbeat after being introduced to Miranda (who betrays some disgust at Johanna's table manners). Oddly enough, though, it is Johanna we feel sorry for as her eating is balm for the pain Nicholas' unsettling behavior causes. Seton's novel describes her as "enormously fat... (and) untidy." The cinematic Johanna is slightly plump, fashionable, and not at all unattractive. Her suffering and tears are demonstrably real as she watches her adored husband waltz with Miranda at the Dragonwyck ball. The actress is also splendid as she whines about being laid up with her cold and doggedly refuses to follow Dr. Turner's sensible suggestion of a light diet. Osborne plays with our emotions once again as she makes us feel Johanna's confusion over Nicholas' mixed messages. (He likes and wants her. He hates her and wishes she would die.) Brava! Daughter Katrine is sensitively played by Connie Marshall. This is a child who tells a relative stranger that she does not love her parents. She is miserable when she is required to be with them and wants to leave right away. The young actress shines in two scenes. In the first one, Miranda has just queried her as to why her father does not like Dr. Turner, and Katrine, without a trace of affectation or overacting says, "Papa never says why not." The second one has her awakened by Azilde's music in the middle of the night with her initial pleasure crumbling rapidly to stark terror.

Glenn Langan turns in a fairly convincing performance as the lovestruck Dr. Turner, but is at a clear disadvantage compared to Vincent Price's bravura turn. Joseph L. Mankiewicz put it best when he said, "The love story is apt to be very unsatisfying in its conclusion. The young doctor cannot be half so glamorous or exciting as his murderous heel/rival. I can imagine no woman preferring the hero to the villain, in this case, for either bed or breakfast..." Langan's moments with Tierney alone are better, especially when he clumsily tries to confess his love before Miranda returns to her family. Jessica Tandy's Peggy O'Malley is unhampered by any such obstacles. Every word and gesture are appropriately articulated: communicating her love

Dragonwyck is one of Vincent Price's 10 best films.

for Miranda, fear of Nicholas and admiration for Dr. Turner. In addition, Ms. Tandy's Irish brogue sounds authentic and her limp is astonishingly lifelike. The actress' gasping horror when Nicholas wheels on her and says, "You loathsome little cripple, why should you have been permitted to live and not my son," is matchless.

Henry Morgan's boisterous Klaas Bleecker is nicely done, particularly his mockery of Nicholas in the tavern as he shouts, "Take off your heads in the presence of the *poltroon*." Spring Byington plays Magda with her trademark good-natured dottiness, but reveals just enough darkness behind the eyeballs to keep us off balance. Of the smaller roles, Grady Sutton as the hoity-toity hotel clerk at the Astor House is a standout. Ephraim and Miranda present themselves at the front desk and he simpers, "And, uh, what can I do for you, my good man?" Ephraim asks him if he is the tavern keeper and he unhesitatingly fires off, "This is not a tavern and I am not a keeper, my good man." Mr. Wells volleys with, "And I am not your good man!" His condescending indifference rapidly changes to obsequiousness when he understands that they are the party being met by the important patroon—"...how stupid of me... a thousand pardons."

Costumes are wonderful, but Miranda's rustling gowns and Nicholas' elegant suits make us sigh for Technicolor. (My favorite is Nicholas' crested velvet robe. This costume gets a lot of mileage as the patroon wears it with full grandeur in the early scenes, is seen with it in the Tower Room and actually dies in it.) Exterior and interior sets are fine as is the attention to detail. Rococo revival furniture was the latest rage in the mid-19th century and we see its intricate, sensuously curving lines in Miranda's bedroom after she becomes the second Mrs. Van Ryn. Alfred Newman's score is lushly romantic as well as eerie. (The discordant celeste sounds and Azilde's harpsichord playing are chilling.)

Reviews were glowing: *Variety*, February 1946: "...its box office chances are assured... grade-A production in every detail... It is one of Vincent Price's best roles to date, and he handles it for all it's worth." *The New York Times*, April 1946, Bosley Crowther "Vincent Price gives a picturesque performance... clean-shaven and elegantly tailored, he still makes a formidable Bluebeard, and his moments of suave diabolism are about the best in the film." *Look*, May 1946: "As *Dragonwyck*'s homicidal aristocrat who tries to murder two wives, [Price] sets a romantic pace which will be a revelation to feminine moviegoers. One of Hollywood's soundest actors, this soft-spoken former member of St. Louis society dominates the picture."

Dragonwyck is one of Vincent Price's 10 best films. (In my opinion, the other contenders are: *The House of the Seven Gables, Laura, The Baron of Arizona, House of Wax, The Mad Magician, The Fall of the House of Usher, The Tomb of Ligeia, The Abominable Dr. Phibes* and *Theater of Blood*.) What a shame that it is not commercially available and is shown infrequently on cable stations. It's an absorbing, tightly spun Gothic romance that deserves to be seen more often.

CREDITS: Producer: Darryl F. Zanuck; Producer (uncredited) Ernst Lubitsch; Director: Joseph L. Mankiewicz; Screenplay: Joseph L. Mankiewicz (Based on the Novel by Anya Seton); Assistant Director: Johnny Johnston; Cinematography: Arthur Miller; Art Directors: Lyle Wheeler, Russell Spencer; Set Decorator: Paul S. Fox, Thomas Little; Music: Alfred Newman; Orchestrator: Edward B. Powell; Editor: Dorothy Spencer; Costumes: Rene Hubert; Makeup: Ben Nye; Sound: W.D. Flick; Special Photographic Effects: Fred Sersen; Choreography: Arthur Appel; Running Time: 103 minutes; Released: April 10, 1946 by Twentieth Century-Fox

CAST: Gene Tierney (Miranda Wells); Walter Houston (Ephraim Wells); Vincent Price (Nicholas Van Ryn); Glenn Langan (Dr. Jeff Turner); Anne Revere (Abigail Wells) Spring Byington (Magda); Connie Marshall (Katrine Van Ryn); Henry Morgan (Klaas Bleecker); Vivienne Osborne (Johanna Van Ryn); Jessica Tandy (Peggy O'Malley); Trudy Marshall (Elizabeth Van Borden); Reinhold Schunzel (Count de Grenier); Jane Nigh (Tabitha); Ruth Ford (Cornelia Van Borden); Scott Elliot (Tom Wells); Boyd Irwin (Tompkins); Maya Van Horn (Countess de Grenier); Keith Hitchcock (Mr. MacNabb); Francis Pierlot (Dr. Brown); Betty Fairfax (Mrs. McNab); Grady Sutton (Hotel Clerk)

Vincent Price as Richelieu in *The Three Musketeers*. (Photofest)

THE THREE MUSKETEERS (1948)
by Susan Svehla

Who better to play the evil Cardinal Richelieu, chief nemesis of the Three Musketeers, than the always elegant Vincent Price? Price joined an all-star cast including Gene Kelly, Lana Turner, June Allyson, Van Heflin, Angela Lansbury, Gig Young, and Frank Morgan in MGM's lavish Technicolor spectacle, *The Three Musketeers*, released in 1948.

> In the year of Our Lord 1625, William Shakespeare was not long dead, America not long settled, and the calm of France not long for this world. A Gascon villager was preparing to go forth and shake that world till its teeth rattled.

So begins the familiar story of the brave Musketeers, the evil Richelieu, the doddering King, the wayward Queen and the seductive Countess de Winter.

Young D'Artagnan (Gene Kelly) leaves his village to travel to Paris hoping to join the legendary Musketeers. During his travels he is accosted by Rochefort (Ian Keith, who portrayed Rochefort also in the 1935 film version) accompanying Countess de Winter (Lana Turner) on a nefarious errand for Richelieu. He picks himself up and continues to Paris where he meets up with Athos (Van Heflin), Porthos (Gig Young) and Aramis (Robert Coote) and in a few short moments manages to agree to meet them all in a duel, Athos at one o'clock, and Porthos and Aramis shortly afterward. But they never get the chance to test their skill with the blade, for Richelieu's men try to arrest them for dueling and the four band together to defeat the soldiers.

D'Artagnan falls in love with the Queen's servant Constance Bonacieux (June Allyson) who begs his help. Queen Anne (Angela Lansbury) had given a set of 12 diamond studs to her English lover, the Duke of Buckingham (John Sutton). Richelieu plans to discredit the Queen by sending Countess de Winter to England to steal two of the diamond studs. Richelieu wants a war with England although the King (Frank Morgan) is against it.

D'Artagnan asks the help of Porthos, Aramis and Athos and, together, the four raise their swords and, in a spectacular shot, the camera pans to an overhead shot as the four look skyward and Athos says, "It's all for one D'Artagnan, and one for all." That scene fades into another impressive bit of cinematography by lensman Robert Planck as the Musketeers and their pages ride in silhouette through the darkened night toward the nearest port. Richelieu's men ambush them along the way and soon only D'Artagnan is left. He manages to retrieve the diamonds, but two are gone. The Duke of Buckingham has a jeweler replace the missing diamonds and D'Artagnan quickly heads back to France. He seeks the help of the Musketeers but Porthos has been wounded in the backside and cannot sit on a horse, Aramis has entered a monastery and Athos is roaring drunk in the cellar of an inn. D'Artagnan manages to sober him up and he accompanies D'Artagnan back to Paris. They get the diamonds to the Queen in the nick of time. But the evil Richelieu does not take defeat gracefully. He has Constance kidnapped and tries to force D'Artagnan to become one of his guards. He uses Countess de Winter to seduce D'Artagnan, who falls for the dangerous damsel. Trying to get information from the Countess, he seduces her maid and impersonates a foppish Count whom the Countess claims to love. Unfortunately his cleverness is for naught for D'Artagnan falls under the spell of the Countess and confesses his impersonation. She is enraged and calls the guards.

D'Artagnan tells all to Constance who has been freed by the Queen and they are married the night before Constance, for her own safety, is sent to England. Richelieu meets Countess de Winter at an inn and subtly orders her to assassinate the Duke of Buckingham while pretending to be a courier of peace from Richelieu. Athos confronts the Countess who turns out to be his runaway wife. He manages to take a letter of carte blanche from the Countess (the letter was one of the demands she had made of Richelieu as a price for her services). The Musketeers learn of this plan and send D'Artagnan's page Planchet (Keenan Wynn, looking much as he would when he impersonates a page in the play within the movie version of *Kiss Me Kate*) to warn Buckingham, who makes Constance the jailer of the evil Countess. When the Musketeers learn of this, Athos comments, "an angel in charge of the devil," and D'Artagnan and Athos head toward England to save Constance.

But they are too late, for the Countess has tricked Constance into helping her escape. She kills Constance, who dies in D'Artagnan's arms, and then assassinates Buckingham. The Musketeers catch up with her in France and send her to her death by beheading. The Musketeers are brought before the King who wishes to be lenient with them, but Richelieu sees his chance to be rid of them and demands he be allowed to give them a harsh sentence. D'Artagnan pulls out the carte blanche and forces Richelieu to change his plans. Richelieu laughs as he accepts the one-upmanship of D'Artagnan and allows Aramis to retire to a monastery, orders a rich widow be found for Porthos, returns Athos' lands and title and sends D'Artagnan to England, where, he implies, things are a little too quiet.

Vincent Price's character of Richelieu would overshadow the previous filmic villains and set the standard for future Richelieus. *The Three Musketeers* had been filmed as a silent film in 1911, 1914, 1916 (with Walt Whitman as Richelieu). The most famous version is the 1921 Douglas Fairbanks rendition with Nigel De Brulier portraying Cardinal Richelieu. In 1935 the novel was again filmed, this time by RKO in the first sound version starring Walter Abel, Paul Lukas, Onslow Stevens and Ian Keith (as de Rochefort). Nigel de Burlier would recreate the role of Cardinal Richelieu once again for this film. De Burlier was a popular character actor who appeared in many costume dramas including *The Man in the Iron Mask* (1939) and worked with Price in *Tower of London* (1939).

Fox would take a stab at *The Three Musketeers* in 1939 with Don Ameche as D'Artagnan and The Ritz Brothers filling in for the rest of the Musketeers. Miles Mander would portray Cardinal Richelieu. Mander also appeared with Price in 1939's *Tower of London* and *The House of the Seven Gables* in 1940. Price's Richelieu would be followed by Charlton Heston as Cardinal Richelieu in the 1973 comedy version that starred Oliver Reed, Raquel Welch, Michael York and Richard Chamberlain. Christopher Lee would portray Rochefort in this version. However, Vincent Price's Richelieu would be most felt in the big-budget 1993 Buena Vista version that used a new generation of stars to portray the well-known characters. Charlie Sheen would star as Aramis, Kiefer Sutherland as Athos, the red-hot Chris O'Donnell as D'Artagnan, Rebecca DeMornay as Milady De Winter and Tim Curry as Cardinal Richelieu. Curry would come closest to the Price interpretation of Richelieu. Although Curry's performance was more over-the-top than Price's, you can easily see a little of Vincent Price in there. Tim Curry is quite like Vincent Price in many ways—he enjoys his work by the glint in his eyes and the tone of his voice, and he is especially adept at loathsome villains.

Although the 1948 version suffered from some ill-conceived casting (Lana Turner is not up to the challenge of portraying the evil Countess de Winter and June Allyson has repeatedly stated she found the role uncomfortable) it is still one of the best. Gene Kelly was perfectly suited to swashbuckling roles and his acrobatics as D'Artagnan are most enjoyable. In 1948 he once again took sword in hand to portray Serafin in *The Pirate* with Judy Garland.

In the scene where D'Artagnan tells Constance he loves her, watch carefully. D'Artagnan has never declared his love before and goes way overboard saying, "I love you. I love you..." Kelly would hilariously use the same tone of voice and over-dramatizing in the silent film segment, "The Dueling Cavalier," with Jean Hagen in *Singin' in the Rain*.

Vincent Price is particularly forbidding in the scene where D'Artagnan is brought before Richelieu. Price softly strokes a cat while doing his insinuating best to try to convince D'Artagnan to join him. His gentleness with the cat does not hide the fact Richelieu is a villain. It's interesting to note other film versions list Richelieu as Cardinal Richelieu but, in *The Films of Gene*

Lana Turner as Countess de Winter and Vincent Price as Richelieu play a game of cat and mouse.

Kelly, author Tony Thomas states the studio was afraid of upsetting religious groups and referred to Richelieu as Prime Minister.

In their review *Variety* noted, "Metro's *The Three Musketeers* is a swaggering, tongue-in-cheek treatment of picturesque fiction, extravagantly presented to capture the fancy of any high romanticist—and there are a lot of them. The Alexandre Dumas classic has always been a blood-quickener. It is even more so in its latest film version and, with a multi-star cast to brighten marquees, there is every indication it will cut a socko boxoffice swath right down the line.

"...There are acrobatics by Gene Kelly that would give the late, great Douglas Fairbanks pause. His first duel with Richelieu's cohorts is almost ballet, yet never loses the feeling of swaggering swordplay... Production wise, Pandro S. Berman has overlooked no angles in dressing up *Musketeers* as a feast for the eyes and a stimulant for chimerical adventuring by an audience... Wise casting has Vincent Price bringing his suave leer and menace to the role of Richelieu. The part is short in the total footage, as is Queen Anne as portrayed by Angela Lansbury."

Director George Sidney used Price effectively in his few scenes. Sidney was more at home directing musicals including *Anchors Aweigh* (again with Kelly), *Annie Get Your Gun*, *Bathing Beauty* and *The Harvey Girls*.

Vincent Price had a dignity and elegant air that would serve him well in costume pictures—especially as Richelieu, a performance by which all future versions will be judged.

CREDITS: Producer: Pandro S. Berman; Director: George Sidney; Writer: Robert Ardrey (Based on the Novel by Alexandre Dumas); Cinematography: Robert Planck; Music Composer: Herbert Stothart; Costume Design: Walter Plunkett; Makeup: Jack Dawn; MGM; 1948; Technicolor; 126 minutes

CAST: Lana Turner (Countess Charlotte de Winters); Gene Kelly (D'Artagnan); June Allyson (Constance Bonacieux); Van Helfin (Robert Athos); Angela Lansbury (Queen Anne); Frank Morgan (King Louis XIII); Vincent Price (Richelieu the Prime Minister); Keenan Wynn (Planchet); John Sutton (Duke of Buckingham); Gig Young (Porthos); Robert Coote (Aramis); Ian Keith (De Rochefort); Reginald Owen (De Treville)

John Sutton as Raizul and Vincent Price as Pasha Al Nadim in *Bagdad*.

BAGDAD (1949)

by Susan Svehla

Universal-International would march out an impressive cast for their desert saga *Bagdad* starring Maureen O'Hara and Vincent Price.

Price stars as Pasha Al Nadim, military governor of Bagdad. The film opens with Price's narration:

> Bagdad. Scheherazade's city of a thousand and one nights. For 5,000 years a fortress in the desert. Crossroad between civilized West and savage East. Legend has it that Adam and Eve built Bagdad when they were expelled from the Garden of Eden. It may be true for in Bagdad all unbelievable things are possible.

Nadim is escorting Princess Marjan (Maureen O'Hara) to Bagdad. She is returning to her people from England where she has been educated. Price is quite dashing in his military uniform complete with fez and sword. They ride through the desert trading barbs until the caravan is attacked by the Black Robes who steal their weapons. Nadim bargains with the outlaws and agrees to their demands. The Princess slyly chastises him. "Apparently the kind lady thinks me a coward," he says. "Oh no, not at all. I think the military governor is a very sensible diplomat." Nadim, annoyed, responds, "But you would prefer me a foolish hero dead." He shakes his head in disgust. "This is pure Bedouin." The Princess replies, "Well, that's what I am."

MAUREEN O'HARA   PAUL CHRISTIAN   VINCENT PRICE

Bagdad

But her feisty manner doesn't put off Nadim who actively pursues the lady. The Princess learns her father has been killed by the Black Robes and her people have no homes and no money. She thinks Hassan (Paul Christian), the Prince of a rival tribe, leads the Black Robes and killed her father and she goes about plotting her revenge. She accepts the protection of Nadim as the two indulge in a game of cat and mouse, each using the other to further their schemes. Hassan forces Nadim to offer him protection and the handsome Prince charms the Princess until she learns his real identity. Nadim, his men being unable to dispose of the Prince, decides to tell the Princess Hassan's identity and allow her to do the dirty work.

Prince Hassan agrees to a trial by the rulers of the tribes who are staying in the home of Nadim. They are all to travel to a desert location the next day but the Prin- cess and one follower overpower Nadim and tie him up. They force a soldier to lead them to Hassan but Black Robes at- tack. Hassan's aide is killed and Prince Hassan is knocked unconscious. The Princess and her fellow tribe member dis- guise themselves in Black Robes and take Hassan with them to torture him for her father's murder. Hassan's cousin Raizul (John Sutton) releases Nadim and we learn that Raizul is really the leader of the Black Robes and Nadim has been assist- ing him.

Fortunately, Hassan convinces the Princess of the truth and they head for the meeting place disguised as Gypsies. The Princess is captured and Nadim sends her to a violent death, but Hassan arrives to save her. He is pleading his case when the Black Robes, led by Raizul, attack. Nadim is quickly disposed of by a gun- shot from one of his own soldiers and Hassan's men arrive to save the day.

Vincent Price, while cutting a dash- ing figure as Nadim, lets the audience know things are not all they seem. Throughout the entire film he uses his eyes as a menacing characteristic of Nadim—his right eye remains wide open, but the left is almost closed, making the handsome man appear menacing and sin- ister. Nadim also constantly slaps those who annoy him. When an officer allows Hassan to escape, Price takes a pair of white gloves and slaps him saying, "fool and father of fools."

Price's best lines are when he is completely disgusted by the cloak and dagger activities of the tribes and denounces the Bedouins and plans to return to civilization.

Director Charles Lamont would work with Price again in *Curtain Call at Cactus Creek* with Donald O'Connor. John Sutton, who portrayed the evil Raizul, appeared with Price in eight films including *The Bat, Hudson's Bay, The Private Lives of Elizabeth and Essex, Tower of London* (1939) and *Return of the Fly*.

Variety was not overly fond of the film in their review. "*Bagdad* is a formula costume film, localed in the city of its title. Promise of adventure may get them in but there's nothing to hold an audience in the plotting. Settings, costumes, and eye appeal of Maureen O'Hara and the beautiful color lensing are the only assets."

While seeing such Anglo actors portray Arabs is disconcerting today, in 1949 it was typical and Price would do justice to his starring role as Nadim. Otherwise the film is standard stuff.

Pasha Al Nadim pursues the lovely Princess Marjan (Maureen O'Hara).

Most critics agree the stars were badly used and the only redeeming feature of the film is its costumes and color photography.

CREDITS: Producer: Robert Arthur; Director: Charles Lamont; Writer: Robert Hardy Andrews (Based on a Story by Tamara Hovey); Cinematography: Russell Metty; Art Direction: Bernard Herzbrun and Alexander Golitzen; Music: Frank Skinner; Makeup: Bud Westmore; Costumes: Yvonne Wood; Universal-International; 1949; 82 minutes

CAST: Maureen O'Hara (Princess Marjan); Vincent Price (Pasha Al Nadim); Paul Christian (Hassan); Jeff Corey (Mohammad Jad); John Sutton (Raizul); Frank Puglia (Saleel); Fritz Leiber (Emir); David Wolfe (Mhamud); Ann Pearce (Tirza)

Vincent Price as James Addison Reavis in *The Baron of Arizona*. (Photofest)

THE BARON OF ARIZONA (1950)
by Gary J. Svehla

While star Vincent Price and director Samuel Fuller are both known for their idiosyncratic style and technique (Price for performing over-the-top lip-smacking performances which, nevertheless, always seem to work; Fuller for establishing a kinky, personal style which is best appreciated in films such as *Shock Corridor* and *Naked Kiss*), in the 1950 Lippert Picture Release, *The Baron of Arizona*, both Price and Fuller (in his directorial debut) create a more restrained artistic statement, but a statement that is effective nonetheless. Essentially a fictionalized historic romantic drama, *The Baron of Arizona* casts Vincent Price in an early starring role as James Addison Reavis, the so-called Baron of Arizona, a forger and a fraud and the man who almost managed to steal the Territory of Arizona from its homegrown citizens.

As told in the film's framing preface, it is 1912 and President Taft has signed the proclamation making Arizona the 48th state in the Union, and as Griff (Reed Hadley), amidst a group of senators and the new state governor, toasts "a real lover of Arizona" and "my friend" James Addison Reavis, the group recoils in shocked amazement. Reminding Griff that the Baron was a "cheap swindler" and seemingly a monster, Griff, keeping his cool, says, "If not for him, you might not have formed your Senatorial Committee for statehood as you did!" Addressing the cheap swindler label, Griff adds: "Swindler—yes; cheap—there was nothing cheap about James Reavis." Asked if they were indeed bitter enemies in the past, Griff responds, "On the contrary, Governor, it was a challenge to have such a man as an adversary."

Citing "ambition" as the reason for his grand swindle, Griff quickly notes Reavis' motive: "It infuriated him that ignorant people inherited land because the United States recognized Spanish Grants... so he decided to steal Arizona with forged documents." Then Griff weaves his engrossing story, beginning where it all started, in a poor man's cabin outside Phoenix in 1872. There Reavis asks about the whereabouts of a young girl Sofia, speaking to her guardian Pepito Alvarez (Vladimir Sokoloff). Reavis, a clerk with the Santa Fe Land Office, knows that Pepito took the young girl in to raise when she was only one year old and has been caring for her ever since. Reavis announces that in 1748 King Ferdinand VI gave Peralta, who was to become the first Baron of Arizona, a grant of land in the U.S. According to Reavis, Sofia is the last surviving member of the Peralta family, and she is the heir to the land grant, literally the entire territory of Arizona; Reavis flashes the papers to prove his claim. Suddenly, a wide-eyed, undernourished dirty child enters, and Reavis invites both Sofia and Pepito to live in his house so he can instruct the growing girl how to act like a Baroness. Almost immediately, Reavis buys expensive clothes for the child and hires a governess, Loma (Beulah Bondi), to teach the young lady the finer things in life.

However, all this is a complex, clever conspiracy fabricated by the scheming Reavis who has studied ancient historic records, learned the art of forgery, studied languages and recreated himself to become a man of culture, fit to later become the Baron to Sofia's Baroness (as his ambitious plan depends upon the young girl, once fully grown, becoming his wife). Reavis' commitment to the plan has few boundaries. When the young Sofia finds a book in Reavis' room which she brings to him, Reavis is very upset at first: "You must never take what is not yours!" However, the harsh surrogate father's temper quickly softens as he invites the child to sit beside him as he supposedly begins to read a fairy tale from the open book. However, as James Wong Howe's camera carefully closes in on the book, we see the title: *Historical Handwriting and Crime of Forgery* by John Griff. One day, at a birthday party for Sofia, Reavis mentions she will be heir to 113,000 square miles, an area as large as Italy, but he has to leave her to get the documents necessary so she can rightfully inherit her land. However the child, deeply in love with Reavis, yells if he has to leave her, she doesn't want the land. Sofia pleads to be able to go with Reavis, but the kind-faced elder tells her that a Baroness doesn't cry and that he must go.

Then in the next 30 minutes, Reavis goes to the Hall of Records and falsifies records of Sofia's noble birth, establishing her family was of royal blood. He falsifies the existence of her now dead parents, paying the caretaker of a cemetery to engrave their names on blank tombstones. Next he sails to Spain to join the Monastery where the Land Grant Record Book of King Ferdinand VI, a hand-written document, is carefully guarded. However, even after joining the monks as Brother Anthony, he still finds the library and record books locked away from him, until he has himself reassigned to the collection of books. There he learns that some monks repair aging bindings while others copy text (using self-created ink whose formula hasn't changed in five centuries). Creating an ammonia-based solution that erases the ink, he uses the centuries-old ink to tamper with the original land records. However, the shocked Reavis learns that another copy of Ferdinand's land records exists in the castle of a Marquis, a secretary to the king, near Madrid. Reavis tells the Father that he is not cut out for this type of life and soon he is running away, stealing the monastery's horse and wagon and driving out of the religious confines like a bat out of hell. However, quickly crashing his carriage, he is taken in and nursed by a tribe of Gypsies, particularly a hot number named Rita (Tina Rome), who addresses the man as Father, because of his dress. But Reavis quickly bonds with the tribe by telling them he had to dress this way to escape from the police. He wins more points by telling a story of receiving a brutal lashing for daring to insult nobility. Rita gives Reavis her money so he will take her away, but he announces that it isn't enough, that they will have to rob the Marquis who lives near Madrid. Of course, in order to get close to the Marquis' library, Reavis becomes friendly with the Marquis' wife who states she is bored with her husband. Reavis reinforces matters by telling her that any man who wastes times with old books, ignoring such a young wife, is a fool. Soon Reavis is doctoring up the King Ferdinand VI land records, deserting the young wife who waits for him at a fountain. But Reavis is long gone.

Reavis returns to the now grown Sofia (Ellen Drew) and Pepito in Paris, where he proposes marriage to her. "Sofia, am I too old for your affections?" The young woman smiles brightly. "Too old! I am grateful to you." Cautiously continuing, Reavis utters, "It would fill my heart if you would become my wife." To which Sofia answers, "I wanted it this way ever since I realized what I wanted!" The two embrace and kiss. However, Reavis delivers the same line to Sofia that he delivered to Gypsy Rita in order to manipulate her: "I've known many women, but with you, I'm afraid."

Soon, the Baron and Baroness arrive in a fancy carriage in Phoenix, ready to stake their claim that they indeed own the Territory of Arizona, something that doesn't sit well with the local citizenry. The arrogant Reavis declares not only does he own the land, but he also owns the right of way (for railroads), mineral rights, grazing land, rivers. When locals challenge him, he smiles and simply states, "You're living on my land!" Soon the territory's leaders admit, "We're whipped," but mob violence develops as the locals think it insane to have to pay to own land for which they already paid hard-earned money, let alone the time and sweat invested. John Griff, our narrator and author of the book on forgery that Reavis pretended to read to Sofia, is assigned the case by the U.S. government to prove that Reavis' land claim is bogus. Griff states to the concerned leaders, "Sometimes a fine wrapper conceals inferior tobacco," telling the assembled that he believes Reavis' official documents are forged. According to Griff's logic, why else would a land office clerk finance a child's education when he could buy the land grant for a few dollars and claim it for himself. According to Griff, the reason for marrying Sofia was for extra protection. As long as a true Spaniard inherits the land, the U.S. government will honor the treaty, but Griff still believes Reavis' claim has "the stench of swindle" all about it.

For the remainder of the film, Griff and Reavis lock horns, such sequences becoming the dramatic center of the movie, showcasing Price's best acting in the film. Leaving a book on Reavis' office desk (a huge map of the territory of Arizona occupies the entire wall behind his

Reavis prepares to pummel a man with the butt of his rifle but is stopped by the cries of Sofia. (Photofest)

desk) and waiting in the shadows for his arrival, Reavis picks up a copy of the book he already knows by heart. "Have you ever read it?" Griff asks. When Reavis answers no, Griff states, "You might like a copy," revealing his trump card from the very beginning. Smiling, Reavis says, "My library is complete." Griff introduces himself as an agent from the Department of the Interior whose specialty is revealing falsified wills, ancient manuscripts and land grants. Turning indignant, Reavis barks, "I have prepared for a thorough investigation of all documents. But I don't appreciate the inference of falsification of papers." Asking Reavis again if he read his book, the tone lightens as the Baron smiles and states, "I really can't recall it." But Griff drops all pretenses and gets directly to the point: "Your penmanship was truly a masterpiece, a work of art... it's a pity your claim is a bad cigar wrapped in a rich Spanish leaf—good day!" Referring to the copy of the book left on the desk, Griff exits saying, "It's autographed." With Griff gone, Reavis' face grows sullen and serious, almost worried. The Baron paces around the office, deep in thought.

Later Griff thinks he has the upper hand, having found the caretaker of the cemetery whom Reavis bribed to engrave bogus tombstones to identify the resting place of Sofia's noble parents. The Spanish engraver is all ready to spill the beans, but Reavis gets to the man first who afterwards denies everything. Soon the Secretary of the Interior is to meet with Reavis at his office.

However, the increasing hatred of the locals necessitates that armed guards accompany the Baron and Baroness everywhere they go, which begins to wear thin with Sofia. "I never want to come here again," she cries, referring to the mob scene which constantly waits outside his office. Quietly, Reavis tells his wife she must come to accept certain terms. To which she answers, "Perhaps I'm not proud enough to accept those terms." Then the nasty Reavis exerts himself: "I forbid you to speak like that!" Sofia then reminds her husband that he now sounds similar to the times "you forbade me to eat raw sugar," referring to her childhood days when Reavis was more like a parent than a lover. Telling Sofia to act like a Baroness, to compose

Realizing he loves Sofia, Reavis confesses to his charade. (Photofest)

herself, the office door is opened to reveal the Secretary of the Interior who offers Reavis a settlement of 25 million dollars, which Reavis readily refuses. In shock the Secretary asks what the Baron wants, and he answers, "Recognition of the Peralta Grant." In a flash, the Secretary is gone. Reavis asks Sofia, "Do you remember the day you sobbed like a little peasant," referring to the time Reavis left the girl to travel abroad. She answers: "I didn't want Arizona; I wanted to be with you!" Reavis proudly declares he won his wife her birth right, but she quickly demands, "What is it you really want," realizing that if money was all he was after, that 25 million was a tidy sum to refuse.

But the ugly mob is getting uglier, as a man on a soapbox rants and raves in front of a banner that reads: "In God We Trust, in Arizona We Trusted." The Baron's carriage approaches and is stopped and confronted by the mob. Forcefully, Reavis states, "Citizens of Arizona. We don't want your homes or shops or livestock... I terrorized no one, I don't want to hurt you. I want to help each of you to help develop Arizona into the richest Barony in the world." To which the spokesperson declares, "That ain't for America, that's for Europe! We ain't slave workers and you ain't our king!" Then in open defiance, Reavis stands erect: "But I am the Baron and what goes with the Barony must and will be recognized by all of you—just as it was recognized 10 minutes ago by the U.S. government." Someone asks what if they don't have the money to pay you, and without missing a beat, Reavis answers, "I shall evict you!" Such a response brings a chorus of *aaahhss* in the background, and when one man in front of the carriage starts to raise his rifle, Reavis jumps down and punches the man, knocking him to the ground, prepared to pummel him with the butt of his rifle, but is stopped by the cries of Sofia.

Sofia, further distressed by the mob scene earlier in the day, goes to speak with her husband later that evening. Angrily she states, "I feel like Caesar's wife before he was murdered... the effort will be worthless if something happens to you. I saw the faces of those people today.

They hate us; they're afraid of you." To which Reavis reminds her, "Once you were afraid of me, remember?" But Sofia corrects him: "I was never afraid of you—I loved you the second you gave me the second piece of candy. I'm not happy to be the Baroness." And Reavis accuses her of having unnecessary guilt, but Sofia pleads with her husband: "Why must we have all the land? I don't want a dead Baron. I want a live husband... I love you... I love you!" As Sofia buries her sobbing face in her husband's lap, Reavis' face assumes a sense of overwhelming worry and concern, almost shock having heard these words and witnessed this outburst of emotion from his wife.

However, when Reavis sues the United States over false accusations and refusing to honor his land grant, going to trial and making a logical and forceful speech, Griff, representing the United States, admits he has no proof to support the government's claims of forgery, yet he dares insult the integrity of the Baron. For the first time, Sofia, totally angered, rises to verbally defend her husband. With burning hatred in her eyes, the Baroness states, "In this room he was accused of being a fake, a forger and a swindler. I will not tolerate such charges, not even by the government. I have nothing to offer him except my love and faith in him. No one calls my husband a thief!"

Later two cowboys visit Reavis in his office, threatening harm unless he signs a confession right here and now. Reavis, at first pretending to write such a letter, swings his elbow to the stomach of the man on his right, and then breaking an object from his desk over the head of the second man, brings both men to the ground in a matter of seconds.

However, the always loyal Pepito confesses to Reavis that he knows his entire story is a hoax ("the miracle in the rain was one big lie"), that Sofia's parents, before they died, told Pepito that she contained Indian blood (a disgrace) and that he must promise to keep the secret quiet. When Reavis entered claiming her heritage of loyal blood, he kept quiet knowing differently because he was a poor man and could not raise Sofia with all the advantages that Reavis promised. However, Pepito confesses he is sick inside and riddled with guilt. "I am sorry for what I did to you, my friend," Pepito confesses to Reavis. Pepito states he will tell the truth to the authorities, and Reavis seems to agree.

Back at home, Reavis is packing, the total truth now known to Sofia. He tells his wife, "I'm a fake," stating Pepito had a reason for lying—for her. But in shame, Reavis confesses he lied to help himself only. But Sofia doesn't seem angered. Reavis, who cannot understand, tries to make everything crystal clear for his wife. "I tell you I'm a forger, the whole scheme is one big fraud... marriage, because it was part of the scheme, not because I loved you... Well, I'm ready for your contempt and your disgust!" But Sofia is still not budging. "I am Mrs. James Reavis, and one of us must have the dignity to accept punishment. One of us must have the dignity to recognize love. I'll always love you, nothing can change that!" With a shocked, dazed look in his eyes, Reavis utters slowly, "You still want me?" To which she responds, "I want you until the day that I die." Reavis turns partially around, almost ready to break down in tears, still dazed, but now beginning to crack a half smile. "Now I know what I was looking for... a lady who would love me for what I am. No man could live without that. No man could ask for more," Reavis utters smiling humbly.

Confronting Griff, Reavis confesses to everything, but moments later Griff acknowledges to him that at last they have the proof that his documents were forged: Reavis used the monastery's five-century-old ink on the document in the section forged where Brother Paul, who wrote the rest of the page, used a different type of ink. Since Reavis wasn't greedy and still had the money he collected from the local citizenry, he agrees to give it all back, thus leading to a lighter prison sentence. Finally Griff asks Reavis if he really ever read his book, and Reavis smiles broadly stating, "It was my Bible!" Asking his worthy adversary why he finally confessed, Reavis admits honestly, "I fell in love with my wife." Before being led off by Griff, Reavis pauses to thank Lama for all she's done for Sofia: "I'm grateful." After he serves six years of hard labor, Reavis' wife, Pepito and Lama are waiting for him in their carriage, ready to resume a new life with a clear conscience.

Yes, the historically based scenario does get bogged down with details which halts the film's momentum; and yes, so many aspects of the plot are overblown and strain credibility; and yes, I admit Samuel Fuller's direction here is formulaic and generic. The direction only suggests a personal style yet to emerge in the hanging sequence where Reavis' head and noose are silhouetted against his gigantic map of the Territory of Arizona. But Price's performance, a starring performance, is uncharacteristically restrained and interesting. In only a few required sequences does he have the opportunity to raise his wonderful voice in contempt and dart his suspicious, fearful eyes from left to right and back again as his face quivers with rage. In the sequence where the town lynch mob lies in wait and then proceed to hang Reavis over the beam in his office, Reavis saves his life with the following impassioned speech:

> "Hang me, you stupid idiots; hang me and this land will never be yours. Go on, hang me! Isn't there one man among you with sense to realize that once I'm dead you won't be able to prove anything. Hang me, and hang your ranches and farms and shops... I've gotta be alive if you want to prove the land is yours. I gotta answer questions... identify documents!"

Vincent Price's powerful speech, as the rope is around his neck bending his head to the side, holds the audience's intense attention.

Price's performance is multi-layered, usually consisting of juxtaposing crafty lines, sinister stares and scenes where he plans deceitful things with sequences where he pretends to be the most pious God-loving monk, the gentlest surrogate father or the most outraged and put-upon government victim on the face of the Earth. Price's sincerity vs. his lying eyes are at the heart of the performance, and even though Price's plan to scam the United States government and the innocent citizens of Arizona is horrid, the man's motives, passion and dedication to his goal almost make the audience root for him to win. John Griff characterizes Reavis, at the movie's beginning, as a criminal, but he's an honorable one that Griff is proud to call a lover of Arizona and a friend. That ambiguity and inability for simple labels is the major reason why Vincent Price shines as James Addison Reavis in *The Baron of Arizona*, one movie that truly demonstrates the versatility of Price's craft.

CREDITS: Presented by: Robert L. Lippert; Producer: Carl K. Hittleman; Writer and Director: Samuel Fuller; Cinematography: James Wong Howe; Art Director: F. Paul Sylos; Set Decorator: Otto Seigel; Music: Paul Dunlap; Editor: Arthur Hilton; Wardrobe: Alfred Berke, Kitty Major; Makeup: Vernon Murdoch; Released 1950 by Lippert Pictures; Running Time: 96 minutes

CAST: Vincent Price (James Addison Reavis, "the Baron"); Ellen Drew (Sofia de Peralta-Reavis, "the Baroness"); Beulah Bondi (Loma Morales); Vladimir Sokoloff (Pepito Alvarez); Reed Hadley (John Griff); Robert H. Barrat (Judge Adams); Robin Short (Lansing); Barbara Woodell (Carry Lansing); Tina Rome (Rita); Gene Roth (Father Guardian); Karen Kester (Sofia, as a child); Jonathan Hale (Governor of Arizona); Angelo Rossitto (Angie); I. Stanford Jolley (Secretary of the Interior); Tristram Coffin (McCleary)

Champagne for Caesar succeeds simply because it's fun to watch Vincent Price enjoying himself. (Photofest)

CHAMPAGNE FOR CAESAR (1950)

by Marty Baumann

Though inexorably identified with horror, Vincent Price was one funny guy. Sadly, the comic performances of Price are often overlooked and decidedly overshadowed by his standing as a fright movie icon. Clearly, his finest shock film performances are colored by an inescapably snide, sometimes winsome way with dialogue that he surely recognized as fey, yet delivered with the utmost respect. An ever-present twinkle sparked his performances in *House on Haunted Hill* and *The Tingler*, and his lilting voice brought a cultured, sardonic depravity to *While the City Sleeps*, *Master of the World* and countless others. No other actor tossed off menacing *bon mots* in quite the same fashion. Even the dialogue of his most good-natured characterizations is delivered with a sinister subtext, a silky thread of menace that snakes fluidly between the lines.

In addition, few performers have taken such relish in skewering their own screen image via public appearances, film cameos or TV guest spots. This winning tactic was second nature to Price, who had invested so many performances with an irresistible gusto, conveying the unmistakable assertion that he was clearly savoring the horrific antics in which he was engaged, no matter how outlandish the situation may be.

In the early '70s, Price slipped easily into the role of the erudite talk show guest, chatting fine art and gourmet cooking with the likes of Mike Douglas and Merv Griffin. When the subject turned to his film career, Price invariably cited some offbeat titles as being among his favorites. In particular, he liked to mention Sam Fuller's *The Baron of Arizona* (1950) as one in which he took pride. His role in the film possesses many of the same aforementioned sardonic qualities and comes from the greatest period of diversity in the actor's long career. Barely a year earlier, he'd lent his formidable nefarity to *The Bribe*, a bona fide film noir classic. His turn as Cardinal Richelieu in *The Three Musketeers* is well regarded, as is his work in *The Adventures of Captain Fabian*. Each role from this three-year period is imbued with the same elegant cynicism he brought to perhaps his finest comic performance in *Champagne for Caesar* (1950), which Price was quick to cite as one of his personal favorite films as well as "one of the funniest scripts I'd ever read."

Though many fans are quick to point out the Corman-Poe films, or Price's immensely enjoyable collaborations with gimmick-meister William Castle as representative of his best work, *Champagne for Caesar* was an important part of a particularly rich period in the actor's career. Employing a fulsome, unfettered, nearly slapstick tone, Price is unforgettable as the megalomaniacal soap tycoon Burnbridge Waters, his eccentricities and borderline hysteria a joy to watch.

Ostensibly, the film belongs to Ronald Colman as Beauregard Bottomley, the world's smartest man. Though he'd won a best actor Oscar for *A Double Life* just two years before, the distinguished actor was nearing the end of a long and rewarding career. His languid comedic skills are still quite sharp, however, especially in several toe-to-toe scenes with a wild-eyed Price who nonetheless dominates the picture.

Price harbored a heartfelt respect for Colman, whom he later recalled as "one of the most charming men in the business." Vincent was justifiably thrilled at the prospect of acting opposite his idol.

Comedic descriptives like "frothy" and "bubbly," though decidedly inappropriate, were used to market the picture which, in actuality, is a social comedy, prophetic in many ways. "The picture was a big success," Price submitted, "but it confused some people because it was so in

LAWRENCE FRENCH: I read a story that the animators screened your old film, *Champagne for Caesar*, thinking they could use Ronald Colman's voice as a guide for Ratigan, and when they heard your voice in the same film, they wanted to cast you in the part.

VINCENT PRICE: (laughing) Really? Well, you know *Champagne for Caesar* is one of my favorite pictures. My favorite actor of all the actors I ever saw on the screen was Ronald Colman. I really worship him. When I was a beginning actor, my first movie, *Service De Luxe* (1938), was a disaster, because I didn't know how to do movie acting. So I went to a woman, Laura Elliot, that everybody in the theater who came out to Hollywood went to. Helen Hayes and so on, we all went to her to study the technique of film acting. It involved learning how to control your face, because when you are thrown up on a huge screen, and your face is 20 feet high, when you start to talk it can suddenly look like you're eating the screen, and a lot of actors do! So she taught us how to control our face, so we don't mug, because actors in the theater tend to mug a bit. She was invaluable, and we learned a great deal from her. One of her recipes for all of us, was to go and see two actors. She said, "I would recommend that you go and see any film that you can, whether it's a new film, or an old film, with Charles Boyer or Ronald Colman." So I went to see every film of theirs that I could, to learn, and I found that Ronald Colman was the master of his craft. He never really eye-contacts anyone. It's always a sort of lower case thing, so you wonder who he's talking to. Then one day I found out I was being cast by my friend, Richard Whorf, in *Champagne for Caesar*, with Ronald Colman. Colman was one of the most charming men in the business, and I did his last picture with him, a little fantasy called *The Story of Mankind*, which was a dreadful picture. Someone came into the dressing room while Ronny, Cedric Hardwicke and I were sitting around, and this interviewer said, "Mr. Colman, where did they get the story for this picture?" He said, "From the jacket of the book." (laughter)

advance of its time." Set in Los Angeles, the Hollywood mentality is ridiculed with little effort, ditzy blondes, flannel-suited "yes men" and vacuous entertainment figuring prominently. Encountering a crowd clustered about an appliance store window to watch the empty-headed game show that Price sponsors, Colman submits with an air of resignation that such electronic spectacles are contributing to the deterioration of civilization. A clownish Art Linkletter as the program's host sports a funny hat and spouts irritatingly unfunny asides at the expense of contestants, aping the hallmarks of the frenzied game shows that dominated radio and early TV.

Unwarily, Colman confronts the very source of the televised vacuity he finds reprehensible. The unemployed genius applies for a job at Price's Milady Soap factory, where he is assailed by the tycoon's belittling insults. Rebuffed but coolly resourceful, Colman vows to exact an intellectual revenge. Armed with an encyclopedic knowledge regarding all subjects, he will appear on the quiz show, doubling his winnings with each correct answer, eventually destroying Milady Soap financially, and Price spiritually.

Week after week, Colman turns the screws tighter on Price. Refusing to take his winnings and run, he's willing to risk losing it all, confident that his massive intellect will make short work of next week's question. As the sum approaches thousands and eventually millions, we're treated to frantic variations on Price's comic mania. An insidious turn of phrase was Price's stock-in-trade, a seamless affectation we've come to take for granted. But bug-eyed double-takes, slow burns and sudden angry eruptions are traits that modern audiences do

Vincent Price as Burnbridge Waters and Ronald Colman as Beauregard Bottomley in *Champagne for Caesar.*

not associate with Vincent Price, who incorporates them smoothly into this energetic performance.

With voyeuristic relish, Price turns to a shady acquaintance, Flame O'Neill, as portrayed by another Oscar winner, Celeste Holm, who'd copped a best supporting Oscar statuette for her role in *Gentleman's Agreement* three years earlier. Here, her feminine wiles are enlisted in hopes of driving Colman to distraction. The ploy works temporarily, though there's little doubt in our minds that true love will eventually emerge from the ostensibly sinister scheme.

Complicating the romantic mix, Barbara Britton, as Colman's sister, falls for Linkletter's unseemly character, to the further consternation of her brother. The casting of Linkletter as a pseudo-romantic lead may be a bit difficult for modern viewers to swallow, as he has since been ensconced in the public consciousness as a cornily garrulous TV host. Britton may be best known to film trivia hounds for her appearance in *Bwana Devil*, the first feature film released in 3-D.

In fact, *Champagne for Caesar* abounds with behind-the-scenes tidbits that enhance its standing as a cultural curio. As Linkletter woos Britton at the local drive-in, the young actor briefly glimpsed on screen is Robert (*Hideous Sun Demon*) Clarke. Ellye Marshall, later cast as one of the infamous *Cat Women of the Moon*, appears as Colman's buxom, airheaded neighbor, an aspiring actress named Frosty. In Britain, barely two years later, co-scripter Hans Jacoby would author *Stranger from Venus*, the poor man's *Day the Earth Stood Still*. Co-producer George Moskov gave the world one of exploitation filmdom's legendary titles, *Chained for Life*, starring the real life, joined-at-the-hip Hilton twins as ostensibly themselves. Muskov's production partner, Harry Popkin, was no stranger to exploitation, with late-'30s programmers like *Reform School* and *Prison Bait* among his credits. It should be noted that Popkin produced a truly indelible bit of film noir, *DOA*, the previous year. Also noteworthy are the vocal talents of Mel Blanc as the carping voice of Colman's adopted, bubbly-guzzling parrot Caesar.

Celeste Holm and Vincent Price paired up for laughs in *Champagne for Caesar*. (Photofest)

Director Richard Whorf had several notable screen comedies under his belt by the time *Caesar* rolled around, but made his real mark the following decade as a prolific television director, piloting episodes of classic series such as *Gunsmoke, Wagon Train, The Untouchables* and *The Wild Wild West*. "Dick Whorf, the director, was a genuine renaissance man," Price recalled. "He was a very fine artist, his brother John Whorf was one of the greatest watercolorists of America." Whorf came from an impressive theatrical background, having designed sets for the legendary Lunts on Broadway. He had, in fact, designed a production of *Richard III*, which featured Price and Jose Ferrer. To his great credit, and the benefit of all concerned, Whorf was smart enough to let the *Caesar* cast drive the film. The eminently capable players show off their comic chops while Whorf does little more than get out of the way, discretion in this case being the better part of directorial valor. Just the same, it is a strangely hands-off approach to theater.

But it is this very atmosphere of dramatic abandon that makes *Champagne for Caesar* the rarity that it is. Nearly all of the lead performances are full-blown and cartoony. There is no anchor character per se, no voice of reason who must survive the insanity of those around him. Every performer seems giddy and playful, pressing the comedic boundaries of his/her role, an approach which in less experienced hands than Price's would be grating if not outright amateurish. Only Britton as Colman's sensible sister approaches restraint, but even she seems smitten with the film's frivolity. That same frivolity, resonating through Price's characterization, might surprise longtime fans who have seen his languorous humor being more subtly employed as a villainous undercurrent. There is little room for subtlety in *Champagne for Caesar*.

My late-night discovery of the film some years back was something of a revelation. Though weaned on the 1960s monster culture of which Price was an undisputed cornerstone, I was originally drawn to the film as a longtime Ronald Colman fan. (There weren't many in my neighborhood.) As a fright film devotee, I was quite familiar with Price's memorable gallery of heavies and was confident that he would turn in the usual superb, sinuous villainy I had come to expect. Though always amused by the patented Price smirk, I wasn't prepared for this uncharacteristic gale of all-out belligerence, delivered with masterful comic timing, employing every inch of his rangy physique.

In the end, *Champagne for Caesar* succeeds simply because it's fun to watch these actors enjoying themselves. There is not a glimmer of credibility in any of it. And who cares? The whole production is delivered with a graceful insanity that never invites probing criticism. In this atmosphere, it falls to the cast to maintain a hold on the audience while romping unbridled through such a fluffy script. The *Caesar* cast, led by two of the more gracious performers in American film, pulls it off. I haven't a clue as to what went on behind the scenes as *Caesar* was being filmed. Perhaps the stars were continually at each other's throats in the time-honored tradition of Tinseltown's clashing egos. The testament to their professionalism is this: They sure seem to be having a great time!

Anyway, *Champagne for Caesar* was one of the funniest scripts I'd ever read. It's about a quiz show, and at that time there was a quiz show on the air called, *The $64,000 Question*. $64.00 with no zeros after it! This was carrying that idea to absurdity. Ronald Colman played this genius who takes on a soap company, like Lux soap or Procter & Gamble, and he gets to the point where it's the soap company itself against his talent.

Dick Whorf, the director was a genuine renaissance man. He was a very fine artist, his brother John Whorf was one of the greatest watercolorists of America. Dick was a man who amused himself by building superb miniature sets. He was also the set director for the Lunts for a long time. When I did a production of *Richard III* on Broadway, with Jose Ferrer playing Richard, and me playing Buckingham, Dick Whorf designed the sets. He was also an actor, and a costume designer. This picture was at the beginning of a not too long career in directing, because unfortunately he died. The picture was a big success, but it confused some people because it was so in advance of its time. —Vincent Price in an interview with Lawrence French

CREDITS: Producers: George Moskov and Harry M. Popkin; Director: Richard Whorf; Screenplay: Fred Brady and Hans Jacoby; Cinematography: Paul Ivano; Editor: Hugh Bennett; Art Director: George Van Marter; Music: Dimitri Tiomkin; Makeup: William Knight and Ted Larson; United Artists; 1950; 99 minutes

CAST: Ronald Colman (Beauregard Bottomley); Vincent Price (Burnbridge Waters); Celeste Holm (Flame O'Neill); Barbara Britton (Gwenn Bottomley); Art Linkletter (Happy Hogan); Ellye Marshall (Frosty); Mel Blanc (voice of Caesar); Byron Foulger (Gerald); Herbert Lytton (Chuck Johnson); Vicki Raaf (Waters' Secretary); Peter Brocco (Fortune Teller); Jack Daly (Scratch); George Meader (Mr. Brown); George Fisher (Announcer); Gabriel Heatter (Announcer); John Eldreidge (Executive); George Leigh (Executive); Lyle Talbot (Executive); John Hart (Executive); Brian O'Hara (Buck); Gordon Nelson (Lecturer)

Robert Mitchum, Jane Russell and Vincent Price star in *His Kind of Woman*.

HIS KIND OF WOMAN (1951)
by Gary J. Svehla

The stylized and shadowy world of film noir was evolving as it expanded into the 1950s, sometimes becoming even more violent, other times toying around with the generally serious and solemn tone created during noir's original decade of the 1940s. *His Kind of Woman*, released by RKO in 1951, features Vincent Price billed third playing Hollywood actor Mark Cardigan, the type of role that became the perfect match for Price's sometimes overly broad and larger-than-life acting style. In fact, Cardigan becomes the type of standout, quirky character that often wins actors Best Supporting Performance Oscars; however, if Price never took that statuette home, his performance certainly warrants "best of year" consideration and becomes one of the defining performances of his career.

Interestingly, the first third of the movie is pure film noir with professional gambler and lone wolf Dan Milner (Robert Mitchum) becoming an archetype noir characterization, as a man world-weary, burned out and in debt to the wrong people. The script, featuring classic noir dialogue by screenwriters Frank Fenton and Jack Leonard, contains the usual intelligent asides and witty turn-downs and come-ons associated with the best of the genre. Over the radio comes reports that criminal Nick Ferrera (Raymond Burr), deported for his crimes and now living in Naples, is planning to return to the United States. Described as former head of the "New York Plunderworld" and "upper crust crumb," Nick is rumored to still be running criminal operations in New York, New Jersey and points west. The first leg of Nick's return scheme involves him flying down to Morro's Lodge in a remote but elegant area of Mexico. But first Dan Milner is being set up as the fall guy. Speaking to Sammy, his black bartender friend, Milner says he went down to Palm Springs "to cure a cold and I wound up doing 30 days." When Sammy asks for what, Milner cries, "For nothing!" Milner plans to go back home to bed where nothing can happen to him.

But when Milner arrives home, three men are playing a game of poker in his living room, something Milner seems to accept as commonplace. "Need a fourth," he deadpans. The men immediately accuse him of owing their boss money, a gambling debt. When they tell Milner it was "called in," Milner tries to make clear that somebody else called it in, not him. Told he owes $600, Milner states "I never bet on a race in my life that wasn't fixed," and when they tell him it was called in last Thursday, Milner responds that unless he had a walkie-talkie he couldn't made the call "because I was digging a road for the law." Milner tells the men to clean up their mess before leaving. The three thugs form a circle around Milner, and knowing what's coming, he picks up a burning butt from the ashtray and sticks it onto the top of one of the thug's hands. Of course Milner gets beat up, but the chief thug reminds the boys to not hurt his face (definitely a clue worth remembering later).

As soon as the thugs finish working Milner over, the phone rings and the disheveled Milner tells the person on the line, "just taking my tie off... wondering if I should hang myself with it." But he is asked to come immediately over to the speaker's house, an elaborate mansion, for a chance to earn big money, $50,000, to come in easy installments as he completes each phase of his task. The plan involves Mitchum catching a bus to Mexico and meeting with up with a fellow named Hernandez, who just happens to be working in the Customs House where the passengers on the bus exit. After introducing himself, Milner tells Hernandez he can be found in the cafe getting a meal. Striking up a conversation with the bartender, Milner eyeballs the cafe singer, a real knockout, Lenore Brent (Jane Russell). He himself doesn't drink, but he wants to buy a drink for the lady and is told she is drinking expensive champagne at $18 per bottle, but with new money burning a hole in his pocket, he springs for a bottle and carries it over, but not before being warned "she's waiting for a chartered plane" and that "she'll be out of your life before the investment pays off!" He uses the great line, his face emotionless and droopy in the best Mitchum manner—"Are you in the oil business or spending your alimony all at once?"— Brent announces she is a spoiled child of the rich. Mitchum counters by stating he is a spoiled child of the poor; immediately, Mitchum and Russell's physical chemistry sizzles, even if she tells the hounddog Milner that she has to leave to board her plane. But not very surprisingly, Hernandez appears and tells Mitchum he too will be flying further down to Mexico to spend some time at Morro's Lodge, on the very same chartered flight and with the same destination as Lenore Brent.

Morro's Lodge turns out to be a playground for the wealthy, with gambling and swimming seemingly the two major activities. Since Milner is a professional gambler with a payoff in his pocket, and more money coming from the same source, he seems content to while away his time, also trying to make time with the delicious Lenore. The host and middle-man for all the nefarious activities occurring at the lodge, Jose Morro, introduces himself to Milner, stating he knows Milner is here by special arrangement with Mr. Arnold (the crime boss who is paying Milner). Milner immediately offers Morro $1,000 for "a helping hand, information," or, in other words, to be kept on the inside and informed of any pertinent information. Asking about Lenore, Morro smiles and tells Milner of her "impeccable background: Boston, New York, Rome, Paris, St. Moritz." Morro then mentions he heard that Milner is from California. And deadpanning once again, "Oh yeah, Pamona, Los Angeles, Glendale, Van Nuys, etc." demonstrating that his lineage is not quite as exotic as Brent's. However, over on the side, a man from the band recognizes Brent as a woman called Liz, but she blows him off quickly saying, "wrong name, sorry." Milner hears this entire exchange.

Snooping around and making acquaintances as rapidly as he can, Milner encounters vacationing investment broker Mr. Winton (Jim Backus) who enjoys a good game of cards. Mr. Krafft (John Mylong) enjoys playing a game of chess alone, hanging out with another mystery man Mr. Thompson (Charles McGraw). But the strangest and yet most important encounter of all occurs when Milner accidentally bumps into vacationing movie star and avid hunter, Mark Cardigan (Vincent Price), who turns out to be a former lover of Lenore Brent. "Sorry, I should have looked where I was going... Say, you're new about here, aren't you. I'm Mark Cardigan... say Milner, do you like to hunt? I'm looking for just one man to come down here who likes to hunt." When Milner calmly announces he likes to hunt, Cardigan's eyes beam and excitement rushes through every fiber in his body. "You do, well, let me tell you something Milner, I've hunted them in the Sierras, in the west lands... down here they have the daddies of them all. A 12 point buck drove me crazy for a week. Yesterday, I nailed him. How about the two of us taking a whack at his brother tomorrow?" To which Milner responds, "What, you have a grudge against the family?" Cardigan laughs, enjoying the dry humor of his companion, offering to show him his Winchester, but is soon called away to greet Lenore Brent. Enthusiastically, Cardigan exits stating, "I'll talk to you later. Don't you get away from me!"

Brent greets him warmly, slowly raising her hand to touch his cheek; surprisingly, Cardigan brushes it away, "Hello my darling—not here... later, when we're alone." Hurt, Brent asks Cardigan why he hasn't written to her—"I have money. I wouldn't have blackmailed you!"—but he smoothes things over by stating, "Does anything else matter now that you're here?" Walking away with her former lover, Cardigan confesses, "I'm like the plague down here... Of all the women in the world, you're the only one who ever loved me for my real self."

That evening all the tourists at the lodge are treated to seeing Mark Cardigan's latest movie, where the beaming-eye hero portrays a Three Musketeers-style swordsman. As the camera focuses in on Cardigan watching his own movie, his eyes shift to see the reactions of his audience. We watch Cardigan smile at his own antics, and when he stabs the villain on screen, he openly applauds his feat of derring-do. At the movie's end, the audience politely applauds and Cardigan rises to greet his fans. "Mr. Cardigan, a brilliant performance"; "I've seen all of your pictures, and this is your best!"; "That was one of the finest movies I've ever seen. They oughta

Mark Cardigan (Vincent Price) greets his fans while Myron Winton (Jim Backus) looks on. (Photofest)

make them all like that. None of this nonsense about social matters. People don't go to the movies to see how miserable the world is." Cardigan does ask Mr. Krafft what he thought, and the unpleasant man gives a curt, snide remark: "It had the message no pigeon would carry." To which Cardigan responds, "At my studio all the messages are handled by Western Union!" To which the most clever line of all follows: "You can't take his opinion on anything... he's an intellectual." Cardigan ventures over to visit with Milner and Brent, asking them what they thought of the movie. Brent quickly snaps out, "It was fine... it was just a little long... about an hour and a half." But Cardigan confesses he should know better than to ask Lenore: "I'm out of my mind to ask her... She hates everything I do!" Cardigan reminds Milner of their hunting date tomorrow morning at 5 a.m., but from his reaction the audience realizes that nightowl Milner will not make this appointment. Milner does remind Cardigan that Morro warned that a hurricane is threatening, but Brent remarks that Cardigan would hunt from a hurricane storm shelter to avoid spending the day with her. The next night, as the storm is blowing up and a private plane makes an emergency landing, Milner chimes, "Fools get away with the impossible," to which Brent responds, "That's because they're the only ones who try." With this come-on, the couple embrace and kiss passionately. But by the next morning, Milner is already apologizing for his actions and Brent is angry that "the nimrod [Cardigan] went hunting again," leaving her alone.

Cardigan's wife Helen (Majorie Reynolds) arrives unexpectedly, along with his personal manager Gerald, who states he is about to negotiate Cardigan's new studio contract but that the press is having a field day with his dalliances with numerous other women, such as Lenore Brent. "I have a right to my happiness too," Cardigan says. But the angry manager states, "I brought Helen down here; you're going to be reconciled! People take marriage pretty seriously,

83

Cardigan rushes to the aid of Milner.

and they expect you to do so too." Before the manager leaves, he approaches Brent and asks, "Are you looking for a settlement?" and the proud woman slaps him hard and leaves, soon followed by Milner. Having prepared a special roast duck for his dinner party, which has now ended abruptly, Cardigan's face sours as he mournfully cries, "And it was going to be such a beautiful dinner."

Milner befriends and escorts the perpetually drunk Mr. Lusk (Tim Holt), the newly arrived airplane pilot, back to his cabin, where Milner confronts the man and states, "You drink like a B girl," meaning, it's all a ruse. Lusk comes clean and admits he's a federal policeman with the immigration service and knows all about Mr. Arnold's plans for Milner. "You're the patsy!" The scheme is for Nick Ferrera, who is aboard a boat just offshore, to use Krafft, who is secretly a plastic surgeon, to give Ferrera Milner's face. Then, quietly getting rid of Milner, Ferrera can return to the States under a new identity. Since Milner is a "lone wolf" without "friends or relatives," the switch will be easy. However, within the next 24 hours, Lusk's body is found murdered, left in the open on the beach.

The film becomes ambiguous from this point onward. Juxtaposed to the hard-hitting noir drama is the lighter tale of the unhappy Hollywood movie star, Cardigan, who wishes to be as brave in real life as he is in the movies. And with all his woman problems suddenly catching up with him, he feels like a man trapped instead of one who is vacationing. But the movie bounces back and forth from the hard-boiled Milner tale to the increasingly comedic tale of Cardigan. For me the film works on both levels, but to fans of film noir the parallel tones may conflict with one another and be off-putting.

We first see Cardigan, glumly dancing with his wife Helen, looking miserable. "Don't look so trapped Mark, surely you didn't intend to marry her, did you?" To which Cardigan responds, "I don't intend to hurt her or embarrass her either." But Helen confesses, "You hurt and embarrassed me!" To which Cardigan answers, "Going to Reno was your idea, Helen... you're not going to tell me you're in love with me?" But Helen stops short of that by saying, "After 10 years we developed a nice kind of tolerance for each other." Finally Cardigan confesses, "Helen, I've never settled for second best. And don't be so sure I'm not in love."

In the parallel sequences, after Lusk is trapped and killed, three men get the jump on Milner and are taking him to Ferrera's boat. However, Brent knocks on the door, and the gangsters tell him to get rid of her fast. "I've spent six months and a lot of money... to try to get Mark Cardigan. I was ready to kiss it all good-bye for you." Brent offers Milner a gun, which he claims he doesn't need, and in a brusque way, shoos her away, for her own good. But as Milner leaves the cabin, Brent waits in the bushes and sees Milner being taken away by force.

For the remainder of the movie, one hard-hitting noir sequence involving Milner will be followed by a lighter-toned sequence involving Cardigan, until both characters are joined again, but quickly separated.

Morro tells Cardigan about the murdered man found on the beach, and almost immediately, Brent enters to report Milner being led off to his supposed death. Gerald the manager wants Cardigan to have no part of this, but Cardigan, in a change of heart, decides to suddenly get tough: "Shut up Gerald and let me think." Of course Helen gets in her jab with, "A little late in life, isn't it?" Then Gerald interrupts further by declaring, "I've been doing your thinking for the last 15 years." Then Cardigan confronts Gerald, "Look, do you want to go out there for me?" But the manager confesses, "I have a wife!" Then Cardigan tells him to shut up again, to let him think. Soon a devilish glee overcomes Cardigan as he recites lines from Shakespeare: "Now might I drink hot blood and do such bitter business that the Earth would quake to look upon... what fools you mortals be!" In the best application of art imitating life, Cardigan begins to see himself as an actual hero and decides to mount a rescue operation to save Milner's life.

Juxtaposed to this sequence, we have Milner arriving by row boat at the foot of the yacht, but he manages to capsize the row boat, jump into the water and swim ashore (dodging bullets all the way), meeting up with Cardigan who is stationed at the shore with rifle in hand. Soon three men are in hot pursuit trying to hunt down Milner and Cardigan. But the movie star seems energized by such dangerous hunting. Handing Milner a pistol he brought along, Cardigan yells out, "Stay with me, bucko, it's my private hunting ground. I know it like an owl knows its tree." But Cardigan is nicked in the shoulder and wondrously admits, "What do you know, I'm really wounded. It's okay!" Then in deep thought, as an occasional shot is fired, Cardigan ponders his life. "You know, all my life I suspected myself of being a phony. Half of it I've been acting, a hundred lives and a hundred stories, all phony. This is the only time the guns were even loaded with something other than blanks." To which Milner asks him how does it feel? Smiling, feeling content and satisfied, Price slowly reveals, as if he's relishing every word, "Fine... you couldn't begin to know how fine." Milner asks Cardigan if he's in love with Brent, and Cardigan responds, "...I've never been in love with anything, except myself." Milner admits he's too young to die, while Cardigan confesses, he's too well known to die. But Milner promises him a first-rate Hollywood funeral. Smiling, Cardigan declares, "I've already had it. My last picture died there." The plan is for Cardigan to keep the three gangsters occupied while Milner swims back to the boat to confront Nick Ferrera.

Again paralleling sequences present contrasting tones and action. Aboard the yacht, Milner is quickly tracked down by the crew who trap him in the engine room, where Milner shoots a hole in the main steam pipe creating a diversion; however, his pursuers still manage to get the drop on him. Milner is taken to confront the sweaty Ferrera and both men detest each other immediately, Ferrera claiming that Milner still owes him money. After slapping Milner around, the gangster chief allows the boys to rough him up, but Krafft reminds them to not damage his face. After toying with the captive, Ferrera wants to kill Milner, forgetting the plan to steal his face.

Back on shore, a different type of tension is mounted as the three gunmen separate to try to get the drop on Cardigan. However, hearing and seeing the rustling of a tree branch nearby,

Cardigan wets and raises his thumb, takes aim and shoots, instantly killing one of the men. Smiling, Cardigan states, "Deceased... gone to heaven." Cardigan soon picks off another gangster, leaving only Thompson alive. Egging on the over-confident criminal, Cardigan taunts Thompson by singing, "Come and get me. Oh, come on... I've been known to miss!" Soon laughter is heard: "Are you coming?" Cardigan creates a trap for Thompson by using a shoestring to tie back a bush, and when Thompson breaks the string and thus snaps the branches, spooking himself and firing off a shot, Cardigan suddenly stands up behind him and points his rifle at him. Thompson attempts another shot, misses, but Cardigan disables the man by shooting him in the shoulder. "How come you didn't finish me off," Thompson curiously asks. "Well, I don't know. Maybe I was confused and forgot what side your heart was on. Or perhaps you don't have one." Leading his captive back to camp, Cardigan raves, "I've taken a prisoner of war. Place him under guard and summon reinforcements at once." By now Morro has assembled his small police force and is confronted by Cardigan and his prisoner, Cardigan delivering each line as though it were dialogue from his latest movie, his hand gestures punctuate each dramatic syllable he delivers. Cardigan tells Morro they must seize the yacht, "Milner is out there alone facing tremendous odds." However, Helen is terrified for her husband's life, and for the first time, Cardigan feels pride in his actions. "Why must I be plagued by yammering magpies on the eve of battle!" he declares. Pleading with her husband to allow the authorities to handle this matter, she finally tells Cardigan he has lost her if he continues. "Such are the fortunes of war. Besides, I thought I had already lost you...," Cardigan states, more than a tad interested in repairing his damaged marriage. Next he lays his heart on the line, speaking honestly: "My dear, you don't understand me, you never have! Do you think I want to go on living in a make-believe world, fighting in Sherwood Forest on Stage 6? Oh no! You go back to Hollywood, while I go on to real life triumphs... or a glorious death!" Helen sees blood and cries out, "You are wounded!" To which Cardigan smiles and answers, "'Tis not as deep as a well nor as wide as a church door." Lenore begs Cardigan to take her with him, but instead he locks her in the closet. "This is men's work, women are for weeping!" Before leaving he announces, "If I'm not here by Wednesday, chop that door down!"

Soon appealing to all the tourists staying at the lodge, Cardigan seeks to create a small army to take on the Ferrera yacht. "A fine example you're setting before these loyal allies of ours. One of your fellow Americans needs help and you stand there gaping. What are you standing in, cement?!!!" Strangely, the assembled guests applaud such impassioned delivery, and those who volunteer are given firearms by Cardigan. "Survivors will get parts in my next picture!" the star promises. Pushing on one policeman's stomach, Cardigan cries out "too flabby, replace him," almost as though he were casting a movie and not fighting for a friend's life. Pointing to another shy policeman standing in the background, Morro explains he is his wife's brother and that he promised to never put the man into danger. "Lieutenant, I am not a patient man. Tell that rascal to fall in. He's drafted!!!" Cardigan declares. Loading the entire army of volunteers into one small boat, Cardigan, now wearing a cape, stands in the front of the boat barking out orders. "Ahoy there, stand by to be commandeered!" Cardigan is warned that the boat is over-full and not ready, but Cardigan orders "full steam ahead" as the boat immediately sinks in about two feet of water. Another literary quote erupts from his lips as he orders, "abandon ship... my kingdom for a ship," as another row boat is readied.

Back aboard the yacht, Milner, who has been stripped to the waist, abandoned in the steam-warmed engine room, and beaten to a pulp, is now being revived by Ferrera who states, "Wake up! I want you to see it coming. I want him to be fully conscious. I want to see the expression on his face when he knows it's coming," a gun pointed at his head. But Cardigan's boat approaches, and since they don't wish to shoot Milner with witnesses in close pursuit, Krafft suggests giving him an overdose of the sedative he was planning to use for the operation, an overdose which will destroy the brain with death to result within a year's time. As Milner is subdued and held tight, Krafft ties a rubber hose around his arm while Cardigan's row boat approaches. As a huge spotlight is shined upon Cardigan and the boat, the crew tells him to order that the light be turned off. Cardigan announces, "I have yet to shun the welcome glare of a spotlight," but Cardigan is convinced, and, taking aim with his rifle, he yells, "out damn spot, out I say," shattering the spotlight. All the lights aboard ship are turned off, making it more difficult for Cardigan's men to hit their targets, but also making it harder for Krafft to find the vein to inject the sedative into Milner.

All-out chaos erupts both on deck and underneath, with Milner finally escaping his captors, and with Cardigan's help, finally shooting Ferrera dead in his tracks. At the resulting press interview, Cardigan is his old self once again, wearing an ornate robe, his shoulder bandaged but shoved outward like a badge of courage—the actor is all pride and swagger. However, when asked what did he use to kill Ferrera, Cardigan's face grows humble and he answers smiling, "A man named Milner."

Of all the roles that Vincent Price ever performed, Mark Cardigan seems the most tailor-made, for Price was never seen as a subtle actor. Thus, Mark Cardigan becomes almost a caricature of the overblown, flamboyant Hollywood actor that Price embodied. However, within the confines of such a stereotype, the screenwriter and Price brought subtlety and sensitivity. Cardigan becomes the man who is loved for his screen image, not the man he really feels he is inside. That's why he is attracted to Lenore Brent, for as he claims, she was the first woman to love him for who he really is. And later in the film, when baring his soul to wife Helen, he tells her that she never knew or understood him. We have the arrogant, overconfident Hollywood star who is actually insecure, unsatisfied and unloved. Price's mock theatrics as he comes up with the clever plan to mount a rescue operation to save Dan Milner is Price at his best, babbling forth literary chestnuts from Shakespeare and other sources, all delivered over-the-top, but deliciously and cleverly rendered. The comic potential of which Price was more than capable is better rendered here amidst a grand cast and intelligent dialogue than it would be in later films such as *A Comedy of Terrors* and *Theater of Blood* or *The Raven*. Here Vincent Price's comic performance is never fully comedical at all, and while he has some serious emotions to convey, the performance is impossible to label as being one or the other. That's why Price's Mark Cardigan is a defining moment in his career, offering him the range and depth that would be lacking in his one-dimensional starring roles to follow later in the decade: *House of Wax, House on Haunted Hill, The Tingler*, etc. While these performances above are still classic and successful in their own right, they seem to pigeon-hole and limit the immense talents of Vincent Price, instead of allowing him to grow in different directions. Perhaps stereotyping, more so than talent (which he possessed in spades), allowed Vincent Price to become a star, but isn't it comforting to see the depth and range that Vincent Price the actor could rise to when the role allowed him to create a different persona. Even though Vincent Price never had many cinematic performances as rich and versatile as the character of Mark Cardigan in *His Kind of Woman,* the simple fact that he did it so well here only demonstrates the immense talent within Vincent Price that was waiting to be tapped.

CREDITS: Producer: Robert Sparks; Director: John Farrow; Screenplay: Frank Fenton and Jack Leonard (Based on the Original Story "Star Sapphire" by Gerald Drayson Adams); Cinematography: Harry J. Wild; Art Director: Albert S. d'Agnostino; Music: Leigh Harline; RKO; 1951; 120 minutes

CAST: Robert Mitchum (Dan Milner); Jane Russell (Lenore Brent); Vincent Price (Mark Cardigan); Tim Holt (Bill Lusk); Charles McGraw (Thompson); Marjorie Reynolds (Helen Cardigan); Raymond Burr (Nick Ferrano); Jim Backus (Myron Winton)

HOUSE OF WAX (1953)
by John E. Parnum

*"Once in his lifetime, every artist feels the hand
of God and creates something that comes to life."*
—Professor Henry Jarrod

House of Wax was as important a film for Warner Bros. and the entire movie industry as it was for Vincent Price. The early 1950s were disastrous for studios as audiences stayed away from theaters to be seduced in their homes by that captivating box known as television. Something dramatic and different was needed to lure these folks out of their houses and back into theaters. One of the answers arrived in New York City in 1952, utilizing three 35 mm projectors and a wraparound screen. Know as Cinerama, the process was limited initially to specialized documentaries in one theater in only about 11 cities. Far more popular were the films produced in CinemaScope the following year. Beginning with 20th Century-Fox's *The Robe*, the process used an anamorphic lens to project images on a large rectangular screen, which was enhanced by strategically placed stereophonic speakers throughout the theaters. But the most dramatic (albeit short-lived) innovation came in the form of 3-D, a medium ideally suited for horror, Western and adventure films.

Certainly there had been three-dimensional films before *House of Wax*, but these had been limited to short subjects such as the Pete Smith comedy short *Third Dimensional Murder* (1941). Early in 1953, United Artists released *Bwana Devil*, produced, written and directed by Arch Oboler and credited as the first feature-length movie in 3-D. While the novelty of having "A Girl in Your Arms" and "A Lion in Your Lap" brought audiences out in droves, the insipid story about two mangy lions harassing railroad workers in colonial Africa left much to be desired. (Ironically, the story was dusted off in 1997, sans 3-D, and made into *The Ghost and the Darkness* with Michael Douglas and Val Kilmer.) Jack Warner, impressed with the box-office receipts for *Bwana Devil*, decided that *his* studio would be the first *major* company to produce and distribute a three-dimensional feature film. After all, hadn't Warner Bros. produced the first talking film, *The Jazz Singer* (1927), and been successful in perfecting the two-strip Technicolor process for *Doctor X* (1932) and 1933's *Mystery of the Wax Museum*?

While screenwriter Crane Wilbur was revising the *Mystery of the Wax Museum* script into *The Wax Works*, the working title for *House of Wax*, Jack Warner offered Vincent Price the starring role in the film's terrifying tale of Henry Jarrod, the burned and scarred sculptor who used wax-covered corpses from the morgue to adorn his Chamber of Horrors. The decision to accept the role was difficult for Price. In his 15 years on the screen, Vincent Price had received star billing only twice: in the 1946 psychological thriller *Shock* and in the 1950 Samuel Fuller-directed historical Western *The Baron of Arizona*. (Although he played the lead in *The Invisible Man Returns* [1940], top billing went to Sir Cedric Hardwicke.) In his film career up until that time, Vincent had capably played a plethora of parts, ranging from Joseph Smith, the founder of the Mormon religion, in *Brigham Young—Frontiersman* (1940) and a president's son-in-law in *Wilson* (1944) to the snobbish missionary of *The Keys to the Kingdom* (1944) and treacherous Cardinal Richelieu in *The Three Musketeers* (1948). The talented actor was even more at home in the legitimate theater, having appeared on Broadway with Helen Hayes in *Victoria Regina* (1935/36) and with Orson Welles and his Mercury Theater in *Heartbreak House* (1938).

In the summer of 1952, Vincent was performing in a West Coast production of Christopher Fry's *The Lady's Not for Burning* and a road tour of *Don Juan in Hell* with Sir Cedric Hardwicke when he was invited by Jose Ferrer to join the Broadway cast of *My Three Angels* (upon which the film *We're No Angels* was based). It was at this time that Jack Warner asked him to appear as the lead in the new gimmick-filled *House of Wax*. It was a tough decision for Price, who had been disappointed in his sagging character-actor screen roles after being lauded for his stage performances. But in the end, Warner won over Jose Ferrer. James Robert Parish and Steven Whitney quote the actor's decision in *Vincent Price Unmasked* (Drake Publishers, Inc., New York, 1974, p. 81). Price said "...that he had grown used to the sunny California climate." But they further reveal that "had Vincent been in a more serious mood at the time, he probably would have explained that his intellectual roots were now in Los Angeles. He was involved in many art programs and organizations on the West Coast, and it would have been extremely difficult to leave them for an entire year, the minimum contractual obligation attached to the contract offer for *My Three Angels*." Although Price returned to his beloved Broadway stage later that year as the Duke of Buckingham in *Richard III* with Jose Ferrer, *House of Wax* would change the course of his career forever.

With Vincent signed on to star in *House of Wax*, Warner remembered that Andre de Toth had expressed an interest in a 3-D project many years before, and selected him to direct the Price vehicle. Ironically, de Toth had lost an eye and was unable to appreciate the astounding effects he had commandeered on the screen. In talking about the film and its one-eyed director in a *Films in Review* article by Michael Buckley ("Vincent Price," June/July, 1988, p. 324), the actor said, "It's almost my favorite Hollywood story!.... Where else in the world would you have a man with one eye... to direct a picture in 3-D? He might as well have been blindfolded!" Then he amends his astonishment by explaining, "If it had been someone with two eyes, it would've been too tricky a picture. That's what ruined 3-D. The producer Bryan Foy wanted a good picture, not a tricky one. There were only, I think, three tricks in the whole thing." Perhaps there is a distinction between "tricks" and 3-D "effects," because *House of Wax* bubbles over with some of the most remarkable and effective 3-D visuals ever committed to the screen, as I'll illustrate later.

There have been many articles comparing *House of Wax* to *Mystery of the Wax Museum* and Price's performance as Henry Jarrod to Lionel Atwill's identical role as Ivan Igor (see Raymond Valinoti's intelligent piece in *Midnight Marquee* #53 for one of the more detailed comparisons). But for this chapter we will concentrate on Price's 1953 remake in which he is first shown as a brilliant and sensitive sculptor of wax figures who abhors the idea that his business partner Matthew Burke (Roy Roberts) wants to cater to the public's morbid fascination and create a Chamber of Horrors. Art critic Sidney Wallace (Paul Cavanagh) appreciates Jarrod's talent to create beautiful figures and the detail that is involved in each piece—each strand of hair is pressed individually into the scalp, and eyes that seem to follow you around the room are inserted through the neck of Marie Antoinette's detached head ("Forgive me my dear for discussing your most intimate secrets," Jarrod apologizes to the wax figure). Jarrod hopes that Wallace will buy out his greedy business partner, but the art critic wants to make his decision after returning from a three-month tour. Burke can't wait that long and suggests to Jarrod that they burn the museum down for insurance money. "Burn? Burn my children? Do you think I'm a murderer? I'll kill you if you try!" Jarrod threatens in a line that most certainly must have amused Price in its contradiction. Price, by the way, was probably quite at home as the benevolent sculptor, having talents and appreciation along the same line. This side of Jarrod most closely reflected Price the man, whereas the later psychopathic Jarrod was represented by Price the actor.

Burke carries out his threat to burn down the museum after scuffling with Jarrod, knocking him out, and, in a macabre touch, even dousing the unconscious sculptor with gasoline. It is in this opening that de Toth establishes the wonders of a 3-D movie, from the raised title credits that project into the audience to the fiery explosion from an escaping gas jet that sends a conflagration of burning debris into the streets of early 1900 New York City. In addition to the chairs and buckets of water thrown from the screen and the collapsing balcony and burning wax heads

Jarrod (Vincent Price) catches Sue Allen (Phyllis Kirk) investigating the Joan of Arc display.

tumbling into the laps of the audience, de Toth masterfully composes the arrangement of the wax sculptures to most effectively utilize the dimensional effects that delighted audiences.

We next see Matthew Burke, flush with insurance money, at a dance hall with his giggly girlfriend Cathy Gray (Carolyn Jones) as he tells her that Jarrod's body was never found. "Yes, they always want a corpse," Carol exclaims in a high squeaky voice that is both amusing and grating. When Burke returns to his office that night, a hideously scarred figure in a black hat and cape emerges from the shadows, garrotes him and dangles his body down the elevator shaft to imply suicide. This is a particularly shocking sequence that had 1953 audiences shrieking in the aisles. There is no question that this is Jarrod, horribly burned and bent on revenge, but the makeup by George Bau is gruesomely effective and totally masks Price's identity behind dead raw skin and bloated lips save for the tell-tale sigh of exertion as he struggles with Burke's body. Since all promotional stills of Price's "phantom" had his made-up face blackened out, this abrupt

LAWRENCE FRENCH: Didn't Jose Ferrer ask you to be in several plays before you did *Richard III* with him?

VINCENT PRICE: Yes, I was offered a play called *My Three Angels*, which Jose Ferrer was going to direct. Later on it was done by Humphrey Bogart as a movie called *We're No Angels*. I couldn't do it, because at the same time I was offered *House of Wax*. At the time, there was a question in my mind about which part would be better for me, because I knew the play was going to be a hit, and it was. But I did *House of Wax* instead, so you never know what's going to be best. I would have liked to have done both.

appearance came as quite a shock to the unsuspecting audience. In *Making a Monster* by Al Taylor and Sue Roy (Crown Publishers, Inc., New York, 1980, p. 38), Price describes the application ordeal: "I'm told it was one of the most elaborate real makeups ever done. Two doctors supervised it to be sure the burns were as real as could be. It took almost three hours to put on and as long to take off... and both processes were very painful. Because the picture was scheduled for only 30 days, I sometimes had to wear makeup for 10 hours. I couldn't eat because my mouth was partially 'scar tissue,' so I drank many liquids and because of the running around in makeup, I fainted one day from lack of oxygen." Also, to heighten the scare quotient, whenever the scarred Jarrod would appear, David Buttolph's eerie score, under the direction of Ray Heindrof and orchestrated by Maurice de Packh, would blast forth from the strategically placed speakers in theaters equipped with stereophonic sound. Price, like Boris Karloff in his Frankenstein Monster days, was banished from the studio commissary on days when he was required to don the monstrous makeup. As he relates in Lucy Chase Williams' excellent filmbook, *The Complete Films of Vincent Price* (A Citadel Press Book, published by Carol Publishing Group, New York, 1995, p. 131), "This cold-shoulder treatment started when I walked into the commissary for lunch the first time. The girl at the cash register turned green and almost fainted. Then the patrons got up and headed for the door. It was bad for business, to say nothing of the indigestion it must have caused a couple of hundred people."

Cathy's roommate, Sue Allen (Phyllis Kirk), returns to her boarding house having been turned down for a hatcheck position. Sue is the complete opposite of her flighty roommate, almost motherly to Cathy, yet naive in the ways of the world. Upon entering her darkened bedroom, she is startled to see that Cathy has been murdered, with the hideous "phantom" preparing to attack her. She escapes out a window into the foggy streets with the lame Jarrod loping after her. In one of the most suspenseful scenes in the film, Price, in his first "monster" role, excels at terrifying us as he waits in a shroud of fog, turning his scarred and distorted body slowly to face the audience and listening for Sue's panicked breathing only a few feet away. The three-dimensional composition, Sue backed into a doorway in the foreground with Jarrod crouched menacingly in the background, actually draws the audience into the film, thereby involving us in the terror.

Sue takes refuge with a friend, Mrs. Andrews (Angela Clarke), and her sculptor son, Scott (Paul Picerni), who provides the love interest in the film. But it is only minutes later that tension returns as morgue attendants file away Cathy's body and the deformed Jarrod "pops up" from beneath a sheet to whisk away her cadaver and scare the bejesus out of the audience. Lieutenant Tom Brennan (Frank Lovejoy, in both a loveless and joyless role) coldly interrogates Sue. He is assisted by Sergeant Jim Shane (Dabbs Greer) who, along with minor characters such as the morgue attendants and Millie (a museum-goer prone to fainting), provides the much-needed comedy relief.

By this time, Sidney Wallace has returned from his extended travels and is invited to meet the owner of a newly opened wax museum. A mute assistant, Igor (a young Charles Bronson whose last name was Buchinski at that time), leads the art critic to a workroom where the propri-

Igor (Charles Bronson) looks on as Jarrod talks to Sidney Wallace (Paul Cavanagh).

etor sits in a wheelchair, his back to us. When he turns, we are as surprised as Wallace that it is Jarrod, not horribly burned, but distinguished in beard and ascot, looking very much like... well, like Vincent Price. "Shaking hands with me is not a pleasant experience," he tells Wallace, who was noticeably taken back by Jarrod's burned hands. "Jarrod is dead; I am his reincarnation." He informs Wallace that he wants to reproduce crimes of violence and exhibit them while they are fresh in the public's minds. "Have you turned your back on beauty?" asks Wallace, to which Jarrod replies, "There will be beauty for contrast," and reflects sadly that he is still searching for his Marie Antoinette. He admits that his burned hands are no longer capable of creating and that Igor and another assistant, Leon Averill (Ned Young) are the artists for the exhibits. He then proceeds to demonstrate how the figures are prepared by having Leon fire up a vat of molten wax that runs through a network of glass tubing with the boiling liquid distributed evenly over the figure, a process especially impressive in 3-D.

One of those three 3-D tricks noted by Price takes place on opening night, with a museum barker (Reggie Rymal) hitting a paddle ball at both spectators on the screen and members of the theater audience. I was sitting in the balcony of Philadelphia's largest theater, the Mastbaum, and the entire audience was screaming and ducking that little ball on a rubber string as it sailed by us toward the projection booth. Many critics have deplored this sequence since the barker stops talking to the screen spectators and addresses the movie audience: "There's someone with a bag of popcorn. Close your mouth, I'm not aiming at your tonsils. Here she comes. Well, look at that; it's in the bag." To me, however, this bit of fluff adds to the film's ability to draw the movie audience into the third dimension and make us a part of this terrifying picture. Once inside the museum, Jarrod takes us on a tour of his ghastly exhibits, and it is here that Price

House of Wax **owed a debt to Price's spellbinding performance.**

shows us another side of the character. As the attendees marvel at the likenesses of Marat Sade, William Kemmler, John Wilkes Booth and Anne Boleyn, Jarrod, as the charming showman, makes quips and quotes about the infamous personages: "A short cut to divorce," Jarrod jokes on passing the about-to-be-decapitated Boleyn, and when weak-kneed Millie (Mary Lou Holloway) faints at his description of Bluebeard's dastardly deeds, he says to her companions, "Smelling salts, ladies; help yourself." Price was having a ball with *this* Jarrod, showing the human side of the psychopath and making the character sympathetic. As Lucy Chase Williams reports in *The Complete Films of Vincent Price* (p. 32), Price believed that "the most interesting villains are those who have been *made* villains through circumstance.... There but for the grace of God go I."

Scott and Sue attend the opening day ceremonies and Sue is shocked to see how closely Joan of Arc resembles her murdered friend Cathy. Jarrod temporarily satisfies her curiosity by saying that he saw Cathy's picture in the newspapers and had Leon base the wax figure on her friend: "Do you really think she'd mind?" he asks. Sue wants to know if the photo showed Cathy wearing earrings and Leon tells her that Jarrod would not forgive him if he missed such a detail. Jarrod is taken by Sue's likeness to his former Marie Antoinette and asks if she will pose for him. He also suggests that Scott become his assistant. As the couple leaves the museum, the barker once again is seen smacking balls into the audience, only this time he catches three of them in his mouth, causing Millie, standing on the sidelines, to faint once more.

The Jarrod "phantom" makes a second but unsuccessful attempt on Sue's life, and the next night Scott takes her to a music hall (a set used as a saloon in so many of those Warner Bros. Westerns) to unwind. This sequence involves the second "trick" that Price referred to, the can-can production number, which was highly promoted in all of the original release posters. "The high kicks of the exuberant girls... will have the theater audience either ducking or reaching for a garter, depending on the sex of the patron," the pressbook warns. It also states that choreographer LeRoy Prinz, "in shooting the dance sequence... qualified as Hollywood's first three-dimensional dance director." When I saw *House of Wax* on a double date and one of the chorus girls thrust her derriere into the audience, my friend Donald Cochran got so excited that his 3-D glasses fell off of his face, much to his embarrassment and our amusement. Sue shows her properness by also being embarrassed and remarking about "all those girls showing their... talents." She tells Scott that Cathy had only *one* ear pierced as did the figure of Joan of Arc, and how could anyone capture that detail from a newspaper photo. They relay this information to Lieutenant Brennan who promises to investigate.

Sue returns to the museum and is caught by Jarrod as she climbs the Joan of Arc exhibit to look for clues. Jarrod again appeases her and then shows her a box that contains a wax likeness of Sue's detached head sculpted by Scott. "What I need for my Antoinette is you—the real you. Nothing less will satisfy me. Will you come to see me again my dear?" he asks in that melodic voice that Price was noted for, and we know that Sue is in deep trouble. Brennan and Sergeant Shane are also at the museum and think that the figure of Booth resembles the deputy city district attorney who disappeared months earlier. Shane recognizes Leon as a paroled alcoholic artist and they decide to pick him up. During Leon's interrogation, they discover the missing attorney's watch, and then torment their suspect by withholding a bottle of whisky from him until he confesses that Jarrod is the monster terrorizing the city.

Meanwhile, Jarrod instructs Scott on how to create more gruesome effects on the head he is sculpting. "A little more bitterness in that face, my boy. Remember this fellow has been badly used by the world and he despises all the people in it. Deepen those lines around the corners of the mouth... not too much... there, that's better. What I wouldn't give to have those fingers of yours." Price, himself talented in sculpture and painting and having had his own works exhibited, most surely was delighted with this role. Then Jarrod sends Scott on an errand, knowing that Sue will soon be waiting to meet him in front of the museum. Sue, thinking that Scott is detained inside on a project, enters the museum and wanders about the macabre exhibits in the dark. This presents another opportunity for de Toth to create suspense and show off the wonders of 3-D through composition and projections into the audience: A hanging skeleton swings an extended bony arm over the patrons, suspended faces and a swinging cherub in the foreground produce an uncanny sense of depth and the wax figure of Matthew Burke (looking very much like Herk Harvey in *Carnival of Souls* [1962]) hangs unceremoniously in an elevator shaft staring out at our heroine.

Sue arrives at the Joan of Arc exhibit and again climbs the funeral pyre to examine the wax figure. She removes the black wig and discovers Cathy's blond hair beneath it just as Jarrod appears. When she turns to flee, he rises from his wheelchair, stands straight and strong and walks quickly and menacingly toward her. This I find to be the only flaw in an otherwise perfect *House of Wax*. Unless it was to conceal from the audience that Jarrod was the crippled and scarred "phantom" who pursued her earlier (a fact that would be revealed in another minute), how could that gimpy "phantom" who hobbled so unsuccessfully after her initially heal himself to pursue her now so effectively? Trapped between Igor and Jarrod, she flails out her fist at the madman, beating his face, which cracks and crumbles, revealing the dead scarred tissue and bloated burned lips of the "phantom" Jarrod. Perhaps because earlier it had been partially concealed by a hat and cape in different lighting, the face appears changed, less elongated and, yes, not as frightening. Still, the surprise (provided you had not seen *Mystery of the Wax Museum*) was quite shocking. Taylor and Ray in *Making a Monster* (p. 38-39) quote Price's feelings about the sequence: "For the famous scene where the girl strikes my face and it cracks and falls off, showing the burnt face underneath—a wax cast of my own face was made—then another of my burnt face—the 'real' one enlarged to fit over the burnt one, and for one hour of horror, I wore two masks while the camera was set up and the director satisfied everything was perfect for hopefully *one* perfect take—it worked and the scene is still remembered as one of the horror highlights of the history of the cinema."

Scott, returning from his errand, searches the museum for Sue. In a bit that caused the most vocal reaction from the theater's patrons, Igor leaps *from* the audience *onto* the screen. It's a kind of reverse three-dimension, and the screams it produced weren't matched in intensity until nearly 15 years later when Alan Arkin leapt out at Audrey Hepburn in *Wait Until Dark*. The fight that follows allows for plenty of projectiles thrown at the audience: Scott hurls an ax at Igor; a blade quickly descends from a guillotine; Scott slams his fist at Igor, missing the mute but connecting with the audience; and Brennan, Shane and the police shove a crowbar through a door that jabs repeatedly at us.

Meanwhile, Jarrod in his cellar workshop has stripped Sue (rather daring for 1953, although Kirk claims she had a flimsy piece of chiffon over her), shackled her naked body in a wooden trough and fired up the old vat of molten wax. He dances excitedly around the imprisoned woman, syringe in hand, deliciously exclaiming, "The end will come quickly, my love. There is a pain beyond pain, an agony so intense that it shocks the mind into instant oblivion. We will find immortality together, and they will remember me through you!" One would think that Price, a cultured Yale graduate who enjoyed Shakespeare and creating culinary delights as well as being a connoisseur of art, would balk at having to say such gibberish. But the mischievous little boy in Vincent persisted throughout his lifetime, and such ludicrous lines and situations only encouraged his penchant to sometimes overact and to play practical jokes. When the police finally break in, they chase Jarrod to a balcony where he is knocked into his vat of boiling wax, and Brennan places his coat over Sue, pushing the trough out of the way of the exploding glass pipettes in the nick of time. At this point the film was to end, but a silly epilogue at detective headquarters was tacked on where Sue thanks Brennan for the use of his coat and blesses Jim Shane when he sneezes. Go figure.

I was 18 when I first saw *House of Wax* in 3-D on the big screen and can attest to the startling effect it had on the audience. I think it might be fair to equate this effect with similar ones experienced by 1925 audiences watching Lon Chaney's *The Phantom of the Opera* and 1931's terrified theater patrons at *Frankenstein*. Time, of course, tempers the terror of these older films, but the innovation of a new dimension, the addition of true surround sound and the classic return to a time when fog-shrouded gas-lit streets concealed unknown terrors provided chills that audiences hadn't experienced for over 20 years. Later I saw both re-releases of *House of Wax*, the first by Sherpix in 1972 and the second by Warner Bros. in 1983. Something was lacking in these versions: The depth was not as great, the prints were either too dark or too faded and the stereo sound was not as dramatic. Or at least it seemed that way. R.M. Hays in his unique book *3-D Movies: A History and Filmography of Steroscopic Cinema* (McFarland & Company, Inc., Jefferson, N.C. and London, 1989, p. 215-218) has this to say about the film: "There have always been two thoughts on *House of Wax*: one, it is a classic film of the horror genre, and two, it is claptrap exploitation of the worst kind. There seems to be no middle ground. Everyone either loves or hates this film. Even if one has followed the middle ground, *House of Wax* has to be considered better than just good. It was expertly mounted, staged, and photographed. The 3-D was wonderful, the surround sound engrossing, the story thrilling. It was old hat but it wore extremely well, and today it is still an exciting film. Stepping beyond the middle ground, it certainly is a classic not only in the horror vein but also of stereoscopic cinematography. It is a must-see in 3-D." As for me, I cherish the memory of having seen *House of Wax* in 1953, in a simpler age at the dawn of exciting new technical developments. It worked.

Jack Warner must have been pleased because *House of Wax* was an instant success. Warner Bros. created one of the most extensive premieres in Hollywood history. As described in Lucy Chase Williams' book (p. 131), "Local transit lines were involved in a tie-in, calling out 'Sixth and Hill, change for *House of Wax!*' as buses and streetcars approached the theater.... Warners set a round-the-clock premiere, with 12 opening ceremonies scheduled during the 24-hour period, starting with a midnight spook premiere.... Warner Bros. even concocted a deal with the Schick Co. to actually make electric razors available in the lobby for any men attending the six a.m. screening." Low-budget producer Alex Gordon arranged to have fading film star Bela Lugosi appear at the Paramount premiere in his Dracula cape, leading a "gorilla" on a chain. Lugosi was even persuaded to accompany Vincent on tour with others in the *House of Wax* cast. While Price, of course, had worked with Boris Karloff in the 1939 *Tower of London*, he also had an interest in meeting Lugosi. *Cinefantastique* in their Vincent Price issue (Steve Biodrowski et al., January 1989, 19[1/20]:49-50) quotes the actor as saying, "We went to Chicago to plug the film and Bela was along.... We all wanted to meet Bela, who was on the same plane, but he was way off somewhere, and he never showed up at any of the press things. So I really just met him briefly."

During these tours, Price exhibited that mischievousness I wrote of earlier. In *Vincent Price Unmasked* (p. 82), Parish and Whitney relate an incident at the Buena Park Wax Museum near Los Angeles. "He took the place of a wax figure of himself in a scene from the movie. 'I was standing in a menacing pose with a hypodermic needle,' he described. 'As the people came closer to look, I squirted water from the needle at them. It was great fun.'" He told Tom Weaver in *Attack of the Monster Movie Makers* (McFarland & Company, Inc., Jefferson, N.C. and London, 1994, p. 270): "While *House of Wax* played for about 30 weeks at the Paramount Theater in New York, I was doing a play [*Richard III*, with Jose Ferrer] and I used to sneak into the back of the movie theater.... I'd always pick two teenage girls to sit behind, cause their reactions were marvelous. At the end of one of these showings, these two girls were riveted and they were moving forward in their seats. And when finally I'm thrown in the vat of wax and I'm burned up and the steam comes up and it says THE END, I leaned forward and I said 'Did you *like* it?' Right up into orbit they went."

Phyllis Kirk was not anxious to be part of a horror film and for several years after *House of Wax* played in Westerns such as *Canyon Crossroads* and *Johnny Concho* and the love interest for Jerry Lewis in *The Sad Sack*. But Kirk made an interesting heroine, with the presence of mind to slip off her shoes during her flight from Jarrod. Her deep, somewhat apologetic voice, almost husky in contrast to Carolyn Jones' high-pitched girlish giggle, offered more personality than the standard scream queens of the 1940s. And watching her fit Jones' character into a corset (Jones was blessed with the most incredibly thin waist ever seen) offers a hint of kinkiness not dreamed of in the early 1950s. Lucy Chase Williams in her book (p. 132) quotes Kirk on Price as saying, "He was very generous with other performers—helpful, not forever hogging everything—he was a real gentleman. He was adorable."

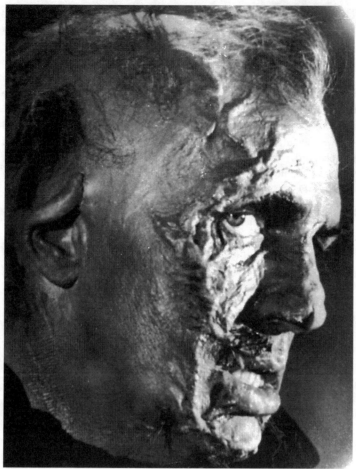

Price wears makeup by Gordon and George Bau in *House of Wax*.

Unfortunately, the two male leads, Frank Lovejoy and Paul Picerni, were saddled with rather lifeless roles. Outside of *Lord of the Jungle* (1956) and *Capricorn One* (1978), Picerni limited his genre roles to television, as in *Alfred Hitchcock Presents* and the *Men into Space*, *Batman* and *The Incredible Hulk* series, among others. Dabbs Greer, likable and funny as Jim Shane, had supporting roles in the 1956 *Invasion of the Body Snatchers*, *The Vampire* (1957) and *It! The Terror from Beyond Space* (1958). Charles Bronson was reunited with Price in Jules Verne's *Master of the World* (1961) in which he plays a hero instead of a heavy. And who could forget Phyllis Kirk passing a line of wax heads on a shelf, and the one resembling Igor moving quickly away to pursue her. The choice of the name Igor is confusing since Lionel Atwill's Jarrod character in *Mystery of the Wax Museum* was named Ivan Igor. Perhaps by this time, Igor was a generic name for any madman's assistant.

All departments acquitted themselves with perfection. Editor Rudi Fehr slips up during one scene at the end when Sue is seen screaming and writhing in the wooden trough. A few minutes later we see her quiet, perhaps even unconscious (has Price sedated her?), and then a moment later she is crying again and scraping the wooden sides of her "coffin" with her nails. Of course, Director de Toth could be faulted also for this gaffe. Andre de Toth had some curiously cryptic comments about Vincent Price in Anthony Slide's interview in *Filmfax* ("Stereoscopic Nightmares," September/October 1995, Number 52, p.41 and 80): "I met him a couple of times before and I liked him. I always thought he was an edge man. You never know which way he was going to go. He didn't have big balls of Errol Flynn, but he was good looking, always. Something was there." The director planned to make a 3-D sequel in 1983 called *Terror in Wax*, but this never came about. The 1966 Warner Bros. film *Chamber of Horrors*, directed by Hy Averback and starring Patrick O'Neal as the one-handed psychotic museum owner, was unofficially a sequel for television and had a working title of *House of Wax #2* before being rejected as too gruesome for that medium.

Price was delighted with his role as Henry Jarrod. As he told Tom Weaver in *Attack of the Monster Movie Makers* (p. 269-270), "I loved *House of Wax*. It was great fun to make. And it was fun to be part of the growing technology of the motion picture industry." Vincent would appear in two more 3-D movies, *Dangerous Mission* and *The Mad Magician*, both in 1954, and enacting a role almost identical to that in *House of Wax* in the latter. Another reason for his appreciation is summed up by Parish and Whitney in *Vincent Price Unmasked* (p. 82): "Not only was it enjoyable, but most importantly it thrust Vincent, who had been in danger of being relegated to the confines of a screen supporting player, back into the top rank of Hollywood performers. His name was once again in prime spots in all the columns and on the lips of the more adventuresome producers. The success of *House of Wax*, which owed a great deal to Price's oversized, outrageous, but spellbinding performance, gave Price's professional career as big a boost as Broadway's *Victoria Regina* had done nearly two decades before." Furthermore, *House of Wax* paved the way for his *starring* performances in over 30 future horror films including his successful association in the American International Poe chillers of the 1960s. By donning the mantle once worn by Boris Karloff and Bela Lugosi, Price became known as the Prince of Terror, something he considered a mixed blessing. But like Karloff, Vincent was not crippled by this association with horror films. He published a much sought after book on gourmet cooking, returned to the stage to give a one-man virtuoso performance as Oscar Wilde in *Diversions and Delights*, and at the twilight of his film career joined three other legends, Bette Davis, Lillian Gish and Ann Sothern, in the highly acclaimed *The Whales of August*.

Wheelchair-bound Henry Jarrod leads his captivated audience on a tour of his exhibits. He stops in front of Marie Antoinette and speaks: "*Once in his lifetime every artist feels the hand of God and creates something that comes to life.*" It may be presumptuous to suggest that the hand of God had anything to do with *House of Wax*, but this innovative little horror picture, with its exciting technical achievements and truly frightening story, breathed new life into Vincent. And while the novelty of 3-D was to fade in only a few years, Vincent Price's career blossomed and endured, providing a varied and fulfilling life for this talented renaissance man.

CREDITS: Executive Producer: Jack L. Warner; Producer: Bryan Foy; Director: Andre de Toth; Screenplay: Crane Wilbur (Based on the Screenplay *Mystery of the Wax Museum* by Don Mullaly and Carl Erickson from the Play *The Wax Museum* by Charles S. Belden); Cinematography: Bert Glennon, J. Peverell Marley and Robert Burks; Natural Vision Supervisor: Milton L. Gunzberg; Natural Vision Camera Operator: Lothrop B. Worth; 3-Dimension Technician: O.S. "Buddy" Bryhn; Editor: Rudi Fehr; Music: David Buttolph; Musical Direction: Ray Heindrof; Orchestration: Maurice de Packh; Art Director: Stanley Fleischer; Set Decorator: Lyle B. Reifsnider; Choreography: LeRoy Prinz; Assistant Director: James McMahon; Makeup: Gordon and George Bau; Wax Sculptress: Katharine Stubergh; Sound: Charles Lang, George R. Groves, William A. Muller and Lloyd Goldman; Wardrobe: Howard Shoup; Wardrobe Department Head: Joseph H. Hiatt; Casting: Hoyt Bowers. A Warner Bros.-First National Picture; Released April 25, 1953 in Natural Vision 3-Dimension and Eastman Color (WarnerColor); 88 minutes

CAST: Vincent Price (Professor Henry Jarrod); Frank Lovejoy (Lieutenant Tom Brennan); Phyllis Kirk (Sue Allen), Paul Picerni (Scott Andrews); Dabbs Greer (Sergeant Jim Shane); Paul Cavanagh (Sidney Wallace); Ned Young (Leon Averill); Roy Roberts (Matthew Burke); Carolyn Jones (Cathy Gray); Angela Clarke (Mrs. Andrews); Charles Buchinski (aka Bronson) (Igor); Reggie Rymal (Museum Barker); Philip Tonge (Bruce); Darwin Greenfield and Jack Kenney (Boarding House Lodgers), Ruth Warren (Scrubwoman); Riza Royce (Ma Flanagan); Richard Benjamin and Jack Mower (Detectives); Grandon Rhodes (Surgeon); Frank Ferguson (Medical Examiner); Eddie Parks and Jack Woody (Morgue Attendants); Oliver Blake (Pompous Man); Leo Curley (Portly Man); Mary Lou Holloway (Millie); Joanne Brown and Shirley Whitney (Girl Friends); Lyle Latell (Waiter); Terry Mitchell, Ruth Whitney, and Trude Taylor (Women); and Merry Townsend (Museum Ticket Taker)

WHILE THE CITY SLEEPS (1956)
by David J. Hogan

While the City Sleeps is predicated on two things that marked American life in 1956, the year of its release: the potent power of big-city newspapers, and America's brief, misguided crusade against comic books. These notions, plus the film's preoccupation with the inbred lust and venality of the human animal, suggest a broad canvas that would seem to be an inviting one for any actor.

Vincent Price, concluding a four-year, non-exclusive contract with RKO, and sixth-billed in this assemblage of "10 top stars," begins the film as an unsympathetic nonentity and then, unexpectedly but with believable motivation, becomes the story's most honest and dimensional character. It's fun to witness his transformation. The shame is that the movie *in toto* is a lot less fun—particularly so because it was directed by one of the giants of cinema, Fritz Lang.

Old Amos Kyne (Robert Warwick) is dying. From a hospital bed set up in his office atop the *New York Sentinel*, the flagship of his media empire, he instructs his top editor, Jon Day Griffith (Thomas Mitchell), to heavily exploit the latest murder by a fiend whom Kyne wishes to dub "The Lipstick Killer" (the culprit leaves behind scrawled crimson messages).

The old man dies shortly thereafter, and his empire is taken over by his dilettante son, Walter (Vincent Price), a thoughtless playboy who nevertheless manages to come up with a novel scheme to make the *Sentinel* an even stronger player in the city. He'll create a new position, Executive Director, and award it to whichever of his top men (his top woman is a mere gossip columnist) cracks the Lipstick Killer case. Veteran newshawk Griffith is one eager candidate; the others are Mark Loving (George Sanders), chief of the worldwide Kyne wire service; and Harry Kritzer (James Craig), head of the Kyne photographic unit. And then there's Edward Mobley (Dana Andrews), a Pulitzer Prize-winning columnist and Kyne-TV commentator who likes the easy respectability of his career, and who doesn't wish to compete at all. In any case, the playboy Walter expects to relish the contest, and anticipates that these men who have always sneered at him will be humbled and humiliated as they scramble for the prize.

The foregoing, if contrived, is not uninteresting, but Lang and screenwriter Casey Robinson indulged themselves in sexual-tomfoolery subplots that clutter the narrative so thoroughly that the story becomes not just annoyingly episodic but, finally, dull and not a little confusing. Get out your scorecard and pay attention: Mobley wants very much to bed his reluctant fiancée, Nancy (Sally Forrest), who is determined to remain a virgin until after she says "I do"; Loving, Nancy's aptly named, octopus-like boss, would like to nibble on her himself; Loving also is carrying on with the paper's dishy gossip writer, Mildred (Ida Lupino); Walter Kyne's gorgeous but conniving wife, Dorothy (Rhonda Fleming), is enduring a rather one-sided affair with the dark-horse candidate, Kritzer; and Mobley takes a cue from Loving and enjoys a piece of the all-too-willing Mildred. Amidst all the ill-advised romance, the characters are double-crossing each other, playing both ends against the middle, feeding each other phony information and doing all those other complicated, unwise sorts of things that movie characters love to do, and that almost never pay off.

Added to all of this is the script's fondness for contrivance. Foremost is that, by purest happenstance, Nancy and Kritzer live in the same apartment building—and across the hall from each other, no less. This proves useful late in the film when the mad killer, Robert Manners (John Barrymore, Jr.), strolls across the hall to confront Dorothy after being thwarted in an attempt to assault Mobley's fiancée.

The killer is physically close to these *Sentinel* people because of two more foolish story contrivances: Mobley's public goading of the murderer on TV (taking his cue from some two-bit psychoanalysis offered by a cop, Mobley declares the killer "a mama's boy"); and the front page of the *Sentinel*'s next edition, which headline's Mobley's attack *and* runs a boxed announcement of Mobley's engagement to Nancy. That's insane, but even crazier is that Nancy's danger is OK with Mobley, who has intended all along to use his fiancée as bait. Lordy, no *wonder* she won't go to bed with this schemer.

Although Mobley eventually chases and subdues the killer in a dark subway tunnel, the Executive Director job is awarded to Kritzer, who has exercised some blackmail muscle against Kyne: *Give me the job or I'll expose you as a weakling who can't hold on to his wife.* But as mentioned earlier in this piece, Price's Kyne turns out to be sympathetic and unexpectedly strong. Tired of being bullied, he publicly changes his mind, telling Kritzer to take a hike and awarding the coveted job to Mobley. Old-time editor Griffith is rewarded as well.

From childhood, director Fritz Lang was attracted to the lurid covers and contents of what he called "ze pulps." He appreciated the visceral power of colorful, lowbrow junk, so the fascination that Barrymore's Manners has with crime comic books is more than a plot device. Lang also was enamored of the psychology of murder, and had long been intrigued by the real-life story of William Heirens, a serial killer who terrorized Chicago in the 1940s. Psychosexually disturbed and thoroughly tormented, Heirens left lipstick messages on mirrors belonging to his female victims; one read, "For heaven's sake catch me before I kill more." The first murder site depicted in *While the City Sleeps* is similarly decorated, with a lipstick message reading, "Ask Mother."

Heirens' inner torment mirrored that of Peter Lorre's child killer in Lang's early triumph, *M* (1931), which was itself inspired by a real-life serial killer, a German named Peter Kurten. Lorre, of course, gave a towering performance in *M*, and there's no doubt that the Heirens case provided Lang with plenty of ripe material for an Americanized version of a similar story (the enormous illuminated "K" that tops the Kyne *Sentinel* skyscraper is a clear link to the "M" iconography of that earlier film). But John Barrymore, Jr., alas, was no Peter Lorre. Stuck at the time in a directionless film career that he never really wanted, the young Barrymore was (briefly) promoted on the strength of his name. If he was no Lorre, he *was* a bit like his father, or at least like the overacting caricature that the elder Barrymore became late in his career.

Costume decisions and Lang's direction did not help the younger Barrymore at all. Lang and writer Casey Robinson envisioned the Lipstick Killer as a psychopathic "Wild One," so Barrymore was dressed in a black leather jacket, peaked motorcycle cap, tight leather gloves and—most humorously—a scarf worn like an ascot. The getup isn't just unintentionally amusing but illogical, too, since even a novice serial killer understands the value of blending in with the crowd. In other words, you don't dress yourself in a way that will cause everybody to take notice of you.

The killer's wardrobe alone, then, makes him look suspicious, and because Manners is atremble with scowls, shifty glances and furtive body language, he's like a hot rod with a license plate that reads *2 FAST*; he's begging to be grabbed by a cop. But according to the fantasy logic of poorly conceived movies, the killer goes about his business for weeks, making drugstore deliveries, slyly fiddling with the door locks of his intended victims when their backs are turned and returning at will to murder.

The killer's motivations are muddled and clichéd. During a restaurant scene in which Mobley and police lieutenant Kaufman (Howard Duff) discuss the theory of murder, Kaufman relates the story of a young man who progressed from thefts of ladies' undergarments to murder—a brand of logic very much like that offered by the comic books that Barrymore reads with such relish (and that the film pretends to condemn). If you're naughty, goes this line of reasoning, you're capable of being evil. If you steal, you can kill. (For more on this sort of dementedly determinist illogic, see media critic Robert Warshow's brilliant book *The Immediate Experience*, which includes the 1954 essay, "Paul, the Horror Comics, and Dr. Wertham.")

Lang and Robinson maintained this train of thought, insisting that Robert Manners' leap to homicide from comic books (which Lt. Kaufman loathes because of what he calls their "instruction manual" approach to mayhem) is perfectly logical.

Further, the script asserts that a criminal will suddenly alter his M.O.—something that nearly never happens in real life. Regardless, Mobley and Lt. Kaufman abruptly dash from the restaurant, having convinced themselves that the killer, who has previously murdered only at night, is now moments away from a daylight crime.

Their hunch is correct, of course, which leads to the story's climax, and the best five minutes of this overlong, 100-minute picture. Andrews surprises Manners just when Dorothy Kyne and Nancy are in peril, and chases him to the street outside. Lang and cinematographer Ernest Laszlo shot from pavement level as the two men scramble and dodge between cars, and as one automobile unexpectedly veers out of control and violently jumps a curb. It's a good, kinetic moment of the sort that this film—composed mainly of static medium- and two-shots on cramped sets, and numberless setups of people talking on the telephone—cries out for desperately.

The on-the-street excitement is carried over into the subway-tunnel climax. Mobley and the killer engage in a furious foot race in the dangerously dark cavern, the scene periodically, shockingly illuminated whenever a train rushes past. The effect is kaleidoscopic and dizzying.

The film's other good moments, while regrettably few, are potent. In the pre-title sequence a young woman (Sandy White) accepts Manners' seemingly innocuous delivery of cosmetics, closes the (now unlocked) door, and pads to the bathroom to kneel at the edge of the tub. The camera holds on her as the door silently opens behind her; as she turns, the camera rapidly dollies in for a tight close-up on her face. She shrieks in fright, one arm sharply upflung to create a frame within the frame. The screen goes black for a beat, and then the film's title and subsequent credits overpower the screen, each "card" quickly moving backwards from the entire frame to its midpoint—*boom, boom, boom!* Herschel Burke Gilbert's music pounds and bleats—it's the sound of the city gone crazy.

Later, after another victim has been discovered, we see only the chalk outline indicating the position of the deceased, her feet and legs on her bed, her upper body sprawled on the floor next to a discarded comic book. The visible lack of the victim herself, and the pitilessness of the crudely rendered police outline, make for a tableau of particular eeriness and disquiet.

Another purely visual moment that works well shows a *Sentinel* front page, with a drawing of a featureless male head and the exhortation, "Fill in This Face, This is the Killer"—and chillingly, the killer has done just that, expertly sketching his own features on the blank template.

It's frustrating that the film's effective set pieces and scenes are buried beneath so much visual dullness and missed opportunity. A particular disappointment is that although *City* is preoccupied with the seamier aspects of sex, it reflects little of Lang's keen personal interest in the subject. Dialogue that was intended to be smart and daring falls flat, and the erotic overtones that Lang strove for are successful only occasionally, as when Rhonda Fleming, in silhouette, performs calisthenics behind an opaque screen, her long legs spread for balance, her magnificent torso twisting this way and that. Later in the sequence, Price massages the bikinied Fleming's naked back while she's recumbent on a chaise lounge. It's the one honestly sexual moment in the film, as these two tall, impressive specimens interact physically.

The subtext of Mobley's attempts to get his fiancée into bed is mildly amusing but fails to spark—an ironic happenstance, since Lang was deeply preoccupied with women and sex during his entire life, and was in fact sexually active nearly until his death at age 85, sometimes with adoring coeds who subscribed to the earthier aspects of the *auteur* theory, and frequently with prostitutes.

While the City Sleeps was produced by Bert Friedlob, an oft-married, onetime Chicago liquor wholesaler who had been bouncing in and out of Hollywood since the 1930s. He began his show business career in California, promoting midget auto racing and roller derby. Later, he brought this low-rent Americana to Europe and the South Pacific. Capital for these and other

Walter Kyne (Vincent Price) discusses the Lipstick Killer with reporter Edward Mobley (Dana Andrews).

ventures came from an early marriage to Harriet Annenberg, of the famous publishing family. Friedlob took his third wife, film star Eleanor Parker, in 1946. She opened Hollywood's respectable doors for him, though Friedlob did not become a producer until 1950; he and Parker divorced three years later.

Despite his unsophisticated professional background, Friedlob produced some not-bad movies. *A Millionaire for Christy* (1951) was a screwball comedy built around Parker, and there were some good, modestly budgeted melodramas, too, including *The Star* (1952), one of Bette Davis' best vehicles of the 1950s; and *The Steel Trap* (1952), an Everyman drama about a bank employee (Joseph Cotten) who steals money, thinking he can cover himself by replacing it over a weekend.

The property that ultimately became *While the City Sleeps* was a "paperback original" by Charles Einstein, a novel called *The Bloody Spur*. Friedlob acquired the book from Einstein and the publisher, Dell, early in 1954. (The title refers to the "bloody spur" of reckless ambition.) As the producer waited for a suitable director, happenstance brought him Fritz Lang.

Lang, despite his love of the violent and tawdry, fancied himself an aristocrat of the film industry, and probably of society at large as well. He didn't warm up to Friedlob, but because of the producer's connections to a number of major Hollywood studios, and Lang's desire to perpetuate his career, the 65-year-old director put himself on his good behavior. His relationship with Friedlob, then, was superficially amicable, partly because Friedlob was a "hands-off" producer who allowed Lang to approach the material as he wished.

Filming began in June 1955 under the provocative shooting title *News is Made at Night*, and continued for five weeks. Friedlob's decision to allow Lang a free hand—surely made on the basis of the director's track record—seems on the surface to have been a smart one, but the sad truth is that by 1955 Lang was tiring, his creative muse leaving him. What Lang and Robinson almost certainly wished to do was establish the killer as more sympathetic than the newsies who are chasing after him, and to show how men will compromise their principles for personal gain. In the event, of course, the killer is only slightly more *un*sympathetic than Mobley and the others; and because none of the latter are shown to have much in the way of principles to begin with, there's nothing for them to compromise.

While the City Sleeps is a thriller that seldom thrills, a psychological study that's illogical and shallow, a piece of would-be social comment that's unable to say what it would like. (As part of a crass promotional tie-in to the script's comic-book angle, Friedlob offered his services to the opportunistic Tennessee senator Estes Kefauver, who was at the time of production squandering taxpayers' money on a foolish investigation of the presumed deleterious effects of comic books.)

In one respect only does the film say something that's of interest to us today, and it does so thanks to the simple passing of years. Despite the fact that television was already a major part of Americans' lives by the mid-1950s (as we've seen, Mobley is a TV personality), the particulars of the script capture American newspapers in the final days of their preeminence as information providers. The *Sentinel* staff constantly presses to get out that next "extra," to beat New York's other papers to the punch, to be the first to hit the streets with a hot story. Today, when most people get their "information" from television and when too many major American cities have just a single daily paper, the film's "newshawk" orientation is a sad reminder of what was. But at least it gives Walter Kyne and the others something that's worth fighting for, even if the fight is conducted for money and personal aggrandizement.

Although it's doubtful that another director could have done much better with Robinson's terminally talky script, Friedlob [1] could not have been entirely pleased. The Friedlob-Lang relationship remained cordial throughout the shoot, then deteriorated sharply on the pair's next collaboration, the considerably more intriguing *Beyond a Reasonable Doubt* (1956), which turned out to be Lang's final American picture.

The creep of age was only one of the roadblocks to Lang's creativity and the success of his personal relationships. The director and Friedlob developed *Beyond a Reasonable Doubt* simultaneously with *City*, so Lang's attention was unwisely divided. Further, Lang was laboring with a neighbor, the celebrated screenwriter and onetime Hitchcock collaborator Charles Bennett, to develop a novel Lang had purchased, Nedra Tyre's *Journey to Nowhere*. Lang was intrigued by the book's premise, that a young girl's obliterated memory of a car crash that killed her entire family hides something sinister. But although he and Bennett met (and drank together) often, the project failed to progress beyond the talking stage.

Despite disappointment, Lang's passion for film remained dominant and pervasive. At the very least, he was intent on noting everything that took place on the *City* set. Ronnie Rondell, the picture's assistant director, noted one day that tiny mirrors attached to Lang's sunglasses gave the director the proverbial eyes in the back of his head. In 1969 Lang commented, "The cinema is my life. Whenever I had to choose between my private life and a film, I chose the film."

Lang was pleased with the cast Friedlob put together for *While the City Sleeps*. The ensemble was flashy, if not exactly as "Top" as the ads declared. Vincent Price was by this time moving easily between top billing in thrillers (*House of Wax* had been released two years before the *City* shoot) to prominent supporting roles in bigger pictures. His impressive performance as Baka in *The Ten Commandments* would be seen the same year as his interpretation of Walter Kyne. This was followed by his colorful turn as Satan in *The Story of Mankind* (1957), and then by a succession of top-billed roles in horror thrillers: *The Fly* (1958); *The Tingler* and *House on Haunted Hill*, a pair by William Castle (both 1958); *The Bat* (1959); and the picture that really catapulted him to important, if ghettoized, stardom, Roger Corman's *The Fall of the House of Usher* (1960). Although these pictures vary considerably in quality (*The Bat*, for instance, is tedious and terribly old-fashioned, while *The Fall of the House of Usher* is perfectly splendid), audiences adored Price, and came to look forward to his portrayals of suave fiends. So successful was this new phase of Price's career, in fact, that he would only rarely win roles in "serious" dramas during the remainder of his career.

Price, of course, had no idea that *While the City Sleeps* would be a sort of ending point for him. He came to the set prepared to work. He respected Lang's talent and the man's sheer presence. And, as always, Price was the consummate professional: practiced with his blocking, ready to go with his dialogue.

Early scenes of the younger Kyne are clearly intended to make the character appear shallow and unsympathetic. When he appears at the *Sentinel* the day after his father's death, foppishly attired as if on the way home from an all-nighter at the Stork Club, he earns derisive glances from the rumpled newshounds. And although he's very clear about his notion of a competition for the Executive Director post, he masks his indecisiveness about other issues with feigned impatience.

The character appears only periodically thereafter, each time seeming a bit stronger. Some of this comes from the script, as when Kyne refers to three peanuts as "Griffith," "Loving," and "Kritzer" before popping them into his mouth. But much of the character's metamorphosis comes from Price, who replaced the unpleasant sharpness apparent in Kyne's early scenes with a demeanor that's increasingly steady and assured. Never mind that he's comically clad in Bermuda shorts and black socks during the chaise-lounge sequence with Rhonda Fleming—he managed to make Kyne not just human, but warm. You suddenly feel for the guy, this self-proclaimed big shot who obviously adores his venal wife, and who has no idea she's cheating on him. By the time Kritzer makes his blackmail play, you're on Kyne's side, and when he eventually does the manly thing by booting Kritzer out on his ass, you're ready to shout, "Right on, Walter!" Price's performance is a subtly effective one that was developed with care. Of all the characters in *City*, Walter Kyne unexpectedly turns out to be the most dimensional. He's certainly the most likable.

Top-billed Dana Andrews, masculine and gruff as Mobley, was deeply sunk into alcoholism by the time of *City*, and showed up on many mornings nursing a fierce hangover. Although his condition is never apparent on screen, neither was he able to summon much fire in his dialogue scenes. Worst of all is that you don't believe for a moment that Mobley is fiercely attracted to his fiancée. The pair generate as much sexual heat as two strangers who strike up an innocuous conversation on a commuter train. (The film's coda, then, in which Mobley marries Nancy in order to have sex with her, is unconvincing as well as embarrassing.) Only during the climactic subway chase does Andrews appear to wake up completely.

Andrews came to Lang via Friedlob, as part of a package that included Lang's next film, *Beyond a Reasonable Doubt*; the actor was even more problematic on that picture, annoying Lang and exasperating co-star Joan Fontaine.

Most others in the *City* cast are effective. Thomas Mitchell is suitably "old school" as the veteran editor; and Ida Lupino, as the gossip columnist, is at once unpleasantly slippery and drop-dead gorgeous. Her real-life husband, Howard Duff, is a convincing cop.

Fritz Lang and Ernest Laszlo film *While the City Sleeps*.

Slick-looking James Craig, a brilliant heavy in Anthony Mann's *Side Street* (1949), is believably smarmy as Kritzer, and luscious Rhonda Fleming, cast opposite Craig, is nearly as impressive physically as that broad-shouldered actor. She makes her usual impression, that is, one that's more visual than thespic. Her best moment other than the difficult-to-ignore calisthenics sequence comes when she finds herself unexpectedly confronted by the killer: She dodges, wrestles, and finally takes the intruder's measure and beats the hell out of him.

The petite Sally Forrest always was a better actress than she was given credit for; although she hasn't much to work with here as Nancy, take a look at her touching performance as an unwed mother in Ida Lupino's *Not Wanted* (1949; direction credited to Elmer Clifton). Silent-screen veteran Mae Marsh, cast as the killer's mother, is unwholesomely effective in her single scene, in which she smothers her boy with affection that's obsessive instead of healthy.

Barrymore, Jr., as discussed, is awful, although this is probably Lang's fault and not the actor's. A cutaway to the killer watching himself being baited on television might have been something special, but Lang filmed Barrymore in a static medium shot with no initial close-up, no camera movement, no attempt at dramatic lighting. You're allowed no idea of what Barrymore might have been capable of achieving. For a hint, watch him as the drawling BMOC in Jack Arnold's *High School Confidential!* (1958) and you'll see a simultaneously edgy and cool screen presence, and a fellow who could effectively underplay. As noted, Barrymore never really desired a place in the Hollywood scene, and eventually retired to a hermit-like existence in the California desert. (His daughter is film star Drew Barrymore.)

Finally, there's the very British George Sanders, a practiced performer who, by this stage of his career, nearly always played George Sanders. He seems out of place, and you wonder how such an arch, condescending fellow ever prospered in the rough and tumble world of New York journalism.

RKO was on its last legs as a production house in 1956, but managed to give *While the City Sleeps* a not-bad publicity campaign. "Ten Top Stars! Ten Peak Performances!" ran the one-sheet's tag line. Come-ons suggestive of plot were more lurid: "A GIRL leaves her door open... A STRANGER tiptoes in... A big city newspaper blazes with murder headlines! Then the chase as newsmen and women feud with each other... to be the first to find the killer!"

While the City Sleeps was a modest financial success, thanks in part, perhaps, to reviews that were puzzlingly kind. A.H. Weiler, writing in *The New York Times*, praised the cast and Casey Robinson's "tight and sophisticated script," and went on to say that "Fritz Lang has kept things moving at a lively clip." A *Hollywood Reporter* review by Donald Gillette noted, "Since it is a tabloid-type story, Fritz Lang has directed it astutely in tabloid style, with short vignettes keeping the action going at a good clip, and the cast is studded with fine troupers, some of them with much less to do than their fans might like but all acquitting themselves with commendable conformity to the requirements of the story.... A very commercial attraction.... Price makes the role of the playboy publisher entertaining." Britain's *Monthly Film Bulletin* noted, "Vincent Price snarls engagingly."

Variety called the picture "a top-flight job," adding that the "old-fashioned 'stop-the-presses' newspaper yarn has been updated with intelligence and considerable authenticity and further brightened with crisp dialogue...."

The *New York Journal-American* called it "[a]n extremely lively melodrama." Finally—and appropriately, one supposes—New York's great tabloid paper, the *Daily News*, flipped over the picture and gave it three-and-a-half stars. Nearly every review noted the potency of the name cast.

A lot of things went wrong with *While the City Sleeps*, and the irony is that Lang, although tiring, still was capable of considerably better. His final film, in fact, *Die tausend Augen des Dr. Mabuse* (1960), is lively fun, with sharp-edged characters, plenty of well-staged action, and marvelously aggressive camerawork.

For Vincent Price, *While the City Sleeps* was just one stop on a remarkable film career that had begun 18 years earlier, and that would continue for nearly another 40 years. The picture is, as Lang historian Paul M. Jensen expressed it in 1969, "profoundly ordinary," and it is neither here nor there in Price's canon, but it does demonstrate the actor's ability to rise above mediocre material, and become a dominant member of a large ensemble cast. Never a grandstander, Price was at the same time too committed to his craft to phone in a performance, and far too talented to be lost in the shuffle. In this movie, *that's* the news that really matters.

CREDITS: Producer: Bert E. Friedlob; Director: Fritz Lang; Screenplay: Casey Robinson (Based on the Novel *The Bloody Spur*, by Charles Einstein); Cinematography: Ernest Laszlo; Editor: Gene Fowler, Jr.; Art Director: Carroll Clark; Set Decorator: Jack Mills; Makeup: Gus Norin;

Music: Herschel Burke Gilbert; Orchestrations: Joseph Mullendore, Walter Sheets; Music Editor: Alfred Perry; Production Supervisor: George Yohalem; Sound: Jack Solomon; Sound Re-recording: Buddy Myers; Sound Editor: Verna Fields; Costumes: Norma; Wardrobe: Bob Martien, Jackie Spitzer; Hair Stylist: Cherie Banks; Assistant Director: Ronnie Rondell; Assistant to the Producer: Leo Taub; Continuity: Joe Franklin, Violet McComan; Technical Adviser: Mike Kaplan; Black and White; SuperScope; 100 minutes; filmed June-August 1955; a Thor Production released by RKO, May 1, 1956. Note: Completely unnecessary "Colorimaged" computer-colored prints exist.

CAST: Dana Andrews (Edward Mobley); Rhonda Fleming (Dorothy Kyne); George Sanders (Mark Loving); Howard Duff (Lt. Burt Kaufman); Thomas Mitchell (Jon Day Griffith); Vincent Price (Walter Kyne); Sally Forrest (Nancy Liggett); John Barrymore, Jr. (Robert Manners); James Craig (Harry Kritzer); Ida Lupino (Mildred Donner); Vladimir Sokoloff (George Pilski); Robert Warwick (Amos Kyne); Ralph Peters (Meade); Mae Marsh (Mrs. Manners); Larry Blake (Police Sergeant); Edward Hinton (O'Leary); Celia Lovsky (Miss Dodd); Sandy White (Judith Felton); Pitt Herbert (Bartender)

[1] Bert Friedlob died at 49, of cancer, in the fall of 1956.

THE FLY (1958)
by Don G. Smith

The Fly is an important film for two reasons. First, it established Vincent Price as a "horror actor" in the public mind; and second, it was one of the most financially and critically successful horror films of the 1950s. In 1958, Price was not yet America's "horror man," the screen's successor to Boris Karloff, Bela Lugosi and Peter Lorre. *The Fly*, however, changed all of that.

In a pressbook interview for *The Fly*, Price responded to the observation that the public was increasingly identifying him with villainy:

> But it's not true. I've done more comedy parts than villains; more straight
> parts than either and only a couple of horror roles... For example, I've done
> only three horror films prior to *The Fly*—and in this my role is straight—but
> *The House of Wax* was a tremendously successful picture and I played such an
> outlandish character that people remember me in it. I've given better perfor-
> mances in a number of better films, but no one remembers that... I don't want
> to be identified with any special type of characterization, certainly not with
> villainy... Shakespeare was right, I must admit, when he wrote: 'The evil men
> do lives after them, the good is oft interred with their bones.' But I wish he
> weren't so precise.

Price had also appeared in some genre television: two episodes of *Science Fiction Theater* and one episode of *Alfred Hitchcock Presents*.

It is still remarkable that *The Fly* was the film that firmly and forever made Price a "horror actor." After all, he plays neither the title creature nor a villain. So why? The answer lies in the success of *The Fly* itself.

Interestingly, Price almost didn't get a role in *The Fly*. His previous film, *The Story of Mankind* (1957), was a financial and critical failure. After that, Vincent left the wide screen for two wildly successful contests on the subject of art history on the television show *The $64,000 Challenge* (a companion show to *The $64,000 Question*). His opponents were jockey Billy Pearson and actor Edward G. Robinson; he settled for a draw against both. Increasing amounts of Price's time were being devoted to art lectures, and Fox executive producer Buddy Adler doubted that the actor retained enough marquee value to boost *The Fly*. Director Kurt Neumann, however, insisted that Price's reputation in horror films would draw crowds, and Vincent was in.

The film was based on a short story of the same name by George Langelaan. Appearing in the June 1957 issue of *Playboy*, "The Fly" provoked a large enthusiastic response from readers and won the magazine's award for best story of the year. Screenwriter James Clavell changed the setting of the story from France to Quebec and altered the ending but otherwise closely followed the short story's structure. A brief summary of the scenario follows:

Helene Delambre (Patricia Owens) awakens her brother-in-law Francois Delambre (Vincent Price) with a phone call and confesses that she has murdered her husband Andre (David Hedison). Since Helene and Andre were, to all appearances, a happily married couple with a son, Francois cannot comprehend why Helene would crush her husband's head and arm under an industrial metal press. Though Helene initially refuses to tell Francois or Inspector Charas (Herbert Marshall) why she did it, she later confides the truth to Francois. It appears that her brilliant husband had succeeded in creating a machine capable of breaking down matter, transferring it to another place, and then reassembling it. Unfortunately, when Andre experimented on himself, a housefly entered the machine with him. When the two were reassembled, Andre had the head and arm of a fly, and the fly had the head and arm of Andre. Andre instructed Helene to find the fly so he could try to undo the tragic error, but when she failed, he destroyed the machine and begged Helene to destroy him. Of course, no one believes her story—until Francois and Inspector Charas see a spider attack a fly with a human head and arm. Charas crushes both creatures and concludes that if Helene is guilty of killing a human that is part fly, then he is guilty of killing a fly that is part human. Case closed.

The Fly was wildly successful, both critically and financially. Filmed on a $400,000 budget, the film grossed $34,000 in its first week of release and eventually earned over $3,000,000. The advertising campaign certainly helped. Note the intriguing lines from the ads and posters:

> "The fly that was buzzing around the house had once been her loving husband!"
> "Once it was human... even as you and I."
> "If she looked upon the horror her husband had become... she would scream for the rest of her life!"
> "It challenged the supreme power of the universe! The monster created by atoms gone wild!"
> "$100 if you prove it can't happen!"

LAWRENCE FRENCH: I remember when *The Conqueror Worm* came out in 1968, quite a few articles cited its excessive blood and violence, but it's really quite tame compared to today's slasher films. What do you think of those films?

VINCENT PRICE: Oh God, you know I go to see those films, because I know people are going to ask me what I think of them (laughter). I find that they have no surprises. They throw so much violence at you, that there's no suspense. You know, violence is something you can only have a little bit of. You can't have somebody ripped apart in the beginning of the show! Where are you going to go from there? They also have no sense of humor, whatsoever! Also, I know how it's all done, so consequently they don't frighten me. I find that some of the old ones, that were made with a sense of suspense, are far better. You didn't know what was going to happen. *The Fly*, for instance. When you saw the fly, you only saw him for a very short while. Then you just saw his claw, and there was a cloth over his head. If that were done today, you'd see him in every frame of the picture, eating his food, and everything. (David Cronenberg's 1986 remake of *The Fly* featured exactly those kind of vivid depictions.) There is such a thing as suggesting something. It's like nude women. Very few women should be caught nude. They should be perfect if they're going to be caught nude.

Though most ads featured the large image of a fly, Vincent Price, billed third, appeared in smaller format in most advertising.

Another reason for the film's success was its timing. The science fiction boom of the 1950s was qualitatively floundering in 1958. England's Hammer Studios had caught the public's attention by producing inexpensive but attractive Gothic horror films, updating the classic films of the 1930s and 1940s for a new audience. America's science fiction films of the late 1950s were almost all in black and white, almost all low budget, and almost all aimed at an adolescent Saturday matinee or drive-in audience. Produced in CinemaScope and color, *The Fly* was effectively hyped to all ages. Adults sent their offspring to see *Attack of the 50 Foot Woman* and *How to Make a Monster* but joined them in seeing *The Fly*.

What interests me most in Price's performance is a lack of any apparent grief at Andre's alarming and totally unexpected death. Indeed, he acts more

Vincent Price stars as Francois Delambre in *The Fly*.

baffled than aggrieved. Francois admits to Inspector Charas that he loves Helene, adding that he didn't marry her because she loved his brother and hardly noticed him. Other conversation indicates that the brothers were quite close. His solicitude for Helene under the circumstances is odd but perhaps understandable since he loves her. Of course, we might argue that the mystery of the whole affair makes odd behavior more believable than it might be otherwise. Then again, perhaps Bill Warren (*Keep Watching the Skies! Volume II*) is on the mark when opining that:

> When Price is miscast, he sometimes almost walks through the role, or flails around trying to find the character. In *The Fly*, he's lost; this quiet, troubled man is just not a role Price should have been asked to play. There's not even a smidgen of excess for him to bounce off. He overacts without the conviction he brings to more flamboyant parts; he's incapable here of registering sorrow, and instead relies on a pained, troubled look through most of the film. Price, who himself is a witty man, is definitely at his best in roles where he can exhibit a sense of humor, either through the character directly or around the edges, doing a mild send-up. Francois Delambre is a totally humorless part, and the only scene in which Price seems comfortable is a brief one in which he listens to the prattling of Charles Herbert as they descend a flight of stairs.

The Fly was released on July 11. Shortly thereafter, Price appeared on *The Red Skelton Show* in a skit with Red as Freddy the Freeloader. While I have not seen this episode since 1958, I remember Vincent barging into Freddy's shack and being covered with falling debris. His

Helene (Patricia Owens) is taken away after the murder of her husband.

features obscured and looking a bit other-worldly, Price ad-libbed, "And don't call me the Fly!" Red laughed in response to Vincent's unexpected promotion.

I was only 10 years old in 1958. Soon after seeing *The Fly*, I wrote a letter addressed to Vincent Price, actor—Hollywood, California. On April 8, 1960, I was thrilled to receive a form letter from Vincent (see illustration) thanking me for writing and informing me of his new book on art, *I Like What I Know* (1959). A publicity photo accompanied the letter. Though the reply was a form letter, the autograph was authentic, the first of many Vincent Price autographs that I would acquire over the years.

Even in 1959, I took positive note of Vincent's interest in art. Art was not discussed in my family, but Vincent's knowledge of and enthusiasm for the subject aroused my curiosity. While I did not acquire *I Like What I Know* immediately after receiving Vincent's letter, I did get the book later and found it an enjoyable and informative read. In fact, I credit Mr. Price for so interesting me in art that I studied art history in Europe in the summer of 1971. After that eye-opening experience, I wrote to the actor and thanked him for writing *I Like What I Know* back in 1959 and for playing a part in broadening my world. Unfortunately his *Treasury of Great Recipes* (1965, with Mary Price) failed to sharpen my culinary skills as I still do well to produce an edible TV dinner.

After 1958, Vincent Price made sporadic references to *The Fly* in his interviews and his writings. For example, in his introduction to *The Ghouls* (1971, edited by Peter Haining), Price discusses the allure of horror monsters in film and literature, recalling *The Fly* by way of illustration:

> The element of 'there but for the grace of God' is the key to the success of *Phantom of the Opera, The Fly, Freaks*, and to me those human monsters will always be more fascinating than the Bloblings and Goblins from outer space.... Tragedy in the dramatic theory of Aristotle and other subsequent playwright-philosophers is the highest element of terror, especially if we can identify with the tragedy. If it could happen to Dr. Jekyll, is it not only possible but probable that there is a monster in every man?... This kind of split personality is the

most challenging problem for the actor, and for the audience too. With *The Beast [from 20,000 Fathoms]*, there was no split personality because there was no personality to begin with, and personality is the actor's only problem. With Frankenstein's monster it was different. He was made up of human parts, and there was some humanity left over—so it was with the Golem. These are not monsters as such, for the trace of man that was left with them was their tragedy, it was outweighed by their inhumanity. This imbalance was also what terrified us. So it was, too, with *The Fly*, a man made into a monster; his sadness was that he could not be rescued back into the race fate had taken him away from. Is that not the ultimate fear of every man, that the end of life, Death itself, may be separation from his identity with man?

The Fly proved such a success that in 1959 Vincent agreed to reprise Francois Delambre in *Return of the Fly*. Though filmed in black and white, the sequel proved to be a critical and financial success. So much was Vincent identified with *The Fly* that fans would often ask him to autograph photos of other actors portraying the title creature. Though he never played The Fly in either film, he would politely sign the photos anyway.

Today, *The Fly* no longer enjoys the critical reputation it had in the late 1950s. The film's obvious inconsistencies have been discussed at length. David (later Al) Hedison has made clear his disagreement with the use of the fly mask and other aspects of the production. And though it isn't the fault of the film, it is hard to watch the spider web finale today without recalling Price's account of how he and Herbert Marshall could not perform the scene with straight faces. Director Cronenberg's 1986 remake of *The Fly* is generally considered superior. In retrospect, while the 1958 *Fly* was not a great film, it remains unforgettable ("Helppp me—helppp me!") and historically important. After *The Fly*, Price solidified his title as new horror film king by starring in several of William Castle's high-profile, financially successful shockers and by becoming, under Roger Corman's direction, the screen's most renowned interpreter of Poe. With Hammer Films ascending, and with 1930s and 1940s classics showing for the first time on television, those were fabulous years for the horror cinema and its fans. We may never see an era like it again—and for that we must forever thank Vincent Price.

CREDITS: Producer/Director: Kurt Neumann; Screenplay: James Clavell (Based on a Story by George Langelaan); Cinematography: Karl Strauss; Art Directors: Lyle R. Wheeler and Theobold Holsopple; Set Decorators: Walter M. Scott and Eli Benneche; Music: Paul Sawtell; Makeup: Ben Nye; Special Effects: L.B. Abbott; Released by 20th Century-Fox; July 1958; 94 minutes

CAST: David [later Al] Hedison (Andre Delambre); Patricia Owens (Helene Delambre); Vincent Price (Francois Delambre); Herbert Marshall (Inspector Charas); Kathleen Freeman (Emma); Betty Lou Gerson (Nurse); Charles Herbert (Philippe Delambre); Eugene Borden (Dr. Ejoute); Torben Meyer (Gaston)

LAWRENCE FRENCH: I understand you had a difficult time saying your lines in the last scene of *The Fly*.

VINCENT PRICE: Oh, it was terrible! It was a very different scene then what we finally ended up with. There was a point where Herbert Marshall and I had a kind of philosophical discussion about what we should do with my brother-in-law (David Hedison), who is a fly with a human head. Now I don't know how many flies you see around the house with human heads, or brother-in-laws, for that matter. But we were playing this scene, looking at the fly saying, "Should we kill it? Should we save it?" and we could never quite get the lines out, because every time that little voice of the fly would say, "Help me. Please, help me," we would just scream with laughter. It was terrible. We ended up doing about 20 takes.

HOUSE ON HAUNTED HILL (1958)

by Gary J. Svehla

House on Haunted Hill, perhaps producer/director William Castle's and screenwriter Robb White's finest cinematic achievement, is considered Vincent Price's *other* major horror film appearance of 1958 (along with *The Fly*). While it does manage to terrify and raise goosebumps, the film is just as much constructed as a mystery/noir as it is a horror film. Quite simply, it was promoted and sold as a horror film, and with a name like *House on Haunted Hill*, how could it be anything but a horror film? Especially since it was released in Emergo, a typical Castle gimmick that required theater operators to send a skeleton on a wire overtop theater patrons during the climax of the film, usually to waves of intense screams, at least from the children in attendance in the audience. However, with a quite clever screenplay written by White, snapping with crisp dialogue, the movie owes more to the world of film noir (its voice-over narration, its despicable characters, its plot involving elaborate crosses and double-crosses, its *femme fatale*, its world of moral ambiguity) than it owes to the world of horror. Because of the intelligent script, Vincent Price is able to deliver perhaps his finest performance in a B movie, horror or otherwise.

The movie addresses its ambivalence as to whether it is horror or noir from the very beginning—the so-called house on haunted hill, externally at least, is in fact a modernistic house that goes against typical haunted house stereotypes (internally, it does conform to expectations). Then the first voice-over introduction, delivered by the house owner Watts Pritchard (Elisha Cook, Jr.), establishes the horror aspect of the production: "The ghosts are moving tonight, restless, hungry... I am Watson Pritchard. In just a minute I will show you the only real haunted house in all the world. Since it was built a century ago, seven people, including my brother, have been murdered in it. Since then I've owned the house. I've only spent one night there, but when they found me in the morning, I was almost dead!" Here dialogue is delivered in a most horrific, ghastly and supernatural expression. But Cook's face vanishes as the sinister face of Vincent Price appears, portraying the film's rich playboy. "I am Frederick Loren and I've rented the house on haunted hill tonight so my wife can give a party, a haunted house party. She's so amusing [with these lines Price cracks a nasty smile]. There'll be food and drink and ghosts— and perhaps even a few murders. You're all invited [to spend 12 hours overnight and collect $10.000]." Price's face disappears as the camera points toward the party guests arriving in the dark, slowly approaching their destination. "It was my wife's idea to have our guests arrive in funeral cars... she's so amusing, her sense of humor is, shall we say, original. I dreamed up the hearse—it's empty now, but after a night in the house on haunted hill, who knows?" In other words, expressed with Price's snide, sarcastic delivery, the tone of the movie has transformed from horror to noir, with haunted houses and supernatural murder being replaced by party pranks and the threat of actual murder. Both narrators instill fear in the audience, but two entirely different forms of fear.

As Robb White's tidy plot advances, the party guests and main cast of characters are introduced by Frederick Loren, who continues with his snide side comments. First we meet test pilot Lance (Richard Long), who Loren describes as a brave man. "Wouldn't you be much braver if you're paid for it," Loren comments, telling the audience that Lance needs the money. Next up is Ruth Bridgers (Julie Mitchum, Robert's sister), a columnist for a newspaper who is writing a feature story on ghosts. According to Loren, "She's desperate for money... gambles." Next we meet Watson Pritchard again, a "man living in mortal fear of a house and yet he is risking his life to spend another night here—I wonder why? He says for money!" Dr. David Trent (Alan Marshal), the next guest, is a psychiatrist and claims "that my ghosts will help him work on hysteria, but don't you see a little touch of greed there, around the mouth and eyes!" Finally, we meet the innocent and young Nora Manning (Carolyn Craig) who was picked from thousands of people who work for Loren since "she needs the $10,000 more than most... she supports her whole family... isn't she pretty." Following the noir tradition, all of these people are in desperate need of quick cash, and while each seems upstanding and honest, Loren colors each introduction with just enough hint of tainting that not any character is above suspicion. Thus, while *House on Haunted Hill* is not film noir in the final appraisal (its dreary tone is used playfully more as a tease, and it never really loses its outrageous horror movie scare sequences), it does allow Vincent Price's character of Frederick Loren to become more sleazily and complexly developed than the typical character of his ilk would be in the traditional horror movie.

And Vincent Price is seldom better (even in a larger-than-life interpretation of a millionaire married for the fourth time to a woman he confesses to hating) than when sparring with wife Annabelle (Carol Ohmart), the two alone up in the bedroom as the party guests gather in the living room below. "Annabelle, our guests are here, unfortunately, still alive. Is your face on yet?"

Annabelle enters from the bathroom, wearing a very tight and revealing outfit, knowing full well that Frederick will not approve. "Dust and dirt everywhere, the water barely trickles. Couldn't you have the place cleaned?" Annabelle complains.

"Atmosphere, darling, you know how ghosts are. They never tidy up [Price smiles broadly]. That's a very fetching outfit but hardly suitable for a party," Frederick complains. Annabelle declares she is not going to his party. But Frederick adds, "This spend-the-night ghost party was your idea, remember? Since it's going to cost me $50,000, I want you to have fun!"

In anger Annabelle reminds her husband, "The party was *my* idea until *you* invited all the guests. Why all the strangers? Why not any of our friends?"

Snidely, Loren counters, "Friends—do we have any friends? Your jealousy took care of that!" Explaining that he invited people from all cross sections of life who needed money, the fun for him is observing if they have the courage to earn the money. "And you call this a party," Annabelle growls. Smiling and nodding his head playfully, Loren states, "Could be!"

Frederick pulls out a bottle of champagne and shakes it. "Why do you always do that, it spoils the champagne," Annabelle again grumbles. "It might explode," Frederick says, aiming the cork of the bottle directly at his wife. "That's not even funny," she pouts. "Makes a good headline: Playboy kills wife with champagne cork... would you join me. Just a sip might improve your humor," Frederick states. "My humor is fine, thanks, and I haven't poisoned it," the wife shockingly adds. Forcing her to take a sip, Frederick insists she will enjoy the party more. "Your trust is so touching [handing the glass back after taking a drink], and I'm not going

"HOUSE ON HAUNTED HILL"

to the party!" Annabelle is now moving the conversation beyond the simple bitchy stage and suggesting that either one of them is capable of doing in the other.

"Of all my wives, you're the least agreeable," Loren declares. "But still alive," Annabelle counters, for two of Loren's young brides died of heart attacks while only in their twenties. "Would you go away for a million dollars, tax free?" Frederick inquires. Annabelle, smiling broadly, moving in closer to her husband, shakes her head no. "You want it all!" Frederick concludes. "I deserve

Vincent Price was not afraid to deliver the performance that *House* needed, and that performance is still a pleasure to watch 40 years later.

it all... your jealousy isn't tax free, your possessiveness is maddening," Annabelle shouts. Losing the snide, sarcastic smile which has accented almost every sentence delivered in this well-written sequence, Loren grows seriously intense and says, "If ever a man had grounds for divorce... the time will come, you'll slip up, one of these days... remember the fun we had when you poisoned me?" In marked contrast to Loren, Annabelle chuckles in the background and remarks, "Something you ate, the doctor said." Returning to form with that twinkle in his eye, Loren states, "Yes, arsenic on the rocks!"

Suddenly, Frederick loses his sense of humor and grabs Annabelle by the arm. He's deadly serious when he says, "Annabelle, you'd do it again if you thought you could get away with it... something about hanging... it's very uncomfortable!" Then Frederick makes comments about all the supposed ghosties and ghouls lurking about this house to which his wife replies, "Darling, the only ghoul in the house is you!" Before exiting the room, Frederick shoots off his final barb: "Don't stay up all night—thinking of ways to get rid of me... it makes wrinkles!"

Such verbal exchange—with all credit going solely to Carol Ohmart, Vincent Price and writer Robb White—is common to the world of film noir, but seldom is this kind of subtlety involving the disintegration of a marriage so complexly verbalized in a standard B horror drama. Vincent Price does over-extend his anger, bitterness and veiled threats a tad, perhaps he might be guilty of smirking, rolling his eyes or even smiling a little too much on cue, almost as if his entire craft as actor has its slip slowing, but this verbal exchange is quite simply classic Vincent Price, his swagger and arrogance meeting its match in wife Annabelle's cleverly worded rebuttals. During these sequences, the screen smolders as each spouse gets down and dirty, deliver-

Frederick Loren (Vincent Price) and wife Annabelle (Carol Ohmart) are a match made in Hell in
House on Haunted Hill.

ing each successive line with more venom and bitterness than the one before. For fans of Vincent
Price, it doesn't get better than this!

At this point, Frederick Loren makes his appearance to his party guests, offering to break
the ice by serving drinks, stating his wife will be joining the party later. Price restates the deal:
Every party member will earn $10,000 by staying in the house overnight; however, if they wish
to leave, they must exit the house by midnight because after then the house is locked up, becoming a virtual tomb, and no one can leave until 8 a.m. tomorrow morning. The warped Watson
reminds the party-goers that the house has claimed seven victims, four men and three women,
the exact same composition of people staying in the house overnight. Watson shares the sordid
history of the house, just moments earlier augmented when the chandelier swayed and fell from
the ceiling, almost crushing Nora Manning. Watson shows the gathering a dried blood stain
from a bedroom ceiling. The spot drips wet blood on Ruth. "Too late, they marked you," Watson
raves. A visit to the wine cellar reveals that the former Mr. Norton, wine maker, could not please
the taste buds of his wife. So filling one underground wine vat with acid, he threw her in.
"Destroys everything with hair and flesh," Watson explains as he throws a dead rat into the vat.

Soon Lance and Nora are investigating empty rooms (in one of which Lance was beamed
by something, knocked unconscious and reawakened with a bloody gash on his forehead), listening for hollow walls. Lance instructs Nora to keep banging on the wall while he listens in the
adjoining room. As he tells her to bang lower, Nora squats down as the classic fright sequence
of the movie is about to occur: First the camera moves in closer on Nora and then shifts slightly
behind and to the left, suddenly revealing the presence of a witchy woman, her arms extended
with hands and nails poised to strike. This causes Nora to scream bloody murder as the woman,
obviously on wheels, frozen in the same position, seems to float out of the room. This sequence
never fails to generate squeals and screams.

So far it seems Nora has been the victim of all the frightful things occurring: the falling chandelier and twice observing the witch-woman. The only help that Dr. Trent can offer is, "hysteria" is the answer for whatever ghosts people see. Nora finds a bloody severed head in a small piece of luggage, and when she fetches the others to share the find, of course the head is gone. Before the night is much older, Nora will be accosted by a spooky old man who attempts to muzzle her with his hand covering her mouth, and she will be visited by a floating corpse outside her bedroom (Annabelle after she commits suicide) as the end of the rope around the corpse's neck mysteriously wraps itself around Nora's feet. Much like Fay Wray and Marilyn Burns before her, all Nora can manage to do is scream and keep screaming. Interestingly, after the old man and witchy woman are later revealed to be caretakers Jonas and his blind wife, director Castle sets up an interesting juxtaposing shot. While the spooky, ugly caretakers are posed standing side by side in the background, Castle cuts to Loren and wife Annabelle in the foreground, to contrast two different types of married couples: The caretakers in back are spooky looking but very much in love, while the handsome Lorens in the foreground are beautiful only on the surface, but hateful and conniving underneath.

After everyone is locked in the house minutes before midnight, Annabelle mysteriously commits suicide by hanging herself from the staircase with a rope—"So beautiful, so greedy, so cold," Frederick utters standing over his wife's corpse, now stored in one of the bedrooms. Loren states the obvious, that one of the assembled guests killed his wife, but Dr. Trent reminds Loren that only he has a motive for murder. Until the house opens tomorrow morning at 8 a.m., each guest agrees to stay alone in his/her bedroom, armed with a pistol provided as a party favor, delivered in oh-so-charming little wooden coffins.

However, in the middle of the night, Trent knocks on Loren's room, telling his host that he hears people wandering around the house, and that Loren should investigate the lower levels while he checks out up here. As soon as Loren disappears downstairs, Trent goes to check in on the corpse of Annabelle: "It's almost over, darling, every detail was perfect... we've done it, the perfect crime," and with these words, Annabelle stirs, coming back to life, showing the audience the hanging harness that she wore to fake her own suicide. Trent's plan is to drive the innocent Nora to hysteria so she will use her gun to kill Loren accidentally. Since Trent knows Nora is downstairs, exactly where Loren is heading, the shooting will occur momentarily, allowing Annabelle to marry her lover Dr. Trent. Trent, who plans to go down to the cellar now, tells Annabelle to come down when she hears the shot.

The plan is apparently working like clockwork. Nora confronts Loren in the cellar and shoots him, screams and runs off. Trent appears and opens the wine vat door, still filled with acid, and prepares to dispose of Loren's body, but just before he throws the body in the vat, the lights go out, a choking/struggling sound is heard and then a splash. When Annabelle arrives in the cellar, no corpses are to be found, but emerging from the vat is a human skeleton.

House on Haunted Hill **is a much more successful and satisfying movie than 1958's other Vincent Price horror release,** *The Fly.*

Annabelle attempts to escape, but all cellar doors are now locked. Loren's voice is heard echoing: "At last you got it all, everything I have—even my life! But you're not going to live to enjoy it. Come with me, murderess, come with me." With these words, the skeleton approaches the hysterical and screaming woman, forcing her to take slow steps backward, inching closer and closer to the vat. When the skeleton's hand lightly touches her on the shoulder, she falls to her death into the acid bath. Moments later Loren is seen emerging from the shadows, reeling in wire and his skeleton on a huge metal harness. Loren's deadly monologue begins: "Good night Doctor, good night Annabelle. The crime you two planned was indeed perfect—only the victim is alive and the murderers are not. It's a pity that when you started your game of murder, I was playing too." The skeleton is thrown back into the vat, concealing the evidence of Annabelle's murder.

Loren, who looks like the cat who just ate the canary, delivers his prepared speech to the party guests, who have just entered the cellar. "I can tell you all now, Trent and my wife were planning to kill me. They failed. Trent tried to throw me in the vat, my wife stumbled and fell. I am ready for justice to decide if I'm innocent or guilty." With these words, Loren slowly ambles up the stairs, secretly secure that he will once again escape the hangman's noose.

Even though released by low-budget Allied Artists, Castle's *House on Haunted Hill* is a much more successful and satisfying movie than 1958's other Vincent Price horror release, *The Fly*, a big-budget release from 20th Century-Fox that ultimately comes off as being too polite for its own good (distilling its horror with melodramatic subplots and fatal doses of romance). The schlocky, gimmick-laden and exploitative *House on Haunted Hill* delivers all the cinematic goods in spades. We have crisp black and white cinematography lensed by Carl E. Guthrie, creating constant creepy mood and the anticipation of fear yet to come. We have red herrings, graphically rendered bloody decapitated heads, creepy people pouncing upon innocent victims in darkened rooms, falling chandeliers, blood dripping from ceilings, corpses floating outside windows lighted by the cracking lightning and thunder of a raging storm. And finally we have the Emergo gimmick, a skeleton dancing above the patrons' heads in the theaters during the climax of the movie, delivering the final one-two punch (quite honestly, the film still works just as successfully without it). Bravo! For audiences in 1958, Castle delivered a total shock package using every ounce of creativity (both within the move itself and also in the presentation) to terrify audiences.

Vincent Price is the glue that holds the entire dramatic structure together, becoming the only recognizable cast member besides Elisha Cook, Jr. and perhaps Richard Long. Fine-tuning and further exploring his most oily and despicable screen persona, Vincent Price's Frederick Loren is not a supporting cad but a leading player, the star of the production, and Price's performance is bolstered by the roll-off-the-tongue dialogue provided him by Robb White, dialogue that is both biting and humorous, delivered by an actor who is not afraid to crack a snide smile or roll his eyes or push the button of melodramatics to the edge. And while many other actors might have simply become too hammy or unbelievable, Vincent Price makes such a broad performance unique and memorable. Sometimes actors bring a *Masterpiece Theater* reverence to a role when the performance requires something more akin to vaudeville or silent movies—*House on Haunted Hill* is certainly no *Masterpiece Theater*, and Frederick Loren's character requires the talents of a professional not afraid to be accused of going slightly over-the-top, for such lip-smacking acting complements the tone of something exploitative enough to be called *House on Haunted Hill*. Quite simply, Vincent Price was not afraid to deliver the performance that *House* needed, and that performance is still a pleasure to watch 40 years later.

CREDITS: Producer and Director: William Castle; Associate Producer: Robb White; Screenplay: Robb White; Cinematography: Carl E. Guthrie; Editor: Roy Livingston; Musical Score: Von Dexter; Theme "House on Haunted Hill": Richard Kayne and Richard Loring; Art Director: David Milton; Set Decorator: Morris Hoffman; Men's Wardrobe: Roger J. Weinberg; Ladies' Wardrobe: Norah Sharpe; Makeup: Jack Dusick; Hairstylist: Gale McGarry; Special Effects: Herbert Townsley; Previewed November 24, 1958; Released by Allied Artists; Running Time: 75 minutes.

CAST: Vincent Price (Frederick Loren); Carol Ohmart (Annabelle Loren); Richard Long (Lance Schroeder); Alan Marshal (Dr. David Trent); Carolyn Craig (Nora Manning); Elisha Cook, Jr. (Watson Pritchard); Julie Mitchum (Ruth Bridgers); Leona Anderson (Mrs. Sykes); Howard Hoffman (Jonas)

RETURN OF THE FLY (1959)

by Mark Clark

Sorry to spoil the mystique, but no sort of collaborative effort goes into these *Midnight Marquee Actors Series* volumes. It's not like we all gather in some big, smoke-filled room to knock back Margaritas and plan who's going to say what about which movies (although that's a pretty cool idea—Gary and Sue, are you listening?).

I mention this since in all likelihood you read Don G. Smith's chapter on *The Fly* earlier in this volume, and I expect to contradict everything Don wrote. I expect this because I'm going to contradict everything else I've ever read about *The Fly* and its sequels.

Conventional wisdom calls *The Fly* a minor classic, an ambitious, well-mounted science fiction thriller. On the other hand, pundits say, *Return of the Fly* is a cheaply made, brain-dead rehash, inferior to the original in every respect. Stated and echoed so many times by so many writers, these perspectives have gained enough analytical momentum that they're now accepted as something just shy of scientific fact. I contend, however, that these popular assertions are more full of baloney than an Oscar Mayer delivery truck.

There's no denying that *The Fly* scared a lot of people and made a lot of money in 1958, but in hindsight it's difficult to fathom why. The film is a tedious, pretentious jumble which plods along interminably. If not for the cachet Vincent Price's presence lends the picture and for the film's powerful climax ("Helllp meee!"), *The Fly* nowadays would be lumped in with other glossy 1950s disappointments such as *Phantom of the Rue Morgue*.

The Fly is an especially difficult picture for me as a Vincent Price fan, since it wastes its star in a meaningless role (confined to an overlong framing sequence) and because Price gives one of his most overrated performances. Price hams and preens mercilessly, perhaps in the mistaken belief that arching his eyebrows and quivering his voice would add depth to his thinly written character. Such arch theatricality often worked for Price when cast as the story's heavy (perhaps most memorably in *The Masque of the Red Death* and *House on Haunted Hill*). But it's asinine to play so flamboyantly a do-nothing character like Price's Francois Delambre. Imagine the burgomaster trying to steal scenes from the Frankenstein Monster.

Worse yet, the movie's slavish devotion to the mystery structure of author George Langelaan's original short story grows tiresome with repeated viewings. Given knowledge of what lies ahead, bored viewers can only twiddle their thumbs until the story's first half ends and the good stuff with David Hedison and his matter disintegrator/reintegrator begins. *The Fly* diminishes each time it runs through your VCR. *Return of the Fly*, on the other hand, retains its low-rent charm.

The biggest thing *Return* has going for it is that it knows what it wants to be. It's an old-fashioned monster movie with no aspirations to high art. Director Kurt Neumann littered *The Fly* with sappy romantic interludes and other highfalutin claptrap intended to establish his film as serious drama. Such madness, thankfully, did not afflict *Return*'s writer/director Edward L. Bernds. *Return* feels and even looks like a leftover from Boris Karloff's days at Columbia 20 years earlier. It's the kind of gloriously schlocky mad doctor opus they just don't make any more (and didn't even in 1959).

Price gives the project a lift with a surprisingly low-key, naturalistic performance. According to James Robert Parish's biography *Vincent Price Unmasked*, Price was excited about the sequel's script, which greatly expanded his role in comparison with *The Fly*. The actor voiced this enthusiasm by delivering a quiet, credible performance miles ahead of his theatrical shenanigans in the original. Sure, watching Price gnaw the scenery can be fun, but his finest performances (such as *Conqueror Worm* and *The Abominable Dr. Phibes*) were his most restrained.

His second turn as Francois Delambre is an overlooked gem, one of Price's most underrated portrayals.

The sequel's plot is smarter than it needed to be, at least for the story's first two thirds. A more accurate title for the film might have been *Son of the Fly*, not only because the story's protagonist is the progeny of the original Fly, but because the scenario's premise recalls that of Universal's classic *Son of Frankenstein*.

The story opens at the funeral of Helene Delambre, widow of original Fly Andre Delambre. Francois (Price) attends the ceremony at the right hand of his grieving nephew, Philippe (Brett Halsey, who bears a striking physical likeness to his screen father, David Hedison). Philippe, now a grown man and a scientist like his old man, demands that Francois explain the secret of his father's research and the details of his mysterious demise.

"If I tell you, Philippe, it will haunt you for the rest of your life," Francois warns. Price's voice resonates loving, parental concern. Grudgingly, Francois takes Philippe on a tour of the ruins of his father's laboratory and provides a capsule synopsis of the first picture. Price shines throughout this sequence, treating Bernds' cliché-rich dialogue as reverently as he would Shakespeare.

The first *Fly* was shot in a flat, antiseptic style, but cinematographer Brydon Baker drapes the sequel in Gothic shadows. The funeral is rain-swept and mournful. The tour of the lab takes place during a thunderstorm and Price's words are punctuated by claps of thunder. "He ventured into areas of knowledge where man was not meant to go," Price cautions as a flash of lightning illuminates his face. Such stylized hokum helps viewers slip into the narrative like they would an old pair of sneakers. The tale is predictable but cozy.

Like Wolf von Frankenstein before him, Philippe Delambre feels compelled to revive his father's experiments. He plans to rebuild the disintegrator/reintegrator, which will serve as his father's "monument—his vindication." Francois wisely disapproves, and at first refuses to aid Philippe. So (in a move he'll soon regret) Philippe teams up with another scientist, Alan Heinz (David Frankham). The pair establish a lab in Philippe's basement and eventually cajole Francois into providing financial support for their project. Philippe and Alan repeat the Andre Delambre's early experiments with an ashtray and a guinea pig. They appear to be working the bugs out of the machine, so to speak.

Then we learn Alan plans to sabotage the project. Turns out he's a British murderer on the run from Scotland Yard. Alan schemes to steal the plans for the disintegrator/reintegrator and sell them through a local mortician (Dan Seymour) who fences stolen property between embalmings.

His plan goes awry when a detective, seen lurking in the background of previous scenes, springs on Alan one evening in the lab. A fight ensues and Alan kills the cop. The scuffle awakens Philippe, who trots down to the lab to investigate. To hide the body, Alan stuffs the cop into the disintegrator and zaps him to atoms.

Later, after Philippe returns to bed, Alan reintegrates his victim. However, the cop's atoms have been fused with those of a guinea pig which had been disintegrated earlier and was awaiting reintegration. Alan is aghast to discover his victim has suddenly obtained the hands and feet of a guinea pig—and that the guinea pig now has human hands and feet! The visual effects throughout this scene are anything but special. The no-frills *Return* can't compete with the original's posh production values.

Philippe's housekeeper spots Alan as the criminal flees to dispose of the policeman's body. Philippe confronts his partner when Alan returns. The two men struggle. Alan cold-cocks Philippe, then shoves him into the disintegrator. With full knowledge of what he's doing, Alan intentionally places a fly in the disintegrator chamber along with Philippe.

This is the single smartest plot point of the film. The crime subplot creates a logical reason for Philippe to have his atoms mixed with those of a fly. It would have been laughable if Philippe had simply duplicated his father's error. This time around, it's not an accident but attempted murder that's behind the human-fly fusion, which is far more believable. (Of course believabil-

Vincent Price gives *Return of the Fly* a lift with his surprisingly low-key, naturalistic performance.

ity is relative when you're talking about a story which features a matter disintegrator/reintegrator, not to mention a six-foot gent with the head of an insect. But you get the point.)

This scene also provides a powerful moment of pure horror: Philippe is awakened from his right cross-induced slumber by *The Fly*, which lands on his cheek. As he struggles to consciousness, Philippe's eyes suddenly bulge with terror. He realizes he's trapped in the disintegrator with the insect, that he's about to suffer the same gruesome fate as his late father.

Francois rushes to Philippe's aid, freeing his Fly-headed nephew from the reintegration chamber only moments before police arrive. For meddling, Alan plugs Francois with a revolver. The lame effects which afflict *Return* extend to the Fly makeup itself. Instead of the icky-looking fuzzy mask used in the original, stuntman Ed Wolff (not Halsey) dons an anatomically accurate Fly headpiece, built in correct proportion to a fly's body. That means the mask is about six times the size of a human head. As a result, the gigantic, spikey dome looks like some bizarre Mardi Gras reject.

The film compensates for its technical deficiencies with old-fashioned chills. While the first Fly never killed anyone but himself, Philippe's Fly immediately seeks bloody retribution against both Alan and his accomplice. His murder of the fence, staged in a dimly lit mortuary, is especially memorable. Philippe lunges out of the shadows, startling his victim, then uses his oversized, flipper-like fly-claw to wring the criminal's neck. After the *coup de grace*. he dumps the body in a convenient coffin! *The Fly* can keep its doomed romance; *Return* has a rampaging monster. Which would you rather watch?

Alas, the relatively sound logic which governs the film's early movements vanishes at this point. First, audiences are asked to swallow the idea that a guy with the bulbous head of an insect could run back and forth across town evading detection, while the police scour the city for him.

RETURN OF THE FLY

VINCENT PRICE
BRETT HALSEY

Produced by Bernard Glasser
Direction and screenplay by
Edward L. Bernds
Released: 1959
Running time: 80 min.

The spine-tingling story of
a man trapped in a nightmare
world of atomic mutation
. . . like his father before
him the young scientist
becomes the monster . . .
the fly.

Then Francois, recovering from his gunshot wound, expresses fear that Philippe may be cursed with "the murderous mind of a fly." Since when are flies murderous? And why is Francois worried about this, since Philippe's old man retained his ability to reason, and even communicated with his wife using a chalkboard and a typewriter? Once again Price can be commended for his earnest delivery, even of this absurd material. Price convinces us Francois is sincere. Unfortunately, viewers must therefore conclude that Francois is an idiot.

Francois' irrational fears are laid to rest when Philippe approaches his sleeping wife (Danielle DeMetz), reaches out and—after a tense pause—tenderly strokes her arm with his human hand. He's not an insane fly-maniac after all. Ironically, this means Philippe was in full control of his faculties when he bumped off Alan and Max and may face murder charges himself!

The picture speeds to its conclusion. Aided by a sympathetic police detective (who, luckily, has captured the human-headed fly), Francois disintegrates and reintegrates Philippe along with the Fly, returning both human and insect to their proper form. Philippe and his wife embrace, Francois looks relieved and the fly buzzes off on in search of tasty road kill. Fade out, roll credits.

Let's review: *Return of the Fly* suffers from bargain basement production values and lapses of good sense. In addition, its acting is uneven (Halsey and Frankham are quite good, the supporting cast is undistinguished and DeMetz is atrocious). But it's briskly paced and zips merrily along the oiled rails of horror convention. It presents its shopworn plot points with disarming enthusiasm. And it boasts a couple of truly thrilling horror sequences.

Best of all, the sequel puts Price to far more significant use than the original. Francois' actions set the chain of events in motion. Later, he becomes embroiled in the action (taking a bullet, no less). Ultimately he rescues Philippe from his Fly state. *Return of the Fly* doesn't belong to Price; it's Halsey's story as much as the original was Hedison's. But at least here Price serves as something more than high-priced window dressing.

The Fly films signaled the launch of an exciting new chapter in Price's career. *House of Wax* transformed Price from a talented character player to a horror star in 1953. Nevertheless Gothic horror pictures remained out of vogue until Hammer Films released its ground-breaking *The Curse of Frankenstein* in 1957. Price bided his time in forgettable pictures like *Dangerous Mission* (1954) and *Serenade* (1956). His only horror film between 1953 and 1958 was *The Mad Magician* (1954), a virtual remake of *House of Wax*.

The Fly and *Return of the Fly* gave Price a much-needed box-office boost as he geared up for the most prolific period of his lifetime. During the next 10 years, Price would star in two wonderfully loopy William Castle gimmick movies; nearly a dozen of American-International Pictures' Edgar Allan Poe adaptations (including most of the finest performances of his career); a handful of other horror shows; and a few Beach Party flicks, among other films. Price was nearing the top of his game when he made *Return of the Fly*, ascending a lofty plateau where he would reside for most of the next decade.

Not that anyone realized he was scaling such heights when *Return of the Fly* hit theaters.

At the time many major newspapers never bothered to review *Return of the Fly*. Most that did panned the sequel. *Variety*, for instance, called the film "inept." Critic Gene Wright's treatment of the film in his book *Horrorshows* is typical. He dismisses *Return* out of hand with a three-sentence capsule review.

Author Bill Warren provides virtually the only in-depth analysis of the sequel on record in his mammoth tome *Keep Watching the Skies!* but spends much of his critique quibbling over the plot's scientific and logical implausibilities. Yet, the sequel isn't any more preposterous than the original, which Warren enjoys. Besides, the usually unflappable Warren suffers curious lapses in his own logic, like when he complains that Alan's "share in the matter transmitter would be far greater (money) than he'd get as a thief." True, but the notoriety which would accompany his involvement with such a landmark invention would certainly attract the attention of detectives. Alan would hardly enjoy his riches while seated in the electric chair.

I'll grant Warren and the other experts that *The Fly* is finer crafted cinema than *Return of the Fly*, but to me that's beside the point. The original might be "better" but the sequel is far more fun. Despite its generous budget and impressive special effects, *The Fly* never achieves its goal of becoming a credible, character-driven drama. *Return*, on the other hand, remains an enjoyable way to burn 78 minutes, which is all the picture ever wanted to be.

CREDITS: Producer: Bernard Glasser; Director: Edward L. Bernds; Screenplay: Edward L. Bernds (Based on George Langelaan's Short Story "The Fly"); Cinematography: Brydon Baker; Assistant Director: Byron Roberts; Editor: Richard C. Meyer; Art Directors: Lyle R. Wheeler and John Mansbridge; Set Decorators: Walter M. Scott and Joseph Kish; Chief Set Electrician: Robert A. Petzoldt; Makeup: Hal Lierley; Music: Paul Sawtell and Bert Shefter; An Associated Producers Production released by 20th Century-Fox, released in 1959 in black and white and CinemaScope (double-billed with *The Alligator People*); Running Time: 78 minutes

CAST: Vincent Price (Francois Delambre); Brett Halsey (Philippe Delambre); John Sutton (Inspector Beacham); David Frankham (Alan Hinds); Dan Seymour (Max Berthold); Danielle De Metz (Cecile Bonnard); Jack Daly (Granville); Janine Grandel (Madame Bonnard); Michael Mark (Gaston); Richard Flato (Sgt. Dubois); Gregg Martell (Policeman); Barry Bernard (Lt. Maclish); Pat O'Hara (Detective Evans); Francisco Villalobas (Priest); Joan Cotton (Nurse), Ed Wolff and Joe Becker as The Fly (uncredited)

Dr. Warren Chapin (Vincent Price) experiments with LSD in *The Tingler*. (Photofest)

THE TINGLER (1959)

by Bruce Dettman

Some 25 years ago while I was going through the motions of a very lukewarm academic career, Vincent Price appeared at my college to give a lecture on acting and the arts. He had initially been booked into the main theater for a single two-hour evening address open to the general public, but without so much as a pause, also agreed at the last moment, and for no extra charge, to present an hour talk late that same afternoon to some 100 drama students in the little theater next door. Many of those who attended were simply interested in seeing a movie star. Others were only familiar with Price as a player in horror films, particularly the popular AIP Poe series. Only a few, it seemed, were aware of the great variety of achievements in Price's professional career: acclaimed performer of the legitimate stage, radio entertainer, memorable character player in dozens of mainstream films, renowned art collector and cook. Still, no matter what one's previous mental image of the actor, his talk that day had something in it for just about everyone. He was warm, intimate and very funny and it was impossible to believe the entire audience was not wholly captivated by this extraordinary man. Afterwards, since at the time I worked at various jobs in the Humanities Department which had sponsored his visit, I was lucky enough to corner the actor backstage for a few seconds of conversation. I had a host of questions in mind, in no particular order of importance, and was bursting to put as many of them before Price as I could before he was mobbed. The first had to do with his work in his earliest fantasy role *The Invisible Man Returns* (1940). It was not a subject which seemed to pique his interest—though he said some nice things about special effects expert John Fulton—and I was on the brink of moving along to my second query when several politicos from the college administration, intent on monopolizing his time, interrupted things and, before I knew it, Price shook my hand, wished me well and was gone. For the record, that second question had nothing to do with his stage work with Orson Welles, the Poe films, the two Dr. Phibes pictures or even his celebrated art collection. It had to do with the film *The Tingler*. What, I was going to ask, had he really thought of this picture which, not only at the time of its release, but even to this day, I still consider to be one of the most bizarrely conceptual films of all time. What were his thoughts when he read the script? Had he reservations? Did he view the project with seriousness or was the premise so outrageous that he opted to just have a good old time with the material and laugh all the way to the bank?

Later that evening, after he had wined and dined with the college's head honchos (none of whom knew Poe from Jacqueline Susann), he delivered his scheduled lecture to a larger but equally receptive audience. Afterwards I tried to worm my way into his company again, but to no avail. The lines for his autograph were nearly as long as the list of questions I had been unable to pose to him.

To this day as I re-watch *The Tingler* I am still bothered by the fact that I never had the opportunity to quiz Vincent Price further about this remarkably oddball film. In a perfect world I would have steered him to some remote watering hole, found a quiet corner, bought him a couple of tall ones (although I doubt that he would have shared my college-age affection for jug red wine with a malt liquor back) and pumped him for all the information I could. A few years later, seeing him portray Oscar Wilde (brilliantly, I may add) in a one-man show in San Francisco, I even thought to play Stage-Door Johnnie and still try to get his thoughts on *The Tingler,* but then decided against it. I'd had my chance and blown it. It was just not to be.

On *The Tingler* Bill came up with another idea called "Percepto," where the seats in the theater were supposed to be wired for electric shocks. Well we opened at a theater in Boston, and it didn't work at all. They couldn't rig the seats, or else you had to be sitting in on one of the seats that was rigged. Then when the tingler gets loose on the screen, I say, "The tingler is loose in the theater, scream for your lives!" It didn't work nearly as well as "Emergo," but remember that wonderful effect Bill had, where there's one color scene, when Judith Evelyn turns on the faucets and out comes red blood.

LAWRENCE FRENCH: In *The Tingler* you pre-dated Timothy Leary by taking LSD.

VINCENT PRICE: Yes, I know it. It's crazy. Of course I never really did LSD. I'm very against it. If I'm a prig about one thing, it's the fact that people don't need that. I didn't do any sort of research for that, because I don't think you have to. Even the people who do take LSD, they don't remember what happens to them, so what good would it do to take it to learn how to play the part?

LAWRENCE FRENCH: So how did you proceed?

VINCENT PRICE: Well, what do you do when you're a little out of your mind? I just did what I thought might happen. *The Tingler* was a pretty good picture, but really the best thing Bill ever did was *Rosemary's Baby*. He was a lot of fun to work with.

With all that has gone on in the arena of fantasy cinema over the last 25 years, one might think that a film like *The Tingler* would be at best a quaint exercise in dated screen terror, an archaic suggestion of what was once considered to be novel, perhaps even genuinely frightening by less sophisticated and demanding audiences. Computer generated special effects have allowed for the visualization of the truly bizarre and grotesque, uncanny celluloid depictions which have brought to the screen supernatural and pseudo-scientific realism which is often as unsettling as it is remarkable. John Carpenter's remake of *The Thing* (1982), and *Re-Animator* (1985), based on the work of H.P. Lovecraft, immediately come to mind. No matter what the outlandish premise, whether set in outer space (*Alien*) or solidly on terra firma (*Nightmare on Elm Street*), modern filmmakers have at their disposal the means to bring to life grotesque images and characters which only a few years ago would have been impossible to realistically create. Nonetheless, plastic, rubber and computers aside, you'd still have to go an awfully long way to come up with a storyline quite as peculiar and unique as that which figures in *The Tingler*.

An empty movie screen, white, immense, waiting for an image to be flashed upon it. Enter Producer/Director William Castle, gray-haired, block-headed, intensely serious, suddenly speaking directly to us, warning us that what we are about to see will be an entirely unique experience and that should the need arise, it is not only suggested but encouraged that we scream for our very lives. After we see a few shots of disembodied heads screaming in total fear the story unfolds.

Warren Chapin (Price), an experimental scientist and working pathologist, has been obsessed for years with the subject of fear. It is his belief that a force exists in the human body so strong that when left unchecked, as in the case of individuals who are literally frightened to death, it is able to assume a solid and very powerful form actually capable of breaking the spinal column. With his assistant Dave (Darryl Hickman) he has been conducting a series of tests on lab animals to secure confirmation of his theory but has been unable to isolate the phenomenon. An episode occurring during a chance encounter with a deaf mute Martha Higgins (Judith Evelyn) and her husband Ollie (Philip Coolidge), in which the woman is unable to verbally vent her fear of the sight of blood and as a consequence passes out, further suggests to Warren that he is on the right track and that this entity (which he has now named the Tingler) really does exist. Using

132

Dr. Chapin searches for the elusive Tingler.

himself for a guinea pig, Warren takes a hallucinogenic drug in order to frighten himself but is unable to control his fear and cannot help but cry out. Later, threatening his two-timing wife Isobel (Patricia Cutts) with a gun, he fires blanks at her causing her to faint. Taking her to his laboratory and X-raying her, he notes on the developed negative the distinct image of some large growth pressing against her spine. Meanwhile Martha is confronted by a series of terrifying manifestations in her apartment. Not able to scream to relieve her hysteria she dies. Warren conducts an autopsy on her and removes from her body the Tingler, a large slug-like creature of immense strength. Subsequently, after Isobel has tried unsuccessfully to kill Warren with the creature (a scream halts its attack), he realizes that its existence is not meant to be and that it must be returned to its original source where it hopefully will either revert to its microscopic size or cease to exist. By this time, having also figured out that Ollie is responsible for his wife's death, he begins to put the Tingler back in Martha's body but realizes it has escaped into a movie theater where it subsequently attacks several members of the audience. Using the public address system Chapin warns the theater patrons that the Tingler is loose and to scream for their lives, which they do, immobilizing it long enough to retrieve it and place it back in the dead woman's corpse. The film closes with Chapin leaving Ollie to turn himself in. Ignoring the doctor's suggestion, Ollie begins to escape when his wife's body suddenly becomes animated and moves toward his screaming form, but he is too paralyzed with fear to scream. Fadeout.

Where to begin when discussing this film? Certainly *The Tingler* is not alone in requiring audiences to suspend a great deal of belief in order to enjoy and accept the central theme. That's what fantasy cinema, despite occasional attempts to provide the rational and logical, is all about. Sometimes the explanations are detailed and on the surface—until one leaves the theater and makes the cardinal mistake of trying to rethink everything one has seen—fairly impressive. In

Price not only goes into some degree of detail as Dr. Chapin, but actually manages to come across as impressively intelligent and credible.

The Fly (1958), for example, the means by which scientist Al (David) Hedison is transformed into half man/half insect is a matter scrambler, a contraption which scatters atomic particles and then re-arranges them. The outcome is, of course, wonderfully ridiculous, but the concept itself is not totally out of the question—it was later exploited weekly on *Star Trek*—and someday some genius will probably come up with a comparable gadget. Then there are those times when the scientific explanation in a fantasy film is almost non-existent, a device to simply toss into the celluloid ring as a momentary nod to those few in the audience who stubbornly require some semblance of a reason, however skimpy and unsatisfying, for what is happening on the screen. In *Attack of the Giant Leeches* (1959) the rationale for the existence of the over-bloated blood-sucking mollusks is dispensed with in a single exchange of dialogue. A secondary character, considering the nature and origin of these nasty critters, simply remarks that Cape Canaveral isn't far away, a fact which seems to satisfy everyone.

The great satisfaction with *The Tingler* lies in the fact that it occupies a kind of half-way point between both these kinds of films, the literate and scientific, and the adolescent and blatantly preposterous. On the one hand, in discussing his theories, however outlandish and absolutely ridiculous, Price not only goes into some degree of detail, but actually manages to come across as impressively intelligent and credible, no small feat when trying to convince both the actors around him and the audience that living within all of us is a microscopic organism, a separate entity which, during periods when we are frightened, grows into a creature which looks like a cross between a giant centipede and a rump roast. I can think of no other actor who could invest such absurd dialogue with as much sincerity, gravity and credibility as Price. No wonder no one argues with the guy. As a kid he almost had me believing that such things might be possible. What better testimonial to the success of a horror film?

Although it is not simply Price's sincerity which makes *The Tingler* work it certainly has a great deal to do with it. The various shadings of this multi-dimensional character makes him constantly unpredictable and worth watching, an unusual trait in fantasy characters who tend to be either black and white creations or flip-flopping incarnations who are misguided until the last reel and then see the light of reason just before the end credits. Price is something quite different here. Thanks to both Robb White's low-key and mostly adult script and the actor's deftly engineered performance, Warren emerges as a man capable of assuming a great many personalities. Like a smoothly running engine he slips, almost undetected, from one emotional gear to another. In his scientist mode he is clinical, detached, dedicated. He is driven by his studies, in particular by his decade-old search to understand the "force" of fear, but he is not maniacal about it, not your typical mad scientist in the Colin Clive vein. With his friends, sister-in-law, colleagues, even strangers he can be generous, kind, thoughtful and genuinely caring and compassionate. But there is another side to this man. In dealings with his wife Isobel he is one unpleasant and vindictive fella, a wounded husband who, beneath his calm and rigidly controlled exterior, is not above venting his disdain and disgust at every turn. Moreover, there is something else, an added pinch of vitriol to Price's attacks which make you think that wifey's misconduct aside, when push comes to shove, the good doctor has a very pronounced dark edge to him as well. At times you can practically taste the venom coming out of him.

> Isobel: "There's a word for you."
> Warren: "There's several for you."

Not that you can blame the guy. This is one dangerous lady, and no slouch with the verbal low blows herself as she continually attempts to emotionally emasculate him with her monetary supremacy and overt sexual two-timing. As Price says to her when they both note a cat in his lab: "Have you two met in an alley perhaps?"

Price is certainly the glue which holds the film together but, as mentioned earlier, his is not the only success story in the picture. As far as the other performers go there is much to recommend. Darryl Hickman and Pamela Lincoln as Price's whiz-kid assistant and the latter's fiancé are mainly along for the ride, attractive window dressing, but both are competent and never annoying as are so many second-fiddle types often in this kind of film. Patricia Cutts as Price's wicked, amoral and dangerous wife is excellent—a slippery, poisonous human viper never to be trifled with. I only question her reaction when she glimpses the Tingler for the first time and eyes it with all the interest of a potholder. Sure, she wants to kill her better half and decides to use the deadly monstrosity for her nefarious pur-

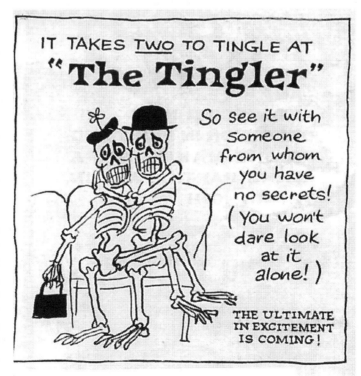

IT TAKES <u>TWO</u> TO TINGLE AT "The Tingler"

So see it with someone from whom you have no secrets! (You won't dare look at it alone!)

THE ULTIMATE IN EXCITEMENT IS COMING!

poses, but a touch of initial revulsion wouldn't have been out of order when first witnessing this mobile meatloaf. The other husband and wife team of the piece are uniformly outstanding: Coolidge, a vulture-faced actor who seems to possess only the slightest membrane of flesh over his skull, is totally convincing as the ultra low-keyed wife-murderer and Judith Evelyn, with her jerky, neurotic mannerisms and big-eyed reactions to everything, appears as someone just dragged out of a nightmare and gives a superb mute performance, truly one of fantasy film's most memorable victims.

Apart from the performers, what really works in *The Tingler* is the movie's overall manner and the sensations this accomplishes. All horror films are miniature mythologies within themselves, celluloid fables. It is up to the producer, director and set designers, often, but not always based on the writer's original intent, to somehow generate a look complementary to the intended mood. Think of the Phantom's Opera House lair, Kong's mist-drenched Skull Island, the fairy tale villages of all the Universal classics, Val Lewton's shadowy New York. Each had a marked and distinct feel, a unique ambiance and style to them. So it is with *The Tingler*. What struck me as a boy, and still does on repeated viewings, was the barrenness of the film, the suggestion of a too-well-organized and sanitary world. Phil Bennett's art direction creates an antiseptic landscape where streets are clean enough to eat off, rooms are ultra tidy and Wilfrid Cline's lighting is intentionally too extreme and harsh giving things a clinical and sterile look like a hospital room just before a bloody body is to be wheeled in. All of this in conjunction with composer Von Dexter's malevolent score, heavy with harp flourishes suggest a skeleton's hand brushing across the strings, accomplishing the somber, uncomfortable look and feel of this film.

On the negative side of things, what hurts *The Tingler* most are those very gimmicks and gestures of over-inflated showmanship on the part of the celebrated William Castle for which the film, particularly in the minds of those baby boomers who saw the picture upon its original release, is best recalled. The creature itself is a great drawback. In this it has much in common with the lesser known but almost equally effective later gem *Island of Terror* (1966) which, in its initial scenes, creates a very suspenseful and successful buildup dissipated somewhat by the appearance of the monsters, turtleish incarnations with ungainly, almost cartoonish appendages like bottle-necked clams. It is a tribute to this film that the appearance of these creatures does not wholly sink the show. The same could be said of *The Tingler*. By any rights, once the slab of rubber with the wobbly feelers pulled in a most obvious and ungainly fashion by strings is glimpsed, even given the acceptability of poor special effects during the period, the game should probably have been up. Remarkably though, thanks to director Castle's steady hand at preserving a mood fully complemented by the performers, the somber, level-headed dialogue, the photography and music, *The Tingler* still manages to succeed. The other drawback is the gimmick of Percepto, a device, highly touted at the time, but in actuality too expensive for most theaters to exploit (certain seats were rigged to vibrate or tingle during key moments in the film, particularly the conclusion in which the thing is loose in the silent movie house). Because of this gimmick, Castle had to momentarily invest the screenplay with some material, both visual and verbal, which is somewhat out of keeping with the otherwise restrained tempo of the movie. This is particularly true when Price, realizing the Tingler is in the movie house, flicks on the public address system and tells everyone to scream for their lives because the Tingler is in the theater—as if anyone would know what the hell the Tingler is. Not that it matters. While I loved this as a kid, I now find it a jarring and unnecessary intrusion in a movie which had up to that point avoided such business.

Although pretty much alone in this, I nonetheless consider *The Tingler* to be one of Vincent Price's best horror roles. Tempered with beautifully modulated restraint, the actor, in the midst of such elevated malarkey, never relinquishes his quiet dignity, forcefulness and pronounced sincerity. At the same time he creates subtle undershadings and slight but intriguing nuances of character and temperament. Only once does he truly go over the top, an acceptable bit of hokum and hysteria when he injects himself—perhaps the first actor on the screen to do so—with LSD. The hooter in this, of course, is that after a bad trip (not that it was called this in the movie—

Vincent Price, Darryl Hickman and Pamela Lincoln star in *The Tingler*. **(Photofest)**

remember, this is 1959), he seems to fully recover his senses in a few moments and is out the door and back to work. In any case, it is hard if not impossible to imagine any other actor who could have held this strange grab-bag of horror, soap opera and science-fantasy together. It is truly an underrated and sadly glossed over performance in the actor's long repertoire of horror roles.

Which brings me to a postscript to my introductory remarks about Price's visit to my college. That same night following the lecture, a group of my cohorts in the department, wishing to reverse the normal autograph ritual, signed the program with all of their names and presented it to the actor backstage. Price roared with laughter while accepting it. A few weeks later on some daytime talk show, I think it was Mike Douglas' series, he was asked by the host if anything interesting had happened to him of late in his travels. At that he pulled out the program and related the story with all the genuineness and charm that was a part of the man. Hearing him relate it and recalling his great warmth and humor was almost as good as having had the chance to have finally asked him about *The Tingler*. Almost but not quite.

CREDITS: Director/Producer: William Castle; Screenplay: Robb White; Cinematography: Wilfrid M. Cline; Music: Von Dexter; Art Director: Phil Bennett; Editor: Chester Schaeffer; Sound: John Livadary, Harry Mills; Makeup Supervisor: Clay Campbell; Columbia, 1959; 81 minutes

CAST: Vincent Price (Dr. Warren Chapin); Judith Evelyn (Martha Higgins); Patricia Cutts (Isabel Chapin); Darryl Hickman (David Morris); Philip Coolidge (Ollie Higgins); Pamela Lincoln (Lucy Stevens)

THE FALL OF THE HOUSE OF USHER (1960)
by Scott Allen Nollen

In 1959, American International Pictures offered Roger Corman a budget of $200,000 to direct two more low-budget horror films. But Corman had grown tired of churning out "quickie" thrillers in a matter of days, something he had been doing for the past five years. He no longer wanted to make unimaginative black-and-white exploitation programmers:

> I started to think that perhaps they had been selling their double bills a bit too long. Although the profits were good, they weren't as big as they once were. I was also getting very restless with this format, partially because of the financial restrictions and, partially, because I simply wanted to make bigger pictures.[1]

A longtime admirer of the works of Edgar Allan Poe, Corman envisioned a lavish Gothic adaptation in rich color and widescreen that would be far more faithful to the legendary author's horrific muse than the earlier Universal productions starring Boris Karloff and Bela Lugosi. Pitching *The Fall of the House of Usher* to James Nicholson and Samuel Z. Arkoff, he intrigued the AIP moguls with the idea of filming a series of Poe adaptations: Not only were the author's sensational tales in the public domain, but their exploitation possibilities and Corman's reputation for turning a modest investment into box-office gold were an irresistible mixture. By the time the negotiations were completed, Corman had scored CinemaScope, color and a $270,000 budget.

Hiring veteran science-fiction author Richard Matheson to write the screenplay for *The Fall of the House of Usher*, Corman began casting the film, thrilling Nicholson and Arkoff when he convinced Vincent Price to play the lead role of Roderick Usher. An admirer of Poe's stories and no stranger to literary adaptations or horror films, Price saw the offer as an opportunity to interpret one of the author's most memorable characters. He later said, "*The Fall of the House of Usher.* I loved that. I loved the white-haired character I was playing because he is the most sensitive of all Poe's heroes. He's hypersensitive."[2]

Matheson had to consider several important elements in adapting the story, which is set primarily in one environment and features more psychology than physical action:

> I knew I would be working within a limited budget but I tried to not let that fact affect my writing. The story was so simple, anyhow. What could they spend money on? You had a few people stuck in an old house. I tried not to write *The Fall of the House of Usher* as a "monster movie." For the sake of suspense, I introduced the factor of Usher's sister going mad and having her placed in a casket prematurely. I had a lot of fun with that.[3]

In fact, Poe already had "introduced" the premature burial element, a personal paranoid obsession and a motif that runs through his literary canon. He wrote "The Fall of the House of Usher," which Poe scholar Kenneth Silverman calls "the definitive tale of horror,"[4] in 1839 when he was 30 years old. Originally published in Burton's *Gentleman's Magazine* in Philadel-

Roderick Usher (Vincent Price) cannot allow Philip Winthrop (Mark Damon) to take Madeline away.

phia, the tale earned him his regular salary of $10 (which he received each week for reviews and articles) plus three dollars per page, hardly sufficient recompense for such a masterpiece. In 1845, the story was included, along with "The Black Cat," "The Gold-Bug," "The Murders in the Rue Morgue," "The Purloined Letter," and other short works, in *Tales*, published by Wiley and Putnam of New York.

Corman decided to reflect the otherworldliness of Poe's prose in the film's overall visual style, including the art direction:

> [T]he world of Poe, to a large extent, was the world of the unconscious. Being the world of the unconscious, I thought it could be recreated better within the artificial confines of a stage than it could be in broad daylight. I didn't want to use location shots. I didn't want the film to be shot realistically. [5]

Art aficionado Price collaborated with Corman and art director Daniel Haller on the selection of a painter to create expressionistic portraits of the Usher ancestors. Burt Schoenburg's paintings became a key visual and narrative component, in that they provide a link between Roderick Usher, his forebears and the House of Usher itself, which Poe created as an actual living, though decaying, entity. All the Ushers and their ancestral home are part of one organism. Poe's clues, such as describing the structure's "eye-like" windows, are represented in the film in several ways, including Philip Winthrop's (Mark Damon) descriptions of the house, Roderick and Madeline's (Myrna Fahey) behavior and the paintings, which include not only deceased Ushers but images of their dying domain.

In the story, Poe describes Roderick Usher in a manner that, in some ways, foreshadows the later appearance of Dracula created by Bram Stoker:

A cadaverousness of complexion; an eye large, liquid, and luminous beyond comparison; lips somewhat thin and very pallid but of a surpassingly beautiful curve; a nose of delicate Hebrew model, but with a breadth of nostril unusual in similar formations; a finely moulded chin, speaking, in its want of prominence, of a want of moral energy; hair of a more than web-like softness and tenuity;—these features, with an inordinate expansion above the regions of the temple, made up altogether a countenance not easily to be forgotten. And now in the mere exaggeration of the prevailing character of these features, and of the expression they were wont to convey, lay so much of change that I doubted to whom I spoke. The now ghastly pallor of the skin, and the now miraculous lustre of the eye, above all things startled and even awed me. The silken hair, too, suffered to grow all unheeded, and as, in its wild gossamer texture, it floated rather than fell about the face, I could not, even with effort, connect its Arabesque expression with any idea of simple humanity.

Price's appearance is far more subdued than this wild creature of Poe's pen; in fact, his physical appearance—including the "ghastly pallor of the skin" but eschewing the large eye and Arabesque expression for a less animated visage—better reflects the character's "morbid acuteness of the senses." (While preparing for the role, Price studied the cadaverous makeup worn by Conrad Veidt—one of his favorite actors—in the German expressionist classic *The Cabinet of Dr. Caligari* [1919].) With his hair dyed white and groomed back neatly, Price's entire head is pale and wan, giving him an otherworldly look—one of ailment and impending death—without making him seem monstrous. His equally quiet performance elicits sympathy both from Usher's visitor and the film audience. (Price scholar Lucy Chase Williams wrote, "Vincent admitted that it was 'real agony' stripping the color from his hair, and described his appearance when the roots began to grow out as 'like a zebra'."[6])

When Usher initially appears from behind his study door, Price, angry and forceful, literally thrusts himself into the Cinemascope image (a far cry from Poe's Roderick, whose introduction is one of "a vivacious warmth which had much in it"), but he then quickly but subtly metamorphoses into the "morbidly acute" man who cannot tolerate even the sounds of music, other than his own bizarre strummings on the lute (a guitar in the story). Throughout the film, Price brilliantly suggests that Usher has intense emotions seething within him but must control them for his own survival, mad passions and urges that cannot be expressed but are reflected in the wild, expressionistic paintings that adorn the walls. Roderick Usher may be Price's most profound cinematic performance: His characterization was achieved not only through the subtlety of his acting but also in his choice of a painter to realize on canvas Usher's inner madness created by his connection with his ancestors and the "melancholy house." It is a character unique in the history of the horror genre, making Oscar Wilde's Dorian Gray (and its impressive 1945 film counterpart) seem simplistic by comparison. Not surprisingly, Price always spoke highly of the character and the film:

> *The House of Usher* was a very enjoyable experience for me. Partially because Roger worked in all this pseudo-psychological symbolism into the story. I truly think he believed in it. At any rate, it made the film a lot more interesting.[7]

Of the director's masterful use of color, author Gary Morris writes,

> Corman's occasional color films during the 1950s could not have prepared us for the sensitivity to color evident in his first Poe film, nor for his skill with the psychology of color, allowing it to express in visual and sensual form the feelings of his characters.[8]

Prior to shooting the film, Corman directed a two-day rehearsal during which he blocked all the scenes and worked closely with Floyd Crosby on mapping out the extensive camera movements. Possessing the ability to visualize entire films in his head, Corman was able to avoid unnecessary re-takes and wasted precious little time during production. The filming, which began on January 13, 1960, was completed in only 15 days.

To stretch the original story to feature-film length, Matheson added a romantic subplot, transforming Poe's narrator from a college friend of Usher's into a young man who is engaged to Madeline. When he arrives at the moribund estate, Philip Winthrop reveals that he intends to take her away with him. Of course, Roderick protests, claiming that she cannot leave (suggesting that the Ushers and the house are not to be separated). The cinematic Roderick has a stronger bond with his sister than does Poe's character, and when Philip is victimized by "accidental" occurrences, such as a falling chandelier and a crumbling balcony railing, Usher, claiming that they are the product of the house's shifting, is depicted as actively attempting to dispose of the young man. When these attempts fail, Usher then intentionally entombs Madeline alive, rather than accidentally doing so after she falls into a cataleptic trance, as does the literary Roderick.

Cleverly integrating a matte painting of the house with a beautifully decorated soundstage set and a "burned out" exterior location (Los Angeles' Griffith Park, which recently had been ravaged by fire), Corman utilized Crosby's cinematographic prowess, Haller's art direction, Phil Mitchell's sound and Les Baxter's evocative score to create an atmosphere that equals Poe's. Although Matheson's screenplay takes liberties with the motivations of the characters (and enlarges the role of the servant, here called "Bristol" [Harry Ellerbe], a butler who knows many of the family secrets), the production never abandons the macabre and doom-laden spirit made famous by the story's tormented author.

The film's most frightening scene is a morbidly mad dream experienced by Philip. The insane Ushers depicted in the paintings appear as ghosts, their mournful wails creating a terrifying ambiance as the young lover frantically attempts to reach his unfortunate fiancée. Later, when the awakened Philip searches for the maniacal Madeline, who has escaped from her coffin, the wails again haunt the soundtrack. To add additional eeriness to the sequence, Crosby shot the horrific, grasping zombies through a blue filter.

As in the story, Madeline vengefully destroys her brother, but the film includes a fiery holocaust (an element that shortly would become a Corman motif in his Gothic AIP films) that precedes the house's sinking into the surrounding swampy ground. The final image is accompanied by the concluding clause of Poe's story:

> and the deep and dark tarn at my feet closed sullenly and silently over the fragments of the House of Usher.

Although Poe purists may object to Matheson's inclusion of a typical "Hollywood" romance, his depiction of Philip as being in love with Madeline makes her premature entombment, madness and horrible death even more powerfully tragic. And though Usher's deliberate act of sealing her in the coffin alters Poe's sympathetic characterization, the viewer still is struck by his grisly end, due in large part to Price's outstanding performance.

Like Boris Karloff, Price had little faith in actors fond of the "method." In fact, he often referred to such formalism as "the mumble school."[9] During the Usher shoot, he often became irked by the limited Mark Damon's method preparations. As Richard Matheson recalled, "Before [Damon] went on the set he would run in place and huff and puff! Then he'd walk in on a scene where Price would be chatting with somebody, and Price would out act the hell out of him!"[10]

Roger Corman said:

> Vincent was the consummate professional. He had been trained in a classical manner, but he had also worked a little bit with the "method." He and I would

Roderick looks on with displeasure as Philip and Madeline (Myrna Fahey) kiss.

discuss the role before shooting; there wouldn't be that much discussion on
the set because we had already worked out the main characteristics. Vincent
would prepare, but... I think it was more of an internal thing. Immediately
before a shot, he would not be making party conversation and then get up and
jump into it. He would sit quietly and think about it and be ready. [11]

Like Price, composer Les Baxter, whose credentials encompassed the jazz, big band, and
pop music worlds, was afforded the opportunity to make a rejuvenating contribution to the genre
of terror. He considered the Usher project, his first film assignment, as "one of the most sensual
scores. It was very sensitive for a horror film." [12]

During the film's initial release in June 1960, AIP sent Price on an extensive publicity tour.
Raking in two million in domestic rentals, the studio did even better business in European mar-
kets, making *The Fall of the House of Usher* one of the box-office champions of the year. Corman
later said:

We were a little surprised that the film was so successful. We had a sneak
preview and the audience loved it. Various people had viewed the rough cut
and liked it. We anticipated that the movie would do well, but not half as well
as it did. [13]

In fact, according to Matheson, none of the studio personnel expected such an enthusiastic response:

The funny thing was that, after the movie was completed, no one at AIP knew what to do with it. They were running it on a double bill with *Psycho*. It made so much money that they couldn't believe their wallets. [14]

Much to Corman's delight, many critics were equally impressed. In his *Variety* review, "Tube" wrote:

> The film has been mounted with care, skill and flair by producer-director Roger Corman and his staff.... Price is a fine fit as Usher, and Miss Fahey successfully conveys the transition from helpless daintiness to insane vengeance.... Those whose combined efforts have succeeded in mounting a flamboyant physical production include special effects man Pat Dinga and production designer Daniel Haller. Their cobweb-ridden, fungus-infected, mist-pervaded atmosphere of cadaverous gloom has been photographed with great skill by Floyd Crosby and enhanced further by Ray Mercer's striking photographic effects and the vivid color, most notably during a woozy dream sequence.... Corman has turned out a go at Poe that is certain to inspire several more cinematic excursions into this author's extremely commercial literary realm. [15]

Paul V. Beckley of *The New York Herald-Tribune* praised "the acting of Price, whose intellectual grasp of this bizarrerie is fine to see.... For aficionados, this is a heartening move in the right direction, a restoration of finesse and craftsmanship to the genre of dread." [16]

But not all reviewers were enthusiastic. Obviously a literary purist, *The New York Times*' Eugene Archer accused Matheson of "blithely ignor[ing] the author's style" and Price and Fahey of "portraying the decadent Ushers with arch affectation." [17] As his subsequent reviews would prove, Archer hated all of Corman's Poe adaptations, and his comments about *The Fall of the House of Usher* suggest that he may have made up his mind before he saw the film; after all, neither Price nor Fahey performs "with arch affectation."

Not only did *The Fall of the House of Usher* garner Corman and Price critical praise, make AIP a great deal of profit, and inaugurate a series of popular literary adaptations, it also resurrected the Gothic horror film in the United States. Following World War II, the horror film was superseded, via the Cold War and the holocausts at Hiroshima and Nagasaki, by a science-fiction oriented genre consisting of two distinct sub-genres: "nuclear terror" and "the other." While the former involved giant bugs and beasts mutated by atomic radiation, the latter focused on outer-space aliens who arrive on Earth to threaten the dominant (American) way of life. The "nuclear terror" category dealt with environmental issues, and "the other" warned audiences of political (Communist) infiltration. A few horror films also were produced, but these tended to be "modern" shockers such as William Castle's *House on Haunted Hill* and *The Tingler*. Even *House*

Madeline tries to destroy Roderick.

of Wax was a remake of an earlier classic, and by no means can be considered a Gothic horror film. Corman's pre-Poe films were all schlock-exploitation films produced for the teenage drive-in market, and *The Fall of the House of Usher* followed the British Gothic revival spurred by Hammer's garish color thrillers *The Curse of Frankenstein* (1957) and *Horror of Dracula* (1958).

A by-product of *The Fall of the House of Usher*'s success was the solidification of Price as the current king of horror films. Boris Karloff had increasingly focused on Broadway and television roles, branching out into as many genres as possible, while still appearing in an occasional horror film, such as *The Haunted Strangler* (1957) and *Corridors of Blood* (1958), both made in England. Interestingly, Price, although often playing a villain, had continually appeared in a wide variety of roles since the late 1930s. Hereafter almost exclusively he would be considered a "horror film star."

CREDITS: Director and Producer: Roger Corman; Presented by James H. Nicholson and Samuel Z. Arkoff; Executive Producer: James H. Nicholson; Screenplay: Richard Matheson (Based on the Short Story by Edgar Allan Poe); Cinematography (Cinemascope and Pathecolor): Floyd Crosby; Editor: Anthony Carras; Production Design/Art Director: Daniel Haller; Musical Score: Les Baxter; Set Decorator: Harry Reif; Wardrobe: Marjorie Corso; Makeup: Fred Phillips; Paintings: Burt Schoenberg; Production Manager: Bartlett A. Carre; Properties: Dick Rubin; Special Effects: Pat Dinga; Sound: Phil Mitchell; Assistant Director: Jack Bohrer; Previewed June 17, 1960; Released by American International Pictures on June 22, 1960; Running Time: 79 minutes

CAST: Vincent Price (Roderick Usher); Mark Damon (Philip Winthrop); Myrna Fahey (Madeline Usher); Harry Ellerbe (Bristol); Bill Borzage; Mike Jordan; Nadajan; Ruth Oklander; George Paul; David Andar; Eleanor Le Faber; Geraldine Paulette; Phil Sylvestre; John Zimeas ("Ghosts")

[1] Ed Naha, *Brilliance on a Budget: The Films of Roger Corman*, New York, Arco Publishing, Inc., 1982, p. 28.

[2] James Parish and Stephen Whitney, *Vincent Price Unmasked*, New York, Drake Publishers, Inc., 1974, p. 104.

[3] Naha, p. 30.

[4] Kenneth Silverman, *Edgar A. Poe: Mournful and Never-Ending Remembrance*, New York, HarperCollins, 1991, p. 149.

[5] Naha, p. 31.

[6] Lucy Chase Williams, *The Complete Films of Vincent Price*, Secaucus, New Jersey, Citadel Press, 1995, p. 163.

[7] Naha, p. 31.

[8] Gary Morris, *Roger Corman*, Boston, Twayne Publishers, 1985, p. 94.

[9] Vincent Price, interview with Scott Allen Nollen, March 1980.

[10] Williams, p. 163.

[11] Williams, p. 164.

[12] Williams, p. 163.

[13] Naha, p. 32.

[14] Naha, p. 32.

[15] *Variety*, June 29, 1960.

[16] Naha, p. 149.

[17] *The New York Times*, 15 September 1960, p. 45.

MASTER OF THE WORLD (1961)
by Dennis Fischer

Back in the 1960s, my favorite working actor was Vincent Price. He and his characterizations delighted me in film after film, so much so that I begin wishing that he could appear in many more films than he already had. (Somehow I managed to miss the worst Price movies of the '60s at the time—my parents would have no time for *Dr. Goldfoot and the Bikini Machine* and others of that ilk.)

It's hard to express just what it was that made him so special, but like the kid in Tim Burton's famed stop-motion tribute *Vincent*, I could really identify with Price in his movies. He typically played men who were smart, commanding, aristocratic, brooding, dedicated, obsessive, sensitive and even a little artistic, and I could readily relate to all those qualities as either ones I possessed or aspired to possess.

The hallmark of a good actor to me was versatility, and who was more versatile than Vincent Price? As far as I was concerned, Vinnie could do it all, not to mention numerous guest appearances on television, performances in plays, proving himself an art expert on TV quiz shows and being hired by Sears for artistic advice, writing books, and cooking gourmet meals. I would dearly have loved him to have played in even more films.

One of the roles I most wanted to see Vincent Price in, for some reason, was Jules Verne's *20,000 Leagues Under the Sea*. Somehow, I pictured a Price-type as Captain Nemo (not having read the sequel, *Mysterious Island*, which revealed Nemo to be an Indian prince), and while James Mason gave a superb performance as the brooding undersea captain in the classic Richard Fleischer/Disney version, I longed to see Price essay the role, which is why I became so pleased with *Master of the World*, AIP's supposed adaptation of two Jules Verne novels, but which was more American International's aerial remake of *20,000 Leagues Under the Sea*.

One of my early passions was science fiction, and one of the first books my parents bought me was a combined edition of *20,000 Leagues Under the Sea* with *Around the Moon* (aka *From the Earth to the Moon*). The preface (by Isaac Asimov) explained that Jules Verne was the father of science fiction and that had me instantly interested. I soon learned to associate Verne's name with the promise of extraordinary voyages and adventures. I watched for Verne films and ended up loving not only *20,000 Leagues*, but also the wondrous *Journey to the Center of the Earth*, the exciting *Mysterious Island* and delightful *The Fabulous World of Jules Verne* (the less said about *Valley of the Dragons* and *From the Earth to the Moon* the better). I even ended up watching an animated Saturday morning cartoon version of *Journey to the Center of the Earth*. A match of Price in a Verne picture seemed like manna from heaven.

April 10, 1997, marked a significant anniversary for science fiction in the United States: the 130th anniversary of Jules Verne's arrival in America. Verne made his only journey to the United States in the spring of 1867, at a time when he was virtually unknown in the English-speaking world, although his books were already best-sellers in France. Only a single short story, "Un Voyage en Ballon" (1851), had been translated into English, along with his third published novel, *From the Earth to the Moon*, which had been serialized a few months earlier in the *New York Weekly Magazine of Popular Literature, Science and Art*, beginning in the January 26, 1867 issue. (By this time Verne had also written several unpublished novels, including the recently-discovered *Paris in the Twentieth Century*.)

Verne traveled in the company of his brother and best friend, Paul, a mariner. Jules and Paul traveled aboard the enormous ocean liner the *Great Eastern*, but the ship's seemingly endemic bad luck caused a series of delays. On board, Jules questioned the crew for details of nautical

Robur (Vincent Price) checks the progress of the *Albatross* as his captives look on.

life and the creatures of the ocean depths, and the responses gave him ideas for the submarine novel he was planning that would become *20,000 Leagues Under the Sea*. Finally, the *Great Eastern* arrived off Long Island on April 10, a week late.

When Jules and Paul Verne checked into the Fifth Avenue Hotel, a fellow guest was named Professor Aronnax and newly arrived from the Nebraska Badlands, two details Verne would remember when writing *20,000 Leagues Under the Sea*. After seeing some of the sights of the city, the Vernes took a paddle steamer up the Hudson, finally arriving after several stops at the fabled Niagara Falls.

Verne was deeply moved by the sight of Niagara, still laden with ice. Recently, the investigations of Stephen Michaluk, Jr. discovered Jules and Paul Verne's signatures in the original guest book at a Niagara hotel.

The memory of Niagara proved so durable that, over 20 years later, Verne laid pivotal episodes in two novels there. The hero and heroine in *Family Without a Name* go over the cataract in a fiery ship. Robur, conqueror of land, sea and air, flies out of Niagara, by instantly transforming his automobile-submarine-airplane, the *Terror*, from a ship into an aircraft, in *Master of the World*. Nor was this all; over a third of Verne's more than 60 novels were set in the United States or the American continent, or featured American characters.

Verne regretted the short period in the United States; he calculated the five days as 192 hours. On April 15, the Vernes embarked on the *Great Eastern* for the return voyage. Jules Verne recounted his journey to America in his novel *A Floating City*, concentrating on the two-week voyage with only minor fictionalization. Verne hoped to return someday, until finally advancing age and ill health made such a trip impossible. [For more details on Verne's trip to America, including quotes from interviews with journalists, see Brian Taves and Stephen Michaluk's *The Jules Verne Encyclopedia* (Scarecrow, 1996)].

There are two novels in the Verne pantheon concerning the character of Robur, "the conqueror of the air." The first novel was published in 1886, as *Robur-le-conquérant*, translated both as *Robur the Conqueror* and *The Clipper of the Clouds*. In it, Robur kidnaps a pair of balloonists who refuse to believe in a heavier-than-air machine, taking them around the world in his *Albatross*, a sort of giant, perpetually-airborne helicopter designed along the lines of a luxury ocean liner. The balloonists blow up the *Albatross*, but Robur survives and returns with a rebuilt *Albatross* to prove his vehicle's superiority over the balloonists' latest hot-air contraption.

In 1904, Verne brought back Robur as the title character in *Maître du Monde* (*Master of the World*), a very short, simple, almost comic-bookish novel. It follows the efforts of U.S. Chief Inspector of Federal Police John Strock to cope with and solve a number of interconnected mysteries. Characterization and detail are minimal as Strock is confronted by reports of smoke and fire coming from an inaccessible mountain crater in Morgantown, North Carolina. An aeronaut attempts to access the area by balloon, but is blown in the wrong direction. Strock gathers the local mayors and two experienced climbers, but they are unable to make the ascent.

Then comes a report of a fast car traveling at the (then) incredible speed of 150 miles per hour that zooms past the fastest cars in a 200-mile race. There is a report of an incredibly fast boat, and then of a submarine, powered by some unknown means that is neither wind nor steam. From the descriptions, Strock puzzles out that all reports are in actuality describing the same ship, an incredible all-terrain vehicle (it later proves capable of flying as well). He receives a letter signed "M.o.W." which threatens his life should he attempt to climb the Great Eyrie, but he regards it as the work of a prankster.

Later, all the major governments of the world attempt to offer enormous sums of money for the secret of the incredible submarine/car, but they are unable to locate the inventor. The inventor finally responds by leaving a letter in Washington, D.C. He writes from his ship, the *Terror*, that his invention will remain his own and that he will use it as it pleases him.

> With it, I hold control of the entire world, and there lies no force within the reach of humanity which is able to resist me, under any circumstances whatsoever.
> Let no one attempt to seize or stop me. It is, and will be, utterly impossible. Whatever injury anyone attempts against me, I will return a hundredfold.
> As to the money which is offered me, I despise it! I have no need of it. Moreover, on the day when it pleases me to have millions or billions, I have but to reach out my hand and take them.
> Let both the Old and the New World realize this: They can accomplish nothing against me; I can accomplish anything against them.
> So I sign this letter:
> The Master of the World.

John recognizes the handwriting and takes the original letter to his superior, Mr. Ward, who orders him to arrest the inventor, an enemy of society against whom all means become justified. The government issues the following proclamation: "Since the commander of the *Terror* has refused to make public his invention at any price whatsoever, since the use which he makes of his machine constitutes a public menace, against which it is impossible to guard, the said commander of the *Terror* is hereby placed beyond the protection of the law. Any measures taken in the effort to capture or destroy either him or his machine will be approved and rewarded," in effect a declaration of war by the United States against the inventor.

John Strock sets off with two of his agents, John Hart and Nab Walker, to track this enemy of freedom down, aided by local man Arthur Wells. Together they head to Black Rock Creek, where Strock is captured and taken aboard the *Terror*, which proceeds to head out across the northeast portion of Lake Erie to the Niagara River. Pursued by a pair of destroyers, it simply sails into the sky after appearing to have fallen over the falls.

Finally, Strock meets with the Master of the World and learns that he is Robur the Conqueror (as in "conqueror of the air") who many years previously in Verne's *Robur the Conqueror* (aka *Clipper of the Clouds* [1886]) had a run-in with the millionaire members, including Uncle Prudent and his secretary Mr. Phillip Evans, over whether the Weldon Institute, a club devoted to aeronautics, should be committed to lighter-than-air ships or heavier-than-air ships. Robur had ridiculed the Institute's plans, pointing out that the only true solution to flight lay in heavier than air machines, and that he had proven this by constructing one.

By force, Robur had abducted the president and secretary of the club and taken them aboard his ship *The Albatross*, manned by a crew of half a dozen men who were absolutely devoted to their leader. After a voyage almost completely around the world, Prudent and Evans managed to escape after arranging an explosion to destroy the ship, which falls into the Pacific Ocean.

The men returned home and constructed their own lighter-than-air ship, the *Goahead*, but the thunder of its launching a year later was destroyed when Robur reappeared in another *Albatross* that hurls itself upon the *Goahead*, which can neither outrun nor outlift its opponent, but instead has its balloon burst when it reaches too great a height. Robur forsook his vengeance and saved the two men, releasing them safely in Fairmount Park while Robur makes the determination that man is not yet ready for the vast increase in power that the conquest of the air will bring him.

Upon Strock's learning all this, the novel ends rather anti-climatically with the haughty Robur and his ship challenging the elements and being destroyed by having its batteries struck by lightning after having ventured into a thunderstorm. The *Terror* falls into the ocean some thousand feet below, and the fortunate Strock survives, left to ponder the significance of Robur and his achievement.

In the 1950s with *20,000 Leagues Under the Sea* and *Around the World in 80 Days*, Jules Verne had proved to be big box-office, inspiring other filmmakers to try their hand at creating Vernean screen adventures. American International saw that its double features were no longer bringing in the same revenues at the drive-ins and such and was hungering for respectability. Having tried their hand at Poe with *The Fall of the House of Usher*, James Nicholson and Samuel Arkoff turned their hand to Verne with their version of *Master of the World*, which featured a Nemo-like captain named Robur and also offered a fabulous airship. In fact, the team hired ace scriptwriter Richard Matheson to transform both Robur books into a low-budget remake.

To direct the film, they hired William Witney, best known for directing serials (including my all-time favorite superhero serial, *Adventures of Captain Marvel*) and Roy Rogers Westerns. Witney slowly transitioned from Westerns to other kinds of low-budget fare, winding up making forgettable exploitation pictures. He was at his best delivering exciting action scenes, but *Master of the World* provides him no real opportunities for that given that its most exciting action material was lifted from other films. He provides no visual pizzazz, but he does keep things moving at a sprightly pace and elicits generally good performances from his cast, headed by AIP's new star, Vincent Price, who excelled at playing such tormented and misunderstood loners.

Interestingly, AIP apparently had big plans for the film and even affixed a prologue detailing, via old newsreel footage, man's dream of flight. (Much of the exact same material later wound up opening Ken Annakin's multimillion dollar comedy *Those Magnificent Men in Their Flying Machines* a few years later.) However, AIP wound up sticking to Price's Poe pictures because they proved a safer bet at the box-office . Nevertheless, one of the things I admire about *Master of the World* is its ambition of trying to create an epic on a shoestring and sort of pulling it off, a tribute to the resourcefulness of the men who made it.

It is quickly apparent in watching the film that Matheson used very little of Verne's original plot. The initial setting is switched to Morgantown, Pennsylvania, probably to avoid the need to cast actors with Southern accents, and to place it in closer proximity to the Weldon Institute of Pennsylvania. Naturally, AIP wanted a love interest, so the character of Dorothy Prudent (Mary Webster) is added, and in addition to Strock (Charles Bronson), who is made a Secretary of the

Strock (Charles Bronson) takes the punishment Robur had intended for Prudent (Henry Hull).

Interior, Matheson adds the characters from *Clipper of the Clouds*. Philip Evans (David Frankham of *Tales of Terror* and *Return of the Fly*) becomes Dorothy's fiancé rather than the club's millionaire secretary. Uncle Prudent (Henry Hull of *Werewolf of London*) is transformed into an arms manufacturer who dabbles in balloons in order to explore their potential as weapons.

Matheson relied on the novel's opening about the mystery of the Great Eyrie. Price is given a great, off-camera introduction, as, over flashes of light upon the clouds above the mountain, we hear him quoting from the Bible, exhorting people to harken unto him, "for the indignation of the Lord is upon all nations and His fury upon all their armies. He shall utterly destroy them," the unseen and amplified Price promises. Clearly, this sets up Robur's concern that the world has become too warlike without giving away too much of the story.

Prudent, Evans, Strock and Dorothy, in a balloon belonging to the Weldon Balloon Society, are fired upon by a missile which brings them crashing into the mountainside. Price is given an effective introduction as Les Baxter's score blasts out ominous bass notes amid swirling strings while director Witney pans up from Robur's white shoes as he surveys the unconscious group before him. Baxter's score is one of his very best and suggests the epic feeling that the film's visuals frequently lack.

Once aboard the *Albatross*, the group is greeted by the captain. He wears a white suit, suggestive of a riverboat captain or Mark Twain, with an artistic cravat (and apart from a brief scene in an Edwardian smoking jacket, this remains his costume throughout the film, perhaps suggesting the purity of Robur's motives). "The name is Robur, sir. Welcome aboard the *Albatross* good people. As to why you are all here, the reason is twofold. Primarily, left within the

Robur investigates the crash his ship had caused in *Master of the World*.

crater of that mountain, you would most likely have perished, and secondarily, in the unlikely event that you survived the crash of your balloon…."

"Which you caused," points out Phillip accusatorily.

"A bit of necessity, sir," returns Robur, unfailingly polite. "However, since you did survive the crash, had you managed to make your way back down the mountain, you might have given knowledge of what you had seen."

"Why should you fear that?"

"That, sir, is my concern alone."

In Robur, Price provides one of his finest performances for an AIP film. The part does not require the sensitivity and brooding intensity of his performances as Roderick Usher or Verden Fell, and he distinguishes the role with admirable restraint, understanding that here less is more. Robur is no tin god or insecure despot. He commands the loyalty and respect of his men, and he is forceful when he needs to be. However, with these unwilling visitors, he is very affable. He is a man who is proud of his achievements and does not get very many opportunities to show off to outsiders. He understands how distressed and disoriented his passengers are, and so shows them courtesy.

Nonetheless, he sets himself apart. Prudent blusters incredulously (a Hull specialty) when Robur proclaims that he has no nationality. "No, sir—my crew and myself like to think of ourselves as citizens of the world."

Overall, the performances in the film are very good with the notable exception of Vito Scotti's comical turn as Topage, the ship's chef. Scotti specialized in playing comic flustered foreign types, and he cannot forsake his old habits here, resulting in a performance that is at odds with the more realistic performances of everyone else. Charles Bronson apparently was not comfortable playing Strock, and typically he does not emote what the character is feeling, but his inward, withdrawn quality proves very good for the cool-headed character (who must mask his feelings), and Bronson does command the audience's attention in a way that the more conventionally attractive Richard Frankham does not.

Apart from the performances, perhaps the most successful element of the film is the *Albatross* itself, designed by Daniel Haller, based on Verne's description of an airship that has both suspension and propulsion blades (i.e., propellers to keep it aloft as well as one to move it forward through the air). The special effects are somewhat variable and were mostly executed by old hands Tim Baar, Wah Chang and Gene Warren, who all had worked previously with producer-director George Pal.

The design does suggest a riverboat of the air, and Haller designed some of the corridors to be easily redecorated and reused. On the upper level, for example, cinematographer Gil Warrenton throws a different colored gel on every section (reminiscent of the multihued rooms from Corman's *The Masque of the Red Death*), while on the level below the same corridor gets bottom supports and more natural lighting to give it a different look.

One thing that does not work well is a split screen shot that shows the giant machinery that powers the airship—obviously close-ups of toy gears turning. Further destroying the effect is a chiming sound on the soundtrack that is heard with every revolution as of a toy bell being struck repeatedly. The ship is supposedly 150 feet long by 20 feet wide, and from the interiors does appear sizable, but the sense of scale is often uncertain. Additionally, a certain condescension seems apparent to me in that the altimeter is labeled a "heightmeter" and the bridge-cockpit is referred to as the steering room.

I love movies that try to evoke a sense of wonder, and *Master of the World* tries to do so with the *Albatross*. We are informed by Robur that it is "powered by electricity created by a mass of metal cutting through what [he calls] the magnetic force lines." Instead of the aluminum that the *Terror* is constructed of, this ship is made entirely of paper, embedded with dextrin and clay and then squeezed in a hydraulic press. Price is great at conveying the pride his character has at having created the world's greatest paper airplane, and his hands helpfully convey the concept of being squeezed by such a press.

Of course, Robur is clever enough not to reveal what he does not want revealed, as when he ignores a query regarding the purpose of his voice magnifier heard at the opening. (Matheson clumsily reveals its existence by having Dorothy scream into it during a turn.) When Strock notes that the *Albatross* is "quite impressive. The government would be interested in this ship," Robur simply returns, "Yes, I'm sure they would" and then makes it clear, "Regarding this ship, I shall inform no government at all."

Though there is always a tendency on the part of subsequent generations to regard the past as a more innocent time, this is not always the case. The essence of Robur's character, derived from other Verne novels more than the original inspiration, is that he is a pacifist who is willing to make war on war. As Price is quoted in James Robert Parish and Steven Whitney's *Vincent Price Unmasked*, "I loved *Master of the World* because I thought it had a marvelous moral philosophy. I adored it. It was a man who saw evil and wanted to destroy it. And if that meant the whole world had to go, then it had to go." America had been through an unpopular war in Korea and was increasing its involvement in another war in Vietnam. The tensions of the Cold War led to frayed nerves and a basic distrust of governments which Robur seems to share. In many ways, Robur represents a classic philosophy, escalate war to the unthinkable (e.g., mutually assured destruction) and thereby bring about its end, and this is brought out in Matheson's crusading screenplay.

Robur finds it highly ironic that one of his passengers proves to be Prudent of Philadelphia, the famous arms manufacturer and precisely the kind of person that Robur hopes to put out of business permanently. Robur reveals his ruthless side after Prudent tries calling down to a passing American warship. Using his voice magnifier, Robur informs the ship, "Officers and crew of the American war vessel, you have exactly 20 minutes to evacuate your ship. At the end of that time, it will be destroyed. I give you this warning because I bear no malice to any man aboard. Believe me in what I say. I do not exaggerate. In 20 minutes your ship will be sent to the bottom."

Naturally, the American crew fails to comply and the ship is bombed to the bottom of the ocean. Robur's mate Turner (Wally Campo) expresses a sense of misgiving, but Robur insists, "It never should have existed, Mr. Turner. It is better destroyed. Destroyed." Robur is a man without compromise, but he is also willing to let his ends justify the means, resulting in the deaths of many otherwise peaceful sailors. He assumes that because his end goal is ultimately good (the end of warfare and its consequent suffering and death) that he maintains the moral high ground rather than being a despicable mass murderer. While one might wish away the devices of destruction, that will never be possible in the real world where we will always have to contend with the danger of despots. Coercion ultimately remains coercion whatever the motives behind it might be.

This act outrages Prudent who confronts Robur. "Do you consider yourself a government unto yourself that you can condemn other nations and wantonly declare war against them?" he asks.

"I am a man unto myself, Mr. Prudent," responds Robur, "who has declared war against war. That is my purpose, the purpose for which this ship was built. To end for all time the scourge of warfare."

"How do you propose to do that, sir?" asks Strock.

"By using the threat of invincible power, or, if necessary, by using the power itself as you saw this afternoon. I have already notified the leaders of your government and instructed them to make plans to scrap their navy and immobilize their army. The government of Great Britain will be similarly notified. Every major government in the world will be given the selfsame ultimatum—disarm or perish."

Prudent retorts, "You, sir, are mad, quite, quite mad."

"How like the reasoning of your kind, Mr. Prudent. All well and sane to be the owner of factories, the products of which cause the violent deaths of millions in warfare and in peace, but to kill hundreds or even thousands with the aim of ending such deaths for all time, this is madness."

"Answer!" demands Prudent. "Do you consider a man who makes a weapon responsible for the action of the one who buys it?"

"Yes, I do, sir," responds Robur. "All men are responsible to all other men."

These, of course, were the sentiments behind the anti-war movement and the push for gun control in the U.S. If soldiers would refuse to fight, how could we continue to have war? (Of course, this overlooks the difficulties entailed when some soldiers might not agree to lay down their arms, as well as the difficulties that the U.S. had in responding to the Nazi threat after extensively disarming after World War I.) Arming yourself simply meant that you expected aggression and thereby invited it. Hence, soldiers were blamed for murdering in the name of the state during the Vietnam conflict.

Gun manufacturers were blamed for the uses to which their products were sometimes put as guns proliferated on the streets of urban centers and at times ended up in the hands of revolutionaries such as the Black Panthers willing to murder for what they saw as the greater good. Prudent is a businessman, but the business of mankind, according to liberal pieties, is man, not business. Indeed, Prudent is later shown to be in shock once he develops a firsthand knowledge of the uses to which his devices are put, though the film does not indicate if this in any way alters his character.

Evans plans a dangerous getaway when the *Albatross* stops above an Irish lake to pump aboard some water. (The landscape does not remotely look Irish but instead resembles the California High Sierra where it was shot.) Fearful that Evans is foolishly endangering his life, Strock informs Robur who decides to punish Evans by dangling him from a rope at the bottom of the ship. Prudent fails to live up to his name by attempting to castigate Robur, who likewise sentences the old man, but Strock volunteers to go in Prudent's place.

A problem with the ship's engines causes it to veer too low. Robur quickly takes the wheel to fend off the emergency, and then demonstrates genuine concern over the two men, who he orders to be retrieved quickly. (Price's body language expresses first weariness, then relief at having saved the ship, and then he raises his head as his eyes dart back and forth. The audience knows that Robur has just remembered the two men he left dangling. It's as though the audience sees the concept literally enter his head.) Evans' rope breaks and Strock saves Evans' life by hanging on to him. Unlike most films of this type, the two men do not instantly recover from their ordeal, a nicely realistic touch.

Vincent Price as Robur.

Prudent tries once more to extricate himself from his predicament. He offers Robur $10 million and amnesty if he will return to the U.S. and sell the ship to the government. Robur casually raises the notion that France might double the price, and the huffy Hull offers on behalf of the U.S. to top any other offer.

Robur simply shakes his head sadly, "It is quite obvious you don't understand me and probably never will. Do you honestly believe I started out on this project with the aim of ultimately selling out to the highest bidder? You're a fool, Mr. Prudent, and worse than that, you are a cynic. A man who has come to regard money as the solution to all human problems.

"Here is the text of a leaflet we will soon drop on London. Quote, To the British government. You will, upon receipt of this message, commence a program of disarmament which is to include the scuttling of all Royal Navy ships, the demobilization of all ground forces, and the elimination of all arms and ammunitions. Failure to comply will mean complete destruction of your armies and navies."

Once more we have reinforced the idea that Robur is principled but unrealistic. Governments are not likely to disarm simply because he asks them to. Robur does what he feels he must do regardless of whether he alienates anyone or whether they understand him or not. As a man of dedication, he is totally committed to doing things his way, and when he approaches Strock, he explains that he admires precisely those qualities in the young Secretary of the Interior.

"I know that you would like to stop me, sir," Robur tells Strock. "For that reason, my impulse is to have you destroyed. My desire, on the other hand, is to have you join me. You're an intelligent man, Mr. Strock. Surely you must appreciate my ultimate objective."

Indeed, Strock does appreciate the objective, but as the hero and the audience stand-in, he questions the methods Robur uses to procure it. "What alternative method is there that would not require centuries more of violence and bloodshed?" asks Robur, as if hoping Strock had an answer, then rejecting it. "No. It is too long to wait. With courage and daring, worldwide peace can be achieved now."

Robur is intelligent enough to know that a man of conviction such as Strock poses the greatest threat to him, but holds back the hope that Strock could be swayed to his side. He asks for and receives Strock's word of honor not to interfere, an act which infuriates Evans, who is dedicated to the concept of honor. Strock tries to get Evans to understand his position that there was little he could do except work covertly to subvert Robur's plans for conquest, and that he took a risk in not simply joining him, but Evans cannot see beyond the idea that Strock sympathizes with Robur's goal.

Indeed, Robur is an inspirational figure.

It is at this point that the lack of budget really brings this confection crashing down. The *Albatross* flies over a model of Elizabethan London that opened Olivier's version of *Henry V*, despite its being two centuries out of date. When it bombs the British Navy, shots of the Tralfalgar naval battle from *That Hamilton Woman,* a black and white film, are tinted blue with the explosions *sometimes* tinted orange. (The attack on the American warship was handled similarly via tinted stock footage from a black and white film.)

To give a sense of scope, Witney superimposes spinning international newspapers with appropriate headlines over peaceful stock shots of London, Paris and Madrid to indicate the *Albatross*' progress as it heads down toward Egypt where stock footage of Africans, Arabs, Hindus and Tartars all seem to have been thrown together. (Strangely, though viewed from the air, all the shots are shown from the ground as armies from different films run every which way on screen.) Just when the film should have given the character some interesting things to do with his fabulous airship, it seems to run out of budget and imagination.

Robur is disgusted with the natives' fondness for war, and in his eagerness to bomb them in a show of force, he lowers his ship too much and it gets damaged by one of its own bombs. Consequently, Robur receives a head wound and the ship veers close to some mountains, forcing the crew to push off with pikes while a cannon fires to clear away a passage for the low-hanging, damaged ship, which heads off to Robur's island base.

While it is anchored to the island Strock sees his opportunity to destroy the vessel and escape with the others. He arranges a slow fuse atop the explosives in the armory. However, the jealous Evans espied him comforting Dorothy during the battle and, once the fuse is set, knocks Strock out and leaves him to die onboard the soon-to-be-exploded ship. Strock wakes him in time to shimmy down the rope to escape, but is shot while trying to cut away the anchor rope. Evans experiences an attack of conscience and aids Strock in finally freeing the anchor from the ship while receiving an arm wound in the process.

The freed *Albatross* heads off over the ocean with several of its suspension propellers still not working. Just then, Strock's bomb goes off and Robur receives the report that his ship is doomed. "Have all men stand by," orders Robur. "Prepare the life rafts. Prepare to abandon ship. [To himself] Strock, if only you'd joined me. I want to thank you for your loyalty, Turner, gentlemen. Abandon ship." He goes to his quarters to watch the approaching ocean's surface as his loyal men enter the room, having for the first time disobeyed one of his orders. As they prepare to die, Robur again quotes from the Bible: "He shall judge among the nations. They shall beat their swords into plowshares and their spears into pruning hooks. Nations shall not lift up sword against nations, neither shall they learn war anywhere."

The ship crashes into the sea while the Weldon Society members look on. The film closes with a quote by Robur from Jules Verne's novel:

> I take my dream with me. But it will not be lost to humanity. It will belong to you the day the world is educated enough to profit by it and wise enough not to abase it.

Though the quote is taken out of context, where it refers not to an end to war but to man's dominion of the air, it does seem an appropriate finish for the film. As an added something extra, after the closing credits, the soundtrack plays the song "Master of the World," sung by Darryl Stevens, music by Lex Baxter and lyrics by Lenny Addison, which is an attempt at a pop song that has very little to do with the film itself.

Ace Books offered a movie tie-in edition of the two Verne novels and Baxter's music was presented on a soundtrack album, something rare for an AIP film, on AIP's own label. In 1975, a more faithful animated version of *Master of the World* was released. In the mid-'90s, Orion Home Video released the Price version at last to videotape and laserdisc, with the laserdisc version presented in its 1.85:1 aspect ratio and featuring stunning Pathecolor and stereophonic sound mixed from the four-track stereo source material.

Master of the World is a flawed but entertaining epic. Like many of Price's lower-budgeted efforts, it tries to make a silk purse out of a sow's ear, and even if it does not fully succeed, it is still worth remembering for Price's performance of the morally ambiguous Robur, who in the book is simply enigmatic and unknowable, and in the film is a Nemo-like warrior for peace who inspires tremendous loyalty in his admirers, much as Price's fine work in pictures had inspired me to seek out his varied work and appreciate Price's consummate professionalism.

I too admired the resourceful intelligence that could create such an airship, inspire such loyalty in his followers, and which would relentlessly pursue the noble cause of peace despite the scorn of those who failed to understand some people's opposition to war. Who could not empathize with a man who sought to make the world a better place for all mankind, however misguided he might be in his methods, a man who is dedicated to his cause and does what he must, the consequences be damned? Indeed, Robur is an inspirational figure and every so often I like to return to be reinspired by Price's masterful performance.

CREDITS: Director: William Witney; Screenplay: Richard Matheson (Based on the Jules Verne Novels *Robur le Conquérant* and *Maître du Monde*; Producer: James H. Nicholson; Executive Producer: Samuel Z. Arkoff; Co-Producer: Anthony Carras; Associate Producers: Bartlett A. Carré and Daniel Haller; Production Design: Daniel Haller; Cinematography: Gil Warrenton; Aerial Photography: Kay Norton; Photographic Effects: Butler-Glouner Inc. and Ray Mercer and Co.; Special Miniature Effects: Tim Baar, Wah Chang, Gene Warren, and (uncredited) Marcel Delgado; Special Props and Mechanical Effects: Pat Dinga; Editor: Anthony Carras; Music: Les Baxter; Music Coordinator: Al Simms; Makeup: Fred Phillips; An Alta Vista Production Released by American International; May 31, 1961; 104 minutes

CAST: Vincent Price (Robur); Charles Bronson (Strock); Henry Hull (Prudent); Mary Webster (Dorothy); David Frankham (Philip); Richard Harrison (Alistair); Vito Scotti (Topage); Wally Campo (Turner); Steve Masino (Weaver); Ken Terrell (Shanks); Peter Besbas (Wilson); Gordon Jones

P-4

158

PIT AND THE PENDULUM (1961)
by Mark A. Miller

In 1960 Roger Corman had ingeniously reached into the public domain and pulled out Edgar Allan Poe's "The Fall of the House of Usher." He convinced AIP's Samuel Z. Arkoff that the house itself was the monster they required, and then he let Vincent Price carry the film to a box office success that surprised everyone involved. Corman's switch to color for this film, with a budget large enough to finance two of his 1950s black and white drive-in features, seemed daring at the time for a small outfit like AIP. It proved a fruitful gamble, however, and insured a second Poe adaptation using the same crew, scriptwriter and leading man. *Pit and the Pendulum* (with *The* dropped) was announced on AIP's production schedule in August 1960. Shot in only 16 days in January 1961, the film cost nearly $1,000,000 to make, an extremely modest budget even at that time.

Writer Richard Matheson, who had previously adapted his novel, *The Shrinking Man*, for the screen, was asked to produce a script based on a short story with even less plot than "The Fall of the House of Usher." "*Pit and the Pendulum* was a lot more of a challenge," recalled the famous author of such novels as *I Am Legend* and *Hell House*. "Poe's story was just one scene of a guy lashed to a table with a blade that's going to cut him in half. And now most people ascribe what I wrote to Edgar Allan Poe!"[1] In interviews, Price often sympathized with Matheson's daunting task: "One of the problems with doing Edgar Allan Poe is that those are short stories, and you've got to make them into long films! And Poe doesn't take the trouble to explain why people are where they are, so you have to explain that." [2]

Edgar Allan Poe (1809-49) wrote "The Pit and the Pendulum" during the six-year period (1838-44) he lived in Philadelphia with his wife (and cousin), Virginia, and her mother, Maria Clemm. Sporadic employment as an assistant editor on periodicals like *Burton's Gentleman's Magazine* did not keep him out of poverty, nor from bitterness over his lack of a literary reputation as lustrous as some of his contemporaries. This latter annoyance he assuaged with scathing and often unfair book reviews that transparently begrudged the success of others, such as William Cullen Bryant, Henry Wadsworth Longfellow, and Washington Irving. Adding to Poe's worries and unhappiness, Virginia began coughing up blood in January 1842 and was diagnosed with tuberculosis. (She died from it five years later.)

Poe's frustration and misery in Philadelphia undoubtedly influenced some of his most famous short stories of this time. "Ligeia" returned to and perfected his theme of the dead returning from the beyond. (Poe earned $10 for the story.) He followed this with "The Fall of the House of Usher" and the psychological thriller "William Wilson." It is not a stretch to proclaim him the only American writer to have invented a genre, the detective story, with his next short tale, "Murders in the Rue Morgue." Coinciding with the discovery of Virginia's illness came "The Masque of the Red Death," with its unmistakable parallel to her condition. Poe's "The Pit and the Pendulum," however, comes closest as a metaphor for his unhappy life of this period.

Set in Toledo during the Spanish Inquisition, "Pit" is a nearly plotless, metaphysical tale of horrifying sensation. The story's nameless first person narrator finds himself imprisoned in a dungeon after having been sentenced to death. He gropes in the pitch blackness, at the mercy of whatever horrible method of death the monks may deliver. The plot consists of the unseen monks' attempt to kill their prisoner in three separate, horrific ways.

First, the monks hope that their condemned prisoner will haplessly fall into a pit. Traversing the dungeon to gain a sense of its width, the narrator stumbles, falling with his chin landing on the slimy stone floor, but with the rest of his head feeling strangely suspended in the air. Thus, by luck, he has "fallen at the very brink of a circular pit...." Dropping a loose piece of masonry into it, he discovers it is extremely deep and partially filled with water. He realizes he has barely escaped "death with its direst physical agonies."

The narrator soon is subjected to the monks' second method of execution. After drinking some drugged water, he awakens in the dungeon, which is now dully lit, to discover himself "upon my back, and at full length, on a species of low framework of wood. To this I was securely bound by a long strap resembling a surcingle. It passed in many convolutions about my limbs and body, leaving at liberty only my head, and my left arm to such extent, that I could, by dint of much exertion, supply myself with food from an earthen dish which lay by my side on the floor." He constantly must use his free hand to defend his meat against hundreds of ravenous rats. Above him is a "crescent of glittering steel, about a foot in length from horn to horn; the horns upward, and the under edge evidently as keen as that of a razor. Like a razor also, it seemed massy and heavy, tapering from the edge into a solid and broad structure above. It was appended to a weighty rod of brass, and the whole *hissed* as it swung through the air." The pendulum slowly descends for days, toward his heart, causing such an exquisite agony of antici- pation that he prays "for its more speedy descent." Then, when the pendulum is only about 10 swings away from reaching his robe, an idea occurs to him. (One wonders why it took so long!) He smears his straps with the spicy meat so that the rats leap onto him, chew on the straps, and free him just as the blade begins to cut. (This is the most sickening part of the story. The rats "writhed upon my throat; their cold lips sought my own....")

Annoyed, the still unseen monks raise the pendulum and try torture number three. The metal dungeon walls heat up and begin to close in on the narrator. He has two choices: die a human waffle or jump into the pit. (Why does the "species of low framework of wood" not prevent the dungeon walls from closing and crushing the prisoner?) When there is "no longer an inch of foothold" separating him from the dreadful abyss, however, the walls quickly recede and he is grabbed just before he falls by General Lasalle, whose French army has entered Toledo in the nick of time.

What prevents Poe's story from becoming only a wet dream for sadomasochists is that it provides a study in human response to terror. The protagonist offers a second-by-second de- scription of his perceptions, which often are metamorphosed or heightened by fear. For ex- ample, as the monks sentence him to death (presumably for heresy, although we are not told), their voices "merged in one dreamy indeterminate hum." Shortly, as though an automatic sur- vival mechanism engages, his hearing fades altogether, but he can still see their thin white lips "writhe with a deadly locution. I saw them fashion the syllables of my name; and I shuddered because no sound succeeded." In the courtroom, seven lit white candles appear as bright angels to him, offering some hope of salvation, but quickly he is overcome with "a most deadly nausea over my spirit" and feels as though "every fiber" of his body is being shocked while the candles become "meaningless spectres, with heads of flame, and I saw that from them there would be no help." His senses alternately provide hope or despair, as though they are directly linked to whatever in the brain deciphers reality from illusion, and now that part of the brain suffers sensory overload from the extreme circumstances, and thus it malfunctions.

A fascinating extension of this transmutation of perception is Poe's motif that not "all of consciousness" ever leaves us—that an indefinable immortality or "gulf" persists when we sleep, faint, or (as in the case of Ligeia in his story of that title) even die. Awakening out of our slumber, Poe's narrator maintains, we find that impressions of our unconscious dreams may linger, or, sometimes, return much later as "shadows of memory." He also entertains, "like a rich musical note," the idea of "what sweet rest there must be in the grave." After he regains consciousness in the dungeon, he experiences one of these "shadows of memory," a vague, literally hellish suggestion of "tall figures [monks]... that lifted and bore me in silence down— down—still down—till a hideous dizziness oppressed me at the mere idea of the interminable- ness of the descent." Not surprisingly, the narrator at first is afraid to open his eyes at the notion

The spirit of Poe never enjoyed a more faithful, potent translator than found in the performance of Vincent Price in *Pit and the Pendulum*.

of a continued absence of light, an indicator that perhaps his punishment has been to be entombed alive, hardly the expected preamble to a "sweet rest." Anyway, no one truly *sleeps* in Poe's stories, and the dead are seldom *dead*. Something of us continues *to be* in the "gulf."

Poe's writing style—a dark, twisted amusement park, where undoubtedly a devil with a thin mustachio sells tickets at the threat of a pitch fork—also elevates his horror stories into a realm above mere sadistic terror. The choice of a first person narrator effectively forces the reader to become the victim who suffers the kiss of the rats and narrowly escapes the black pit, the soaring pendulum and the searing walls. (Poe's first person narrators of "The Tell-Tale Heart," "Cask of Amontillado" and "The Black Cat" are all murderous madmen—thus, so is the reader.) His syntax (simpler in "Pit" than in earlier stories) and diction are eloquent and potent (which renders his subject matter all the more disturbing), particularly in his use of repetition, alliteration and rhythm. In one paragraph, Poe begins sentence after sentence with *Then* to achieve a detailed, hammered, stair step-like impression of the narrator's slowly awakening to consciousness, then blacking out again and reviving, after the altogether exhausting, terrifying court appearance.

Repetition is used again to accentuate the torturous anticipation and endless swing of the deadly pendulum: "What boots it to tell of the long, long hours of horror more than mortal, during which I counted the rushing oscillations of the steel! Inch by inch—line by line—with a descent only appreciable at intervals that seemed ages—down it came!" Besides mimicking the back and forth motion by reiterating *long*, *inch*, and *line*, Poe includes alliterative *s* sounds that evoke the *swoosh* and *hiss* of the blade's passing. The onomatopoeic *rushing* contributes to the sensation. Add to this the sometimes animated anapestic and iambic quality of his prose that suggests the rhythm of the inexorable pendulum. All of these devices intensify the narrator's (and thus reader's) agony of anticipation.

Poe understood torture.

Little wonder that he did. During this time his financial woes and Virginia's slow death by consumption fueled his drinking, which could only have inflamed the guilt and failure he must have felt. Efforts to raise capital for his own literary magazine and to secure financial stability with a government job both failed. Poverty stood in for his own personal deep pit from which he could not escape for any length of time.

Unlike his famous contemporaries, for the most part, Poe could place his stories and poems only in low-paying, often short-lived periodicals. Some of his tales were pirated by other periodicals, for which he received no remuneration. Yes, life's indiscriminate, sharp pendulum was in full swing over Poe, and his reaction could sometimes be ugly. In anger and envy, he lambasted successful writers in his sometimes anonymous reviews, even accusing Longfellow in print of blatantly plagiarizing Tennyson.

The red-hot steel walls of disappointment, hard luck and spite closed in on Poe. It is easy to see him as the narrator of "The Pit and the Pendulum" because the protagonist is persecuted and tortured for an unspecified crime in the name of religion or God. The irony and unjustness of it certainly must reflect Poe's frustrations over the slow, painful fate of his wife and, in his opinion, the unfair lack of literary and financial success he suffered while others, less deserving, gained money and fame.

Yet Poe's tale ends on a sudden note of sunny optimism as the narrator is abruptly saved. Perhaps Poe believed that salvation was still possible for him. If so, it later proved unfounded. He perished, poor and lonely, probably of exposure and brain inflammation, in a Baltimore hospital, less than three years after Virgina's death.

Like characters in so many of his tales, if Poe resides in an ethereal "gulf" of paradoxical unconscious consciousness, I hope he at least senses the everlasting popularity of his work posthumously. It may just be that General Lasalle represented a Destiny so incongruously prodigious that even Poe could not have imagined it in his lifetime—an everlasting fame—republished time and time again and reincarnated on stage, radio and television—and film.

Matheson's script takes the centerpiece of Poe's tale, the pendulum, for its climax, and appropriately includes many of the terrifying motifs of Poe's canon to reach it. Premature burial; black, ironic humor; wild, morbid imagery; the dead who do not die; gradual insanity—all of these qualities are logical, intrinsic components of Matheson's plotline. (He earned $5,000 for his script, plus a bonus from director Roger Corman who greatly appreciated his superb job.)

In 1546, Francis Barnard (John Kerr) travels from London to the remote Spanish castle of his brother-in-law, Nicholas Medina (Vincent Price), to learn about the mysterious death of his sister, Elizabeth Bernard Medina. Francis is told that she died of "something in her blood." However, Nicholas's physician and close friend, Dr. Charles Leon (Antony Carbone), visits and tells Francis that Elizabeth really died of shock.

As a result, Nicholas explains (in a flashback sequence) the terrible truth that he had wished to spare the now skeptical Francis: Nicholas's father, the infamous Sebastian Medina, had been a cruel inquisitor who tortured people to death in a dungeon beneath the castle, and Elizabeth (Barbara Steele) became obsessed with Sebastian's torture chamber. One night when Nicholas found her there, she died in his arms, whispering, "Sebastian."

Soon Nicholas's sister, Catherine (Luana Anders), confides to Francis that Nicholas, as a boy, had seen his father murder their uncle, Bartolome (Sebastian's brother), and torture their mother, Isabella, to death for their adulterous affair. (Much of this is seen in a flashback.) That night, the harpsichord is heard throughout the castle, yet only Elizabeth knew how to play it.

Later, the doctor tells Catherine that Nicholas believes Elizabeth may have been interred alive. The doctor also reveals that her mother was not tortured to death but was walled up in her tomb still alive. "The very thought of premature interment," he warns Catherine, has become "enough to drive your brother into convulsions of horror." Next, the maid runs screaming from Elizabeth's room, claiming that she heard her voice. The doctor and Francis theorize that the servants may have conspired to trick Nicholas into believing that Elizabeth was buried alive, perhaps to drive him mad.

162

Then crashes are heard from Elizabeth's room, which has since been locked, drawing everyone except Nicholas. It is in a shambles, and Nicholas's portrait of Elizabeth has been slashed. Searching the room, Francis discovers a secret passageway that leads to Nicholas' room.

This prompts Francis to wonder if Nicholas has been "creating evidence of Elizabeth's revengeful return" during periods of insanity, brought on by guilt that he may have buried her alive. Nicholas insists that the only way to be sure this is *not* so is to exhume her body.

Once the crypt is opened, the face of Elizabeth's partially decomposed corpse suggests a scream, frozen in death. Her hands reach out in a claw-like position. The doctor blames himself, claiming the case is unprecedented. Nevertheless, Nicholas is consumed with guilt.

That night, ghostly calls draw Nicholas to the tomb, where Elizabeth (no longer decomposed) rises from her coffin and chases him until he stumbles down the torture chamber's stairs. Apparently he is dead.

The doctor appears and embraces Elizabeth. Their conversation reveals that they have been lovers and have conspired all along to drive Nicholas to insanity or his death. To their horror, however, Nicholas is not dead, only stunned. Completely insane, he *becomes* his father and re-enacts the murder and torture of Isabella and Bartolome, for whom he mistakes Elizabeth and the doctor. Nicholas locks Elizabeth in an iron maiden and the doctor stumbles to his death into the pit. When Francis enters the dungeon, Nicholas now believes that *he* is Bartolome.

Nicholas straps Francis under the pendulum. Only seconds away from death, he is saved by Catherine and a servant, who wrestles with Nicholas and inadvertently sends him to his doom into the pit.

Matheson's script cleverly has Nicholas, Catherine, and the doctor give Francis incomplete facts piecemeal, to place viewers into Francis' position of frustrated curiosity, which is tantamount to turning the audience into a participatory first person narrator of the sort that is so effective in Poe's stories. Also, the flashbacks are Poesque because they intrude into the reality of the moment, reshaping it with new, sometimes shocking information. Poe, himself, would have appreciated some of Matheson's mocking irony. For instance, the doctor, who falsely declares Elizabeth dead then fakes her premature burial, later proves that he really *is* an incompetent physician when he mistakes Nicholas for dead.

Roger Corman—with the inestimable talents of cinematographer Floyd Crosby, production designer/art director Daniel Haller, and editor Anthony Carras—fashioned Matheson's script into one of the genre's masterpieces. Corman and his team were able to do this, in part, because the director imbued the film with what Price called the "spirit of Poe, the psychological overtones that have been discovered in Poe...."[3]

Corman had begun to study Freud, and so he overlaid some of his theories of the unconscious mind on the works of Poe. Hence, in his autobiography, he spoke of a character's journey down a castle's cobweb-strewn corridors, haunted by spiders and rats, as functioning

> on an unconscious, symbolic plane.... Horror can be a reenactment of some long-suppressed fear that has seized a child, even a baby. A dream. A taboo. A fear gets locked in the subconscious. In dealing with suspense at a later stage of development the house can be seen as a woman's body with its openings—windows, doors, arches. The corridor becomes a woman's vagina. The deeper you go into the dark hallways, then the deeper you are delving into, say, an adolescent boy's first sexual stirrings. These are contradictory urges—an irresistible attraction and desire for sex and the fear of the unknown and illicit. The very ambivalence builds tension.
>
> Put together correctly, the classic horror sequence is the equivalent of the sexual act. The sharp, shocking event at the end that releases the tension is the equivalent of the orgasmic climax.... [T]here is growing tension and release—all analogous to the rhythms of a sexual act.[4]

Nicholas Medina (Vincent Price) is obsessed with his dead wife Elizabeth.

Of course, it is tempting to dismiss such armchair psychology as so much after-the-fact hogwash, but it does rings true in *Pit*. The sequence that involves the seductive yet terrifying voice of Elizabeth coaxing Nicholas down into the tomb is a perfect example. Price's face simultaneously expresses a deep longing for and loathing of her; he may be anxious and terrified, but nevertheless he *still* slowly descends into her crypt. The climax of his journey will literally be the discovery of a woman. Whether the chord struck here is sexual or not, its overtones are deep-rooted and real. Elizabeth is beautiful but also terrifying and ghastly, her hands covered in blood. She pursues him and he stumbles away in near paralyzed terror. Perhaps this is the ultimate symbol of a terrible sexual experience, perhaps not. Each individual viewer has his or her own private, subconscious "monsters" to live with, and Corman is the Freudian technician who releases them.

Corman's use of special filters and optics, his staging in Panavision, his camera movement, and his editing (with Carras) display an imagination dedicated not only to telling a story well and economically but also to creating or underlining the tension, suspense and terror that must be animated from the pages of the script. "Roger did make pictures very quickly," recalled Price, "but they were made thoroughly. They were brilliantly designed and brilliantly thought out. He was one of the best directors I ever worked with in my life."[5]

Corman opens his film with a Panavision vista of paints on glass—purples, reds, blues and yellows that wash up and swirl like an ocean coastline. This projects a surreal, otherworldly quality upon the real coastline that he cuts to next, with shots of a coach traveling along the shore to take Francis to the castle. The clear blue sky and the water, which crests in foamy, white spills on the beach and against the rocks around the castle, take on a quality of quiet deception. This is because Corman juxtaposes the images with Les Baxter's weird musical score of kettle drums and string plucks, devoid of any melody. The unsettling contrast of image and sound suggests that what is seen may be quite different from what is real, a marvelously appropriate preamble for the deceptive events at the castle.

Corman's use of images and words enhances ideas. A close-up of Nicholas' portrait of Elizabeth dissolves into a long shot of Nicholas, Catherine and Francis, framed through a fireplace. The flames make the portrait appear to be afire. The transition suggests the relationship between Elizabeth and Nicholas, a paradoxical blend of strong passion and yet cold distance implied by the long shot. In the flashback sequence of Nicholas as a child, we hear Catherine's narration, "And there before my brother's very eyes, his mother was tortured to death." On the word "eyes," Corman zooms in from a close-up of the boy to an extreme close-up of his eyes; then he cuts out of the flashback to a shot of Catherine staring directly into the camera. The sequence creates an intensity that evokes the idea that perception must, by its very nature, equal terror.

Corman, in fact, underlines this notion throughout the film with an unrelenting emphasis on close-ups of eyes. (In his stories, Poe also frequently used eyes in a context of horror and revulsion, most memorably in "The Tell-Tale Heart.") Each of Corman's flashbacks begins with an optical effect that reduces his entire frame to a small, rectangular area around the eyes of the narrator. This technique serves as both transition and highlighter of shock. For example, at the film's end, Catherine leaves the torture chamber, announcing, "No one will ever enter this room again." In the editing room, Corman created a dizzying pan from Catherine to the iron maiden, in which we see Elizabeth, poking her fingers through the facial grating, her mouth bandaged and her eyes in a wide panic. An optical rectangle closes all of the frame but her eyes, which then turn purple through use of a filter. These optical and filter effects powerfully convey Elizabeth's insurmountable, intractable fear, as this time she really is "buried alive." Remember, too, that these are actress Barbara Steele's unsurpassed eyes! (I vividly recall my eight-year-old brother John screaming and running from our living room at the sight of those eyes when the film first ran on network television.)

Corman's tricks with the camera do not come off as gimmicky because he uses them wisely. For instance, in the flashbacks, he uses blue filters that give the image a distorted, dream-like quality around the edges of his frame. This nightmarish effect significantly underscores the horror that usually takes place in them. Also, he includes red filtered images that slant and stretch to the right or left to accentuate the violence of Sebastian beating his brother with a red hot poker, then closing in on his wife.

Corman's most ingenious use of filters occurs in the sequence where Nicholas and Francis use pickaxes to break through the wall of Elizabeth's tomb. Like a ticking time bomb, the scene rhythmically intercuts shots of the striking pickaxes with close-ups of the two men, until stopping on an extreme close-up of Nicholas' eyes that fill the Panavision frame.[6] Between his eyes, Corman superimposes a blue filtered shot of Nicholas as a boy, witnessing his father wall up his mother alive. This memory, literally emerging from Nicholas' head, raises the tension considerably. *Did Nicholas' wife suffer the same hideous death as his mother?*

By constantly but unobtrusively moving his camera in and out, right and left, Corman gives a tremendous depth and height to his interior castle sets. For one memorable, extended sequence, a series of moving camera shots dissolve one into another: from Elizabeth's tomb to a dungeon wall with a crucifix hanging on it; to the torture chamber; to the large, empty dining room; and finally to the ornate altar of the castle's sanctuary. The camera dollies away from the altar (distancing us from the religious icons) and dissolves to a pan revealing Francis reading in his room. During this entire sequence we hear Elizabeth's harpsichord. While this sequence evokes the enormity of the castle, the religious icons and music in it also suggest that perhaps Elizabeth exists in spirit throughout the entire castle. The separation we feel as the camera tracks out of the sanctuary also implies that Elizabeth's spirit may be malicious.

Corman often preferred a mobile camera, especially in sequences with actors. "I always liked camera movements to lead people into and through scenes," wrote Corman in his autobiography. "The point-of-view (POV) shot was always a key in heightening tension. The critical shots then are with the camera in front of the actor, tracking back as he moves forward and then the POV reverse shot along the same dolly track, as the camera 'sees' what he sees. And I would mix up the angles and distances, keeping the camera in motion."[7] Certainly this technique enhances the suspense as Nicholas descends into the castle's catacombs, drawn by Elizabeth's beckoning. His terrified reactions as he faces the camera increase our anticipation for a shot of "what he sees."

By no means does Corman always move his camera. During dialogue scenes, for instance, Corman sometimes fills his frame with a master shot of all his characters, then takes the time to insert the many needed close-ups, one shots and two shots. On a shooting schedule as short as this film's, his planning must have been painstaking because the numerous inserts cleverly and quietly observe the nuances of the script and underscore certain ideas and emotions.

The climactic sequence involving the pit and pendulum epitomizes Corman's masterful workmanship. "Do you know where you are, Bartolome?" the deluded Nicholas asks Francis. "You are about to enter Hell, Bartolome." This is seen in a shot of Price hovering over actor John Kerr, who is strapped down to Poe's "species of low framework of wood." Corman then cuts to an extreme long shot revealing that Price and Kerr are on a small wooden platform, the pendulum above them, the immense Pit (a matting) below, as Nicholas reiterates, "Hell!" It is a beautiful cut because the long shot does, indeed, reveal a convincing image of what Hell could resemble.

When Nicholas triumphantly announces that Bartolome is about to experience the pendulum, Francis looks up in horror and Corman cuts to an awesome shot that places us under the threatening pendulum, staring directly up at it. (Again, this mirrors Poe's use of the first person narrator.) The horror is compounded as the pendulum begins to swing. According to Corman, "The contraption was actually operated from above, a very large mechanical system that didn't work as quickly as I liked. So I skip-framed it with an optical printer later, taking every other frame out optically to make the blade appear to move twice as fast."[8] As a result, the pendulum swings with a slightly surreal and nightmarish jumpiness.

Unlike Poe's pit, Corman's is a Gothic netherworld of flambeaux and huge shadows of the pendulum's clinking and clanking clockwork and swishing and swooshing blade. Murals of ghastly, hooded monks, with only their piercing eyes visible, haunt the walls. (This *is* in keeping with Poe's story: "The figures of fiends in aspects of menace... overspread and disfigured the walls.") To express the twisted, terrifying perspective of Francis as he lies there in Hell, Corman inserts a selection of slanted, colored filter shots of the walls, pendulum and Nicholas. "We did that sequence in a day," wrote Corman. "The end was fun. I used a crane and just started to make up shots as we got to the last hour or so, knowing I'd cut it all together in editing. We got a shot off every two or three minutes, or thirty or forty shots in the last two hours. I got shots of the blade from above it and below it; I had the camera panning and swooping. Danny [Haller] had murals painted along the walls and so I had the camera zoom along the walls. These cutaway montage shots would give the sequence color, vitality, and a dynamic tension."[9] The uncharacteristically large amount of footage Corman had in the can for this sequence marked a rare occasion on which he could edit a sequence with the luxury of many possible choices. The result is a splendidly horrifying sequence, one of his best ever. Richard Matheson was pleased with Corman's results: "That was a very well-executed and well-edited and very effective scene."[10]

Corman's skillful techniques create and intensify drama, and, in fact, in *Pit* we do see a master technician at work much more than a performance coach. If *Pit* has a weakness, it may be some of the acting. Richard Matheson felt that Corman "was good with the camera, he knew how to move with it, but... I don't think I ever saw him work with actors."[11] Hazel Court, who later acted in three of Corman's Poe films, remembered "Roger once telling me that he was going to UCLA for a course on how to handle actors." Barbara Steele liked working with him but found him "very shy."[12]

Whether or not Corman lacked the necessary skills to direct actors on more than a traffic cop basis is difficult to assess. He was actually wearing two hats, director and producer. Although the quality of his art obviously transcended his budgets and schedules, Corman was also an incredibly astute businessman who understood that sticking to budgets and schedules was an absolute essential for profit margins. (Sneer at this if you wish, but Corman almost never lost money on his movies and is a *very* rich man.) On such a short schedule, Corman would have needed to depend on his actors to take charge of their own interpretations while he dealt with camera set-ups and other technical concerns.

Luckily, none of the performances is poor, but they do range from fair to outstanding. Part of the difficulty is that the dialogue possesses a highly stylized, elevated syntax and vocabulary intended to seem upper crust and authentic for the time period. Such lines can be difficult. John Kerr, in particular, has trouble with this. A fine actor, he still woodenly stumbles through such lines as "Too many things need fuller explanation [unnatural pause] before I can be satisfied that what you say is true." Some of his lines risk sounding ridiculous if not spoken just right, and it is difficult not to smile when he asserts, "My sister was a strong and willful woman, not subject to the influence of atmospheres." Perhaps the problem is that Kerr is too "modern" a person to be convincing in a period piece.

Luana Anders fares much better. Soft spoken yet with an expressive voice, she delivers the dialogue wonderfully, no matter how potentially awkward it could sound, in a moving performance. Her character, too, has suffered from the knowledge that her father was an infamous torturer who entombed her mother alive, but she hides her unhappiness from her haunted brother as she tries to help him. Anders' subtle style embraces this dramatic role of repression and unselfish love. Antony Carbone, too, handles the dialogue of his treacherous character with conviction. He plays the smiling crocodile role with reserved deviousness.

Barbara Steele's performance is a special case. Fresh from a starring dual role in Mario Bava's *Black Sunday*, which AIP distributed in the U.S., she was deservedly an overnight sensation with genre fans. Her unusual beauty projected both sizzling sexuality and threatening evil, a combination that doomed her to be cast in strong, sinister roles for most of her career. (She proved to be a capable producer, however, in the early 1980s on two sweeping TV miniseries, *The Winds of War* and *War and Remembrance*.)

Most of Steele's low-budget horror films were produced in Europe, so her voice frequently was dubbed by others for the films' American release. Surprisingly, her voice is also dubbed in *Pit*, her first American film. Corman reportedly felt that she possessed a British working class accent that contrasted too much with the voices of the others.[13] Interestingly, her posh, aristocratic accent in one of her earlier British films, *Upstairs and Downstairs* (1959), seems to contradict this notion. Still, Steele has described herself while making *Pit* as "very shy during that period. I was extremely frightened when I did that film, because I was struck by the idea of working in the States.... I think I was frozen in my own particular panic at the time; I was myopic. I wasn't sure of what was going on around me...."[14] Perhaps her fears somehow undermined her vocal performance. Nevertheless, whoever did dub Steele's voice was perfect. This is a wicked, sadistic voice that purrs with sexuality and blends deliciously with Steele's physical performance. When that voice beckons Price into the crypt—"Nich-ol-as"—it is a terrifying mixture of malicious coaxing and playful seduction, like an invitation to play hide-and-seek in Hell. "Elizabeth, where are you?" Nicholas asks in a soft, apprehensive response, descending deeper and deeper toward her tomb.

At the heart of the good script and superb technical work is the dominating performance and presence of Vincent Price, who earned $125,000 for his part, plus a box office percentage. Corman knew well that Price was the star of his picture, and his camerawork and editing promote the actor's presence. The build-up to first meeting Price in *Pit* is a prime example. Following Catherine down into the dungeon, Francis hears terrifying clacks of immense clockwork and rattling chains. "In the name of heaven, what's that noise?" he asks her. He abruptly turns from her path and walks toward the door from behind which the noise comes. Corman uses a quick dolly to this door (a subjective shot of Francis' approach) then cuts to Francis reaching it as the noise stops. In a close-up, the door suddenly bursts open and out pops the face of Vincent Price to the deep, brassy sound of Baxter's *Du-du du dom*! followed by Price's formidable voice, asking sinisterly, "Who are you?" No doubt about who stars in this film! It is a worthy introduction to Nicholas, a tortured, unbalanced and greatly wronged man.

Price is the only actor possessing the unique skills necessary to play such a role as Nicholas. Only he, dressed in tights and sporting a collar that makes him look like a French poodle, could with complete seriousness and believability deliver such lines as "Shock and grief restrained me from more adequate communication. You have every right to be provoked" or "Am I not the spawn of his depraved blood?" Price transforms such dialogue into a realm of Poesque poetry. His deep, emotional, mellifluous voice is perfectly suited to Poe's haunted characters, and Price expertly conveys the complexity of Nicholas. His character's tragic experiences of the past must govern his actions and reactions in the present, which slowly pushes him toward madness, but with the unexpected result of transforming him into his sadistic father. Such a role is so dramatically charged that it is impossible to imagine anyone else doing it without turning in a somewhat hammy performance. Price's precise portrayal avoids this. He brings a respectable verisimilitude to his role's impossibly long gauntlet of sensations and passions, including an emotional breakdown into cries of heartbreak, a resigned stoicism toward Elizabeth's impending vengeance, his moans like a hurt animal as he collapses into a pathetic heap upon the sight of Elizabeth rising from her tomb, and his rage, violence, and insanity.

Price is the only actor possessing the unique skills necessary to play such a role as Nicholas.

Price's countenance is often imbued with an underlying torment. Antony Carbone, who is now a director at the American Academy of Dramatic Art, recognized and appreciated Price's often underrated abilities in such complex roles. "Certain actors have an instinct," observed Carbone. "There's always something else going on that they're not sharing with the audience. Vincent had that gift. He was always thinking of two or three things at the same time, and that keeps you guessing, will he do this or will he do that? That element keeps you totally focused on the image."[15] This is particularly evident when Nicholas deceives Francis about his sister's death. Even as he lies, Nicholas' visage suggests that her real cause of death is unimaginably sinister and unspeakable, and that the truth haunts him. As a result, he seems unpredictable, capable of anything.

One of Price's finest moments occurs when he appears

dead after his fall down the steps. Elizabeth, caressing his face in mock affection, gloats over him, "I have you exactly as I want you—helpless. Is it not ironic, oh my husband? Your wife an adulteress, your mother an adulteress, your uncle an adulterer, your closest friend an adulterer—do you not find that amusing, dear Nicholas?" In one of the most bloodcurdling close-ups in screen history, Price, his face immobile with blankly staring eyes, suddenly forms a diabolical smile and answers, "Yes." It is a worthy resurrection that mocks Elizabeth's fake return from the beyond with startling, unspoken promises of ghastly doom.

When Price clutches Steele, he strokes her hair one second, then chokes her the next. "I am going to torture you, Isabella," he says in a voice dripping with contradictory affection and sadism. "I'm going to make you suffer for your faithlessness to me. Before this day is out you will be begging me to kill you, to relieve you of the agony of Hell into which your husband is about to plunge you." Price then violently kisses her while he chokes her. "Harlot! You will die in agony. Die!" Price electrifies the scene with a sexual, psychopathic power that is hair raising. (When I screened this scene for a group of teenagers working on a Poe unit in the fall of 1997, they stared in absolute silence with open mouths and eyes as big as silver dollars.)

Steele remembered that this confrontation "was done in one take, with a brief rehearsal beforehand. He really went at me and I had the bruises on my throat to prove it. Afterwards, he was so concerned he had hurt me—such a gentleman—a truly kind figure in spite of his image."[16]

Price's co-workers genuinely admired and respected him on *Pit*. To Carbone, he was "one of the most professional people I've ever worked with. He knew his lines better than anyone else, he was always ready to go. He could get *in* there—wonderful, just wonderful. If I had a scene to do [and Price's lines were delivered off camera], he was always there. He had a wonderful sense of humor, wonderful stories. You could sit around and talk to him for hours.... It's almost unfortunate that Vincent was so good in this kind of film, because he could have done anything. He was a wonderful actor. I'm sure anyone has to have a great deal of affection and respect for the man."[17]

Steele described Price as "completely charming and a fabulous actor. He is glorious and bright; he could have been great in Shakespeare. He's very compassionate and intuitive, very protective and kind... and wickedly funny."[18] Perhaps Samuel Z. Arkoff sums up Vincent Price best in the brief but succinct: "He was a spectacular man in every respect."[19]

Vincent Price noted that "part of Roger's genius... is the fact that he surrounded himself with incredibly talented people."[20] Tom Matsumoto's gorgeous matte paintings of the castle and pit do not look realistic, but this in fact adds to the film's unworldly, surreal atmosphere that is so essential in interpreting Poe's horrific tale. Corman's cinematographer, Floyd Crosby, who had won an Academy Award for *Tabu* (1931), bathes the sets in his luxuriant color photography of foreboding shadows and shuddery hues. Daniel Haller's beautiful, rich sets, adorned with Harry Reif's exquisite period furniture, coats of armor, clocks, wall tapestries, weapons, candlesticks and paintings, almost match the high standard of Bernard Robinson's famous Hammer sets. Price, in particular, recognized Haller's importance to Corman. "The thing about Danny Haller," recalled Price, "is that [he] was one of the art directors who really was capable of taking nothing and turning it into a terribly exciting thing. In *Pit and the Pendulum*, I think he was the first person ever to use a complete stage. He went right up to the ceiling and removed the catwalks, which gave an enormous sense of depth and height to the [pit]. He is a very talented man.... I do think that Danny is responsible for a lot of the success of these [Poe] pictures."[21]

Haller's pit set meets all expectations of the sensational. He researched and, he said, found "that such a pendulum actually was used during the Spanish and German inquisitions."[22] This pendulum was constructed under the supervision of Ross Hahn, Jr., working from Haller's designs. Eighteen feet long and weighing over a ton, it was rigged from the top of a sound stage, 35 feet up,[23] and it took four strong men to operate it.

John Kerr's job was to act frightened of the pendulum as it soared in the air above him. Not much acting would be necessary because some danger was real. "At first we tried to use a

Vincent Price as the doomed Nicholas Medina.

rubberized blade," remembered Haller, "and that's why it got stuck on Kerr's chest. We then switched to a sharp metalized blade covered with steel paint. The problem was to get it in exactly the right position so it would slash John's shirt without actually cutting him. To guard against this we put a steel band around his waist where the pendulum crosses. He was a good sport about it but I noticed him perspiring a good bit and no wonder. That pendulum was carving out a 50 foot arc just above his body."[24] In reflecting on the danger to John Kerr, producer Samuel Z. Arkoff quipped, "I had nightmares of trying to explain this one to our Blue Cross insurance agent."[25]

Pit and the Pendulum garnered mainly sterling reviews, although a few notable Philistines (Charles Stinson of the *Los Angeles Times* for one) panned it entirely. Arkoff has called *Pit* his personal favorite[26] and the most successful of the Poe pictures at the box office.[27] (No wonder it is his favorite!) Richard Matheson recalled that when *Pit* "made even more money than [*Usher*], they said, 'Hey! Let's try one more!' It went on and on like that for years. It was like making shoes or something."[28] Matheson wrote two more Poe films, Corman directed six more (five with Price), and Price participated in nine more, if film titles alone qualify as Poe movies (e.g., *Conqueror Worm*).[29]

At the climax of *Pit and the Pendulum*, Vincent Price, Richard Matheson and Roger Corman, with his exemplary crew, compose a filmic requiem to Poe that is deeply moving. "The razor edge of destiny," Price sadly announces with malignant resignation as he introduces the pendulum about to descend upon Kerr, "thus the condition of man: bound on an island from which he can never have hope to escape, surrounded by the waiting pit of Hell, subject to the inexorable pendulum of fate, which must destroy him finally." This melancholy metaphor is unmistakably the epitaph for Edgar Allan Poe, and the spirit of Poe never enjoyed a more faithful, potent translator than found in the performance of Vincent Price in *Pit and the Pendulum*.

CREDITS: Producer and Director: Roger Corman; Screenplay: Richard Matheson (Based on Edgar Allan Poe's Short Story, "The Pit and the Pendulum"); Production Manager: Bartlett A. Carre; Executive Producers: James H. Nicholson and Samuel Z. Arkoff; Music: Les Baxter; Music Coordinator: Al Simms; Director of Photography: Floyd Crosby; Production Designer/Art Director: Daniel Haller; Film Editor: Anthony Carras; Sound Editor: Kay Rose; Music Editor: Eve Newman; Scenic Effects: Tom Matsumoto; Photographic Effects: Butler-Glouner, Inc., and Ray Mercer; Special Effects: Pat Dinga; Assistant Director: Jack Bohrer; Sound Recording: Roy Meadows; Makeup: Ted Coodley; Wardrobe: Marjorie Corso; Properties: Richard M. Rubin;

Set Decorator: Harry Reif; Released 1961 by American International Pictures; filmed in Panavision; Color by Pathe; 80 minutes

CAST: Vincent Price (Nicholas Medina); John Kerr (Francis Barnard); Barbara Steele (Elizabeth Barnard Medina); Luana Anders (Catherine Medina); Antony Carbone (Dr. Charles Leon); Patrick Westwood (Maximillian); Lynne Bernay (Maria); Larry Turner (Nicholas as a child); Mary Menzies (Isabella Medina); Charles Victor (Bartolome Medina)

[1] Weaver, Tom. *Science Fiction Stars and Horror Heroes*. Jefferson, NC: McFarland, 1991: 303.

[2] Weaver, Tom. *Attack of the Monster Movie Makers*. Jefferson, NC: McFarland: 1994: 275-76.

[3] French, Larry. "Vincent Price: The Corman Years, Part One:" *Fangoria 6* (June 1980): 24.

[4] Corman, Roger with Jim Jerome. *How I Made a Hundred Movies in Hollywood and Never Lost a Dime*. New York: Random House, 1990: 80.

[5] Weaver, *Attack*, 275.

[6] Because Corman's compositions utilize so beautifully and intelligently the entire Panavision widescreen frame, the scan-and-pan versions seen on television and released to video are to be avoided. Luckily, the film has been released on laser disc in its original widescreen format. This is the version that *must* be seen and the one discussed in this chapter.

[7] Corman, 80.

[8] Ibid., 83.

[9] Ibid.

[10] Weaver, *Science Fiction Stars*, 303.

[11] Ibid., 310.

[12] Dietrich, Christopher S. with Peter Beckman. "The Barbara Steele Interview." *Video Watchdog* 7 (Sept/Oct. 1991): 55.

[13] Williams, Lucy Chase. *The Complete Films of Vincent Price*. New York: Carol Publishing Group, 1995: 166.

[14] Dietrich, 55.

[15] Williams, 170.

[16] McGee, Mark Thomas. *Faster and Furiouser*. Jefferson, NC: McFarland, 1996: 191. (Quoted from an article/interview by Steve Biodrowski, David Del Valle and Lawrence French in *Cinefantastique*.)

[17] Williams, 170.

[18] Warren, Bill. "Princess of Darkness." *Fangoria* 102 (May 1991): 18.

[19] Weaver, Tom. *Interviews with B Science Fiction and Horror Movie Makers*. Jefferson, NC: McFarland, 1988: 31.

[20] Yaccarino, Michael Orlando. "Vincent Price: The Merchant of Menace." *Scarlet Street* 7 (Summer 1992): 58.

[21] French, 24-25.

[22] McGee, 191.

[23] Ibid.

[24] Ibid.

[25] Arkoff, Sam with Richard Trubo, *Flying Through Hollywood by the Seat of My Pants*. New York: Carol Publishing Group, 1992: 115.

[26] Weaver, *Interviews*, 35.

[27] Arkoff, 115.

[28] Naha, Ed. *The Films of Roger Corman: Brilliance on a Budget*. New York: Arco, 1982: 32.

[29] Poe's "The Pit and the Pendulum" has been adapted to film several other times, twice in France as short films, in 1910 and 1963. Director Stuart Gordon made a version in 1991.

The 1968 ABC network broadcast of *Pit* included 10 minutes of additional footage of Catherine Medina (Luana Anders) in a madhouse, telling the horrifying story, with the original film presented as her flashback. Corman's assistant, Tamara Asseyev, shot the added segments, probably in 1967 or 1968.

Footage of Price from *Pit* shows up in *Dr. Goldfoot and the Bikini Machine* (1965, Norman Taurog), which also stars Price.

•Source for Poe information: Silverman, Kenneth. *Edgar A. Poe: Mournful and Never-ending Remembrance*. NY: HarperCollins, 1991.

TOWER OF LONDON
(1939 and 1962)
by Bryan Senn

When Hollywood handles history, it usually does so with kid gloves, whitewashing its subject in broad strokes of thrilling adventure and heroism. With a certain historical personage of the English monarchy, however, the exact opposite has been true. In 1483, Richard III became King of England amid the civil unrest and political upheaval of the Wars of the Roses. The last of the Plantagenet kings, Richard fell in battle less than three years later and the monarchy passed into the hands of the Tudors (of whom Henry VIII is the best known).

If one recognizes the name of Richard III at all, it is probably as one of history's vilest villains, a humpbacked usurper who murdered members of his own family—including his two prepubescent nephews—to gain the crown. This is the Richard of William Shakespeare, who based his fictionalized account of *Richard III* largely upon the highly biased and inaccurate tracts of Tudor chroniclers (who were naturally anti-Plantagenet). Disregarding the fact that Richard was at the time of his reign a well-loved reformer (and also personally well-formed; i.e., no hump) who showed more mercy to his enemies than good sense would dictate, Shakespeare's popular play has forever cast him in the public eye as an evil, scheming nephew-killer (despite a complete lack of evidence [1]). Never one to fly in the face of popular opinion (not to mention established literature), it comes as no surprise that Hollywood took the same tack in its two (non-Shakespearean) takes on the tarnished tale. [2]

Besides sharing the same attitude toward its main maligned character, the two *Tower*s of *London* (1939 and 1962) also featured the same actor—though in different roles. In 1939, rising stage star Vincent Price had just embarked upon his five-decade-long movie career. In fact, he had made only two previous films (*Service De Luxe*, 1938, and *The Private Lives of Elizabeth and Essex*, 1939) before Universal cast him in their new historical horror, *Tower of London*.

"I had what we call today a cameo part, which means very little money," quipped Price about his horror film debut (in a 1989 *Cinefantastique* interview). At the time, this suited the relatively green actor well, particularly as he "wanted to get established playing character parts. I really didn't think I fit in the mold of a leading man in terms of Hollywood. I'm a character actor; that's what I like to do."

Apart from launching Vincent Price's silver scream career, the year 1939 saw Hollywood horror revived. For nearly two years big-screen terror had lain quiescent in its self-imposed tomb (due to the new anti-horror owners at Universal—the home of horror—and to the British moratorium on terror films) until flying forth like the proverbial bat out of hell with the reissue of the original *Dracula* and *Frankenstein* to booming box-office. With the money pouring in, Universal quickly set about creating a new batch of terror tales to feed the hungry horror houses clamoring for more product to show their eager patrons. First up was the belated sequel *Son of Frankenstein* (1939) directed by Rowland V. Lee, followed closely by Universal's take on the "evil" Richard III mythos, *Tower of London* (also with Lee at the helm).

Though more a historical melodrama than outright horror movie, Universal made sure to include all the nefarious trappings (such as a plethora of tortures and murders) which would slot it firmly into the now-revived genre. Scripter Robert N. Lee also created a pivotal role for the king of horror himself, Boris Karloff (who plays the fictitious figure of Mord the Executioner, Richard's right-hand [and club-footed] man). Much more than your average chiller, however, *Tower of London* proved to be one of the best costume dramas of the age. Superb acting, grand spectacle (as well as some chilling, intimate moments of terror), precise photography, a classic storyline and deft direction make *Tower of London* one of the most impressively mounted productions from the golden age of horror.

The story follows the clever and ruthless machinations of Richard (Basil Rathbone), brother of usurper King Edward IV (Ian Hunter), who claimed the English crown in 1471. With the aid of the Tower of London's chief torturer/executioner, Mord (Boris Karloff), Richard sets about murdering all those who stand in the way of his accession to the throne, including his own brother Clarence (Vincent Price) and his two young nephews. Winning his prize at last, Richard soon meets his fate at the hands of Henry Tudor (Ralph Forbes) at the battle of Bosworth field.

Almost immediately, the viewer is whisked inside Jack Otterson's magnificent castle sets whose authenticity is only matched by their size and grandeur. Immense walls and towers rise 75 feet above the castle courtyard while the spacious-yet-forbidding interiors are made even more ominous by the huge stone fireplaces, mammoth pillars and massive wooden doors. Otterson even built an authentic replica of the watery "Traitor's Gate" which leads to the river Thames, an imposing structure that opens and closes like the mouth of a great beast to devour the characters.

The excellent screenplay by Robert N. Lee (brother of director Rowland V. Lee) is full of well-drawn, contrasting characterizations, the most notable being the strong King Edward (ebulliently played by Ian Hunter) and his cunning brother, Richard. Edward is a hearty, guileless, even good-humored man, whose misdeeds arise not from malice or forethought, but from the weight of leadership and the willingness to take the most expedient route. With an engaging impishness, he plays along with Richard's ploys, blind to his sibling's darker motivations. Richard, however, schemes and plots to achieve his ends, drawing his brother in when necessary but never revealing to anyone but himself his true intent. One truly likes Edward, and wishes that he had a nobler advisor than Richard.

Though Richard is definitely the villain of the piece (with Mord as a physical extension of his antagonism), he is not thoroughly evil. He exhibits a genuine affection for the woman he loves, and while we abhor his vile deeds, we also admire his cunning and even feel a pang of pity for this brilliant but misguided man.

Little fault can be found with Rowland V. Lee's grand direction. Though creating a lavish spectacle filled with costumed extras, Lee does not neglect any attention to detail. As the herald mounts the execution platform, for example, the man casually reaches out to the body-sized wicker basket lying on the stage's corner to flip open the lid, readying the container for its imminent use. With a small but forbidding gesture, Lee adds a subtle shudder to the somber scene.

Tower of London sports more than its fair share of thrilling battle scenes, all wind and rain and clashing swords. Lee utilizes a montage of images (men swarming over a hill, knights battling hip-deep through a muddy stream) to create a sense of chaotic urgency, heightened by the driving rain and sounds of trumpets mixed with the clang of metal and the screams of dying men. (The director had great difficulty in shooting these sequences. Three hundred extras were there ready for battle only to have their cardboard helmets and shields disintegrate under the onslaught of the rain machines. Lee finally overcame these obstacles by filming small bands of men fighting and transposing them against a background of battle scenes already shot to create the montage effect.)

Though Price characterized his director as "fun and adventurous," Rowland V. Lee apparently took

The Duke of Clarence (Vincent Price) confronts King Edward IV (Ian Hunter) in 1939's *Tower of London*.

his job very seriously. "Every time a director looks through his camera lens," theorized the filmmaker in a studio publicity piece, "he is looking directly into the eyes of millions upon millions of people all over the world... The vast audience is countless times greater than all the persons who saw and heard Moses, Buddha, Jesus, Mohammed and all other prophets combined. What a privilege! What an obligation!" With *Tower of London*, Lee fulfilled his obligation admirably.

Basil Rathbone was forced to decline a principal role in RKO's 1939 remake of *The Hunchback of Notre Dame* due to his Universal commitments. *Notre Dame*'s loss was the *Tower*'s gain, as he gives a vibrant performance to bring the character of Richard to full malevolent life. Rathbone's steely gaze and black eyes are like the stare of a snake. In an early execution scene, his gaze never wavers as the headsman's ax falls, though his eyes seem to glitter evilly and flicker with excitement while a barely detectable half-smirk deepens on his cold countenance.

Though for the most part a forbidding figure, Boris Karloff gives Mord a soul nonetheless. With gestures and hesitations at the murder of the young nephews, for instance, Karloff imbues his character with some small sympathy. When Mord picks up the young Prince fallen asleep at his prayers, the sleeping child's arm trustingly goes around the executioner's neck. At this, Karloff's face softens slightly and one can almost see the compassion struggling behind his eyes—before he again sets his face grimly and forcibly hardens his heart. For a brief moment, Karloff shows the man beneath the brute, adding a key dimension to his despicable character.

Vincent Price's supporting role as the Duke of Clarence offered the fledgling screen actor a chance to stretch his histrionic muscles—and stretch he did. Though on-screen for only about one-tenth of the film's 92-minute running time, Price manages to make an impression as the shiftless, pouting Clarence. In his very first scene, the actor establishes his character's sulky yet explosive nature (as well as defining the me-against-them attitude he holds toward his two siblings—a sentiment obviously reciprocated by them as well). While Clarence watches Edward and Richard sparring with halberds, a wild swipe from Richard's weapon narrowly misses his head. "Careful Richard, you *swine*!" shouts Clarence, "I think you meant that for me!" Afterwards, Clarence goes to Edward and complains, "Edward, did you see Richard try to brain me?" Price edges his adult indignation with the whiny tattletale tones of an outraged baby brother—a peevish attribute the actor emphasizes in several scenes.

In another sequence, the foppish Clarence strokes a poodle while he verbally spars with Richard. At this point, Price's half-lidded eyes look like those of a reptile, visually emphasizing the man's scheming and untrustworthy nature. When Richard turns a threatening gaze on Clarence, Price reveals his character's thinly veiled cowardice by inadvertently pulling back in his chair and clutching the dog in front of him—almost like a shield.

Price adds yet another facet to Clarence's character when Edward awards Richard's new bride some land previously held by Clarence. As the indignant brother, Price is at first hotly petulant, shouting "That isn't fair!" with lower lip extended and eyes flashing in anger. But when Edward proves unbending, Price's face goes hard and his eyes narrow. A bit of steel creeps into his voice as he warns in low tones, "You'll be sorry." Unlike his previously pouty protests, this ominous, determined warning carries real strength, transforming Clarence from a harmless, whiny bore into a real and significant threat—one with which Edward (and especially Richard) must now deal.

Next, when Clarence entices a group of lords in a tavern to back his treasonous claim to the throne, Price's smooth voice and smiling promises cement his character's position as someone to take seriously. The actor's silky charm serves him well here (as it would in so many of his later performances) as he infuses Clarence with a hint of the devious pleasure his screen villains would so often convey.

Price's big scene (lasting nearly four-and-a-half minutes—half of his total screen time) comes when an angry Richard challenges Clarence to mortal combat, even offering to use Clarence's "beloved wine" as the weapon. Laughing with giddy enthusiasm, Clarence accepts the challenge, gloating, "You haven't the liver of a first-class wine-bibber!" During the drinking bout, Price plays Clarence as a man in his element, obviously enjoying himself as he laughs into his cup while his brother labors painfully to quaff yet another flagon. Even after Richard passes out and Price titters triumphantly, "I've won!", he takes yet *another* drink—just for the pleasure of it.

This boisterous jocularity quickly dies in his throat, however, when Richard raises his head and fixes his wine-clouded-but-hate-filled gaze on Clarence. Price's demeanor abruptly changes to a near-panic as he cries, "Richard—Richard you promised!" his voice high and cracking with fear. (Richard had assured his suspicious sibling that "Malmsey will be the only weapon used" in their "duel.") Emotions surge forth, and Price's frightened face suddenly darkens with anger. "Richard, you swine!" he spits as he lunges across the table at his brother, who with one hand sends him crashing to the floor—where Clarence lies unconscious until Mord arrives to help Richard drop him into a vat of malmsey wine to drown. (Ironically, Richard *does* keep his promise.)

"Vincent Price is excellent as the Duke of Clarence," opined *Variety*.

"Vincent Price is excellent as the weakly Duke of Clarence," opined *Variety*. Indeed, Price's brief-but-effective characterization brings to life this childish and despicable—yet very dangerous—man, who wears his emotions not only on his sleeve but stamped upon his expressive face as well.

"I saw [*Tower of London*] again only recently and found it ponderous but interesting," Price himself offered years later (to *Universal Horrors* authors Michael Brunas, John Brunas, and Tom Weaver). "The drinking match was all ad-libbed and had to be done in a very few shots to heighten credibility. We shot it in one day."

For Vincent Price, *Tower of London* proved a happy introduction to big-screen horror, and he held his two "horror" co-stars in high regard. "Boris was a great professional," Price told *Filmfax*'s Gregory J.M. Catsos. "I was very fond of him. He was a man who loved his work and knew exactly what he was doing. Off the set, he was a very funny man." Basil Rathbone "was an intelligent person and a brilliant actor."

In a letter to Cynthia Lindsay (a close friend of the Karloffs), published in her book *Dear Boris*, Vincent Price wrote a tribute "to one of the few (very select) of my Hollywood life I'd even care to mention. Boris came into it early on—my second or third film, *Tower of London*, and he and Basil Rathbone introduced me to a kind of joyousness of picture-making I too seldom encountered in the hundred films that came later."

Price's fellow actors returned the affection. As Rose Hobart (who played Richard's love interest, Anne Neville, in the film) observed years later in *Universal Horrors*, "Why [Boris Karloff] and Vinnie Price should end up as monsters when they're two of the gentlest people I've ever known is incredible."

Often unfairly overlooked by the strict "horror" fan, *Tower of London* remains a grand historical epic boasting intense performances from two horror favorites of the time, Basil Rathbone and Boris Karloff, and enough blood and thunder to please any genre fan. As an added bonus, it also sports an effective early turn from the screen's *future* number-one bogeyman, Vincent Price, in a role very different from those he would come to play…

Things had definitely changed in the near-quarter century since Universal's 1939 production—including big-screen horror. By the late 1950s and early 1960s, the classic Teutonic-style horror spearheaded by Universal had largely given way to invading aliens and mutant bugs. Golden horror icon Bela Lugosi was dead, while the two aging horror stars of the original *Tower of London*, Boris Karloff and Basil Rathbone, found themselves appearing in puerile produc-

Price advanced from supporting player (Clarence) to lead villain (Richard) when Roger Corman took a (low-budget) stab at historical horror by remaking Universal's *Tower of London*.

tions like *The Black Sleep* (1956), *Frankenstein 1970* (1958) and *The Magic Sword* (1962)–when they could get movie work at all.

One *Tower of London* alumnus, however, found himself a hot horror property since his watershed year of 1958–which saw Vincent Price starring in both *The Fly* and *House on Haunted Hill*, two highly successful genre entries. In rapid succession, Price confirmed his "Master of Menace" title with appearances in *Return of the Fly* (1959), *The Tingler* (1959), *The Bat* (1959), *Master of the World* (1961), and the beginnings of the Corman/Poe cycle: *The Fall of the House of Usher* (1960), *Pit and the Pendulum* (1961) and *Tales of Terror* (1962).

Indicative of his rise to terror prominence was Price's advancement from supporting player (Clarence) to lead villain (Richard) when Roger Corman took a (low-budget) stab at historical horror by remaking Universal's *Tower of London*.

"[Writer] Leo Gordon and I were trying to come up with a variation on that genre—not to do Edgar Allan Poe," related producer Gene Corman (brother of Roger) to interviewer Tom Weaver, "because it seemed to me that Vincent Price had done enough of those. We were looking to find another venue; we talked about Nathaniel Hawthorne, and three or four other ideas. Then I said to Leo, 'Why don't we go to Shakespeare and see where that takes us?' *MacBeth* didn't serve us, but the story of *Richard III* did. So that was how that came about—we were exploring the same genre, but a different author." (Interestingly, a significant theme from the "unserviceable" *Macbeth* did ultimately creep into the *Tower of London* scenario—the torment of inescapable guilt.)

With their subject and star chosen, Corman and Gordon needed financial backing. Over at United Artists, independent producer Eddie Small had been greedily eyeing AIP's substantial profits on their Price/Poe series. At the time, however, Vincent Price had an agreement with AIP that he not make a Poe movie for any other studio. Small apparently saw the films more as Price pictures than Poe productions and so jumped at the idea of backing a small-scale (non-Poe) Vincent Price costume horror movie in an effort to capitalize on the AIP films. As insurance, in addition to Price, Small also signed Gene's brother Roger to direct, thus keeping the Corman/Price team (which was experiencing so much success with the Poe series) intact. "Eddie liked the Poe films," related Roger in *The Films of Roger Corman* by Ed Naha, "and wanted to bankroll a similar picture. He figured the *Tower of London* story would be fine. I said sure. I wasn't doing anything at the time."

"I'd been to London," commented frequent Corman writer/actor Leo Gordon (*The Wasp Woman, Attack of the Giant Leeches, The Terror*, etc.) in Mark Thomas McGee's *Roger Corman, the Best of the Cheap Acts*. "The damn Tower. I had a feel for it. I'd have liked to have had Basil Rathbone but Rathbone wasn't to be had, you know."

In any case, Rathbone had already had *his* turn back in 1939, and this time it was Vincent Price in the 15th-century driver's seat.

"Recent roles in hit horror pictures, including the successful series of Poe translations to the screen... prove that Price is right for his latest role," began a *Tower of London* pressbook article. "Such experience in raising the hackles on the audience's collective neck was the warm-up for his portrayal of Richard the Stonehearted.

"'Every trick of dastardly I ever learned,' Vincent says, 'was preparation for my role in *Tower of London*. Then we added some new, diabolic devices to fill out Richard's character as one of the 10 meanest men in the world.

"'I'd have to live in a fortress and drive to work in an armored car if people thought I was as horrible as the character I portray,' Price said. 'I'm grateful that people recognize the difference between me and Richard, for instance, and I'm glad that I'm one of the villains audiences love to hate.'"

First announced in February 1962 as *A Dream of Kings*, the film (retitled *Tower of London*) began shooting in mid-March.

"The Tower of London, a monument to the corruption of the soul..." begins the narrator (omnipresent 1950s voice-over artist/actor Paul Frees) at the film's opening. What follows is a tale of murder and ghosts and conscience, in which Richard kills his brother, his political rivals, his nephews and (accidentally) even his own loving wife—with his own hand this time. (Since this version dispenses with the extraneous character of Mord the executioner, Richard must do his own dirty work.) In another change from the earlier film, the ghosts of his victims appear to Richard (or at least are conjured up out of his own guilt-riddled mind) to bedevil his existence and ultimately lead him to his death at the battle of Bosworth.

As might be expected, Corman's remake comes nowhere close to the earlier film in production quality; but then the 1939 version was a relatively high-priced effort ($580,000) from a major studio whereas Corman's project was a low-budget (less than $200,000 25 years later!) independent entry. (Corman even borrowed some of the original's battle footage to flesh out his minimalist fight scenes.) The tones of the two films are miles apart as well, the earlier version being a historical melodrama with horrific overtones while the latter focused on the themes of madness, guilt, and death—more in the vein of Edgar Allan Poe than medieval history (undoubtedly intentional, considering the personnel involved).

Corman's proved the more intimate of the two, with the weight of the film resting on the humped shoulders of Vincent Price (who, unlike in the earlier film, appears in nearly every scene). In contrast to Rathbone's calculating and remorseless machiavellian, Price plays Richard as a man who tortures and murders to achieve his ends yet suffers from his own conscience to the point of madness. Even more so than in the first version, the role of Richard in the Corman film is a fascinating one, with the script portraying him as a man who knows what is right and what is wrong, but chooses the path of evil anyway. "Is it what men do that darkens the sky, or do the skies blacken the souls of men?" asks this reflective villain (rephrasing the age-old "nature vs. nurture" question). This makes Richard a much more intriguing figure, one who is

"'Every trick of dastardly I ever learned,' Vincent says, 'was preparation for my role in *Tower of London.*'"

not totally evil but who embraces it nonetheless and therefore orchestrates his own destruction. Richard has a conscience, and out of it he creates his own guilt-ridden hell by conjuring up the ghosts of his victims to torment him. As a morality play, the message could not be clearer: No one, no matter how corrupt, can truly escape his/her own conscience. And in the end, despite the somber, often brutal trappings, the film delivers an upbeat message (perhaps hidden under the surface but there nonetheless): That Man, despite his savagery and cruelty, is basically good, and this goodness will triumph in the end—whether it be by love... or by self-punishment meted out by one's own mind.

Praiseworthy missives aside, this *Tower of London* fails to live up to its potential. The script is structured so that the film will rise or fall with the performance of Vincent Price in the pivotal role of Richard (who is the focus of nearly every scene). Though at times Price sublimely points the production heavenwards, it never quite takes wing—due to that actor's uneven playing.

"I had done one Shakespearean play in my life," revealed Vincent Price in *Scarlet Street* magazine. And yes, it was *Richard III*. (The play, which lasted only 15 performances at the New York City Center Theater in December of 1953, starred Jose Ferrer as Richard and Staats Cotsworth as the Duke of Clarence. Also in the cast were Maureen Stapleton [later of TV's *All in the Family*] and Tom [*I Married a Monster from Outer Space*] Tryon. Price played the Duke of Buckingham.)

In the Corman film, Price sometimes acts as if he were back treading the boards, playing to the balcony's back row, indulging in overblown arm-waving, lip trembling and histrionics that lessen the impact that a more subtle performance could have generated. He too often relies, for instance, on a near-imbecilic half-grin—mouth open, one corner of his fleshy lips curled upwards—to portray both confusion and terror when confronted with his ghosts. The blame in part should rest with Roger Corman, never noted as an actor's director, who failed to properly rein in the actor when he should have. ("He was very creative," commented Price of his director in *Cinefantastique* magazine, "but more concerned with the story and effects than the actors. He hired actors whom he thought knew what they were doing.") A subtle straight performance is certainly not beyond Vincent Price, as he's demonstrated on many occasions (director Michael Reeves, for example, got one for *Witchfinder General*, though by all accounts he had to fight for it).

This is not to say that Price spoils this particular cinematic broth. Far from it; as Price's *Tower of London* co-star Michael Pate told interviewer Tom Weaver, "Any Price performance is always worth seeing," and the actor spices his particular brand of ham with dashes of evocative subtlety that ultimately saves this celluloid entree.

In the opening sequence, for instance, when the dying Edward names his brother Clarence as Protector of the Realm rather than Richard, Price's reverentially bowed chin snaps up and his face hardens into an almost stoic mask. He grasps Clarence's shoulder in recognition, saying, "Clarence my—dear brother," with just the slightest of pauses between "my" and "dear," subtly suggesting the effort it took to say and the contrary sentiment lurking beneath.

Price shines during the scene of Clarence's murder. In the wine cellar, Richard and Clarence talk of their childhood. "We were so different," marvels Richard, "yet our love for each other was the same." Clarence warmly answers, "That, at least, will never change." At this Price adds quietly, contemplatively, "as long as we both shall live." The actor's voice goes low and smooth, almost wistful in its tone yet carrying an ominous undercurrent. A moment later Richard plunges a dagger into his brother's back as they embrace.

Even in this first act of violent treachery, Richard knows the evil he commits and, as his brother dies in his arms, pleads, "Don't blame me Clarence, blame Edward's choice." By shutting his eyes tight and letting his head droop slightly—seemingly in shame—even as his hand pushes the dagger deeper, Price foreshadows the self-loathing to come—even as his words try to shift the blame.

In another sequence, Richard's aged mother displays her disdain for him. "You think I am not [capable of love]?" demands Richard. "You think my affection is as *warped* as my back?" Price's wounded, almost accusatory tone, tinged with anger and self-pity, provides handles of insight and sympathy that the viewer can readily grasp to draw him or herself into the plight of the complex character of Richard III.

When the ghosts of Richard's murdered nephews entice him over to the edge of the battlements, his faithful retainer stops him just in time. "Why did you stop me?" Richard implores. "They wanted to play with me; they won't wait." Price's voice is a mixture of confusion and longing (for lost innocence?) that inspires genuine pity.

In the end, Vincent Price provides a larger-than-life portrayal, sprinkling his wild-eyed, open-mouthed, full-blooded delivery with moments of subtlety and emotion. It's an enjoyable performance without doubt, but an uneven one.

"Horror, to a large extent," commented Roger Corman (in *Cinefantastique*), "has to do with loss of control. There's crude horror, which is just brutality, but there is a more subtle horror, which represents a higher intelligence, a higher sensitivity, a mysticism which can take over. I felt Vincent was very good at portraying that. Being a cultivated man, he was able to portray a person of intelligence, of sensitivity, of sensitivity carried beyond obsession."

"I thought Vincent was very good in *Tower of London*," opined producer Gene Corman. "It seemed that he had a real feeling for that period, and for that character. I kind of liked that film, and I know Vincent was always pleased with that performance."

Co-star Michael Pate, on the other hand, felt that Price's portrayal "doesn't rank with some of his other, incredibly wonderful performances... His style is totally unique." Indeed.

As a setting for Vincent Price's histrionics, art director Daniel Haller's somewhat cramped but grimly evocative sets greatly add to the visual power of the film. The wonderful castle

Despite its flaws, 1962's *Tower of London* is still an entertaining movie, filled with intrigue and shock and bizarre situations.

interiors, for instance, are full of long corridors, billowing curtains and dank dungeons. Not so wonderful, however, are the obvious studio-bound exteriors of papier mache forests and the unconvincing Tower model employed for long shots (which only serve as blatant visual reminders of the film's constraining budget).

The script contains many effective touches, such as having Richard attack and strangle one of his ghostly tormentors, only to find the neck of his loyal wife in his hands—the one person he loved and the only one who ever loved him. He projected his guilt-conjured demons onto her, perhaps in a further bit of unconscious self-punishment. Unfortunately, the screenplay also presents an overabundance of lurid sequences as well, with a rather gratuitous emphasis on torture—the rack, whippings, even a hungry rat in a box placed over the head of a political rival (a horrific concept also used in George Orwell's *1984*)—that cheapens the picture's tone.

The film has an additional problem, one that a few more dollars could have easily alleviated. It greatly suffers from a lack of color, with the black and white photography making it seem an even smaller production than it actually was. Roger Corman apparently did not know it was to be shot in black and white when he signed on. He later said, "To my great surprise, I found that I was supposed to shoot the picture in black and white. Somehow, nobody had bothered to tell me that! I was flabbergasted... I shot the movie, but I think that it suffered from the lack of color... The film just didn't have the impact it could have had."

Despite its flaws, 1962's *Tower of London* is still an entertaining movie, filled with intrigue and shock and bizarre situations. More importantly, something worthwhile lurks beneath the garish surface. "He escaped the headsman's block, but he could not escape his own conscience." At least it's something to think about.

The two *Towers of London* served Vincent Price well. The first offered the fledgling actor a grand opportunity to hone his craft among seasoned professionals and to construct an effective "cameo" in his introduction to screen terror. The second provided a veritable one-man-show to the now veteran horror star, who took full advantage to barnstorm his way through the role, synthesizing both broad and subtle techniques into an entertaining whole that, while perhaps not his *best* work, effectively encapsulates Vincent Price's indomitable enthusiasm and style.

TOWER OF LONDON (1939)
CREDITS: Director/Producer: Rowland V. Lee; Screenplay: Robert N. Lee; Cinematography: George Robinson; Art Director: Jack Otterson; Associate: Richard H. Riedel; Set Decorator: R.A. Gausman; Editor: Edward Curtiss; Musical Director: Charles Previn; Orchestrations: Frank Skinner; Sound Supervisor: Bernard B. Brown; Technician: William Hedgcock; Gowns: Vera West; Assistant Director: Fred Frank; Technical Advisors: Major G.O.T. Bagley and Sir Gerald Grove; Universal; Released November 16, 1939; 92 minutes

CAST: Basil Rathbone (Richard, Duke of Gloucester); Boris Karloff (Mord); Barbara O'Neil (Queen Elizabeth); Ian Hunter (King Edward IV); Vincent Price (Duke of Clarence); Nan Grey (Lady Alice Barton); Ernest Cossart (Tom Clink); John Sutton (John Wyatt); Leo G. Carroll (Lord Hastings); Miles Mander (King Henry VI); Lionel Belmore (Beacon); Rose Hobart (Anne Neville); Ronald Sinclair (Boy King Edward); John Herbert-Bond (Young Prince Richard); Ralph Forbes (Henry Tudor); Frances Robinson (Duchess Isobel); G.P. Huntley (Prince of Wales); John Rodion (Lord DeVere); Walter Tetley (Chimney Sweep); Donnie Dunagan (Baby Prince)

TOWER OF LONDON (1962)
CREDITS: Director: Roger Corman; Producer: Gene Corman; Screenwriters: Leo V. Gordon, F. Amos Powell, James B. Gordon; Story by Leo Gordon and Amos Powell; Cinematography: Arch R. Dalzell; Art Director: Daniel Haller; Editor: Ronald Sinclair; Musical Director: Michael Anderson; Production Manager: Joseph Small; Costumes: Marjorie Corso; Makeup: Ted Coodley; Assistant Director: Jack Bohrer; Set Decorator: Ray Boltz; Sound: Phil Mitchell; Special Effects: Dialogue Director: Francis Ford Coppola; Modern Film Effects; An Admiral Pictures production released by United Artists October 24, 1962; 79 minutes

CAST: Vincent Price (Richard of Gloucester); Michael Pate (Sir Ratcliffe); Joan Freeman (Margaret); Robert Brown (Sir Justin); Bruce Gordon (Earl of Buckingham); Joan Camden (Anne); Richard Hale (Tyrus); Sandra Knight (Mistress Shaw); Charles Macaulay (George, Duke of Clarence); Justice Watson (Edward IV); Sara Selby (Queen); Donald Losby (Richard); Sara Taft (Richard of Gloucester's Mother); Eugene Martin (Edward V); Morris Ankrum (Cardinal)

[1] In fact, in mock trial arguments held at the U.S. Supreme Court on June 4, 1997, United States Supreme Court Justices William Rehnquist, Ruth Bader Ginsberg and Stephen G. Breyer acquitted Richard III of the murders of the two Princes.

[2] There have been numerous straight screen adaptations of Shakespeare's play, including 1955's *Richard III* (starring Laurence Olivier), Sir Ian McKellen's critically praised 1996 adaptation, Al Pacino's *Looking for Richard* (1996) and a recently re-discovered 1912 version starring Frederick Warde (believed to be the oldest surviving complete American feature film). For those wishing to delve more deeply into the fascinating history (rather than fantasy) surrounding Richard III, I recommend the book *Good King Richard* by Jeremy Potter (Constable, 1985) as one of the best and most balanced on the subject.

TALES OF TERROR (1962)
THE RAVEN (1963)
THE COMEDY OF TERRORS (1963)

by Paul Castiglia

Laurel and Hardy... Abbott and Costello... Hope and Crosby... Martin and Lewis... *Price and Lorre?!* It may seem odd to some to see Price and Lorre's names among this list of beloved comedy teams, but the very definition of the phrase "comedy team" has been open to debate. There are those who would argue that Laurel and Hardy and Abbott and Costello qualify while Hope and Crosby and Martin and Lewis—and for that matter television's Gleason and Carney—don't. Simply because they were performers and/or actors who just happened to team occasionally and didn't necessarily come from a comedy background (a great example of a present-day team who fit that bill is Jack Lemmon and Walter Matthau—who in addition to their pairings have a large body of work independent of one another in both the comedy and drama genres). The same argument could be leveled at Price and Lorre. Another way to look at it, however, is to ask yourself one very simple question: Did two or more performers act in concert with one another, sharing a considerable amount of screen time together, with the singular purpose of making the audience laugh? If your answer is a resounding yes, then as far as this writer is concerned, you've just enjoyed a comedy team—at least for the duration of the particular film or TV show you may be watching. And if you're enjoying Price and Lorre in one of their heralded outings, you're enjoying the horror genre's all time classic comedy *scream team!*

On top of the fact that people have differing views concerning who qualifies as a comedy team, lies another point: There are different *types* of comedy teams. The most common, and to many minds, the only proper teams are those consisting of a "straight man" and a "clown" (or buffoon, stooge, or patsy). The straight man is the character who more or less has a reasonable head on his shoulders. He is are responsible for leading his partner through a plot as well as providing "set-up" lines for the clown's punchlines. In addition to punchlines, the clown is also responsible for the wild detours he and the straight man may take. In other words, he has to completely screw up the hard work of the straight man and throw a monkey wrench into the works, insuring that they are no longer stuck in the straight man's boring plotline, but thrust into wild scenarios for the ultimate comic effect. The perfect example of a "straight man/clown" team is Abbott and Costello. Other teams that seem to fit the bill are Martin and Lewis and Hope and Crosby. But those teams show just how tenuous such labels could be, since Dean Martin and Bing Crosby (the "serious" crooners and love interests in most of their films) also contributed mightily to the comedy with verbal barbs or physical gags of their own.

Another type of comedy team is one wherein there is no clear-cut "straight man"—those teams where all parties can be equally funny—or equally inept. These include The Marx Brothers, The Three Stooges, and the preeminent comedy team, Laurel and Hardy. Many people have made the mistake of considering Laurel and Hardy a "straight man/clown" team, but they are clearly not. The misconception arises from the fact that Oliver Hardy would take "command" of whatever situation he and Stan Laurel were in. He appeared to be the "leader," calling all the shots. But notice where his take-charge attitude often led him: into (slapstick) harm's way!

American International presents
EDGAR ALLAN POE'S
TALES of TERROR
in COLOR
and PANAVISION
STARRING
VINCENT PRICE
PETER LORRE
BASIL RATHBONE
Special Guest Star DEBRA PAGET

"...and there was an oozing liquid putrescence, all that remained of Mr. Valdemar." --POE

"I had walled the black monster up within the tomb!" --POE

Laurel and Hardy themselves often admitted that, looked upon from a certain angle, Hardy's character was actually dumber than Laurel's: "The dumbest type of dumb guy there is—the dumb guy who *thinks* he's smart."

This leads us back to Price and Lorre. Were they a "straight man/clown" team or purely a funny team? Well, the truth is that in the three films in which they teamed, they were a little of both. Interestingly enough, they seem to be most evenly matched in the laugh department in their first team-up, *Tales of Terror* (1962). *The Raven* (1963) found a more subdued Price in league with Lorre's riotous character (who for a portion of the movie is actually the title character, due to a vengeful enchantment—but more on that later). Last but not least, *The Comedy of Terrors* (1963) brings us Price as a ruthlessly funny man (and I might add, a hilariously ruthless man!), while Lorre's turn as his assistant is a more sympathetic character. Even so, both actors manage to get laughs in all three films. We'll examine those films in a moment, after we take a look at Price and Lorre's overall accomplishments within the comedy genre.

Over an impressively lengthy career, Price's name, of course, became synonymous with horror cinema. But that was just one facet of his career. Many people have fond memories of the latter 25 years of Price's output—where a tongue-in-cheek Price could be seen on TV shows such as *Batman, Get Smart, The Brady Bunch* and *The Muppet Show* while also cavorting on the big screen in over-the-top and somewhat campy roles such as the title character in *The Abominable Dr. Phibes,* its sequel, *Dr. Phibes Rises Again,* and scorned Shakespearean ham Edward Lionheart in the scrumptious *Theater of Blood.* This was a period where Vincent's horror image was constantly lampooned—often with the actor's blessing and participation. In fact, the "king of horror rock," Alice Cooper—who had lapsed into self-parody as well—used Price to great effect as a morbid-but-merry master of ceremonies to his *Welcome To My Nightmare* TV special in 1975 and accompanying soundtrack album. And speaking of kings, let us not forget Vincent's "rap" in the "king of pop," Michael Jackson's song, "Thriller" (while performed by Price with earnest intent, how could it ever be taken seriously given its context in a song and video that are, regardless of what Mr. Jackson's intentions may have been, inevitably light and fluffy, with any potentially terrifying moments buried under the weight of all the pomp and spectacle as well as by what many consider Michael's odd persona). These are the types of performances which have endeared Vincent in the hearts of young and old alike as a friendly "uncle" type who has never really meant any harm and whose "threats" are not only idle, but in good fun as well.

What the general public may not be aware of, however, are Mr. Price's previous comedy outings. Even before being teamed with Lorre, Price took aim at moviegoers' funny bones with several notable performances. His very first film, in fact, was the romantic screwball comedy, *Service De Luxe,* wherein he has the lead role of an inventor who has vowed not to let a women control his life, and spends the rest of the picture fending off several chanteuses while trying to get his inventions off the ground. Chief among his other pre-1960s comedic gems are *Champagne for Caesar, Curtain Call at Cactus Creek* and *His Kind of Woman* (1951). In *Cham-*

pagne for Caesar, Price is a scream as a the president of a soap company sponsoring a quiz show where a contestant's winnings are creeping dangerously close to the value of the soap company itself! *Curtain Call at Cactus Creek* finds Vincent in a role he would find himself playing many times in the years to come: a ham actor! This time, it's in the Old West as Vincent heads up a traveling theatrical troupe performing the melodramatic saga, "Ruined By Drink" in all its deliriously drippy glory! Price immediately followed this portrayal with yet another "ham" role in *His Kind of Woman.* While not a comedy in and of itself, this film contains moments of high comedy from Vincent. A noirish crime drama vehicle for Robert Mitchum—the film also flirts with romance (as Mitchum flirts with Price's mistress, Jane Russell) and satire, as Vincent not only portrays an overzealous actor, but also gets to parody the type of swashbuckling roles he himself had played early on, as the actor attempts to become a "real" as opposed to "reel" hero! A film that is nearly un-categorical, much of its appeal lies in Price's tour de force comedic performance, which is in sharp contrast to the film's other elements. Another performance from this period that bears mentioning is Vincent's comedic voice-over as The Invisible Man in the closing scene of the classic horror-comedy, *Abbott & Costello Meet Frankenstein.* Of particular note is that his one line of dialogue resonates much more today *after* his many successive horror offerings than it ever could have when originally released.

As for Peter Lorre, he had a spate of turns as a supporting actor, playing quirky characters who, often more odd than comedic, occasionally served as comic relief just the same. In fact, his career was a bit more scattershot than Price's when it comes to chronology. Where Price would often get typecast in a string of similar roles after a successful picture, Lorre, with the exception of stints teamed with Sydney Greenstreet in crime thrillers (including, of course, such classics as *The Maltese Falcon* and *Casablanca* as well as the title detective in the Mr. Moto series, would jump genres more often. From his breakout role as the despicable child killer in Fritz Lang's classic *M,* to Raskolnikov in the filmed adaptation of the literary masterpiece *Crime and Punishment,* to a variety of parts in war movies, dramas and period pieces, Lorre had the opportunity to exercise his versatility in the first couple of decades of his career. He even directed a film, *The Lost One.* Ironically enough, two of his 1940s efforts foreshadowed his later horror spoofs with Price, namely *You'll Find Out* and *Arsenic and Old Lace.* In his final years, the comic aspects of his characters really came into fruition, first in adventures such as *20,000 Leagues Under The Sea, Around the World in 80 Days* (1956) and *Voyage to the Bottom of the Sea* (1961), then in his films with Price, and finally in his last two films, *Muscle Beach Party* (1964) and Jerry Lewis' *The Patsy* (1964), wherein he played a director of comedy films!

When American International Pictures and director Roger Corman launched their series of Edgar Allan Poe adaptations with Price in *The Fall of the House of Usher* (1960), they hit paydirt. The film was an enormous critical hit *and* performed well at the box office, insuring that movie audiences hadn't seen the last of these newfangled, usually far-from-faithful interpretations of stories from the mind of Baltimore's brooding bard. Following *Pit and the Pendulum* (1961), Corman enlisted Price to appear in not one but three Poe stories. Dubbing the anthology *Tales of Terror,* it began and ended on suitably creepy notes for a horror film: Price is eerily effective both as a beleaguered widower haunted by his un-dead wife in the opening tale, *Morella,* and in the closer, *The Case of M. Valdemar,* as a terminally ill man who is put into a trance by a doctor who just can't wait for him to die so he can get his surgical mitts around Price's wife! It is the middle segment, however, that makes this no ordinary sandwich. *The Black Cat* will always be remembered as the beginning of a wonderful teaming: Vincent Price and Peter Lorre—together! Sure, they were previously both in *The Story of Mankind* (1957), but in separate stories. Here now was a story they could share, and sink their teeth into with all the comic flair they could muster. It was a task they relished! And while it is the shortest of the projects they appeared in together, it is perhaps the richest in terms of their humorous performances, and therefore the one to which we'll pay the most attention.

The segment, actually inspired by Poe's *Cask of Amontillado* as well as (or maybe more than) *The Black Cat,* opens on the sight of a drunken Lorre staggering down the street. Right off the bat, we know we're in for comic delights as Lorre punctuates his inebriated state not only with body language, but facial tics and muttering asides as well. His quips are especially curt—delivered in a slur, but not incoherent, and quite clever and acerbic: "Why don't you watch where *I'm* going?!" he intones, as he stumbles into someone. The ever-expressive Lorre eyes are also in service, ever opening, closing, bulging. There has been much conjecture over the years as to how much of this performance—as well as Lorre's work in *The Raven, The Comedy of Terrors,* and his other films from this period—featured Lorre actually acting or being genuinely inebriated!

Following Lorre as he floats along the street is the title character, a black cat. The trail leads back to his flat, where his ever-patient wife is waiting. Inside the apartment, Lorre's lovable drunk shows a nastier side, as the unemployed slacker demands money from his wife so he can go back out and drink some more. She claims they have no money to spare, but he's convinced she's got it stashed away.

> "What about your sewing money?" Lorre asks.
> "We need it for food," she replies.
> "Food? That's exactly what I need it for—I *drink* my food!"

Exchanges such as this illustrate Lorre's ability to be extremely funny while simultaneously having more than a hint of pathos about him. To be sure, this was a time in Lorre's personal life when things were not going well—including substance, alcohol and diet abuse, so both his physical health and mental demeanor were affected. Don't get me wrong—Lorre's dialogue, whether scripted or ad-libbed, is delivered hysterically. However, you just can't help but feel that he's a pathetic character. It is this element that made Lorre so perfect for the type of lovable yet troubled sods that populated Richard Matheson's comedic screenplays. In a way, these characters are a more lighthearted mirror image of the ones Vincent Price played in Matheson's "serious" Poe films (which were the embodiment of the noble, perhaps romantic yet ultimately tortured soul with a skeleton or two in his closet and a dark spot in his heart). These conflicting emotions are also at the heart of Poe himself, so the spirit of Poe is there, if not always the content.

Fortunato (Vincent Price) is challenged to a wine tasting duel in *Tales of Terror.*

Of course, sewing money in hand, Lorre proceeds to drink it all away, culminating in getting (bodily) thrown out of a local watering hole. A parade of passers-by are accosted by Lorre, as he implores them to cough up their hard-earned cash so he can earn a hard-drinking rash! He doesn't even hide his intentions: "Could you spare a coin for a moral cripple?" is a typical inquiry. "Get away from me, you drunken fool!" is the typical response. Each rejection is punctuated by a juicy raspberry from the portly souse! This scene also contains a classic gem of a line that is both riotous and poignant, as Lorre angrily exclaims, "If I had a pistol...," then, quietly "...I'd probably sell it and buy more wine."

Fate plays a major role in any Poe story, even one that is as loosely "based" upon the source material as this one is. In this case, fate comes in the form of a "Wine Merchant's Convention" which Lorre stumbles across. A demonstration in "expert wine tasting" by Price is about to commence. Lorre is aghast at the notion that anyone could have a more intimate knowledge of the spirits of the grape than him, and challenges Vincent to a wine tasting duel! Once again, the high comic genius of Lorre resonates: "Afraid to try me, coward?" Then, almost as a delicious afterthought, his face contorts with an air of privileged femininity, and he slowly pronounces, "...poseur!," with all the pompousness of a French art critic!

Vincent is taken aback and brilliantly conveys his character's astonishment in a role that is classic Price. He once again lampoons the "aristocratic" sort he'd often played in dramas, with such an air of hoity-toity exaggeration, that it is clear that this material is being played as pure farce. Particularly amusing are Price's grandiose mouth "exercises" as he prepares to taste the wine. The actual tasting of the wine is just as flamboyant. Price and Lorre, in fact, use a comedic style that had more or less fallen out of favor with adult moviegoers of the time. The broad nature of their characters was always more prevalent in the theater and on radio, anyway, but if you examine them closely, you'll find that they are precursors to the frantic sketch comedy characters that arose in such ground-breaking 1970s TV programs as *Saturday Night Live, Monty Python's Flying Circus* and *Second City Television.*

LAWRENCE FRENCH: Later on, you had another drinking bout, this time with Peter Lorre, in *The Black Cat* episode of *Tales of Terror*.

VINCENT PRICE: Yes, that one scene of wine tasting was really something that has remained in people's minds. Peter and I played two drunks, but before we did it they brought in this very famous wine taster to show us how it was done. We enjoyed that enormously; we got very drunk in the afternoons (laughter). Roger really allowed us to comedy it up on that scene. I did it exactly the way (the wine taster) showed us, but added just a little bit more, and Peter was doing it the way they didn't do it, which made for a very funny scene.

To everyone's surprise, Lorre actually manages to match Price vintage for vintage in identifying the wines—even as he's way past the point of intoxication! His heights of delirium invoke memories of such classic Laurel and Hardy films as *Blotto* (1930), *Fra Diavolo* (*The Brother's Devil*) (1933), *Them Thar Hills* (1934) and *The Bohemian Girl* (1936). The main difference, however, is that Stan and Ollie almost never intended to get plastered!

Three sheets to the wind, Lorre is in no shape to walk home, so Price graciously accompanies his opponent, who at this point is so far gone he's referring to his new-found acquaintance as an old and dear friend! Once at Lorre's place, there is an immediate attraction between Vincent and Lorre's wife. This attraction is heightened as Vincent also gets on famously with the cat, admitting, "I have several of my own at home." In a matter of moments, Lorre inevitably passes out, and as Vinnie and wifey struggle to carry him to bed, a bond forms between them. A bond which (the audience left to fill in the blanks) goes beyond polite conversation. Joyce Jameson as Lorre's wife proves to be a real pro in Vincent and Peter's company, exuding innocence on the outside but burning need within—and played for laughs just the same.

Lorre himself fills in the blanks on his wife's affair when, returning early from another night of revelry, he spots Price leaving the premises. Waiting until after Vincent has gone, he walks in and confronts his wife, who admits the affair and announces her intentions to become Vincent's wife. Lorre has something else in mind, however...

Once again, Price and Lorre share the screen and fill it with rich, comic delights as Vincent answers Peter's "dinner invitation." They immediately begin imbibing the bubbly, with Price particularly giddy over the offerings. Another scene filled with hysterical Lorre asides, such as when he proposes a toast to Vincent's "long life," then immediately follows it under his breath with, "right now I have a better chance than you have!" As funny as it sounds, he's not kidding: After gulping enough "whammy juice" to down a pony, Price falls to the floor. It is a moment of pure slapstick, as Vincent's eyes roll and his face collapses in on itself. The choice of the screenwriter and the actors to play this with such lunacy only enforces the fine line between drama and comedy. Dialogue and body language require precision, and only the most skillful

Herringbone (Peter Lorre) imagines Fortunato and Annabel (Joyce Jameson) attacking him after he has walled them up in *Tales of Terror*.

writers with the best actors at their disposal can accurately distinguish between the two. This doesn't always happen, of course, which explains why so many so-called dramas are often unintentionally funny.

As he proceeds to seal Price and Jameson behind the wall, brick by brick, Lorre's deadpan barbs continue. He answers Price's incredulous pleas with yet another classic line: "Haven't I convinced you of my sincerity yet? I'm genuinely dedicated to your destruction!" Equally funny is the follow-up sequence where Lorre imagines Price and Jameson ripping his head off and tossing it like a football, as he screams, "Keep that cat away from my head!" Of course, this is a still a horror story, albeit a comedic *horror* story, so while the comedy is very black the tale still ends on a jarring note as the Black Cat exposes Lorre's crime to the authorities.

As it turns out, the *Black Cat* sequence proved to be the most popular of the three *Tales of Terror.* With that knowledge in hand, Matheson decided to dive head-first into comedy for the next Poe film, *The Raven,* and once again had the team of Price and Lorre at his disposal. Adding to the frivolity this time around were a young Jack Nicholson, a vampy Hazel Court, and one of the all-time horror greats, the inimitable Boris Karloff.

The film's opening is rather serious and melodramatic, hardly hinting at the high jinks to come, as a dour Price laments the absence of his beloved Lenore. The tone shifts gears as Price opens the window to let the raven in. Believing the bird to be a "dark-winged messenger from beyond," Price asks, "Shall I ever hold again that radiant beauty who the angels call Lenore?"

The solemnity is shattered by the bird's unexpected reply, courtesy of Lorre's voice-over: "How the hell should I know? What am I—a fortune teller?" Yes, folks, we've officially been launched into comedy—horror style, via Price and Lorre! This leads to a riotous scene where

Lorre barrages Price with a series of insults and demands that would make Don Rickles proud as he implores Price, who we soon learn is a sorcerer, to change him back to his human form. Even in the midst of Price's attempts to do just that, Lorre badgers him with sarcastic banter that is so fast and furious, it could very well take a whole book to record and analyze. Not to mention Lorre's in-between stage, wherein his transformation's only halfway complete, he helplessly—and hilariously—flaps the wings that remain on his human body! With the limited space afforded this essay, you are encouraged to track this film down and partake of this wonderful sequence yourselves.

One criticism that has been leveled at *The Raven* is that it contains only the barest of plots. But let's face it, how many films of the comedy teams mentioned earlier were heavily plotted? They, like the television sitcoms which followed in their wake, existed on the simplest of premises, and *The Raven* is no exception: Lorre wants revenge on Karloff for turning him into a bird (which he claims would never have happened, "If I was only sober, which I admit doesn't happen often"); while Price is trying to win back his wife, whom Karloff stole (Lenore wasn't dead after all!). Likewise, Karloff maintains a grudge against Price's family, as Vincent's father was always his chief rival in the brotherhood of sorcerers.

Once the unlikely duo decide to confront Karloff, an inspired bit of tomfoolery follows as Price encourages Lorre to dress warmly for their trip and offers him his choice of hat and cloak. For someone who has no wardrobe, Lorre sure is picky, and delivers his objections in quite a genteel fashion! There is such spontaneity and sparkle to this scene that it is hard to imagine it could ever have been scripted. It is likely that this was one of the famous Lorre ad-lib scenes, and it is also the sequence wherein Price's persona starts loosening up a bit, as he ties to keep pace with Lorre's clever improvisational inventions. Price allows himself to be overtaken by the comedy bug as a his manservant becomes obsessed and attacks him. Knocked out in a slapstick fight, he allows his eyes to roll back into his head. Once he's made that turn, Price alternates from the character's earlier serious leanings to one capable of quips and visual humor of his own.

Shades of Lorre's *Black Cat* character emerge as his son, played by Nicholson, arrives to drive them (via horse and carriage, of course) to Karloff's castle. Even before he becomes obsessed himself, Nicholson is a lousy driver, resulting in more classic Lorre insults and exaggerated faces.

Arriving at Karloff's castle, a wonderful set piece follows as the seemingly gracious Karloff treats his "guests" to dinner. Karloff's beautifully understated performance, suggesting a kindly old, cultured gentleman, is nothing short of brilliant comedy itself. It is easy to see how the characters may be deceived by him, even as we the audience sense it's an act from the start. But we're not the only ones who see right through him: The irascible Lorre is suspicious as well! This inevitably leads to more Lorre gyrations, as he challenges Karloff on the spot. The fit of mayhem that unfolds, as Lorre attempts to awe the room with the magic he's conjured, will make your sides burst. Incredibly, even at his advanced weight, Lorre was able to pull off not only facial but body distortions as well, with all the manic energy of rubber-limbed Jim Carrey! For his troubles, he winds up hocus pocusing himself right into thin air. We later learn it's all a ruse—a literal smokescreen thrown for his cover, as we discover he's really a rat who has sold Vincent out. The way the character is written makes you wonder if Matheson purposely injected personality traits which he knew Lorre would run off with, given his performance in *The Black Cat*. Namely, that of the crafty, conniving coward—a cousin to Daffy Duck, Bob Hope and George Costanza. Only pickled!

As previously mentioned, a recurring aspect of the Price/Lorre teamings is the contrast between them. Not only their height and weight differences, but the way they carry themselves and speak as well. As in *The Black Cat,* there are some wonderful verbal exchanges between them, that highlight not only their comedy chops, but really point out what fine, underrated actors they were. Witness Lorre deflating Price's ponderous pontifications as if with a single pin prick:

Dr. Erasmus Craven (Vincent Price) tries to help Dr. Adolphus Bedlo (Peter Lorre) in *The Raven*.

"Instead of facing life, I turned my back on it. I know now why my father resisted Scarabus—because he knew that one cannot fight evil by hiding from it. Men like Scarabus thrive on the apathy of others—he thrived on mine, and that offends me. By avoiding contact with the brotherhood I've given him freedom to commit his atrocities unopposed..."

"You sure have!" Lorre leaps in, in no uncertain terms. It is the perfect punctuation, reminiscent of the classic scene in Disney's *Pinocchio*, wherein the blue fairy tries to explain why the little puppet's woes have been mounting: "Perhaps you haven't been telling the truth, Pinocchio!" Official conscience Jiminy Cricket, staring at the tree trunk that used to be Pinocchio's nose, can only exclaim, *"Perhaps?!?!"*

The difference here is that Price rolls with the comedy punches, and with the same candor as Lorre, answers back: "I'm sorry!" But not as sorry as Lorre—who is soon turned back into a raven by Karloff!

Lorre's earlier magic tricks were but a teaser for the comic delights yet to come: a magical duel to the death between Vincent and Boris! It is in this segment that Vincent's goofy side shines once more, and the aging Karloff proves more than game for this test of not only their character's powers, but for the actors' abilities to make us laugh as well. In a modern day film, the actors might let the special effects wizards do all the work for them. But Price and Karloff come from a tradition of stage acting, and in Karloff's case, the silent screen, so the special effects are only half the battle. They are accompanied by wild gesticulations and facial tics that involve the audience and invite them to take sides, while simultaneously entertaining with their clever wit and invention.

Having vanquished Karloff, the film ends in Price's study, where Lorre is pushing his luck. Shooting off his wise mouth and offering his services (unsolicited, of course) as Price's right-hand magician, he once again pleads to be restored to human form. Price says he'll take it under advisement, but can only tolerate so much of Lorre's banter. With a wave of his hand, he commands, "Shut your beak!" It is a fitting ending for what still remains a first-class romp to this day. It is a testament to the actors, writers and directors that material such as this, attacked by the principals with such understanding and passion, survives as an undated farce sure to entertain generations to come.

The final film in the Price/Lorre oeuvre is *The Comedy of Terrors*. This time, we're actually treated to an original story *not* based on Poe, although it does contain a satirical homage as a drunken Vincent recites *The Raven* poem, albeit changing a few lines: "...dreamed of gently, gently rapping... rapping gently with a hammer on a baby's skull." This film begins right off the bat with a role reversal: Whereas Vincent was the reserved one in *The Raven* playing off Lorre's clown, Lorre is now subdued and subject to Price's antics. This even extended to Price's

LAWRENCE FRENCH: It must have been tough for (screenwriter) Richard Matheson trying to adapt Poe's poem *The Raven* into a script.

VINCENT PRICE: Well when Boris, Peter and I heard we were going to be in *The Raven* together we were really very excited, and we called each other up and Boris said to me, "have you read (the poem) lately?" and I said, "Yes" and he said, "What's the plot?" (laughter). Of course there is no plot. So we just had fun with it, and send it up. It ended up being a very funny black comedy.

LAWRENCE FRENCH: It's too bad you couldn't have done a few more pictures with Boris Karloff.

VINCENT PRICE: Yes, Boris has been gone some 20 years now, and I've been around and almost gone for nearly as long. I've always given him credit for an awful lot. He was really the first one, and he had a great pride in doing these pictures. I felt an enormous closeness as a friend, and a co-worker in Boris, and this marvelous sort of warmth as a human being. We used to go out to dinner in London, which was wonderful fun, because the two of us would walk into a restaurant and we would clear the place (laughter). We never had to make reservations, because we had our choice of any table! Then one time I got on an airplane to go somewhere, and people came up to me and said, "Oh Mr. Price, may I have your autograph," and I was very flattered, and finally one man came up to me and said, "Mr. Karloff I have always wanted your autograph." So I gave him Boris Karloff's autograph! (laughter).

character's fondness for getting drunk, a character trait shared by Lorre's characters in both *The Black Cat* and *The Raven*. And drunk he is, hurling insult after insult at his pretty, young wife. When told he only berates her when he drinks, Price responds with glassy cool: "We escape the unendurable however we can!" Although assuming the drunken mantle previously held by Lorre, Price's is a different sort of drunk. He is more eloquent, and while his barbs sting as much as Lorre's, his are made with the fanciful vocabulary of an educated man, while Lorre's drunks usually speak in the tongue of the Everyman. Price even admits he courted his wife to get a shot at her father's undertaker business. Meanwhile, Price's assistant Lorre holds a special place in his heart for the woman his boss so disdains.

One gets the notion that Price feels liberated after two films with Lorre where he remained restrained in his co-star's presence, not to mention the tortured souls he played in the various Poe films. Price really cuts loose this time, delivering his lines with the most severe sarcasm and venom: "What I wouldn't do to get her [his wife] down here as a customer!" he sneers as he peers into the coffin workshop. He also mugs and vamps much more than in previous entries, a style he would perfect a couple year's later on the *Batman* TV show as the egg-centric and egg-citable Egghead.

Once again, the film has a simple premise, but one which lends itself to great comic possibilities: faced with eviction, Price must raise funds, and since the undertaker business isn't exactly knockin' 'em dead, well, Vincent figures he and Peter better start doing the knocking to get those customers in those coffins!

Price and Lorre receive game support once again. Boris Karloff is back as Price's wife's seemingly deaf, decrepit father. Once again, he steals many scenes. Fellow character actor (and veteran of a few horror films, as well as the most famous of all Sherlock Holmes) Basil Rathbone tears the screen apart as a man who just can't quite seem to stay dead. It is a tour de force performance that also illustrates how underrated a comedy talent Rathbone was. Joyce Jameson is back and robust as ever as Price's wife and opera singer wanna-be. And last but not least, a crazy cameo by wide-mouthed Joe E. Brown as a Cockney cemetery keeper who just can't get over the fact that for a place filled with stiffs, there's sure a lot going on!

The mechanisms of this film's plot, more so than the others, force Price and Lorre to literally spend more time on screen *teamed up* in their endeavors. These scenes of the pair breaking and entering and attempting murder are among the most hilarious ever committed to film, and rate favorably with the best of Laurel and Hardy and Abbott and Costello for sheer verbal and visual virtuosity. For example, a staircase of one of their prospective victims is lined with statues of busts on every step. Just as in a Laurel and Hardy film, we see the gag coming, but even though it's been telegraphed, the site of Peter Lorre bumping into the first statue to topple each one in a domino effect still elicits laughter!

The laughable pompousness of Vincent's gentleman drunk is beautifully underscored in the scene that follows, as Vincent attempts to explain his services to the widow:

Waldo Trumbull (Vincent Price) checks to see if John F. Black (Basil Rathbone) is really dead in *The Comedy of Terrors*.

"Allow me Madame in this moment of your most desolate bereavement to lift from your sorrow laden shoulders the burdensome tasks..."

"What?!" the confused widow answers, her head reeling.

"I'll bury him for you," shoots forth Price, all manner of proper speech suddenly shut down as if by remote control!

The Comedy of Terrors does lack one element that made *The Black Cat* and especially *The Raven* so special. It sticks to a linear though amusing plot, and for the most part seems played as scripted, with little or no evidence of improvisation, which is a real shame after becoming accustomed to Lorre's delightful musings in the previous films. Still, Lorre is given some choice dialogue from time to time: "Why did I ever escape from prison—it was so peaceful there!" he laments.

The plot's stakes are raised when Vincent decides he'll kill two birds with one stone: By killing the wealthy landlord, the fee he'll attain from his estate will help pay off his debt, *and* the landlord himself will be off his back! Ah, but this is Basil Rathbone—the man who won't stay "dead!" He's also the man who won't let Shakespeare die, as he spends the rest of the film not only spouting olde William's soliloquies, but brandishing a sword as well! It is just what the doctor ordered, as a film with funny but murderous undertakers would be a horror film and not a comedy if the victims were all serious.

Lorre startles Rathbone, who seemingly succumbs on the bed, but Lorre is much more afraid of the sword-wielding fanatic, and falls out the window—landing right on top of Price! As if this visual wasn't enough of a nod to Laurel and Hardy, Price punctuates the scene with an emphatic exclamation: "A fine mess you've made of things again!"

LAWRENCE FRENCH: You must have enjoyed doing *The Comedy of Terrors* with Boris Karloff, Peter Lorre and Basil Rathbone.

VINCENT PRICE: Oh Yes! They were all divine people, with great senses of humor. We used to sit around and say very seriously, "How can we scare the little bastards!" (laughter). We'd say, "Let's do this, let's do that, let's do the other thing." We had a wonderful time. One time, one of the big magazines, *Look* or *Life*, sent out a reporter, to try and make fun of us. He came on the set and was really sort of grand you know, and when he saw that we were really enjoying making the picture, he wrote the most wonderful article about the joy we had in making something that was really pure entertainment. The premise for *The Comedy of Terrors* was really very funny. It shows you how simple comedy is. It's about a family of out-of-work undertakers. Now what do you do? You kill somebody! So you kill the richest man in town, who was Basil, and you have the most expensive funeral. That's all the plot was.

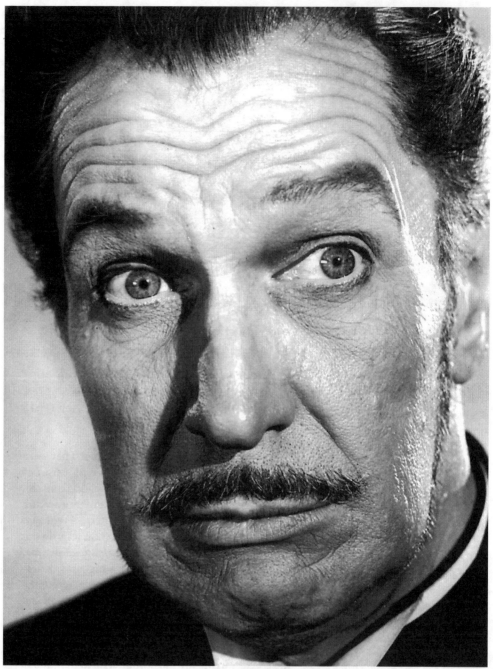

Vincent Price as Waldo Trumbull in *The Comedy of Terrors*.

The film becomes a test of wills, as Price insists on burying Rathbone while Rathbone insists on resurrecting himself over and over again, apparently a recurring condition which Rathbone's manservant is quick to point out to the ambivalent doctor. Price and Lorre then get to shift gears from Laurel and Hardy to Abbott and Costello, with Lorre taking on the jittery Lou Costello role and Price assuring him, à la Bud Abbott, that there is nothing to be afraid of. This also effectively changes the tone of the film, as what started out as a black comedy becomes pure burlesque. It all leads up to perhaps the longest death scene in movie history, as Rathbone, down for the count, keeps re-emerging to spout one last line of Shakespeare... and then some!

This isn't the last showdown, as Price appears to kill his wife, and then Lorre. But appearances can be deceiving—they end up more alive than Rathbone on a bad night! It's Karloff, however, who gets the last laugh and simultaneously plunges the film back into black comedy. All throughout the picture, Vincent has threatened to feed Karloff the vial of poison he keeps in his pocket, calling it his "medicine." Karloff, seeing Vincent crumpled at the bottom of the stairs, figures he could use a good drink: "Drunk again, eh? What you need is a dose of your own medicine. You keep it in your waistcoat, don't you?" Vincent unwittingly gulps down the toxic fluid, as Karloff offers, "...that ought to take care of you nicely!" Several minutes later, Rathbone sneezes—punctuation as afterthought!

The Comedy of Terrors is a nice, amusing finale to the Price/Lorre trilogy. However, despite the word "comedy" in the title, it is perhaps the weakest of the three, and not ageless like *The Raven*. Still, Price and Lorre should be commended for treading on ground where so many geniuses tread before. They prove that they are just as qualified to play on that field. If you reacquaint yourself with their films, you may agree—Price and Lorre, though short-lived, were one of the funniest comedy teams of all!

TALES OF TERROR (1962)
CREDITS: Producer/Director: Roger Corman; Screenplay: Richard Matheson (Based on Stories by Edgar Allan Poe); Cinematography: Floyd Crosby; Production Design/Art Director: Daniel Haller; Set Decorator: Harry Reif; Music: Les Baxter; Editor: Anthony Carras; Wardrobe: Marjorie Corso; Makeup: Lou LaCava; Executive Producers: James H. Nicholson and Samuel Z. Arkoff; AIP 1962, 85 minutes; color and Panavision

CAST (for *The Black Cat* segment only): Vincent Price (Fortunato); Peter Lorre (Montresor Herringbone); Joyce Jameson (Annabel); Wally Campo (Bartender); Alan DeWit (Chairman); John Hackett (Policeman)

THE RAVEN (1963)
CREDITS: Producer/Director: Roger Corman; Screenplay: Richard Matheson; Cinematography: Floyd Crosby; Art Director: Daniel Haller; Set Decorator: Harry Reif; Music: Les Baxter; Editor: Ronald Sinclair; Wardrobe: Marjorie Corso; Makeup: Ted Coodley; Special Effects: Pat Dinga; Raven Trainer: Moe Disesso; Executive Producers: James H. Nicholson and Samuel Z. Arkoff; AIP 1963, 86 minutes; color and Panavision

CAST: Vincent Price (Dr. Erasmus Craven); Peter Lorre (Dr. Adolphus Bedlo); Boris Karloff (Dr. Scarabus) Hazel Court (Lenore Craven); Olive Sturgess (Estelle Craven); Jack Nicholson (Rexford Bedlo); Jim Jr. (The Raven)

THE COMEDY OF TERRORS (1963)
CREDITS: Director: Jacques Tourneur; Writer/Associate Producer: Richard Matheson; Cinematography: Floyd Crosby; Production Designer/Art Director: Daniel Haller; Set Decorator: Harry Reif; Music: Les Baxter; Editor: Anthony Carras; Costume Supervisor: Marjorie Corso; Makeup: Carlie Taylor; Hairstyles: Betty Pedretti, Scotty Rackin; Special Effects: Pat Dinga; Producers: James H. Nicholson and Samuel Z. Arkoff; Co-Producer: Anthony Carras; AIP 1963, 84 minutes; color and Panavision

CAST: Vincent Price (Waldo Trumbull); Peter Lorre (Felix Gillie); Boris Karloff (Amos Hinchley); Joyce Jameson (Amaryllis Trumbull); Basil Rathbone (John F. Black); Joe E. Brown (Cemetery Keeper); Rhubarb the Cat (Cleopatra)

THE LAST MAN ON EARTH (1964)
by David H. Smith

By the mid-1960s, the rules for casting Vincent Price in a horror movie were almost as established as British common law, unwritten and yet completely understood.

Vincent Price became the Vincent Price audiences love (and most fans have fond memories of) in the 1960s. Even after having trod sound stages for more than 20 years, it was not until then he became, for a new generation who looked past his uppity Yale education and august London stage dues, the closest thing we in America had to a homegrown horror institution. He was, as *Variety* so pithily put it, "the rock-generation's Boris Karloff."

The 1960s, as everyone knows, were a turbulent time in which old traditions were exploded, establishments razed and consciousness raised. Every icon or symbol or embodiment of the status quo was subjected to ferocious scrutiny. Doubt was the watchword and questions hung like storm clouds in the air.

Into this culture of anxiety and revolution came director Roger Corman's adaptations of Edgar Allan Poe—films that were both tributes to the horror movies of years gone by and, at the same time, indicative of the changing tastes of the filmgoing public. They were both of their time and ahead of their time, praised by some and damned by others who were sure they recognized the claptrappings of kitsch.

Lost amid their sumptuous sets and costume design came another, very different Vincent Price vehicle, *The Last Man on Earth* (1964), one of the great ignored science fiction horror films of the 1960s. It was ill-received by the critics of the time despite the ingeniously original plot, done to death by others since. Nowadays, those same critics have rethought many of their earlier barbs, recognizing the movie's influence on the genre, and have grudgingly forgiven the budget's (and locale's) shortcomings.

It wasn't until 1969 and *Night of the Living Dead* came along that *The Last Man on Earth* was rediscovered after a fashion by horror film fans. But by then the momentum (and influence) of the later film was too unstoppable for fans and filmmakers to look anywhere but forward, much less back at what seemed by then to be just another chintzy Italian B-movie.

On looking at *The Last Man on Earth* today, with the benefit of hindsight, it is easy to see why 1964 audiences couldn't come to grips with the picture. Despite it being in black-and-white, more than anything it resembles a movie from the middle of the 1980s' cannibal zombie boom. In common with many of those pictures it has the same basic story structure (outnumbered normal people under siege from supernatural predators), which immediately brings to mind the plot of the later *Night of the Living Dead* (whose creators have always pooh-poohed a connection).

But, when compared to its horror film contemporaries, *The Last Man on Earth* is certainly a film that was ahead of its time. How odd that its origins, convoluted as they are, stemmed from a decade earlier.

Richard Matheson, born 1926 in Allendale, New Jersey, was already well regarded as a short story writer for the plethora of science fiction magazines flourishing in the mid-1950s (there were then about 35 genre magazines published regularly in the U.S.). With this resume, he sold his first novel *I Am Legend* to Gold Medal Books for a $3,000 advance; Matheson's writing career truly took off with the book's July 1954 publication. In that period of McCarthyism and the Cold War, Matheson's doomsday scenario was irresistible, the main thrust of the story being the question of the existence of the lone survivor of a bacteriological catastrophe.

The Shrinking Man soon followed, both as a book (1956) and, with the proviso he write the screenplay (thus gaining an entry into the film business), adapted to the big screen (1957), to similarly high acclaim. From there, Matheson would become increasingly recognized as one of the most significant modern creators of terror and fantasy in both fiction and film.

Despite its first-person title, *I Am Legend* is the third-person narrative of Robert Neville, who survives a viral plague which has turned everyone on Earth into a vampire but him. By day, Neville heads out in his station wagon, disposing of the corpses (slowpoke vampires!) lying about, visiting the local supermarket for fresh garlic bulbs, then going about the deserted metropolis hunting down and staking his fellow vampire-citizens. At night, he locks himself in his fortified suburban domicile to lathe wooden stakes for the next day's hunt. Outside, the undead stalk the deserted streets, beckoning him to join their ranks ("...crawling, shambling through empty streets whimpering, pleading, begging for his blood!" said the movie ads).

The element of horror almost overrides the perfunctory science fiction base of *I Am Legend*. Combining the folkloric conventions of vampirism with the sleek scientific notions of modern day has often produced truly mixed literary and cinematic results in writers' and producers' attempts to satisfy monster-lovers of all stripes.

But as the horror and science fiction genres came to overlap in the 1950s, few novels were as filmable as written as was *I Am Legend*. In *Horrorshows*, author Gene Wright remarked Matheson's novel "broke with the past and set vampires free (almost) of its ties with Christian mythology by providing a believable science fiction explanation for the malady." Philip Strick, in *Science Fiction Movies*, found it "a magnificent idea, repeating once more the Matheson theme of the beleaguered individual."

The dominant theme in Matheson's work has always been paranoia, whether imagined in Gothic or in science fiction terms. *I Am Legend* is, in its obsessive images of persecution, perhaps the very peak of all paranoid science fiction. Genre literate Leonard Wolf, in *Horror: A Connoisseur's Guide to Literature and Film*, examined the book and found it "a nearly classic example of the way in which a primordial image like the vampire can be eroded when it is put under the spotlight of contemporary rationalism."

But the novel also works on another, less obvious level. In *V Is for Vampire: The A-Z Guide to Everything Undead*, David J. Skal said Matheson's work "also provides a subtextual commentary on the anxious underside of American society in the fifties. Instead of the good life, Matheson gives us unlife."

Indeed, by the middle of that decade, America had become almost a mythical country of picket fences, strong families, upward mobility and well-placed optimism—but what did it all matter when, to survive, those pickets had to be driven into the chests of your bloodthirsty neighbors?

In 1957, England's Hammer Films was riding high on new success with horror and science fiction. Since 1935 it had been a small, relatively nondescript company making low-budget adaptations of popular British radio programs, as well as conventional comedy, crime and romantic stories.

Most of these movies were routine productions for domestic British consumption, often geared to the unsophisticated taste of the small-town populace. Hammer's fortunes teetered on the brink of solvency for years as the studio never strayed from this safe but unimaginative course. But a wildly successful 1955 film version (*The Creeping Unknown*) of the BBC's six-part TV serial *The Quatermass Experiment* convinced company head James Carreras there was money in horror.

Their fortunes turned and spirits buoyed, the next year Carreras and producer Anthony Hinds went for broke with an astonishingly successful rehash of the familiar Frankenstein tale. It introduced to international audiences Peter Cushing as the wan, cold-blooded doctor and Christopher Lee as his scarred, spastic creation. The die was cast for Hammer, and the company never looked back.

Hinds took out an option on *I Am Legend* and, recognizing Matheson's talent for writing scripts from Universal-International's *The Incredible Shrinking Man* (though shorn of three of its 81 minutes of running time for its release in England), offered the author $10,000 up front,

Robert Morgan (Vincent Price) keeps audio records of his vampire hunting.

passage and a generous £50-a-week allowance to come to London and adapt *I Am Legend* for the screen. Agreeing, Matheson completed his screenplay after a two-month sojourn and re-titled it *The Night Creatures*, feeling confident of another cinematic success.

Getting ahead of himself, studio head Carreras signed Val Guest to direct the *I Am Legend* project, recognizing Matheson's themes of science fiction paranoia had already been filmed to good effect by Guest in the first Quatermass sequel (*Enemy From Space*) earlier that year.

However, behind the scenes, Matheson's efforts fast came undone. Following procedure, Hammer submitted the script to the British Board of Film Classification for approval. The BBFC, still feeling skittish from its recent sanction of Hammer's graphic *Horror of Dracula*, took no chances and flatly turned down *The Night Creatures*. There were to be no second chances for the screenplay, no revisions made, no alterations allowed. If the movie was made as it was written, it would not be passed for exhibition in England.

Similarly, in December 1957, Geoffrey Shurlock of the Motion Picture Association of America raised doubts about the script's "overemphasis on gruesomeness," and submitted a detailed list of objections which included brutality, profanity, bad language and immorality.

Told of the censors' edicts, Matheson at first thought Hammer was being kind trying to spare his feelings about the filmability of his book, but later grudgingly accepted the truth. As recently as in a 1996 interview, he found Hammer's kowtowing to the BBFC and the MPAA self-contradictory. "Their Dracula films had much more violence. But who can argue with a censor?"

Thus, Carreras was forced to abandon the project (but retained the copyrighted title, eventually using it for Universal-International's American release of Hammer's lively and suspenseful, non-horror *Captain Clegg* in 1962).

Robert is attacked by one of the night creatures in _The Last Man on Earth_.

Since the script was commissioned, written, and paid for, but was ultimately unusable, Hammer sold it at a bargain price to an American associate they knew from their salad days. Robert L. Lippert, under the aegis of one of 20th Century-Fox's subsidiaries, had provided budget-conscious scripts and low-rent American stars—like Richard Carlson and Dan Duryea—and directors—like Sam Newfield and Reginald LeBorg—for Hammer productions.

In turn, Lippert had been given exclusive American distribution rights to these films. From 1951 till 1955, Lippert gave the American major studios acceptable second features to fill out their double features, albeit with limited appeal to U.S. audiences (though they sufficed as inexpensive late-night TV fodder as the decade progressed). Unfortunately for Lippert, the liaison dissolved shortly before Hammer's emergence as England's (and the world's) preeminent horror film factory.

Lippert kept his finger on the pulse of science fiction in the interim, serving as executive producer for _The Alligator People_ in 1959. Lippert had intended to shoot Matheson's script as early as 1959, going so far as to announce it in the trades with the exploitable (if inapt) title of _Naked Terror_. (As with _The Night Creatures_ and the waste not, want not philosophy of producers, that title was also eventually used for a completely unrelated movie, this time a 1961 feature "documentary" of the Zulu tribes of Africa... narrated by Vincent Price!)

However, budget-wise, for _The Night Creatures_ to be brought to the screen was beyond the meager means of Lippert's Screen Guild Pictures. In 1961 he decided to take advantage of the lower production costs in Italy and government subsidy incentives, and entered into a co-production agreement with Produzioni La Regina in Rome. Again, title shenanigans came into play, with parent company 20th Century-Fox opting to reuse their own _The Last Man on Earth_, a silent movie which had starred Earle Fox as the only fertile man living in a society ruled by women in various stages of undress. John G. Blystone directed this 1924 sexist fantasy.

Matheson was told at first that Expressionist director Fritz Lang was being sought to handle the project, and performed some rewrites to, in his estimation, make the script even better. By this point in Lang's life, however, the Austria-born director's failing eyesight prevented the contemplation of any film projects, and one has to suppose Lippert's chicanery may have served only to heighten anticipation and attract investors.

But, to meet the demands of the European unions and navigate the linguistic barriers faced by a "name" English-speaking star (a prerequisite for any sort of ka-ching at the U.S. box office), Lippert instead enlisted Ubaldo Ragona (who had directed only one other film, and that was back in 1958) to handle the Italian cast and crew, and hired Harvard-educated Sidney Salkow to supervise the U.S. version. And one guaranteed box-office star was available, whether he was appropriate for the part or not.

Because of the international success of American International Pictures' first two adaptations of Poe (*The Fall of the House of Usher* and *Pit and the Pendulum*) and of a Jules Verne novel (*Master of the World*), star Vincent Price was asked to appear in three movies filmed back-to-back in Italy (his contract with AIP nonexclusive), among them the stillborn Hammer project. Price, like some modern-day Maecenas, and then-wife Mary looked forward to spending an entire year in Rome. They would be free (when he was not summoned before the ponderous, non-synchronized sound Italian cameras) to explore the city's renowned ancient ruins and to go in quest of the country's art treasure-troves.

Price's other two films made overseas (*Queen of the Nile* and *Rage of the Buccaneers*), made with fellow Americans Jeanne Crain and Ricardo Montalban respectively, are of negligible interest to horror film fans (Price found the scripts absolutely awful even before embarkation). But of the three, *The Last Man on Earth* has emerged as one of the most hotly contested titles in the actor's filmography.

Price read and enjoyed the original novel, and was no doubt aware that other film luminaries were similarly impressed. No less a talent than Orson Welles had often said it was one of the most interesting ideas in the horror genre.

But even before the first scenes were shot, Lippert's penny-pinching would begin to take its toll, and the end result would suffer accordingly.

Still not satisfied with the script, Lippert brought in erstwhile movie and TV actor William Leicester to lend a hand with further revisions. With that, Matheson washed his hands of the project. He had his screen credit changed to "Logan Swanson," a composite of his mother-in-law's maiden name and the American version of his mother's last name. "I thought it was terrible," Matheson said of the script used. "I had written a good screenplay, but they had someone rewrite it and make it abysmal."

LAWRENCE FRENCH: When you did *The Last Man on Earth*, why did they change the setting to Rome?

VINCENT PRICE: They couldn't do it in Los Angeles, it would have been just impossible to do. It's based on Richard Matheson's story *I Am Legend*, and it's supposed to be Los Angeles after the atomic bomb. Well Los Angeles sometimes looks to me like the atomic bomb has already fallen (laughter). So we did it in Rome, which is as little like Los Angeles as is humanly possible. Funnily enough, the picture came off fairly well. I think it was better than *The Omega Man*, that Charlton Heston did later on from the same story. It had a kind of amateur quality about it. We worked in a studio that was so cold, that before each scene we had to go and take ice water in our mouths, so that when we talked you wouldn't see our breath. Seriously, it was that cold in Rome while we were filming. It was an interesting film, a very difficult story to make, to really make. It should be done as a great spectacular, just buy a city and empty it out.

It's far from that. In fact, given the budgetary constraints and production shortcomings, *The Last Man on Earth* is far better than it has any right to be.

Contrary to Matheson's dismissal, the movie follows the novel very closely (though compressing some events for running time's sake; e.g., the hero's finding and befriending a stray dog). Even now, while no faint praise, author Stephen King cites *The Last Man on Earth* as "an example of the ultimate political horror film."

Despite the visible drawbacks, *The Last Man on Earth* still manages to convey an atmosphere of despair. Regrettably, it replaces the paranoia of the original novel with maudlin stream-of-consciousness shopping lists ("I need more mirrors. And this garlic has lost its pungency.") and mawkish, middle-aged wistfulness ("This convertible would be nice. Probably handles well. But I can't think of comfort. There was a time I shopped for a car; now I'm looking for a hearse."). It's a mixed bag of a movie, to be sure, and a mixed blessing of results.

To its thespian undoing, Salkow (and Price) fall back on the tried and true, with the actor reverting to his trademark (by 1964 at any rate) wide-eyed, aghast double-takes, especially when his dead wife (Emma Danieli) shows up on his doorstep. Price's reaction comfortably if none-too-originally echoes his Francois Delambre (*The Fly*) at finding his miniaturized brother, Roderick Usher recoiling from his revived sister, or Prince Prospero (*The Masque of the Red Death*) pulling the hood off of Death and revealing... himself!

Rechristened "Robert Morgan" for the movie (a homonymous play on the word "morgue"?) and now a scientist (for faster plot exposition) instead of a garden-variety factory worker, Price's performance has always been the biggest bone of contention with fans of the novel and critics of the film. Extremes ranged from the contemporary *Hollywood Citizen News* review saying *The Last Man on Earth* contained "his most restrained performance in some time," to the modern-day and Steven Puchalski's *Slimetime* taking him to task for reaching "the hammiest heights of angst."

Why this dissent? As mentioned before, for better or worse, the image of Vincent Price was pretty much set in audiences' minds by this point in his versatile career. He was the haughty high-muck-a-muck, generally seen strutting about in an Inverness cape, attended to by regiments in medieval livery or riding imperiously by the proletariat in a horse-drawn carriage.

In filmgoers' eyes, Price did not seem the "Everyman" the titular role of *The Last Man on Earth* seemed to be crying out for. At a well-groomed, erudite 50 years of age, he was the antithesis of Matheson's envisioned scruffy blonde, unshaven, 30-something factory worker. Price's look was too dapper, his attitude too cultured, his delivery too refined. Audiences didn't expect (or want) to see Price refilling gasoline generators or hefting corpses into the back of a station wagon. Where were his minions when he needed them?

Nevertheless, Price's performance does have its proponents. Chief among them are genre film aficionados Dennis Fischer and Don Leifert. Fischer found Price's take on the role "powerful" and "low-key" in *Midnight Marquee* #49, sentiments shared by Leifert in the second issue of *Movie Club*. Leifert continued, "He was quite subtle on occasion, and [this] is a case in point." (Conversely, Phil Hardy, in *The Encyclopedia of Science Fiction Movies*, found the same "oddly low-key performance" unsatisfactory.)

The prolific Tom Weaver leapt foursquare to the actor's defense in *Cult Movies* #16: "The casting works better than the bad-mouthers like to admit. A more robust, 'conventional' leading man would look out-of-place spending his life scouring an urban wasteland for walking corpses."

Vincent Price fan Lucy Chase Williams championed his "resigned, restrained, matter-of-fact performance" in her exemplary *The Complete Films of Vincent Price*; later, in correspondence, Ms. Williams elaborated to me she thought Price "was wonderfully downbeat and, surprisingly, perfectly 'ordinary' in *The Last Man on Earth*: droopy shouldered, unshaven, lip curled, bored, his clothes just hanging on his large frame."

Evaluating the quality of performance of Price's co-stars is just as difficult, but for a very different reason: the unremarkable English dubbing of their parts. Fourth-billed Italian actor Giacomo Rossi-Stuart, usually anglicized in the U.S. as "Jack Stuart," was a veritable mainstay

Robert Morgan grabs Ruth Collins (Franca Bettoia).

of U.S.-imported Italian fantasy cinema. Among the actor's other genre films were starring roles in *Caltiki, the Immortal Monster* (1959), *Planet on the Prowl* (1965), *The Night Evelyn Came Out of the Grave* (1971), and *War of the Robots* (1978), along with many others.

As Morgan's friend, confidante and scientific collaborator (in life), the coifed and square-jawed Rossi-Stuart seems just as miscast as Price—he is the polar opposite of the Matheson description (a rotund Oliver Hardy look-alike). Returned from the grave, it is he who nightly beckons his old friend to slake his and his comrades' thirst.

Actress Franca Bettoia, despite her character's two-facedness, still manages to make her part a sympathetic one, as she nicely disguises her ulterior motive behind a facade of fear and apprehension at Morgan's (nonsexual) proposals of kinship. Bettoia is perhaps more known for her marriage to Italian leading screen personality Ugo Tognazzi than for her real acting on her part. Tognazzi was one of the leads in *La Cage aux Folles* (1978) and its two sequels. He and Bettoia were married from 1972 until his death.

Producer Robert L. Lippert did stack the deck in the movie's favor as much as he feasibly could. He commissioned a moody score from Poland-born Paul Sawtell, whose themes had already graced a wealth of Westerns and Tarzan movies, as well as several science fiction films from the 1950s, including *The Black Scorpion* (1957), *It! The Terror From Beyond Space* (1958) and *The Cosmic Man* (1959), to say nothing of his work on Vincent Price's two entries in the Fly trilogy of films. Sawtell also composed the theme to the Sunday night staple ABC-TV series *Voyage to the Bottom of the Sea* (1964-8).

Cinematographer Franco Delli Colli evoked some nice claustrophobic touches in Morgan's cluttered home (though the two years' worth of calendars scrawled by hand on the kitchen Sheetrock are a bit much—no blank paper to be found anywhere?), and made the litter- and

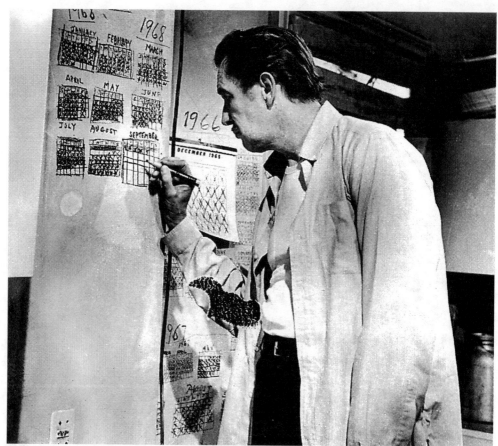

Following production of *The Last Man on Earth* (but before its U.S. premiere), Price returned to America.

body-strewn streets look suitably, post-apocalyptically deserted (filmed as they were in the wee hours of the morning). In his long career, Delli Colli would return to the genre on occasion, acting as director of photography for such horror movies as *The Night Child* (1975), *Frozen Terror* (1980) and *Revenge of the Dead* (1983).

Based on the pressbook's acknowledgments, Lippert probably assumed the movie's stateside release would be managed by 20th Century-Fox (the studio did handle the foreign distribution, however), but he was in for a rude awakening. Both of Price's other Italian films played U.S. theaters before *The Last Man on Earth* was picked up by AIP, which put it out on a doublebill in May 1964 with a re-release of the company's British chestnut *Circus of Horrors* (1960). Here that grisly thriller was on its third go-around (it had already been re-released once before, paired in 1962 with a re-release of the Grand Guignol *Horrors of the Black Museum* [1959]). In black-and-white and with all its poor technical work, *The Last Man on Earth* paled beside its garish co-feature's bold hyperbole of "Spectacular Towering Terror!"

(Someone in the AIP publicity department was asleep at the switch, missing out on a golden marketing opportunity by not pairing it with Filmgroup's colorful 1960 postnuclear love triangle, *The Last Woman on Earth*, a two-week wonder made in Puerto Rico by Roger Corman for many of the same cost incentives that lured Lippert to Italy.)

Following production of *The Last Man on Earth* (but before its U.S. premiere), Price returned to America, to a short-lived post on the White House Fine Arts Committee, and to his contractually obliged AIP thrillers. Besides a reunion with the Roger Corman regime, Price worked again with director Sidney Salkow in 1963's atmospheric and imaginative *Twice-Told Tales*.

Similarly, Lippert kept busy in the genre by producing *Witchcraft* (1964) with a bacchanal and bloated Lon Chaney, Jr., and by executive-producing *The Earth Dies Screaming* (1964), directed by then–Hammer persona non grata Terence Fisher. Associate producer Harold E. Knox worked as the production supervisor on *The Day Mars Invaded Earth* and *Hand of Death* (both 1962).

Price's memories of his trio of Italian film ventures were less than fond. "I made some dreadful pictures in Italy. They were terrible," he reminisced in Williams' book. The primitive conditions of the movies' production were always clear in his mind, with the acquisition of a host of European art collectibles acting as the trip's sole saving grace.

Elsewhere, interviewed by Lawrence French (published in a commemorative issue of *Famous Monsters of Filmland*), Price recalled, "We worked in a studio that was so cold that before each scene we had to go take ice water in our mouth, so that when we talked you wouldn't see our breath."

The inhospitable weather was evidently Price's strongest recollection of *The Last Man on Earth* when he told interviewer Tom Weaver, "I was never so cold in my life as I was on that picture. I used to tip my driver a big sum to keep the car running, so I could change my clothes in the back seat."

Throughout his long career, Price salvaged more than his fair share of fantasy films with an urbane elegance that belied his middle-class upbringing as the son of a Missouri candy manufacturer. But here, as *The Last Man on Earth*, he looked out of his element.

Casting actors against type sometimes allows them to appear on-screen to be discovering their characters even as they play them, and that can give a film a tension that might not have been expected. However, while the part of Robert Morgan and *The Last Man on Earth* only just tapped into Price's dramatic talents, here the milieu was too foreign (figuratively) for him to look comfortable in and for audiences to accept.

CREDITS: Produced by Robert L. Lippert; Associate Producer: Harold E. Knox; Directed by Sidney Salkow and (uncredited) Ubaldo Ragona; Cinematography: Franco Delli Colli; Film Editor: Gene Ruggiero; Production Manager: Vico Vaccaro; Assistant Director: Carlo Grandone; Art Director: Giorgio Giovannini; Makeup: Piero Mecacci; Music Composed by Paul Sawtell and Bert Shefter; Orchestration by Alfonso D'Artega; Music Editor: Norman Schwartz; Screenplay by Logan Swanson, Richard Matheson and William F. Leicester (Based on the Novel *I Am Legend* by Richard Matheson); a co-production of Associated Producers Inc. and Produzioni La Regina Sp.A. in Italy in 1961; Copyrighted 1964 by Alta Vista Productions and released by American International Pictures in the U.S. on a double bill with *Circus of Horrors*; overseas distribution by 20th Century-Fox Film Corporation; 86 minutes; released in Italy as *L'Ultimo Uomo della Terra* (*The Last Man on Earth*); also known as *Vento di Morte* (*Wind of Death*)

CAST: Vincent Price (Robert Morgan); Franca Bettoia (Ruth Collins); Emma Danieli (Virginia Morgan); Giacomo-Rossi-Stuart (Ben Cortman); Umberto Rau; Christi Courtland (Kathy Morgan); Tony Corevi; Hector Ribotta

THE MASQUE
OF THE RED DEATH (1964)
by Scott Allen Nollen

In August 1958, independent schlock filmmaker Alex Gordon planned to adapt Edgar Allan Poe's "The Masque of the Red Death" for the screen. Announcing that Vincent Price would star in the picture, to be titled *The Mask of the Red Death*, he hired the duo of Gordon and Mildred Gordon to write the script. Fortunately for Poe's tormented soul, the producer was unable to raise the budget before Roger Corman employed Charles Beaumont in February 1961 to write the ultimate adaptation. That script became a hybrid of "Masque" and another Poe medieval tale, "Hop Frog," after a second writer, R. Wright ("Bob") Campbell, was brought in to provide "a final polish of the script."[1]

During October 1963, American International announced that following unsuccessful negotiations with Ingmar Bergman (perhaps this was only a publicity stunt), Roger Corman had been given the green light for yet another Vincent Price–Poe extravaganza, to be shot in London the following month. Emigrating to Elstree Studios, Corman solidified a deal between Nicholson-Arkoff and Anglo-Amalgamated that ensured that *The Masque of the Red Death* would be filmed entirely in Great Britain.

Afforded nearly twice as much shooting time as usual (five weeks instead of three), Corman assumed that he would be allowed to make, in his words, a "bigger picture."[2] But he did not realize, until well into production, that "English crews work much slower than American ones. So, five weeks in England was, roughly, the equivalent of four in the United States." As compensation, Corman injected some new creative blood into the Poe series by hiring the masterful Nicholas Roeg to capture, in glorious Panavision and color, the magnificence of Daniel Haller's sets (which were recycled from those built for Paramount's *Becket* [1964]), and David Lee to compose a powerful musical score incorporating medieval elements (rather than again using the reliable but predictable Les Baxter).

While AIP mogul Samuel Z. Arkoff claimed that Price spent his London per diem on artwork, therefore lodging in a seedy hotel, co-star Hazel Court exposed this "reminiscence" as a lot of rubbish:

> Vincent loved London. We'd have a bite on the way home. But we did work awfully hard—it was fast and furious. It was wonderful... He stayed at the Cadogan on Sloane Street... I liked Vincent best as a heavy. He had a sinister quality which he could portray which was quite marvelous and penetrating. He was a sexy man; he had an aura about him, a sensuality. The other side was fun, the comedies, but the dramatic qualities that he always brought to the movies should have been put to use in pictures that were not horror films.[3]

Some critics have faulted Charles Beaumont for working the revenge tale "Hop Frog" into the screenplay, but it would not be possible for anyone to adapt a four-page, nearly action-less story like "The Masque of the Red Death" into a 90-minute feature film. Beaumont had to add something; and rather than fabricate an hour's worth of material, he incorporated another Poe medieval tale featuring a masked ball, as well as an extraneous subplot involving Prospero and Juliana's (Hazel Court) devil worship. In each story, a nobleman (a pompous prince in "Masque" and a corpulent king in "Hop Frog") is hideously killed after demonstrating abuses of power and egocentric assumptions about superiority and invincibility.

Poe opens "Masque," one of the most morose tales ever penned, with a paragraph permeated with words such as "blood," "death," "pestilence," "fatal," "hideous," "horror" and "termination." Any reader sinking his teeth into a Poe work has some idea what to expect, but this story begins, rather than ends, with a catastrophic circumstance and grows more moribund as the words pass. Like many of his tales, "Masque" (which originally was spelled "Mask") is highly autobiographical, a fictionalized catharsis for a terrible experience the author was suffering through at the time. During the spring of 1842, Poe's beloved young bride, Virginia, began hemorrhaging as a result of tuberculosis; and as she lay dying in Philadelphia, he literally saw "the red death" on a daily basis. In April of that year, he left the staff of *Graham* magazine, which published several of his works, including "The Mask of the Red Death," over a 13-month period.

After opening "Masque" with his paragraph of death, Poe counters it with a description of the prince's belief that, with his exalted position in the Great Chain of Being, he can safeguard himself and 1,000 of his friends from the ravages of the external world. The Red Death may have laid waste all of Europe, "But the Prince Prospero was happy and dauntless and sagacious."

Poe cleverly foreshadows the characters' imminent ends by using the device of an "ebony clock," a symbol, each time it clangs, of their having lived another hour. When it sounds, the revelers all stop in their tracks and remain motionless until it has finished. While Poe depicts the emissary of Death as a shrouded corpse, Corman chose to make him "a mysterious cowled figure which, essentially, is the same representation made famous by Ingmar Bergman in *The Seventh Seal*."[4] But while Bergman's reaper is stark black-and-white, Corman's is robed, hooded and masked in blood red. And though Price's Prince Prospero is a feudal overlord capable of great evil, Poe's is even more arrogant and seemingly impervious to Death:

> Who dares... who dares insult us with this blasphemous mockery? Seize him
> and unmask him—that we may know whom we have to hang, at sunrise, from
> the battlements!

Throughout his life, Poe was at odds with authority figures, his employers, publishers, other critics and writers. By setting stories in a bygone era, he could create catharses for his frustrations through depictions of pompous noblemen receiving their "just rewards," sometimes from the inevitable death that comes to both commoner and king, sometimes from an "inferior" being far down the rungs of society's ladder. In "Hop Frog," set during a period in which "fools and jesters are still in fashion," the title character has a value "trebled in the eyes of the king, by the fact of his being also a dwarf and a cripple."

Originally titled "Hop Frog: or, The Eight Chained Orang-Outangs," this tale also resulted from Poe's mighty self-torture, penned during the spring of 1849, just a few months before his delirious death in Baltimore. Published in the *Flag*, the story, in the words of Poe biographer Kenneth Silverman, "dramatizes years of accumulated gripes and griefs."[5]

"Hop Frog" depicts a king and his seven ministers who all are fat and lazy, doing nothing but supping and desiring witty entertainment from their jester slaves. The current favorites are Hop Frog, so named because of his gait—"something between a leap and a wriggle"—and Tripetta, an exquisite tiny dancer, both of whom were captured from adjoining provinces and presented by a victorious general as gifts to the king.

Beaumont's adaptation of "Hop Frog" is very faithful to Poe, its one major deviation being a change of the character's name to "Hop Toad," which sounds more unattractive (although the excellent actor Skip Martin is far from being the creature described by Poe). Whereas Poe's king forces Hop Frog to drink wine and then throws it in Trippetta's face when she pleads for mercy, Beaumont's version transfers this humiliating action to Prospero's decadent friend Alfredo

Prince Prospero (Vincent Price) is quite taken with Francesca (Jane Asher) in *The Masque of the Red Death*.

(Patrick Magee), who becomes enraged when the dancer (here called "Esmeralda" [Verina Greenlaw, a girl whose voice was over-dubbed with that of an adult]) accidentally kicks over his goblet of vino.

In the story, Hop Frog convinces the king and his ministers to masquerade as the "Eight Chained Orang-Outangs," which he creates by covering them with tar and flax. The film offers only one victim, Alfredo, whom Hop Toad dresses in an ape pelt. Interestingly, while Poe's version is a mass murder, he depicts Hop Frog attempting to make the killings look like an accident as the dwarf appears to identify the figures hanging from the chandelier before "inadvertently" setting them aflame with his torch. By contrast, the film version depicts Hop Toad maliciously hauling the ape up on the chandelier mount and deliberately torching him. Though shocking, this visualization is not as horrendous as Poe's description of the formerly obese aristocrats: "The eight corpses swung in their chains, a fetid, blackened, hideous, and indistinguishable mass." When Alfredo's flaming body is lowered to the floor, Corman and Beaumont offer some gallows humor, beautifully played by Price: "Guards, clear that out of the way. How can I expect my guests to dance around that?" Prospero, having enjoyed the "entertaining jest," then orders £5 to be awarded the dwarf, who, with Esmeralda, already has made his getaway through a skylight.

The Masque of the Red Death opens with a prologue in which the red messenger of eternity turns a rose bloody and hands it to an old crone, telling her, "The day of your deliverance is at hand." Soon someone orders, "Make way for the Prince Prospero!" and Price emerges from behind a curtain in the royal coach to survey the villagers of Catagna, who are brewing thoughts of rebellion. After Gino (David Weston) and Ludovico (Nigel Green) claim that they all will be delivered from the prince's tyranny, Prospero orders his guards to garrote them. Francesca (Jane Asher), a beautiful young redhead, pleads for mercy, but the prince insists that one must die. Offered a choice, Francesca cannot make a decision: Gino is her lover, Ludovico her father.

When the Red Death appears at the masque, Prospero believes that his master, the Lord of Flies, has arrived.

"Silence that!" Prospero orders after a hideous scream interrupts their harrowing negotiation. Led into a tent, the prince is shocked to find the old crone in the final throes of the Red Death.

To escape the plague, Prospero, accompanied by his guards and all three prisoners, heads for the safety of his castle. As her father and lover languish in a dungeon, Francesca is bathed in a solid-gold tub and dressed in the clothes and jewels of the jealous Juliana, Prospero's red-headed mistress and fellow Satan worshipper. Beaumont's addition of the Francesca and Gino subplot shifts some of the focus away from Prospero, adding a degree of hope to a depressing story. Later, when she speaks to Prospero about the positive aspects of life, including love and faith, the prince laments that God is dead and that someone, some*thing*, rules in his place; hence the constant presence of "famine, pestilence, war, disease, and death."

Daniel Haller's art direction includes the "ebony clock" of Poe's story, which is visually foregrounded in several of Nicholas Roeg's widescreen compositions showing characters in the expanse of the castle's great hall in the background. The clock, featuring an ax-like pendulum not unlike the blade in *Pit and the Pendulum*, serves the same purpose as its literary counterpart, with Prospero remarking, "What is terror? Come. Silence. Listen. Is it to awaken and hear the passage of time? Or is it the failing beat of your own heart? Or is it the footsteps of someone who, just a moment before, was in your room?" Later, after Juliana dies violently in front of the clock, he paraphrases his earlier rhetoric: "Hush. Listen. The passage of time. The beating of a heart. The footstep of an assassin—destiny!"

The fluidity of Roeg's camera is as impressive as his framing, making the most out of Haller's architectural realizations of Poe's prose. Several shots have a deep-focus effect, particularly those showing the series of contiguous rooms, each of which is a different color (yellow, purple, white, black), with their doors leading from one to the next. The black room, appropriately where Prospero and Juliana hold their black masses, also features blood-red lighting, which, streaming in through a Gothic window, illuminates the faces of those present.

Prospero begins celebrating his "triumph" over the Red Death by offering music, dancing, food and drink. During the soiree, he commands his guests to behave like animals, one like a snake, another a worm, others a pig and a jackass.

In his study of Corman's films, Gary Morris writes:

> These "entertainments"...reinforce his position above the rabble, his godlike status, since he is proving how backward, ignorant, unevolved people are by making them act like animals, and they provide a "lesson" for Francesca in the sordidness of life, allowing Prospero to remake her in his own image. [6]

Price's acting in this scene is vintage Vincent, and no other actor could have pulled it off with quite the same mixture of believability and relish. Prospero's desire to see his "friends" act out "the lives and loves of the animals" also effectively foreshadows Alfredo's later wearing of the ape skin during the "Hop Frog" vignette.

Corman and editor Ann Chegwidden use shock effects throughout the film: People literally lunge into shots at times, and transitions often are abrupt and jarring (a tambourine struck by a dancer ends the "be an animal" sequence, for instance). There also is a high degree of suspense, particularly in a scene in which Gino and Ludovico are forced to play a "suicide" game with five daggers, each man cutting his arm with one of the blades until one dies, all in view of the bloodthirsty guests. Of course, the contest is decided by the final knife; but when Ludovico attempts to retaliate with it, he is killed by Prospero's sword. Corman also managed to work in another of his surreal dream sequences, during Juliana's "wedding" to Satan. Similar in content to a scene that was scripted and shot for Universal's *The Mummy* (1932), the sequence, featuring a foggy, black-and-white look, depicts Juliana reincarnated and murdered in various eras and cultures, including African, Hebrew and Asian.

When the Red Death appears at the masque, Prospero (rather than wanting to execute the interloper, as in the story) believes that his master, the Lord of Flies, has arrived. Believing himself to be all-knowing, the prince learns a thing or two from the crimson-cowled figure, including the fact that Satan "does not rule alone."

"Let me see your face," Prospero pleads.

"There is no face of Death, until the moment of your own death," it replies. "Each man creates his own God—his own heaven and his own hell."

Even as his 1,000 "friends" begin to turn blood red and dance themselves stiff onto the ornate floor of the great hall, Prospero still believes he will be spared.

"Why should you be afraid to die?" the Red Death asks. "Your soul has been dead for a long time."

The resulting danse macabre is one of the best scenes in horror cinema, a masterful, chilling, hair-raising combination of choreography, color, camera movement, acting, and music. The image of Prospero falling dead under a sea of groping hands is unforgettable, and far more effective than Poe's original depiction, which simply has the prince fall dead before his guests begin to pile up. Corman's version offers a strong visual symbol for the price Prospero has paid for faith in his own twisted decadence and his failure to save others of his social station, "all rich and greedy for more."

Convening at the spot where the old crone had received word of "the day of deliverance," several emissaries of Death report the numbers of people they have reaped in their wanderings. The Red Death took all, save for Francesca, Gino and the small child, the only person spared by Prospero. The film closes with Poe's words: "And darkness and decay and the Red Death held illimitable dominion over all."

Shooting in England unquestionably allowed Corman to make a better film, as well as a "bigger" one. Mounted on the same scale, *The Masque of the Red Death* would have cost far

Jane Asher and Price do a little shopping during their time off.

more to produce in Hollywood; and the addition of Roeg and Lee, in particular, as well as the leftover *Becket* sets, were in large part responsible for the increase in quality from the previous Poe films. But improved production values were not the only step forward for the director.

Masque differs from the earlier Poe adaptations in its depiction of the "real" world existing outside the realm of a Gothic castle (wherein the conflicts between "good" and "evil" occur in *The Fall of the House of Usher*, *Pit and the Pendulum* and *The Premature Burial* [1962]). Morris writes:

> The opposition of two worlds—the larger, conformist world in harmony with natural law, and the smaller, individual world in violent opposition to it—forms the basis of all the films in the series, but... *Masque*... substantiate[s] both worlds, rather than mak[ing] the larger world a fantasy or a memory, visualized by unmistakable matte shots or set off from the story proper by montage, that only triumphs at the end. *Masque*... reenacts the basic struggle between the worlds of good and evil, within a framework of religious/existential questioning. Both forces exist precariously in perhaps the most complex character in the series, the ironically named Prince Prospero...[7]

But Morris also identifies a Corman motif that ties *Masque* to the earlier Poe entries:

> In many of its conventions, *Masque* falls in line... The kind of rotting plushness associated with a decadent world, headed by a corrupt aesthete, which we saw in the earlier films is also present here. Likewise we see an "innocent" whose unwilling entry into this world both brings about its destruction, and educates the innocent into the corruption that exists in the world.[8]

Indeed, Jane Asher takes up where her predecessors—Mark Damon, John Kerr, Richard Ney and Jack Nicholson—left off, performing the eternal Corman motif of walking around the late-night corridors of an eerie castle, here medieval rather than Gothic. In all the Poe films, as well as *The Terror* (1963), a good portion of the running time is devoted to these near-silent perambulations.

Undoubtedly the most complex character in Corman's Poe series, Prospero is also one of Price's finest characterizations, a role he could play with some flair yet take seriously; less sympathetic than his superb Roderick Usher interpretation, but just as engaging for the viewer. Although Prospero is an evil man, executing both nobles and commoners alike, rather than offering them sanctuary, he correctly identifies his own kind as rich and greedy, and he shows some morality by refusing to have a child executed along with his parents. Morris notes:

> Prospero is no ordinary devil-worshipper, embracing evil for the sake of evil. It becomes increasingly clear that he has embraced Satan as a more "realistic" alternative to a Christian God by turns evil or missing entirely. He is a kind of theoretician of evil, obsessed with the dark side of human nature as a path to enlightenment, having given up—bitterly— on the concept of a humane Creator.[9]

Prospero also shows his "good" side late in the film, when he appears to genuinely care about Francesca, rather than merely desiring to possess her. When the Red Death tells her to wait on the battlements, she gently kisses the prince, who fully expects to be joining her in a matter of moments. Instead, Prospero joins the revelers in a surreal crimson death, pulled down by the grasping hands of those he stood above for so long.

Just before the film was released, Alex Gordon filed a lawsuit against American International, Anglo-Amalgamated, Corman and Price, charging that his script had been plagiarized. Asking a Los Angeles superior court judge to order an injunction against *Masque*, Gordon was denied on grounds that all similarities emanated from two sources: the original story and the fact that Corman used the same plot in all the Poe–Price films!

Like the earlier films in the series, *Masque* was considered quite lurid by some contemporary reviewers, but this time the increase in quality was immediately apparent. *Variety*'s "Whit" even mentioned the complexity of Price's characterization:

> Latest [Poe film] catches the flavor of past offerings in this field of horror and exploitation and should carry the same lure, particularly with the name of Vincent Price, star of most of AIP's Poe program, to build on.... Price is the very essence of evil, albeit charming when need be, and as film progresses the dark workings of his mind are stressed... [10]

Corman closes the film with an end-titles graphic that reinforces the final scene, during which the Red Death plays with a deck of tarot cards. As the credits change from one panel to the next, an animated hand places tarot cards around the words, ultimately placing down the death card before David Lee's music crescendos dramatically and the image fades out.

CREDITS: Director-Producer: Roger Corman; Associate Producer: George Willoughby; Screenplay: Charles Beaumont and R. Wright Campbell (Based on the Short Stories "The Masque of the Red Death" and "Hop Frog" by Edgar Allan Poe); Cinematography (Panavision): Nicholas Roeg; Editor: Ann Chegwidden; Musical Score: David Lee; Production Designer: Daniel Haller; Art Director: Robert Jones; Set Dresser: Colin Southcott; Costume Supervisor: Laura Nightingale; Makeup: George Partleton; Hairstyles: Elsie Alder; Choreography: Jack Carter; Special Effects: George Blackwell; An Alta Vista Production; Released June 24, 1964, by American International Pictures; Running Time: 90 minutes.

CAST: Vincent Price (Prince Prospero); Hazel Court (Juliana); Jane Asher (Francesca); David Weston (Gino); Patrick Magee (Alfredo); Nigel Green (Ludovico); Skip Martin (Hop Toad); John Westbrook (Man in Red); Gay Brown (Senora Escobar); Julian Burton (Senor Veronese); Doreen Dawn (Anna-Maria); Paul Whitsun-Jones (Scarlatti); Jean Lodge (Scarlatti's Wife); Verina Greenlaw (Esmeralda); Brian Hewlett (Lampredi); Harvey Hall (Clistor); Robert Brown (Guard); David Davies; Sarah Brackett

[1] Lucy Chase Williams, *The Complete Films of Vincent Price*, Secaucus, New Jersey: Citadel Press, 1995, p. 193.
[2] Ed Naha, *Brilliance on a Budget: The Films of Roger Corman*. New York: Arco Publishing, Inc., 1982, p. 179.
[3] Williams, p. 195.
[4] Naha, p. 180.
[5] Kenneth Silverman, *Edgar A. Poe: Mournful and Never-ending Remembrance*, New York: Harper Collins Publishers, 1991, p. 407.
[6] Gary Morris, *Roger Corman*, Boston: Twayne Publishers, 1985, p. 125
[7] Morris, p. 121.
[8] Morris, p. 123.
[9] Morris, p. 124.
[10] *Variety*, 24 June 1964.

Even on her wedding night she must share the man she loved with the "Female Thing" that lived in the Tomb of the Cat!

AMERICAN INTERNATIONAL
presents

VINCENT PRICE
ELIZABETH SHEPHERD
STARRING IN

EDGAR ALLAN POE'S

TOMB OF LIGEIA

IN COLORSCOPE

THE TOMB OF LIGEIA (1964)
by Jonathan Malcolm Lampley

"The boundaries which divide life from death are at best shadowy and vague.
Who shall say where the one ends and where the other begins?"
> —Edgar Allan Poe, as quoted in the film

England, 1821: In the churchyard of a crumbling abbey, a small funeral procession conveys a coffin to its final resting place. Abruptly the ceremonies are interrupted by the village parson; he claims the deceased, Ligeia Fell, is not a Christian and therefore cannot be buried in consecrated ground. Husband Verden Fell (Vincent Price) steps forth to confront the clergyman, and during their conversation a black cat growls and leaps onto the newly carved tombstone. Beneath the coffin's face plate, Ligeia's eyes fly open. "A muscular contraction," Fell explains.

Some months later, a fox hunt is in progress near Fell's abbey. Tiring of the sport, Lady Rowena Trevanion (Elizabeth Shepherd, who also plays Ligeia) wanders off, becoming fascinated by Ligeia's tomb. The black cat suddenly appears, spooking Rowena's horse. Thrown to the ground but unhurt, Rowena tries to regain her composure, only to be startled by the appearance of Verden Fell, clad entirely in black and wearing dark glasses. Rowena's surprised cry brings her companion Christopher Gough (John Westbrook) running; when Fell greets him by name, Christopher recognizes his childhood friend.

Rowena's ankle is sprained, so Fell literally sweeps her off her feet and carries her into his home. Playfully the young woman removes her host's glasses, causing him to drop her and stumble away in pain. Embarrassed, Rowena returns them; Fell explains that he must wear them due to "a rather morbid reaction to sunlight." Verden expertly bandages Rowena's foot—so well, in fact, that her father, Lord Trevanion (Derek Francis), mistakenly assumes Verden is a physician.

Rowena finds herself strangely attracted to the mysterious owner of the abbey. When Verden sends Christopher a note a few days later, Rowena takes it upon herself to personally deliver the reply. She enters the abbey unannounced, and Verden, in a trance-like state, attacks her. Rowena's screams bring Fell back to his senses, and he tries to comfort her as best he can.

Verden and Rowena marry, and the groom announces his plan to sell his gloomy estate and provide a more cheerful home for his new bride. Yet soon after the honeymoon, Verden resumes his old ways. He starts wearing the dark glasses again and neglects his wife. When Christopher (acting as the couple's attorney) tries to arrange the estate sale, he discovers the property is in Ligeia's name. No certificate of Ligeia's death can be found, and without it, the sale cannot take place; legally, *Ligeia is still alive*.

Bad dreams plague Rowena, and when Verden attempts to hypnotize her following a dinner party, Rowena suddenly begins speaking in Ligeia's voice. The black cat stalks the new Mrs. Fell—is it possessed by the spirit of Ligeia? With the assistance of Verden's loyal servant Kenrick (Oliver Johnson), Christopher digs up Ligeia's grave, only to find a wax effigy in the coffin. Kenrick confesses that just before she died, Ligeia mesmerized Verden, convincing him that she would not die and would always be his wife. For months Verden's subconscious has been fighting off this post-hypnotic suggestion, and the struggle is driving him mad.

Meanwhile Rowena discovers why her husband has not been sharing her bed—he has been sleeping with the corpse of Ligeia! Christopher and Kenrick burst into the abbey's living quarters, only to discover Verden choking the life out of Rowena, whom he has once again mistaken for Ligeia. Fell dismisses his friends, urging them to take Rowena's body with them. Verden insists on destroying the black cat, which he is now convinced contains his first wife's evil soul.

In the ensuing melee the cat scratches Fell's eyes out, and a fire soon blazes out of control. Rowena finally stirs in Christopher's arms, and the film closes with a final shot of Verden Fell lying among the flames, embracing the body of Ligeia.

The Tomb of Ligeia is an interesting film in many ways. It is the eighth and final entry in Roger Corman's celebrated Edgar Allan Poe cycle; American International Pictures would continue to borrow Poe's titles for later Price vehicles, but none of these have anything to do with Poe's writings. It is one of two (the other is *The Masque of the Red Death*) Corman/Price/Poe projects shot on location in England. And in many ways, it is the best entry in the series.

I admire this movie over its companions because I feel it captures the spirit of Poe's works better than any other adaptation yet committed to film. Because Poe was more concerned with creating a specific mood or atmosphere in his writing, his stories are often short on plot; consequently, filmmakers have been required to take enormous liberties with the tales in order to stretch them into full-length features. In *The Tomb of Ligeia*, director Roger Corman and screenwriter Robert Towne have added material and characters Poe would never dream of, yet all of these additions contribute to what Poe himself called "a certain unique or single *effect*."

Corman and Towne tweak the horror formula by presenting a pure Gothic tale in the traditional style. What this means is that the filmmakers incorporate the trappings of a traditional Gothic tale: the mysterious protagonist, the endangered heroine, the ruined castle (or abbey, in this case), evidence of supernatural visitation and the "realistic" explanation (hypnotism). Most significantly, Corman and Towne emphasize the romantic elements of the Gothic tradition, perhaps best exemplified by the love story at the heart of Charlotte Bronte's *Jane Eyre*.

Christopher (John Westbrook) bursts into the abbey's living quarters, only to discover Verden (Vincent Price) choking the life out of Rowena (Elizabeth Shepherd).

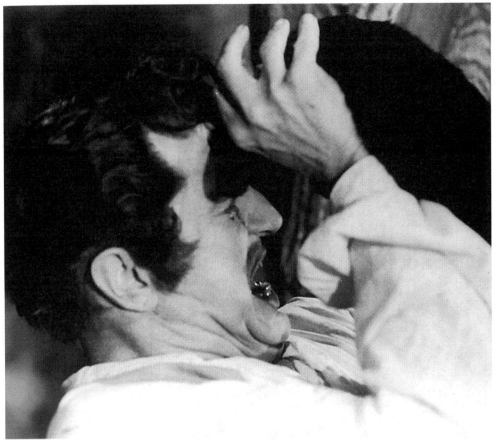

Ligeia's cat attacks Verden.

There's no mistake about it: *The Tomb of Ligeia* is a love story, albeit a somewhat twisted one. Although his condition is exaggerated by Ligeia's hypnotic influence, Verden Fell is clearly still in love with his first wife—to the point of obsession. His dark aspect and nature—his air of mystery, even of danger—are the very qualities that draw the innocent Rowena to his side. At one point she even states that it is possible to be in love with a person one doesn't even like. This suggests an element of obsession on her part as well. Finally, Ligeia lives on, either supernaturally or psychologically, precisely because her indomitable will refuses to release the life she loves so passionately. The obsessive qualities of romantic love are at the heart of Poe's short story, and they have been successfully transferred to the screen in *The Tomb of Ligeia*. The Master would be proud.

Vincent Price considered the picture to be the best of the cycle, and it is easy to see why. For one thing, the love story emphasis gives the aging matinee idol one last shot as a romantic leading man, and he makes the most out of it, perhaps recalling his earlier success in the similarly themed *Dragonwyck* (1946). Eschewing his famous but sinister mustache, the clean-shaven Price is still quite handsome in spite of his 53 years. Decked out entirely in black, he seems a precursor to the recent Goth craze in contemporary American culture. I suspect it is this gloomy, love-struck image that Tim Burton had in mind when he made *Vincent* (1982), his early animated tribute to the Merchant of Menace. Certainly for once Price is as much victim as villain; in later films such as *The Abominable Dr. Phibes* (1971) and *Madhouse* (1974), the actor would go on to perfect this portrayal of "ambiguous sympathies."

As always it is the presence of Vincent Price that contributes most to the production's success. Who else could recite a line of dialogue such as "If only I could lay open my own brain as easily as I did that vegetable! What rot would be freed from its gray leaves?" Out of anybody

Verden thinks he is choking his deceased wife Ligeia.

else's mouth the line would inspire derisive laughter; from Price's lips it conjures forth grue-some imagery. However, the use of location shooting (a ruined abbey in Norfolk) and seasoned British professionals (much superior to the amateurish supporting casts of earlier Corman/Poe films) help elevate *The Tomb of Ligeia* above the typical AIP release of the period.

This early screenplay by Robert Towne happily foreshadows his later triumphs, including such a morally complex script as *Chinatown* (1974), for which he won an Oscar. Towne makes good symbolic use of vision and perception. What characters see—or fail to see—is of consid-erable importance. Again and again characters do not realize the significance of events that unfold before their very eyes. When Lord Trevanion arrives to check on his daughter, he is more concerned with the rare fox he's captured. Trevanion fails to acknowledge his child's injuries, and he assumes Fell is a doctor simply because the bespeckled stranger is bandaging Rowena's foot. Then the fox (an Egyptian pet of Ligeia's, it is revealed) disappears; Fell suggests the cat made off with the carcass, even though someone in the group would surely have noticed such an odd physical phenomenon. Later, Verden fails to recognize Rowena on two occasions, as his perceptions are muddied by Ligeia's evil influence.

From the very first, eyes play an important role in the film. Ligeia's eyes pop open when the cat causes a commotion at her funeral; this disturbing event suggests Ligeia is not really dead, one of the central themes of the movie. The only spot of color on the black cat is its eyes, which glow a baleful green while the beast prowls. Of course, Verden Fell's eyes—the windows to the soul—remain hidden behind his glasses whenever he stands in sunlight (a visual symbol for purity and goodness), and ultimately he is blinded during his climactic battle with the cat.

Perhaps most chillingly, when Rowena revives at the denouement, Christopher joyfully embraces her. Rowena stares placidly over his shoulder, smiling faintly. The expression is similar to Ligeia's face when her body is disturbed by the cat early on—could it be that her spirit lives on in Rowena? It is an intriguing possibility.

To its credit, *The Tomb of Ligeia* successfully evokes the dreamlike, Gothic feel of Poe's short story. However, if there is a criticism of the film, it is that it is light on moments of pure terror. Compared to Corman's other Poe adaptations, the sense of horror is considerably milder, due in part to the emphasis on romance. There are plenty of sudden shocks, mostly courtesy of the black cat, and there is one supremely disturbing scene where Rowena discovers Ligeia's stolen body. Recoiling in terror, Rowena gets tangled in the bedclothes and accidentally stumbles into her rival's cold embrace. Overall, however, Corman is more concerned with the psychological terrors of his tale; here he concentrates on the unsettling and odd rather than the grotesque and terrifying.

This interest in "quiet horror" is actually a nice change of pace from the more physical scares associated with Corman's earlier work. This approach may not find favor with everyone, but for fans interested in seeing a purely Gothic film, as opposed to a Gothic *horror* film, it is well worth checking out. For fans of Poe, it is proof that film can do a credible job of capturing the author's spooky intentions. For fans of Vincent Price, *The Tomb of Ligeia* contains one of the actor's most significant performances, and as such it is nothing less than required viewing.

CREDITS: Director: Roger Corman; Producers: Pat Green, Roger Corman; Screenplay: Robert Towne (Based on the Story "Ligeia" by Edgar Allan Poe); Cinematography: Arthur Grant; Art Director: Colin Southcott; Music: Kenneth V. Jones; Editor: Alfred Cox; Wardrobe: Mary Gibson; Makeup: George Blackler; Special Effects: Ted Samuels; Cat Trainer: John Holmes; An Alta Vista Production, distributed by American International Pictures; Released in November 1964 (UK) and January 1965 (US); Filmed in WideScreen Colorscope; Running Time: 82 minutes

CAST: Vincent Price (Verden Fell); Elizabeth Shepherd (Ligeia/Lady Rowena Trevanion); John Westbrook (Christopher Gough); Oliver Johnson (Kenrick); Derek Francis (Lord Trevanion); Richard Vernon (Dr. Vivian); Ronald Adam (Parson)

CREDITS SOURCE: Lucy Chase Williams, *The Complete Films of Vincent Price* (New York: Citadel, 1995)

LEAVE THE CHILDREN HOME!
...AND IF *YOU* ARE SQUEAMISH
STAY HOME WITH THEM!

A crawling shape intrude!
A blood-red thing that writhes
from out The scenic solitude!
It writhes! — it writhes! —
with mortal pangs
The mimes become its food,
And seraphs sob at vermin fangs
In human gore imbued.

EDGAR ALLAN POE

EDGAR ALLAN POE'S

THE CONQUEROR WORM

FROM AMERICAN INTERNATIONAL IN **COLOR** by PERFEC

STARRING
VINCENT **PRICE** · IAN **OGILVY** · RUPERT **DAVIES** · HILARY **DWYER**

AND INTRODUCING

"Based on a book entitled 'Witchfinder General' by Ronald Bassett and the poem by Edgar Allan Poe

EXECUTIVE PRODUCER **TONY** TENSER · PRODUCED BY **LOUIS M. HEYWARD** · DIRECTED BY **MICHAEL REEVES** · SCREENPLAY BY **MICHAEL REEVES & TOM BAKE**

© 1968 American International Pictures
AD MAT 313

222

WITCHFINDER GENERAL (1968)

by Bryan Senn

Witchfinder General (renamed *Conqueror Worm* in America) may be Vincent Price's finest performance in a terror film. It is certainly one of his most *unusual* portrayals in that he eschews the buttery charm and smooth flamboyance for which he had become so well known (and loved) to deliver a steely, subdued and intensely menacing performance that becomes utterly convincing. While it may not be every Price fan's *favorite* role, it is undoubtedly his most powerful.

The film, based on Ronald Bassett's historical novel of the same name, began with producer Tony Tenser, head of Tigon British Film Productions (a cut-rate competitor of England's Hammer Films). "I thought it would make a wonderful film," recalled Tenser in *Fangoria* magazine, "but a lot more expensive than my other pictures, so I would have to look for a partner." Tenser found said partner in American International Pictures.

"I showed the novel to Michael Reeves [whose previous film, *The Sorcerers*, Tenser had co-produced] who was very keen on it. I then spoke to 'Deke' Heyward [head of AIP's British division], and we made a deal." The deal involved AIP kicking in £32,000 to enhance the £50,000 Tenser had already raised. One condition the Americans imposed was to insist that their current contract star, Vincent Price, play the title role. "AIP felt that it would enhance their market if Vincent Price played Matthew Hopkins," explained Tenser. "They paid for his salary [reportedly £12,000]. I was totally happy with that, because Price would enhance my market as well."

"All screen villainy is fun," declared Vincent Price in the film's American pressbook. "That is why I enjoy doing it so much. It gives me as big a kick as comedy, which I also love doing, besides being so much easier."

On *Witchfinder General*, however, nothing apparently was "easy" for Price. While *Witchfinder* stands as one of his finest cinematic moments, it also proved to be one of the actor's most disagreeable filming experiences. For instance, on the first day of shooting, Price was thrown from his horse and had to spend the rest of the day in bed recovering from the various bumps and bruises. But the pain inflicted by an uncooperative animal was nothing compared to the mental anguish inspired by *Witchfinder General*'s disgruntled director...

When AIP first approached Price about the project, it was with an air of optimistic enthusiasm. In August 1967, producer Louis M. "Deke" Heyward sent a letter to Price (quoted in *The Complete Films of Vincent Price* by Lucy Chase Williams) in order to sell the actor on the proposed production. In it Heyward plays up the extensive location shooting (ironically, Price preferred studio shoots to location filming), the strong script and the film's young director, Michael Reeves, whom Heyward felt Price would find "one of the most inspiring things that's happened to you as an actor in a long time. He is not only bright, imaginative and well-organized, but he has the *cujones* [sic] to force a crew through to doing things the way he wants to... He wafted off in a faerylike cloud of ecstasy when he heard we were casting you in the lead."

Unfortunately for Price, Heyward's description of Reeves' reaction was somewhat exaggerated. In fact, Heyward out and out *lied*, for Michael Reeves emphatically did *not* want Price in the title role—and was not at all circumspect about his displeasure when the actor showed up to begin filming. "When I went on location to meet [Reeves] for the first time," recalled Price at the 1990 *Fangoria Weekend of Horrors* in Los Angeles, "he said, 'I didn't want you and I *still* don't want you, but I'm stuck with you!' That's the way to gain confidence! He had no idea how to talk to actors. He came up to me one day after a take and he said, 'Don't shake your head!' I said, 'What do you mean? I'm not shaking my head.' He said, 'You're shaking your head!! Just don't shake your head.' Well, that made me so self-conscious that I was poker-

Matthew Hopkins (Vincent Price) uses his power to get what he wants in *Witchfinder General*.

faced—and, as it turned out, he was right! He wanted it *that* concentrated, so it would be that much more menacing. He could have been a wonderful director... such a sad, sad death." (Reeves died of an overdose of barbiturates and alcohol in early 1969; it is uncertain to this day whether it was an accident or suicide.)

Reeves had actually wanted Donald Pleasence for the part of Matthew Hopkins (he'd already approached the actor about doing the role) and resented bitterly AIP's thrusting Price upon him. "To Mike, the character of Matthew Hopkins was a little, ugly, ineffectual man," explained *Witchfinder General* co-star and longtime Reeves friend Ian Ogilvy to *Fangoria*'s Steve Swires. (Ogilvy was the only actor to star in all three of Reeves' films, and their friendship stretched back to their prep school days.) "When Donald was going to do it," continued Ogilvy, "Mike was going to have a scene in which he would get up on his horse in front of a group of villagers and fall off the other side, because he couldn't even ride. He was meant to be a pathetic Napoleonic figure, who was bitter about his own inadequacies. But that all changed when Vincent came along, since he is rather handsome and virile-looking."

This "handsome and virile-looking" image and (more importantly) Price's grandiose acting style proved anathema to Michael Reeves. "[Reeves] felt that Vincent was having too good a time at whatever part he was playing," explained Deke Heyward in *Cinefantastique* magazine, "and however horrible the man he was portraying was, there would be an overtone of 'You and I both know we're kidding' which Michael didn't want.... Reeves did not feel Vincent could do the acting job necessary." Fortunately, Reeves was wrong, and he managed to wring a harrowingly sinister portrayal from the recalcitrant actor.

Price put the unpleasant friction between himself and his young 24-year-old director down to Reeves' inexperience (Reeves had only directed two previous features, *The She Beast* and *The Sorcerers*). "He hadn't the experience, or talked to enough [actors] to know how," Price later stated (in *Cinefantastique*). "Afterwards, I realized what he wanted was a low-key, very laid-back, menacing performance. He did get it, but I was fighting with him almost every step of the way. Had I known what he wanted, I could have cooperated."

It seems likely that Reeves' animosity toward his star was strictly a professional concern rather than a personal dislike, and his directing style regarding actors made it difficult for him to adjust to this awkward situation. "Mike never directed the actors," remembered Ian Ogilvy. "He always said he didn't know anything about acting and preferred to leave it up to us. If it wasn't good, he would tell us, but he wouldn't know how to make it better. The only direction he ever gave was, 'A bit quicker' or 'A bit slower.' If he trusted you, he left you alone." Obviously, he didn't trust Vincent Price and apparently could only badger him into the type of performance he wanted. Though unpleasant for Price, Reeves' relentless and unforgiving approach ultimately proved highly effective. Willing to give credit where credit is due, Vincent Price admitted that, "I realized only after I saw the finished film how talented [Reeves] was."

Shooting began September 17, 1967, and wrapped on November 13. Advertised as Vincent Price's 92nd film (it was actually his 75th), *Witchfinder General* begins with a brutal pre-credit sequence in which villagers drag an old woman, screaming and clawing, to a scaffold where she's hanged. The dark, vio-

LAWRENCE FRENCH: The director of *The Conqueror Worm* was Michael Reeves. How did you like working with him?

VINCENT PRICE: He was only 24 years old when he did that film. He had only done two other films. Well he hated me. He didn't want me at all for that part. He wanted some other actor, and he got me and that was it. I didn't like him, either, and it was one of the first times in my life that I've been in a picture where really the director and I clashed (twists his hands), like that. He didn't know how to talk to actors, he hadn't had the experience, or talked to enough of them, so all the actors on the picture had a very bad time. I knew though, that in a funny, uneducated sort of way, he was right, in his desire for me to approach the part in a certain way. He wanted it very serious and straight, and he was right, but he just didn't know how to communicate with actors. Actors are very sensitive people. I'll never forget one time he came up and said, "Don't shake your head." I said, "What do you mean, I don't shake my head." He said "Yes, you do." So we didn't get along at all. He was a funny young man, brilliant, but he had a lot of problems. Really mixed-up problems: one of them being dope, another being an unhappy romance, and he killed himself. It was a great loss to the cinema, because had he been disciplined he could have become a very good director. Believe me, this profession takes enormous discipline. You're out there at six in the morning, and you're up till midnight, and back at six the next morning, so there's no fooling around. If you want to last, you're disciplined.

LAWRENCE FRENCH: Wasn't he going to direct you and Christopher Lee in *The Oblong Box*?

VINCENT PRICE: Yes, that one, and then *Scream and Scream Again*, but he had this terrible problem of suicide. He tried about four times, and finally they thought they had him cured, but when we started to do costume tests and all the preparations for *The Oblong Box*, he tried it again, and they just said, "He's too unstable." It was a shame. He couldn't control himself, and he was on the flip, and then his girlfriend ditched him, because she couldn't put up with him. He was just completely determined to destroy himself.

lent tone established, an off-screen narrator (Patrick Wymark, who later appears *on*-screen in a brief cameo as Oliver Cromwell) then sets the historical stage: "The year is 1645. England is in the grip of bloody civil war. On the one side stand the Royalist party of King Charles; on the other, Cromwell's Parliamentary party, the Roundheads. The structure of law and order has collapsed. Local magistrates indulge their individual whims. Justice and injustice are dispensed in more or less equal quantities and without opposition. An atmosphere in which the unscrupulous rebel and the likes of Matthew Hopkins take full advantage of the situation. In a time where the superstitions of country folk are still a powerful factor, Hopkins preys upon them, torturing and killing in a supposed drive to eliminate witchcraft from the country—and doing so with the full blessing of what law there is."

The cleverly constructed story that follows is dual-pronged, one branch following the brutal activities of "witchfinder" Matthew Hopkins (Vincent Price) and his assistant John Stearne (Robert Russell), while the other follows the (also sometimes brutal) activities of neophyte Parliamentary soldier Richard Marshall (Ian Ogilvy). The two story threads soon cross and become inexorably intertwined when Hopkins descends upon the village of Marshall's fiancée, Sarah (Hilary Dwyer). Hopkins not only tortures and kills Sarah's guardian, the local priest (against whom several of the disgruntled townsfolk have brought the spurious charge of witchcraft), but also seduces Sarah by (falsely) promising to go easy on the old man if she acquiesces.

Visiting on leave, Richard learns from the traumatized Sarah what has happened and swears vengeance, then sets about tracking down the pair of witchfinders. Once found, however, Hopkins turns the tables and accuses Richard *and* Sarah of consorting with the Devil. In the shocking climax, Hopkins meets his bloody fate at the hands of Richard—but not without cost to both the hero and heroine.

"Grim" is the watchword for *Witchfinder General*. "By far it was our most violent—and least humorous—Poe picture," remarked AIP head Sam Arkoff. "There wasn't much funny about torture, hangings and burnings at the stake. But it was effective." Effective indeed, thanks to an unflinching approach by director Michael Reeves. Rather than softening the edges of violence, or even making it appear almost *attractive* as so many pictures do, Reeves displays it for the brutish and ugly thing it is. "Mike didn't believe, as John Wayne believed, that a saloon brawl is okay, and everybody can bash each other and hurl each other through windows, and nobody seriously gets hurt," explained Ian Ogilvy to *Cinefantastique*'s Bill Kelley. "Mike said this philosophy is very wrong. He said, 'This will surely teach kids they can go into a place and start hitting people and think they're not actually hurting anyone. I think if you hit somebody in a film, you should see the knuckles break and the teeth fly out and the blood spurt and somebody possibly getting a broken jaw before he leaves—just once. This idea of banging away at people's chins for hours is ludicrous. It's inclined to make violence seem rather jolly.' Mike always believed violence should be seen to be horrible, to put people off, not to glorify it." And the violence seen in *Witchfinder General* is indeed horrible, from the intimately sickening sight of Stearne thrusting a long needle into the bare back of the old priest (searching for "the Devil's mark") to the horrific scene of a screaming woman tied to a wooden ladder and lowered face first into a blazing fire.

LAWRENCE FRENCH: Reeves did that wonderful film with Boris Karloff, *The Sorcerers*, which was really a metaphor for the cinema.

VINCENT PRICE: Yes, he showed great promise. He was a wonderful director, but these problems he had. He called me after *The Witchfinder General* was released in England, and it got very good notices. It was really a hit for him. He said, "There, you see, I told you so!" It was a mad kind of thing to do. Then when we got together on *The Oblong Box*, I said, "Well, I think you were wonderful, you made a marvelous picture, now let's get along on this one," but we didn't because he got sick again and killed himself.

Though a "funny, funny guy" off-screen, Vincent Price (under Michael Reeves' fractious hand) delivered a deadly serious performance as Matthew Hopkins.

Such an unshrinking approach to portraying violence generated a lot of heat from the critics of the day. Britain's *Sunday Telegraph*, for instance, denounced the film as "a sadistic extravagance," while the London *Sunday Times* labeled it "peculiarly nauseating." Even Tinseltown reviewers seemed offended, as the *Hollywood Citizen News* called it "a film with such bestial brutality and orgiastic sadism, one wonders how it ever passed customs to be released in this country." But these critics missed the point: by not turning away from the violence inherent in the story, Reeves forces the viewer to see it for the sickening act it is. The brutality in *Witchfinder General* is never appealing (much less "orgiastic" as the *Hollywood Citizen News* labeled it) but rather is repulsive in its realism. Perhaps it was the discomfort caused by this unsentimental approach to something that has so often been glossed over and stylized beyond recognition that so offended the reviewers.

Ironically, all this critical outrage became a prominent factor in the film's financial success. "Deke" Heyward related to interviewer Tom Weaver that, though a resounding success in the U.S., the film only became a hit in England "after all the horrified letters came in to *The London Times*."

In fact, Reeves had actually toned down his film's violence quotient before release at the behest of the British censors, trimming four to seven minutes [sources differ] from such scenes as the torturing of the priest, the witch-burning scene and the hero's climactic savage attack on Hopkins. (Though he initially opposed the cuts, Reeves later admitted to Ogilvy that they actually improved the film, since some of the violence was so protracted and sadistic that it "stopped the show.")

Director Michael Reeves responded to the critical attacks on his film with newspaper letters of his own. In one he wrote, "Violence is horrible, degrading and sordid. It should be presented as such—and the more people it shocks into sickened recognition of these facts the better."

Despite the critics' complaints, *Witchfinder General*'s ultimate tone is one of *anti*-violence, as evidenced not only by the repulsive depiction of the act, but by the effect it has on the story's characters. Hopkins, of course, though seemingly repelled initially by the undisguised sadism of his assistant, comes to welcome it as he sinks deeper and deeper into his hypocritical malaise and loses what little vestige of humanity and self-righteousness he possesses.

But the most tragic transformation occurs in both the hero and heroine (the audience identification figures) after they themselves embrace violence. When Richard shoots and kills an enemy soldier at the film's beginning, his face registers not pleasure at his accomplishment nor pride in his marksmanship (despite compliments from his comrades) but a bewildered, even appalled expression, his brow knit with confusion and surprise at the ugly outcome of his violent act. This obvious abhorrence of violence on the part of the hero makes the climactic denouement (in which Richard gives way to his bestial hatred and savagely attacks Hopkins with an ax) that much more powerful. And the result? When a sickened soldier shoots the mutilated Hopkins to put him out of his misery, Richard's bloodlust gives way to madness as he screams like an animal, "You took him away from me!" over and over. Thus from violence (even though it may *seem* like a just retribution) springs only horror and madness—for both Richard and the watching Sarah (upon whose hysterically screaming face the film freezes and ends) cannot participate in such ferocious violence and escape with their sanity intact. By showing the awful wages of brutality, *Witchfinder General* carries an effective message.

TONY TENSER presents
VINCENT PRICE
IAN OGILVY RUPERT DAVIES
WILFRID BRAMBELL

WITH
PATRICK WYMARK
AS CROMWELL

AND INTRODUCING
HILARY DWYER

Beyond its overt anti-violence stance, *Witchfinder General* holds further thematic relevance for modern viewers. Though ostensibly about the archaic subject of the persecution of witches, the film raises the broader issue of the abuse of authority. It's not much of an imaginative stretch to go from the lawfully empowered Matthew Hopkins and his assistant brutalizing and torturing an innocent woman in 1645 to a group of Brooklyn policemen brutalizing and torturing a Haitian immigrant in 1997 (as detailed in recent headlines). One reason *Witchfinder General* remains so disturbing (and it does disturb as evidenced by the occasional critical backlash even today) is that it touches on the horrors of power brutally misused.

What makes such an uncompromising and disturbing treatment palatable, however, are the well-drawn characters and the efficacious acting that so effectively draws the viewer into their cruel world. At the top of the list, of course, stands the inimitable Vincent Price.

"I was surprised how terrifying Vincent was in that," commented AIP head Sam Arkoff to *Cinefantastique* magazine. Indeed, Price does terrify with his cold presence and forbidding manner, bringing his character to full malevolent life. Garbed in black hat and cloak, sporting a long and luxuriant mane of graying chestnut hair and a close-cropped, well-combed silver beard, wearing spotless white gloves and mounted on a white steed, Price cuts an extremely imposing figure.

About his character of Matthew Hopkins, Price had this to say in the film's pressbook:

> Despite his macabre and revolting occupation, this man Hopkins was not just a sadist. Else, I wouldn't have been interested in playing him. He was a human being—not a humane one, perhaps—but he had all the usual weaknesses, including a fondness for young women.
>
> I saw him as a man who, at first, really believed in the Christian justness of his cause, but who, when he found he could turn it to profit through the credulity of local magistrates in those lawless times, degenerated into an ogre whose lust for power and greed for money ran away with him.
>
> Having begun, he had to keep on, and finally his atrocities became more and more terrible. He became the complete hypocrite—cowardly as well as demoniac.

From his very first scene, Price's skillful playing establishes his character's fascinating and diverse dichotomy. When Stearne asks, "How much farther, Matthew?" Hopkins reacts forcefully with, "You'll not call me 'Matthew.' I'm not one of your drinking cronies carousing and wenching in the taverns." Price's voice is hard, his flinty tones ringing with both authority and superiority. Obviously, Hopkins sees himself as one who stands above those around him.

A revealing verbal exchange quickly follows:

"Remember, John Stearne," states Hopkins, "you ride with me only because you help me in my work."

"You call it *work*," sneers Stearne.

"It's the Lord's work," replies Hopkins, "a noble thing."

"And a profitable one," Stearne shoots back, "the good Lord paying in silver for every hanging."

"That's blasphemy Stearne; hold your tongue!" Hopkins orders.

LAWRENCE FRENCH: Why was it called *Witchfinder General* in England, and *The Conqueror Worm* in America?

VINCENT PRICE: They just picked a title that they thought would sell. I thought *Witchfinder General* was a wonderful title, because that's what Matthew Hopkins was, but *The Conqueror Worm* was the title of a poem by Poe, so they could sell the film as Edgar Allan Poe in America. I didn't really know where the poem came from, until one day I was re-reading *Ligeia*, and in it is the poem, *The Conqueror Worm*, which I had completely forgotten about.

LAWRENCE FRENCH: At the end of *The Conqueror Worm* you meet with a very bloody death. You get hacked to pieces with an ax.

VINCENT PRICE: Oh yes, that was terrible. Remember though, this was a very violent time in English history. The story is set in 17th century England, during the bloody civil war between Oliver Cromwell and King Charles I.

Obviously (at this early stage, anyway), Hopkins still has *some* belief in the rightness of his "work."

The scene concludes with Hopkins commenting on his assistant's enthusiasm: "You enjoy torture, don't you Stearne?" Price's hard voice carries a hint of disdain as he turns his face away from his compatriot to stare straight ahead.

"And you?" asks Stearne, sneering, before insolently adding, "Sir." At this, Price's head jerks around, almost angrily, at the question. But instead of a reply, he simply turns forward again, his face stony and unreadable. Perhaps Stearne has hit a nerve.

Hopkins is a man that does not sully his own hands. That is why he has Stearne working for him. When he arrives in Sarah's village, Hopkins leads a gaggle of villagers to the house of their first victim. Hopkins stops at the threshold, however, and glances at Stearne, who dutifully steps forward and bangs on the portal. Hopkins disdains to even knock on the door!

Price reveals further aspects of Hopkins' character when Stearne and he begin questioning the old priest. After Stearne slaps the old man, Price closes his eyes for a moment and turns his head slightly—as if momentarily repulsed by his assistant's debasing and violent action. Reeves provides no close-up here (which perhaps would have been too overtly blatant), choosing instead to stay in medium shot on all three of the actors, so one could easily miss Price's subtle manner. (Ever the professional, Price gives that extra effort even when not on center stage.) Moments later, when the priest rejects their accusations, Price's head snaps back and he shouts with venom, "All you reject is the true God! Take him Stearne, look for the Devil's marks upon him." Then, tellingly, Hopkins turns away so that his assistant (rather than himself) can get on with his cruel work.

Hopkins obviously enjoys the power he wields and (on at least some superficial level) believes in his profession. Yet (unlike his coarse compatriot) he does not necessarily revel in the brutality that comes along with it. Price's subtle playing reveals the multi-faceted character hiding beneath the cold mantle of "Witchfinder General."

Price and his fellow actors are aided by Reeves' sure-handed direction and a squeeze-every-dollar-(or £, actually)-attitude from its production staff, who create a realistic stage upon which their players can move. *Witchfinder General* looks much more lavish than its meager £82,000 (roughly $250,000) budget would normally allow—thanks to the ingenuity and creativity of Michael Reeves and his production crew. For instance, during the Lavenham witch-burning sequence, Reeves found that they couldn't afford an expensive camera crane, so for a mere £10 he rented a cherrypicker from the local utility company instead. Also, rather than rent costly studio space for the interiors, the production leased two abandoned aircraft hangers outside of St. Edmunds for the bargain rate of £1,500 a month. (Of course, since the tin roofs caused an echo sound, this necessitated significant dialogue re-dubbing later on; but it still proved far cheaper than shooting in a film studio.) And filming at actual historic locations (such as Orford Castle in East Anglia) added immensely to the realism.

When released on video in the late 1980s, American fans of *Witchfinder General* were in for a shock, for Paul Ferris' original orchestral score had been replaced by a synthesizer composition by Kendall Schmidt. Apparently, this was done by Orion Pictures when they acquired the rights to the AIP catalogue in 1983—and neglected to obtain the musical rights as well, so that some films had to be re-scored or royalties paid to their original composers. "I pretty much like what I did with [*Conqueror Worm*]," commented Schmidt in *Gorezone* magazine. "I took an acoustic approach, used mostly strings, did a contrapuntal kind of score. I think it fits dramatically, but if you've seen the film 20,000 times the way it used to be…" Indeed, the melancholy "new" score works quite well within the context of the film.

In America, of course, AIP re-titled the film *Conqueror Worm* (after a poem by Edgar Allan Poe) to ride the tail end of their ongoing Poe series. It proved a financial boon for AIP, grossing over $1.5 million in domestic rentals (no doubt buttressed by all the inflammatory reviews complaining of excessive violence and bad taste). Ever the opportunists, AIP played up the film's

Hopkins seduces Sarah (Hilary Dwyer) by promising to go easy on Sarah's guardian if she acquiesces.

gruesome qualities in its advertising. "LEAVE THE CHILDREN HOME!" screamed the ads, "...and if YOU are SQUEAMISH STAY HOME WITH THEM!!!!!!!" Underneath this incendiary ad-line sat a repulsive rendering of a grinning, partially decayed skull and a particularly grotesque passage from Poe's poem "The Conqueror Worm":

> A crawling shape intrude!
> A blood-red thing that writhes
> from out the scenic solitude!
> It writhes!—it writhes!—
> with mortal pangs
> The mimes become its food,
> And seraphs sob at vermin fangs
> In human gore imbued.

Though AIP's ads loudly proclaimed it "Edgar Allan Poe's *The Conqueror Worm*," small print at the bottom admitted that the film was "Based on a book entitled 'Witchfinder General' by Ronald Bassett and [ahem] the poem by Edgar Allan Poe."

"Although the story had a Poe flavor to it," explained Sam Arkoff in his autobiography *Flying Through Hollywood by the Seat of My Pants*, "we had worried that *The Witchfinder General* was an English tale that wouldn't have much appeal on this side of the Atlantic... However, we came across an Edgar Allan Poe verse which included a line that spoke of a 'conqueror worm.' We weren't exactly sure what it meant [Poe uses the term as a metaphor for death], but it was pure Poe and seemed to fit with *The Witchfinder General*'s story line. We felt

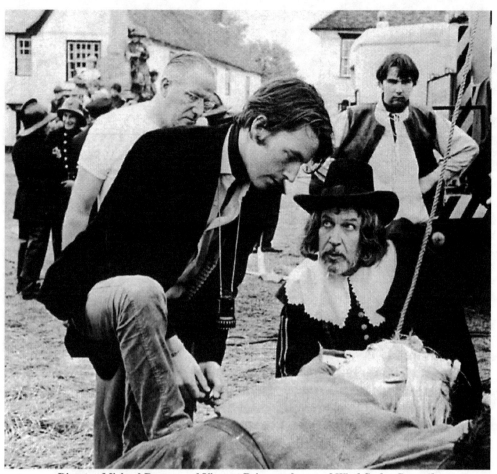

Director Michael Reeves and Vincent Price on the set of *Witchfinder General*.

if we had Vincent recite the poem at the beginning of the film, we could legitimately call the picture a Poe movie."

Price himself, however (as well as just about everyone else), failed to see the "legitimacy" of calling *Witchfinder General* a Poe picture, commenting to interviewer Michael Orlando Yaccarino in *Scarlet Street* magazine that "*The Conqueror Worm* was the most ridiculous title for *Witchfinder General*. It took me six months to find the goddamn poem!"

Apart from the expected seat-selling slants of midnight showings, bookstore tie-ins and attendant "nurses," AIP came up with a suggestion that was sure to warm the cockles of Vincent Price's art-loving heart. "Tie in with your local Sears stores," recommended the film's pressbook, "for a Vincent Price 'Paint In' with local artists duplicating the art work from *The Conqueror Worm*." (At the time, Price was in the middle of a decade-long affiliation with Sears, Roebuck and Company in which the art-loving actor bought over 55,000 pieces of fine art for The Vincent Price Collection sold at Sears stores throughout America in an effort to "bring art to people in their daily living.") On second thought, considering the *Conqueror Worm* "artwork" in question, such a suggested stunt must have sent a cold shiver down the actor's artistic spine.

While filming *Witchfinder General* in England, Price signed to appear in a small role in *The Magic Christian* (1970) alongside the likes of Christopher Lee, Yul Brynner and Raquel Welch. Unfortunately, *Witchfinder General* went over schedule and Price was unable to keep his cameo commitment.

Commenting on his co-star, Ian Ogilvy told *Scarlet Street* magazine, "I remember [Vincent Price] was a funny, funny guy, but a lot of it was fairly unprintable, the stuff he came out with.

He was extremely forbearing. I had to kill him with an ax, and we had this very hard rubber ax. I hit him and Vincent died gracefully."

Though a "funny, funny guy" off-screen, Vincent Price (under Michael Reeves' fractious hand) delivered a deadly serious performance as Matthew Hopkins. His powerful portrayal, combined with Reeves' inventive direction and hard-line approach to violence, turned this tale of a *Witchfinder General* into a film of significant thematic and artistic integrity.

"I think *Conqueror Worm* is a good film for that genre and that time," commented "Deke" Heyward, "and it may be one of the better things that Vincent Price has done."

Sam Arkoff concurred: "Michael Reeves brought out some element in Vincent that hadn't been seen in a long time. Vincent was more savage in that picture. Michael really brought out the balls in him."

And what did Vincent Price himself think of his work in *Witchfinder General*?: "I think it's one of the best performances I've ever given." Indeed.

CREDITS: U.S. Title: *Conqueror Worm* (Note: On the film print itself the title actually appears as *Matthew Hopkins, Conqueror Worm*); Director: Michael Reeves; Executive Producer: Tony Tenser; Producers: Louis M. Heyward, Philip Waddilove, Arnold Miller; Screenplay: Tom Baker, Michael Reeves; Additional Scenes: Louis M. Heyward (From the Novel *Witchfinder General* by Ronald Bassett); Cinematography: John Coquillon; Art Director: Jim Morahan; Set Dressers: Jimmy James, Andrew Low; Film Editor: Howard Lanning; Dubbing Editor: Dennis Lanning; Music: Paul Ferris (Kendall Schmidt for video release); Production Manager: Ricky Coward; Location Manager: Ewan Pearson; Wardrobe: Jill Thomson; Hairdresser: Henry Montsash; Makeup: Dore Hamilton; Special Effects: Roger Dicken; A Tigon British Film production released May 15, 1968 by American International Pictures; 87 minutes

CAST: Vincent Price (Matthew Hopkins); Ian Ogilvy (Richard Marshall); Robert Russell (John Stearne); Nicky Henson (Trooper Swallow); Hilary Dwyer (Sarah); Rupert Davies (John Lowes); Patrick Wymark (Oliver Cromwell); Wilfred Brambell (Master Loach); Tony Selby (Salter); Michael Beint (Captain Gordon); Bernard Kay (Fisherman); Beaufoy Milton (Priest); John Trenaman (Trooper Harcourt); Bill Maxwell (Trooper Gifford); Peter Thomas (Farrier); Maggie Kimberly (Elizabeth Clark); Ann Tirard (Old Woman); Gillian Aldham; Hira Talfrey (Hanged Woman); Jack Lynn (Brandeston Innkeeper); Michael Segal; David Webb (Jailer); Sally Douglas; Edward Palmer (Shepherd); Lee Peters (Infantry Sergeant); Peter Haigh (Lavenham Magistrate); Godfrey James (Webb); Morris Jar [Paul Ferris] (Paul); David Lyell (Foot Soldier); Alf Joint (Sentry); John Kidd (Magistrate); Susi Field; Margaret Nolan; Philip Waddilove; Tony Lemmon; Martin Terry; Derek Ware

SCREAM AND SCREAM AGAIN (1970)

by David H. Smith

Baseball great Jackie Robinson was a pioneering man. Besides being an outstanding player who was elected to the Hall of Fame, he was the first African-American to shatter the sport's segregated system. There's a weird irony about his life, though. "To tell the truth," said Jackie's widow Rachel, "he preferred football."

However *non sequitur* it may sound, Vincent Price circa 1969 was a lot like the former Brooklyn Dodger. Even then, it was no secret Price appeared in so many horror films because they made money, and this allowed him to cultivate his eclectic interests in art and cuisine. The intelligentsia forgave his mercenary presence in those films because, outside of them, Price did so much to encourage appreciation by the layman for those finer things in life.

An art connoisseur, gourmet chef, television personality, author and lecturer, Vincent Price was nevertheless practical and down-to-earth about his typecasting. "I'd prefer to make more artistic, important pictures," he conceded. "Who wouldn't? But in a period where few people go to the movies, it's good to be appearing in films that are well attended." Like some entertainment dervish, Price moved from film sets to location shoots to the *Hollywood Squares* game show, episodes of *Here's Lucy* and *The Mod Squad*, to the demo kitchenette of *Dinah's Place*, all without missing a beat.

Unfortunately, as Marshall McLuhan used to say, "We drive into the future using only our rearview mirror"—at the time, Vincent Price had no reason to suspect American International Pictures of steering his movie career wrong. The "company" had never treated him shabbily before, and, even in the least film, his image had never suffered any lasting damage.

But with *Scream and Scream Again*, however good it may have looked on paper, behind-closed-doors machinations and AIP's indefatigable marketing department worked overtime against one another. The casting promised so much more than it delivered, and the movie itself was as jumbled a production mess as they come.

Early in the 1960s, expatriate American Milton Subotsky produced a couple of cheapie feature films designed to cash in on the craze for traditional jazz that was briefly flowering in Britain. After a couple of those—like *It's Trad, Dad!* (1962), directed by Richard Lester (who found Subotsky a "cartoon American innocent abroad") and *Just For Fun* (1963)—Subotsky decided to stake a claim in the lucrative horror territory strip-mined by Hammer Films. He found a collaborator in Max J. Rosenberg, and together they formed Amicus (Latin for "friend") Productions to give Hammer a run for its sterling with a series of 19 chillers that would run up to the early 1970s.

Unlike the period Hammer films, however, Amicus kept its horrors modern-day (saving on costumes and sets), but unabashedly used many of Hammer's regular stars and character actors, as well as behind-the-scenes personnel. To good effect and profit, Amicus frequently used the anthology format of four or five stories told under the pretense of a larger, arguably scarier clincher at the end.

Subotsky was the creative force behind he and Rosenberg. He was keen on recognizing box-office potential in forgotten horror properties like 1950s E.C. Comics, acquiring the scriptwriting services of contemporary genre masters like Robert Bloch (1917-94), or banking on the future success of then-unknowns like Stephen King (born 1947). (Rights purchased in perpetuity explain Subotsky's "co-producer" credit on several films based on early King stories, even *Sometimes They Come Back... Again*—made five years after his death!) Subotsky acquired the rights for Amicus of an obscure science fiction novel which laid the groundwork for *Scream and Scream Again*.

The Disorientated Man was a short, almost unwieldy pulp novel written by "Peter Saxon" and published in 1966. Saxon was initially the personal pseudonym of Irish journalist, editor and author W. Howard Baker. Under the Saxon *nom de plume*, Baker wrote many titles for Amalgamated Press, mainly stories in the Sexton Blake series (a kind of second-rate Sherlock Holmes) before its cancellation in 1963.

Baker then took the name to Mayflower Books in 1965, where the series flourished briefly, written by him and others under what was now a house name (much like author Lester Dent did with "Kenneth Robeson" and the Doc Savage pulp series in America). *The Disorientated Man*, first published in the U.S. in 1967, was actually written by U.K. publisher and pulp writer Stephen Frances, with heavy revisions by Baker.

Securing the rights, Subotsky tried his hand at adapting *The Disorientated Man* into screenplay form, but soon came to realize—even after eliminating the original's outer space aliens (!) responsible for the Frankensteinian science—it would prove to be beyond the limited wherewithal of Amicus to produce anything that did justice to the book's themes of cold-war politics, vampires, fascists and mad science.

In 1969, Subotsky brought the project to Louis M. "Deke" Heyward, the head of AIP's English production division, who promptly announced in the trades "*Screamer*, a super-suspense mystery feature" for its production schedule. Filming was to begin in May 1969, with Gordon Hessler directing.

Born in 1930 in Germany, Hessler was first a story editor for the TV series *Alfred Hitchcock Presents* (1955-62) and later served as a producer and director on *The Alfred Hitchcock Hour* (1962-65). He made his feature film directing debut in 1964 with *The Woman Who Wouldn't Die* starring Gary Merrill. Heyward remembered Hessler from when they had both worked at Universal and brought him over to England to sit in the abandoned director's chair of *The Oblong Box* (1969) when Michael Reeves balked at the script, got up and left (and died from a barbiturate overdose soon after).

This time, Hessler nearly threw in the towel himself because of Subotsky's script—he found it "unplayable" (a familiar complaint about Subotsky screenplays, first lodged by Richard Lester, who early on thought the unstructured 23 pages sent him for *It's Trad, Dad!* were a rough outline not, as Subotsky contended, the full shooting script). Hessler was allowed to bring in his friend Christopher Wicking, who had contributed "additional dialogue" and all those bawdy, ersatz-Hammer tavern scenes to *The Oblong Box*, to make sense of it all. It was Wicking who built up the political aspect and gave *Scream and Scream Again* its unsettling outlook on the future.

As AIP executives were wont to do, Heyward was looking for a marketing *coup de grace* for his next picture, and inexplicably saw the foundering Subotsky project as a seaworthy vessel to launch it in. Heyward had already struck gold by teaming Boris Karloff with Christopher Lee alongside horror starlet Barbara Steele for *The Crimson Cult* (1968), a Lovecraftian witchcraft thriller. The period melodrama *The Oblong Box*, full of black magic (not voodoo, per se), premature burial and fisheye lens shots galore, boasted a variation of the casting formula, pairing Lee with Vincent Price.

Surely the third time would have just as much box-office charm, so Heyward would reuse the "more is better" casting maxim again; alas, Karloff had recently passed away, consequently passing the sputtering torch of horror superstardom to Vincent Price and his British contemporaries, Peter Cushing and a reluctant Lee.

Price was already in England, having agreed to a three-film deal with Heyward, and effortlessly donned the bloodied surgical scrubs of mad medico Dr. Browning for *Scream and Scream Again*. Price recognized the importance of his role and his screen brethren to the genre: "If all the mad doctors were extracted from crime, horror, and science fiction, you wouldn't have much

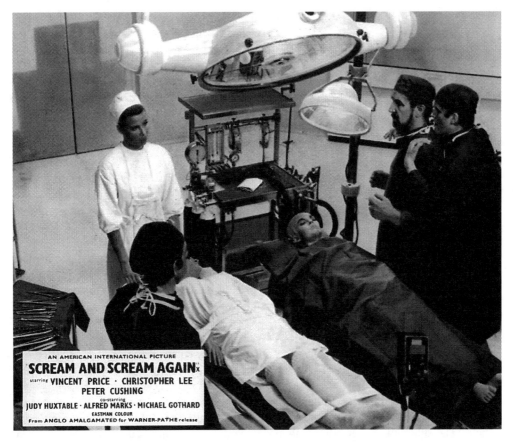

left. Think of Dr. Jekyll, Dr. Fu Manchu, Dr. Cyclops, Dr. Caligari, Dr. No, Dr. Strangelove, etc. People are wary of doctors, anyway, and mystified by the paraphernalia of surgery and medical research. It's always been a rich field for horror stories."

Nowadays, opinions of *Scream and Scream Again* (as it was finally entitled) seem to have an all or nothing air about them. Critics either admire it for its kinetic direction and paranoid political subtext (one, David Pirie in *A Heritage of Horror: The English Gothic Cinema 1946-1972*, said it was "quite on a par with the work of Nigel Kneale or Richard Matheson"), or they reject it outright for its confusing and disjointed narrative. Hessler himself said the film was ahead of its time, a conceit to which studio chronicler Mark Thomas McGee (*Faster and Furiouser: The Revised and Fattened Fable of American International Pictures*) rejoined, "How much longer do we have to wait?" The movie is lurid and sometimes unpleasant, but there are occasional flashes of power.

It's difficult to summarize the full plot of *Scream and Scream Again* without becoming embroiled in detail and nuance. As it pertains to Vincent Price, however, there are only a couple of scenes that bear discussion.

Private researcher Dr. Browning (Dr. Sanders in the book) is introduced about 10 minutes into *Scream and Scream Again*, questioned by the police about a nurse in his employ found dead and drained of blood on his estate. There is no sense of foreboding in the scene, no hint that Price's character knows more than the ignorance he pleads to the investigators. (No surprise the police can't put two and two together, as these police are remarkably naive. One scene later has an undercover policewoman, wired with a hidden microphone, parked in a secluded area with a handsome young man in testosterone-soaked leather trousers, and the dimbulb peace officers all sit and puzzle over what could possibly be making that "sucking" sound they hear!) Yet, because it is *Vincent Price,* not some anonymous character actor in a tweed jacket, you just know there's more to it.

TRIPLE
DISTILLED
HORROR
...as powerful
as a vat
of boiling
ACID!

SCREAM
and SCREAM AGAIN

VINCENT PRICE · CHRISTOPHER LEE · PETER CUSHING
an American International Picture

In point of fact, *Scream and Scream Again* squanders the talents of all three of its "big name" horror stars. The trio are never even on-screen together, but AIP seems to be following horror-film precedent set years before by keeping them apart. Universal upperclassmen Boris Karloff and Bela Lugosi never crossed paths in their fifth pairing, *Black Friday* (1940), in spite of their *quid pro quo* top billing.

The same goes for genre sophomores John Carradine and Lon Chaney, Jr. in the all-star monster rally *House of Frankenstein* (1944), their respective "Dracula" haunts and "Wolf Man" rampages kept separate and distinct; Carradine and Chaney, their roles as brothers notwithstanding, never met in the *House of the Black Death* (1966) either.

Cushing and Lee never encountered one another in *The House that Dripped Blood* (1970) or in *Arabian Adventure* (1979). Cushing and Carradine were strangers to one another in *Shock Waves* (1977), and Cushing (again!) and veteran European horror star Paul Naschy (born 1934) never shared a scene in *Mystery on Monster Island* (1980), disappointing fans on two continents.

Scream and Scream Again's biggest casting profligacy comes with Cushing, relegated to a three-minute cameo as an officer in the government of a neighboring, unnamed fascist nation (Nazi black and red color schemes, brassards and banners with vaguely swastikaed emblems). When a sadistic subordinate (Marshall Jones), taken to task by Cushing, does him in with a sham of *Star Trek*'s Vulcan nerve pinch (or "three-finger salute"), Cushing disappears from the action. The subordinate then usurps his position, still acting on his own, unknown agenda. (Cushing and Price wouldn't share a scene until, believe it or not, their *third* movie together, 1974's *Madhouse*.)

Time-wise, Christopher Lee fares little better as the British government official who knows more than he tells, but his part is more substantial. If anything, Lee's performance in *Scream and Scream Again* seems to substantiate everything his detractors have said for years about his real-life egotism. Haughty and aloof, Lee seems to treat the small role (however pivotal it is in the end) as unworthy of his thespian talent.

Of the three stars, Price comes off best, but that's damning him with faint praise. It isn't until the final confrontation with an intuitive coroner's assistant (Christopher Matthews) that Price really gets a chance to show his dynamism. In a scene that very easily could have degenerated into the most savory honey-baked spiral-sliced vainglorious ham, Price instead is the epitome of cordial reserve. His matter-of-fact rationale is absolutely chilling and, at the same time, ingratiating.

"It's the old mad scientist's dream: 'Let's Play God,'" Matthews shakes his head after Price, like a proud parent, gives the young man a tour of his mansion's hidden operating room and expounds on his method of creating half-human, half-synthetic "composites."

"My dear young man," Price replies without patronage, "you know as well as I do that God is dying all over the world. Man invented Him but doesn't need him anymore. Man is God now. As a matter of fact, he always was."

For what has, up till now, been a routine, dated thriller, full of miniskirted nymphets, car chases, and libidinous "vampires" in neo-Romantic poet blouses, *Scream and Scream Again* suddenly immerses itself in metaphysics. However briefly, here Wicking's helter-skelter screenplay borrows from Nietzsche ("Is man only a blunder of God, or God only a blunder of man?") and Voltaire ("If God does not exist, it would be necessary to invent Him.") in an outlandish juxtaposition of the drive-in and the art-house crowds.

Suddenly, jarringly, all of Wicking's disparate plotlines come together in the last 10 minutes, with Cushing's murderer attacking Price, who reveals himself to be a superhuman composite as well. Even as the unwelcome intruder finds himself submerged in a vat of murky yellow acid, Christopher Lee pops in to reprimand Price for allowing his earlier, unaccountably vampiric creation (Michael Gothard) to run amuck in London's most psychedelic discotheques (which occupied the bulk of the movie's running time).

"But what of the dream?" Price challenges his superior.

"There is only nightmare," Lee answers cryptically and, with his most perfunctory, non-contact-lensed Dracula hypnotic gaze, forces Price to lie down in the same vile-looking liquid. "In horror films the odds are always heavily against me," Price said in an on-set interview. "But then I'm always evil in a keen, clean way."

Price comes off as anything but (literally) clean in his demise, however. In his autobiography *Tall, Dark and Gruesome,* Christopher Lee recalled "the yellow tinge of the acid made it look like Vincent had suffered some terrible natural mishap on a grand scale, so the first take we did was completely ruined by our both laughing as we fought to the death." Neglecting to use nose plugs, Price felt he suffered respiratory problems for the rest of his life from the scene.

After Dr. Browning's suicide, Lee escorts the bewildered Matthews and his girlfriend (Judi Bloom) out to a waiting limousine. Presumably, the government conspiracy to replace humankind has suffered only a temporary setback, but, with reorganization, will someday start anew. Or something.

Milton Subotsky was at a loss himself to explain it all. "Strangely enough, *Scream and Scream Again* made a lot of money," he said in a 1973 *Cinefantastique* interview. "I don't know why, it wasn't all that good. It might have been because we used three top horror stars and it had a very good title."

Even the stars of *Scream and Scream Again* are unable to explain the appeal. Price, interviewed in *Cinefantastique*, shrugged, "I know it [that the film was a favorite of Fritz Lang]. I never knew what it was all about, but Fritz really loved it. It was a strange story. Strange movie."

Indeed, Fritz Lang admired *Scream and Scream Again* because of its political subtext. Its depiction of an impersonal, highly technological "Big Brother" state was reminiscent of the Austrian-born director's own *Metropolis* (1926), *Spione* (1928) and Dr. Mabuse films *Dr. Mabuse der Spieler* (1922), *Das Testament des Dr. Mabuse* (1933) and *Die tausend Augen des Dr. Mabuse* (1960).

Even more so than his German Expressionist classics, Lang's American *The Big Heat* (1953) echoes the theme with a bulldogged homicide sergeant (Glenn Ford) who finds but cannot defeat the evil at the top of the crime syndicate strangling his city and its administration. Here, in *Scream and Scream Again,* that theme is taken still further—our political masters are literally monsters.

Executive producer Heyward, ever stacking the movie's deck for potential audience favor, thought he had dealt *Scream and Scream Again* a straight (after his three of a kind) by signing 1960s teenybopper band The Amen Corner to perform two songs in the discotheque scenes. Originating from the Cardiff area, The Amen Corner, a seven-piece band that included a small brass section, had shot to national prominence in the U.K. with "Gin House" and continued with a string of Brit-

---

LAWRENCE FRENCH: You did *Madhouse* with Peter Cushing, but what else?

VINCENT PRICE: We did a radio show in England called *Aliens of the Mind* (broadcast in six parts in January, 1977), and were in a picture called *Scream and Scream Again*

LAWRENCE FRENCH: Yes, but you never appeared in any scenes with Peter Cushing in *Scream and Scream Again.* Cushing was only on screen for about two minutes.

VINCENT PRICE: Yes, and Chris Lee was in it as well.

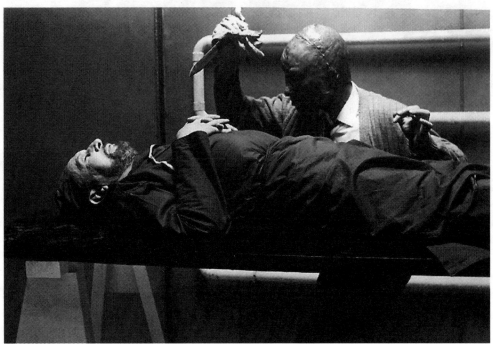

Dr. Browning (Vincent Price) is attacked in *Scream and Scream Again*.

ish Top 10 successes. As the hits dried up, the group splintered in 1970, with the brass section joining Judas Jump, and the remainder becoming Fairweather (named for Welsh-born lead singer Andy Fairweather-Low), which itself disbanded after only one hit. Neither song performed in *Scream and Scream Again* was a chart hit, and none of The Amen Corner's LPs remain in print today.

Shortsighted AIP, the idea of home video in 1970 being as farfetched as the science fiction trappings the company banked on in its films, failed to secure the rights to the music soundtrack in perpetuity. Ergo, nowadays, David Whitaker's original music score—a tribute to the eerie jazz soundtracks of the German Edgar Wallace krimi films of the early 1960s—has been replaced by a synthesized pastiche. (Italian director Mario Bava's gorgeously atmospheric *Planet of the Vampires* suffers a similar videocassette fate.)

The soundtrack substitution isn't too noticeable (though there is a conspicuous jump-cut in the opening credits between the "car stunts" and the screenplay credits), save for one scene when the bloodcurdling scream of a captured defector (Yutte Stensgaard) segues into The Amen Corner's singer belting out the movie's homonymous-title song. Unfortunately on cable and video, the original cleverness looks rather silly, as he seems to be lip-synching a Moog synthesizer wail. As *Video Watchdog* pointed out, after this tinkering, "The scuffling shoes of the dancing audience [are] actually louder than the music they're dancing to!"

Pulling what he thought would be another trump card, Heyward got a friend of his, a pre-*Monty Python's Flying Circus* Terry Gilliam, to create some animated titles for *Scream and Scream Again*. Filled as they were with humor and violence, poker-faced AIP head honcho James H. Nicholson promptly deleted them in favor of stock lettering.

His literary contribution ingloriously removed from the very project he begat, Milton Subotsky contented himself with a producer credit (alongside Rosenberg), With hindsight and honesty, Subotsky conceded that "it was a bit of a cheat to advertise [Price, Lee and Cushing] as 'stars' rather than 'guest stars'" in an interview published in the second issue of *Little Shoppe of Horrors*.

Christopher Wicking, even with all the critical dirt heaped on him, managed to exhume himself and carve a successful screenwriting career in 1970s British horror, scripting *Cry of the*

Banshee (1970) (the last of Price's "period" horror films, and a return to snarling, eye-rolling form), *Murders in the Rue Morgue*, *Demons of the Mind* (both 1971*), Blood from the Mummy's Tomb* (1972) and Hammer's swan song *To the Devil a Daughter* (1976). Wicking also wrote the legendary unproduced Hammer Films version of *Vampirella*, based on the fantasy pop comic created by *Famous Monsters of Filmland* editor Forrest J Ackerman.

Composer David Whitaker similarly saw cinematic justice in the 1970s, contributing soundtracks to *Vampire Circus* (1971), *Dr. Jekyll and Sister Hyde* (1972), *Old Dracula* (1974) and *Dominique* (1978). None of them suffered any post-production retrenchment and remain (so far) intact for future TV and video generations.

Actor Michael Gothard, who received the best notices for *Scream and Scream Again* as the dynamic and desperate vampire, also appeared in *Who Slew Auntie Roo?* and *The Devils* (both 1971), *Warlords of Atlantis* (1978), the twelfth James Bond adventure *For Your Eyes Only* (1981), *Lifeforce* (1985) and others. He was found hanged in his London apartment, an apparent suicide, in 1993.

Danish bit player Yutte Stensgaard —married to Amicus resident art director Tony Curtis— went on to no little genre immortality as the topless, blood-drenched, anagrammatical reincarnation of J. Sheridan Le Fanu's Carmilla in *Lust For a Vampire* (1971).

Bland, blond leading man Christopher Matthews appeared only in *Scars of Dracula* (1970) and *See No Evil* (1971) before vanishing from the screen altogether.

Already ill-treated for its home video release, the Vestron Video package design further disserviced the legacy of *Scream and Scream Again* with a starburst proclaiming "Vincent Price in his 92nd thriller!" It wasn't even his 92nd *film*.

As it stands, *Scream and Scream Again* is a letdown for what it might have been, but it is a mere detail in Vincent Price's career. His uncondescending performance in such a superficial thriller is, however, a reminder of why that career was so rich.

CREDITS: Produced by Max J. Rosenberg and Milton Subotsky; Executive Producer: Louis M. Heyward; Director: Gordon Hessler; Lighting Cameraman: John Coquillon, B.F.C.; Production Designer: Bill Constable; Photographed in Eastmancolor; Processed at Humphries Laboratories; Color: Movielab; Editor: Peter Elliott; Production Manager: Teresa Bolland; Art Director: Don Mingaye; 1st Assistant Director: Ariel Levy; Camera Operator: Les Young; Continuity: Eileen Bead; Makeup: Jimmie Evans; Hairdresser: Betty Sherriff; Wardrobe: Evelyn Gibbs; Dubbing Editor: Michael Redbourne; Dubbing Mixer: Hugh Strain; Construction Manager: Bill Waldron; Special Operating Theatre Equipment: Matburn Surgical Supply; Police Car Chase arranged and executed by Joe Wadham; Music Director: Shel Talmy; Music: David Whitaker; Song "Scream and Scream Again" by Dominic King; Song "When We Make Love" by Dominic King and Tim Hayes; Music on Video Release: Kendall Schmidt; Screenplay: Christopher Wicking (From Press Editorial Services' Novel "The Disorientated Man" by Peter Saxon); Copyrighted 1969 by American International Productions England Ltd.; Released in the U.S. in February 1970 on a double bill with *The Dunwich Horror*; Released in the U.K. by Pathe-Warner; 95 minutes; released in France as *Lachez les Monstres!* (*Free the Monsters!*); released on French video as *Docteur Diabolic* (*Dr. Diabolic*)

CAST: Vincent Price (Dr. Browning); Christopher Lee (Fremont); Peter Cushing (Major Benedek); Alfred Marks (Detective Superintendent Bellaver); Michael Gothard (Keith); Christopher Matthews (Dr. David Sorel); Judy Huxtable (Sylvia); Anthony Newland (Ludwig); Kenneth Benda (Professor Kingsmill); Marshall Jones (Konratz); Uta Levka (Jane); Yutte Stensgaard (Erika); Julian Holloway (Griffin); Judi Bloom (Helen Bradford); Peter Sallis (Schweitz); David Lodge (Detective Inspector Strickland); Clifford Earl (Detective Sergeant Jimmy Joyce); Nigel Lambert (Ken Sparten); Edgar D. Davies (Rogers); Lincoln Webb (Wrestler); Steve Preston (Fryer); Lee Hudson (Matron); Leslie Ewin (Tramp); Kay Adrian (Nurse); Rosalind Elliott (Valerie); The Amen Corner (Themselves)

242

CRY OF THE BANSHEE (1970)
by Susan Svehla

Cry of the Banshee seems to be to Vincent Price's film canon what an embarrassing relative is to families—we know it's there but perhaps if we ignore it, it will go away. There are no two ways about it, this movie is just plain nasty.

The film opens with the standard salute to Poe, hoping to convince audiences the well-known scribe's work actually had something to do with the film.

> In the startled ear of night
> > How they screamed out their affright!
> Too much horrified to speak
> > They can only shriek, shriek
> Out of tune—EDGAR ALLAN POE

We're off to a pretentious start but the film immediately hits rock bottom and stays there as half-clothed pagans (all beautiful young men and women, of course) perform some kind of orgy/sacrifice or something. Lord Edward Whitman (Vincent Price) and his evil henchmen spy from the surrounding bushes. "More treason against God."

A net is thrown over the worshipers and many are slaughtered. A few remain along with their leader Oona (Elisabeth Bergner). Whitman releases her, telling her to warn the others of the fate that awaits those practicing witchcraft. "If your sorcery was so strong Oona, why didn't you use it to save your children?" Whitman asks to mock her. Immediately the audience is supposed to associate the innocent witches with the early Christians (if your God is so powerful, why do terrible things happen?) and to see Whitman as the disbelieving enemy. That's really about as deep as the film gets (although at times it seems we may be standing knee deep in a dung pile).

Of course, Oona places a curse on Whitman. "I curse his flesh, his blood, his wife, his children and his house. I conjure you Lord Satan to send me an avenger!" Wait a minute, I thought the witches were good. What are they doing calling forth Satan?

A title card now announces:

> "England in the Sixteenth Century—a dark and violent time. Witchcraft and the ghosts of the old religion still hold sway in the minds of the people, pre-occupying both the Law and the Church. For, who can be sure that this is just primitive superstition and childish fear?"

Lord Whitman is truly an evil man. He terrorizes the village, sadistically enjoying the agony of innocent villagers accused of witchcraft and tortured for his amusement while justifying the dirty deeds as God's will. When the daughter and son of Oona are brought in he forces them to dance and allows the girl to be abused. When she pleads for help he pulls her to him and roughly kisses her, casting a superior look at his young wife who is the only one who protests the treatment of the pair. He murders the boy in cold blood when he springs to the aid of his sister. The sister is then shot by one of the henchmen.

Stableboy Roderick (Patrick Mower),who is sleeping with Whitman's daughter Maureen (Hilary Dwyer) has the ability to soothe Whitman's wife Patricia (Essy Persson), who is fast going over the deep end. Unfortunately, Roderick is the avenger sent to destroy the family. First victim is evil son Sean (Stephen Chase), as despicable a villain as his father. As Whitman walks back from the funeral with Father Tom he says, "I suppose you know we're cursed from Hell to Christmas." This is a classic Vincent Price line and in any other film with an ounce of humor he would have given the line the justice it deserved. But in this travesty there is no opportunity for Price to bring that distinctive voice into play and use those delightful witty intonations that put the spark in his other characters. There is no humanity in either Lord Whitman nor this grim movie, and Price plays the role that way—low-key and evil. I think the script was so hideous it probably just depressed him, I know it depressed me. I hope the salary bought him some great artwork and a few bottles of a really fine wine. Joining Price in his depression was Elisabeth Bergner as Oona. Bergner was an international stage and screen star who first appeared in German films in the 1920s. She was nominated for an Oscar for *Escape Me Never*. She also appeared in *As You Like It* with Laurence Olivier. Not only did she earn the distinction of adding this title to her resume, but to add insult to injury they even spelled her name wrong (as Elizabeth) in the credits.

Lady Patricia is the next victim even though she seems to have an affinity with Roderick. Meanwhile, second son Harry (Carl Rigg) and the new village priest Father Tom (Marshall Jones) find the gathering place of the witches and Harry stabs Oona in the neck. Unfortunately it is too late for the cursed Whitmans.

Roderick attacks Maureen and she, instead of following the orders of Harry and Father Tom, opens the door to Roderick again and leads him to her father where the Banshee attacks Whitman. Maureen shoots Roderick in the face with a gun and Whitman thinks he is saved. He tells Maureen now they can leave this cursed place.

The remaining family, Maureen, Harry and Whitman, drive away from the castle with faithful servant Bully Boy (Andrew McCullouch) at the reins. Whitman stops at the cemetery to check the casket containing Roderick's body. Surprise! It's gone!

Father Tom tells him, "Born by fire and by the fire he must be consumed." Well, now's a really nice time to tell Whitman this. Whitman enters his carriage and finds Maureen and Harry both dead. The audiences sees Bully Boy (nice name) mauled and Roderick driving the carriage into the forest.

Finally "The End" flashes on the screen. Without a doubt the best part of the film. After 87 minutes of ceaseless violence, with a sigh of relief, we find ourselves reprieved.

There isn't a decent person in this entire film. Maureen and Harry seem a little more benign then the rest of the family, but that does them no good for they are killed by the witches anyway even though Maureen is the lover of Roderick and Harry tried to save one of Whitman's victims. But Maureen and Harry are not pure of heart for we witness many of the family's worst traits in them also. And what a family; father and brothers and sister seem a little too friendly toward each other in a *Hotel New Hampshire* sort of way.

Whitman, his children and his henchmen are not the only villains in this film. The witches kill completely innocent people to get to Whitman and the villagers taunt falsely condemned witches, while pelting them and trying to stay in the good graces of Whitman.

AIP and screenwriters Christopher Wicking and Tim Kelly threw in everything they were allowed to at the time—gore, rapes, whippings, witch burnings, a branding, half-naked women. Well, there's just something for everybody—unless you're looking for a decent story and a single redeeming character. Another torment forced upon the audience is when slow spots are filled with dancing, but not just any dancing, the worst dancing you may have ever seen.

Enough of the movie. What about Vincent Price you ask? Well, he turns in his usual professional performance. And with a lighter directorial touch the film could almost have been fun (I did say almost) for several lines are crying out for that well-known Price knack of humorous deliveries, but the grisly script kept any lightness at bay in this dark nightmare known as *Cry of the Banshee*.

CREDITS: Producer/Director: Gordon Hessler; Writers: Tim Kelly and Christopher Wicking (Based on a Story by Tim Kelly); Cinematography: John Coquillon; Music Composer: Les Baxter; Makeup: Tim Smith; AIP; 1970; 87 minutes

CAST: Vincent Price (Lord Edward Whitman); Elisabeth Bergner (Oona); Essy Persson (Lady Patricia); Patrick Mower (Roderick); Hilary Dwyer (Maureen); Carl Rigg (Harry); Stephan Chase (Sean); Marshall Jones (Father Tom); Andrew McCullouch (Bully Boy)

THE ABOMINABLE DR. PHIBES (1971)
DR. PHIBES RISES AGAIN (1972)
by John E. Parnum

For the second time in his acting career, Vincent Price in *The Abominable Dr. Phibes* (1971) and *Dr. Phibes Rises Again* (1972) portrays a character whose face has been horribly burned. And like Henry Jarrod in the 1953 *House of Wax*, he must wear a "Vincent Price" disguise to cover his disfigurement. But in *Wax*, Price submitted to hours of painful makeup when Jarrod's burned visage was on the screen, and his "disguise" turns out to be a mask as Phyllis Kirk pummels it with her fists. In a kind of reverse, Phibes's applies *his* "disguise" as makeup, and the burned visage is a mask that Price the actor donned in less than two minutes. To be perfectly frank, it was a far inferior burn covering than in *Wax*, and for that reason was shown only briefly in the *Phibes* films.

Also, as in *House of Wax* nearly 20 years prior, *Dr. Phibes* was another turning point in Price's career. *House of Wax* led the way for numerous horror roles for the actor, garnering him the title of Prince of Terror. But with the *Phibes* films, Price showed that he could successfully blend giggles with his ghoulishness. As noted by James Robert Parish and Steven Whitney in *Vincent Price Unmasked* (Drake Publishers, Inc., New York, 1974, pp. 131-132), "More than anything, the movie served to bridge Price's screen image from the Poesian figure of the 1960s to the mock-horror figure of the 1970s, with the on-camera character generally as much to be pitied as to be abhorred." Ironically, he was nearly passed up for the Phibes role because of a feud with producer Samuel Z. Arkoff over the absence of intelligent scripts he had been given at American International. The two patched up matters with *The Abominable Dr. Phibes*, and Price declared that the character ranked high on his list of favorites.

As directed by Robert Fuest with a witty script by James Whiton and William Goldstein, the first *Phibes* was a welcome change for horror enthusiasts, especially since they were seeing Price as they'd never seen him before. Not much on plot, the attraction of *The Abominable Dr. Phibes* rests on a creative pairing of humor and horror, with much of the humor as black as the inside of a buzzard's bowels. Basically, it is the story of one man's revenge (and it is hinted that Phibes is a *dead* man) against the nine medical professionals who were unable to save his beloved wife, Victoria. The charm of the film resides in the outrageous methods that Phibes uses to dispatch his victims (he invokes the nine Biblical plagues visited upon the Egyptians before Exodus on each) and also in the incredible Art Deco sets in Maldine Square where Phibes resides with his automated Clockwork Wizards band and his beautiful assistant Vulnavia (Virginia North). In addition, the inclusion of many period tunes, such as "Elmer's Tune," "All I Do is Dream of You," "100 Years from Today," "Charmaine," and others, provides amusement for older audiences who can better appreciate their appropriate placement in the film.

The first of the curses we witness involves bats, which dispatch Dr. Dunwoody (Edward Burnham). A butler brings Dunwoody his breakfast and discovers his employer's bloodied corpse as a frightened bat sails into a plate of fried eggs on toast. Detectives inform Inspector Trout (Peter Jeffrey) that another bizarre murder occurred recently in which a Dr. Thorton was stung to death by bees in his library. All the while, Phibes plays Mendelssohn's "War March of the Priests" on a Wurlitzer organ (with pink Lucite pipes) that rises and descends from his mansion's cellar. He directs his mechanical band or dances with the white-gowned Vulnavia, and after each murder, Phibes ritualistically drapes an amulet around a clay bust of the victim and blow torches it.

Phibes next attends a masquerade ball, wearing a hawk half-mask, and offers an impressive frog head covering to psychiatrist Dr. Hargraves (Alex Scott). He places it on the doctor, sets a mechanism in motion and watches hawklike as the disguise crushes the headshrinker's skull. Next, Terry-Thomas as Dr. Longstreet is bled to death one night while watching some recently purchased girly films. Phibes sets each quart bottle of blood he extracts on the mantel and even returns to count them to be sure he had bled the physician dry. But during a scuffle with the victim, the amulet for Dr. Longstreet is dropped, and Phibes is unable to complete the ritual for the curse of blood. Detective Trout, who is sometimes referred to as Pike by his superior Waverly (John Cater) and others, takes the amulet to a goldsmith (Julian Grant Woods) and a rabbi (Hugh Griffith) who explains the nine curses. They also learn that all four doctors served under a Dr. Vesalius (Joseph Cotten), the chief surgeon who operated unsuccessfully upon Victoria Phibes. They mistakenly eliminate Anton Phibes as a suspect since he was supposedly killed in a fiery car crash while rushing to the hospital.

On a deserted country road, Vulnavia waylays Dr. Hedgepath (David Hutcheson) in a limousine. Phibes, wearing a handsome fox fur collar, sets up a sleet machine in the vehicle which pelts the doctor to death with ice. Later, as Phibes and Vulnavia celebrate amidst purple curtains and night club backdrops, the doctor plugs a microphone into a socket in his neck and speaks via an RCA victrola. Using his vast knowledge of music and acoustics to reproduce his voice, Phibes intones: "Nine killed her; nine shall die!" Meanwhile, Trout and Vesalius open a mausoleum and discover that Victoria's body is missing and that Phibes' ashes may belong to someone else. Trout's assistant Schenley (Norman Jones) rushes to the London Aeroplane Club to warn Dr. Kitaj (Peter Gilmore) that he may be next. Arriving too late, Kitaj, already in flight, is attacked by rats in the cockpit and crashes. All this is watched by Vulnavia and Phibes through a telescope on a nearby hill. There are nice macabre touches as Phibes tries to keep the plummeting plane in the scope's sights, rubs a daisy tenderly against his cheek as the rats tear apart Kitaj's face and applauds when the plane hits the ground. Later, while drinking champagne with Vulnavia, he lifts the glass to his neck and pours it into the socket.

Trout and Schenley take one of the remaining physicians, Dr. Witcomb (Maurice Kaufmann), into protective custody, but as they are leaving his club, a brass unicorn head is catapulted across the street, impaling the doctor to the door. Staring at the screw-like horn protruding from the other side of the door, they mutter something about it being a left-handed thread, and proceed to rotate the body to unscrew him from the door, while an unaware club member complains about all the noise. This may be the funniest but most bizarre of all the murders.

Gazing sadly at slides of Victoria, Phibes continues to eulogize his departed wife saying they will "soon be reunited in a secluded corner of the great Elysium field in the beautiful beyond." Then, he is off, carting a wheelbarrow full of cabbages and brussels sprouts to his laboratory, where he boils them in kettles, casually tossing aside any of the vegetables that do not meet his culinary expectations.

The eighth member of the surgical team, Nurse Allan (Susan Travers) is given a sedative to calm her nerves and locked in a hospital room with a guard standing outside. Phibes, disguised as an orderly, gains entrance to the room above her. Placing a diagram of a naked woman on the floor above where he thinks she sleeps, he drills a hole in the drawing's forehead through the ceiling, and pours the green vegetable glob down the hole, completely covering Nurse Allen. Finally, he encourages a swarm of locusts through a glass tubing down to where the poor woman is sleeping, where they proceed to strip her flesh to the bone.

It isn't until this point that Trout and Vesalius realize that the final curse, the curse of the first born, doesn't refer to Vesalius but rather to the surgeon's son. Sure enough, Phibes kidnaps young Lem Vesalius (Sean Bury), implants a key to the shackles that bind him behind the boy's heart, and challenges Vesalius to surgically remove the key within six minutes before acid snakes

Dr. Phibes (Vincent Price) resides with his automated Clockwork Wizards band.

down a glass spiral over Lem's face. As Vesalius operates feverishly on his son, Phibes follows the slow moving acid with his finger, and tells the surgeon: "Don't cry upon God, Doctor Vesalius; He is on my side. He led me, showed me the way in my quest for vengeance. Not God, Doctor—look to yourself." Phibes, who in addition to being one of the world's greatest organists, also has a degree in theology. Then he promises that in a few minutes Lem's face will resemble his, and removes the wig and makeup to reveal the hideously burned skull-like face.

Vesalius, naturally, retrieves the key and unlocks the chains that secure Lem as the police break in. Vulnavia, who has been demolishing the place with an ax, is doused with the acid. Phibes, on the other hand, descends to his tomb below, lies down next to the perfectly preserved body of his dear Victoria (Caroline Munro in an uncredited lifeless role) and embalms himself, fulfilling the final curse of darkness. Unusual credits roll to the strains of "Over the Rainbow," and as Tim Lucas points out in *Video Watchdog* (Number 31, 1996, p. 58), "...the Phibes films were an attempt to reinvent the silent fantastic crime serials innovated by Louis Feuillade (*Fantomas, Judex*) for the sound era.... The formality of homage extends to the end titles, which formally group the players into The Protagonists, The Victims, The Law, and Interested Parties." It is significant that no Antagonists are listed, with Price being credited as a Protagonist along with Joseph Cotten. It is a ploy to have audiences sympathize with Phibes in his agony of loneliness. And for those patrons who stay until the AIP logo appears on the screen, they are rewarded with Price's final malevolent chuckle on the soundtrack, foretelling the inevitable sequel.

American International touted *The Abominable Dr. Phibes* as Price's 100th film in 35 years on the screen. It would have been a nice tribute had it been true. The prestigious *MD* magazines for physicians called the film "a minor movie masterpiece of the macabre" and *Film Bulletin*

LAWRENCE FRENCH: *Madhouse* (1974) was your last film for AIP. Why did they stop making horror movies in England?

VINCENT PRICE: Well, it's a hard job to get a picture done in England these days. It's so expensive, and the reason they did them over there was that it was cheaper. I think, also, AIP decided that they were going to be classy. They were trying to go high class, which never worked. The film they did with Ingrid Bergman and Liza Minnelli (*A Matter of Time*) was a disaster. That really isn't there forte, or their medium. They should just turn out good entertainment pictures and let it go at that. But you know they all become grand sooner or later. There is a marvelous third script for *Dr. Phibes*, called *Dr. Phibes in the Holy Land* (laughter). I was talking with Milt Moritz (a Vice-President at AIP), and I said to him, "Why don't you make it?" The other two films have a tremendous following and it's a very funny script. Remember at the end of the last one (*Dr. Phibes Rises Again*), we were in Egypt and I sang, "Over the Rainbow" (unfortunately, in a dispute over the music rights, Price's singing of "Over the Rainbow" has been eliminated from all the videotapes of *Dr. Phibes Rises Again*). I won't do another *Phibes* film, unless Robert Fuest directs it. He's the only person in the world, who is mad enough to direct the Dr. Phibes films. He's a genuine, registered nut! He even looks like a madman. He's all over the place, like an unmade bed. What imagination he has. They were all his ideas.

noted that the screenplay was filled with "...fruitily funny moments and bizarre images." The *Philadelphia Inquirer* praised the film saying "Dr. Phibes reaches pinnacle of absurd glory. They should strike a magenta Oscar for this one. See the movie with some friends when you're all in a party mood. This film's distinction is in its satisfying giddy mingling of the laughable with the horrible." One detractor was David Pirie, who in his book *A Heritage of Horror* (Gordon Fraser, London, 1973, p.175) called it "...the worst horror film made in England since 1945."

The Abominable Dr. Phibes is a camp classic that holds up well today, especially with older audiences. There are several basic reasons why this is so. First is the humor (quite dark at times), refreshing and outrageous for 1990s audiences weaned on British comedies in their youth. Phibes patiently taps on the glass tube containing the locusts to precipitate their drop into the room below to feed on Nurse Allan; Phibes has a phone in his Wurlizer with a picture of the deceased Victoria on the dial, and there is a profile of him outlined on the shades of his limousine. But does the macabre go too far to achieve laughs? When Dr. Hargraves gets his head crushed in the frog mask, Norman Warwick's camera gives us a point of view shot through a red filter. The key embedded in young Lem seems in questionable taste, especially since we are not shown if the boy survives *two* operations. In the *Cinefantastique* Vincent Price issue (Steve Biodrowski, David Del Valle and Lawrence French, January 1989, Vol 19 [nos. 1 & 2], p. 75), the cover article states that the humor in Phibes "...is a result not so much of contents as of style: there are not a lot of punchlines, and audiences laugh not at what happens but at how it happens." They cite how director Fuest encouraged creativity on the set and how Vincent himself was responsible for many of the clever extemporaneous bits, such as drinking champagne through his neck.

The second reason that the film works are the imaginative sets by Brian Eatwell. They are colorful, totally unexpected, and most of all... fun. William N. Harrison in *Monsterscene* (Number 10, Summer 1997, p. 7) further elaborates: "Brian Eatwell's ballroom, with art nouveau flourishes topped with an illuminated, elevating art deco theater organ is the visual height of the film. The mixing of the two styles, art nouveau and art deco, seems not to accurately indicate a specific time and place, but instead create a general mood, an ambiance for a bygone era, not like the era itself, but like a dream about it. It is that atmosphere that is one of the key attributes of the film."

The extravagant sets nicely complement the imaginative script by Whiton and Goldstein, the third reason for the film's popularity and box-office success. *Monsterscene* (p. 8 & 9) also reports that the original script was much darker: The curse of the first born occurred at the beginning with Lem actually being drowned; Victoria dies of metastatic cancer of the uterus (Could the name of Phibes' substitute for Victoria, Vulnavia, then be derived from a combination of vulva and navel?); the Clockwork Wizards actually defend the estate in Maldine Square against the police, using their musical instruments as weapons, and Phibes himself turns out to be a kind of robot that leaks oil when shot. (This last may even have been carried over to the advertising since the promotion for the 22 x 28 poster reads: "Behind Anton Phibes was the lovely Vulnavia, winding him up, plugging him in, cleaning his electrodes and changing his oil. Without her, Phibes couldn't have committed one dinky little murder." The insert reflected a similar theme, but the one-sheet satirized the popular and then current movie *Love Story* with the line "Love means never having to say you're ugly [instead of 'sorry']."

Fourth, former set designer and sometime director of *The Avengers* TV series, Robert Fuest, brings an impressive look to Phibes. As seen in some of his later films, such as *The Final Program* (*The Last Days of Man on Earth*) (1973) and *The Devil's Rain* (1975), his imagination is unbridled.

Price, the fifth and most important reason for *Phibes'* success, is being overly kind. Many of the memorable bits were his, created extemporaneously by his fertile mind during the shoot. But perhaps the highest praise for his talent can be reserved for his being able to convey emotions through limited facial expressions and pantomime. Unlike Henry Jarrod in *House of Wax*, Price's face in *The Abominable Dr. Phibes* is supposed to consist of pieces of synthetic makeup: skin patches, false ears and nose and a mustache and wig. The flaw in Price's Henry Jarrod is that the character's "Price mask" appears as "smooth" and he is able to speak distinctly. Anton Phibes's face looks like both makeup and Price, with the actor dubbing in his voice later in a sound studio to simulate words produced electronically from motionless lips. Price had to visually show slight movement of vocal cords, even though he was not speaking on camera, and convey his feelings through movement of his head and eye expressions. As he relates in *The Complete Films of Vincent Price* (Lucy Chase Williams, A Citadel Press Book, Published By Carol Publishing Group, New York, 1995, p. 228), "...Phibes is an entirely different thing [from characterizations in the Corman Poe films]. Phibes is all inside, seething and boiling, and you can't do too much of that because movies are too facial, so it all had to be sublimated. I had to do a lot with my eyes and hands."

Price admitted that the makeup was both fun and problematic for him. As we have seen elsewhere in this book, Price had a marvelous sense of humor. This had disastrous effects on the makeup, as he explains in *Vincent Price Unmasked* (p. 134): "...it was agony for me because my face was covered with plastic, and I giggled and laughed the whole time, day and night, and the makeup man and I were practically married because the makeup kept dissolving and he had to patch me up every five minutes." Sometimes his humor took on a tad of mischievousness, like tormenting Joseph Cotten, as he related in *Cinefantastique* (p. 76): "...I learned the lines but never had to speak them, which made Joe very angry. He used to come up to me and say, 'It's not fair. You're not speaking the lines, and I'm having to remember all mine and say them.' I said 'Well, I remember them, Joe.'" Vincent continued this teasing with Robert Quarry in the 1972 sequel, *Dr. Phibes Rises Again*.

While *The Abominable Dr. Phibes* did well at the box-office, it probably could have done a lot better if it had been marketed properly. Newspaper promotion was geared toward the horror audiences with ad copy proclaiming: "Probably the most terrifying film you will ever see" and "There are two sides to Dr. Phibes—both of them evil!" Posters stressed the satirical side, with the *Love Story* theme spoof and the fact that Vulnavia cleaned her boss' electrodes and checked

Vincent Price rises again as Dr. Phibes.

his oil: "Although Phibes is entirely synthetic, Vulnavia—Hoo Boy!—*isn't*!" A full page ad in *Variety* played both angles, showing Phibes attaching facial parts to his bony skull with the copy line, "Evil Dr. Phibes is a man of parts... if he can only get them all together." In Britain, ads showed the *Love Story* embrace between Vulnavia and the burned Phibes with a white circle hiding the latter's face and warning, "The authorities will not permit this face to be shown on advertisements." Trade journals such as *Film Bulletin* agreed that the fun of the first Phibes was discovered too late, but that the sophisticated world was ready for the sequel and that it should be promoted to both the exploitative audiences as well as those selective and off-campus theaters that respond to off-beat humor. Unfortunately, *Dr. Phibes Rises Again* achieved nowhere near the success that the producers anticipated.

Production values for the sequel are on a par with those of the first *Phibes*. Most of the film takes place in Egypt in Phibes' impressive temple located inside a mountain. Too bad that costs had to be kept down and only the feet of a gigantic statue at the tomb's entrance could be shown. The primary fault of *Rises Again* rests in the script concocted by director Fuest and Robert Blees. Like the director's unbridled imagination, the story is all over the place, quite disjointed, with no direction. The deaths that Phibes causes are imaginative to be sure, but there is no uniformity as in the first film, some of the murders are so far fetched they seem ludicrous. There is a lot of gibberish concerning elixirs, a wondrous shrine in the Valley of the Pharaohs, a river of life, appointed tides revealing secret doors and a mysterious key ejected from a gold snake, but they seem only to drag down a lifeless plot. Even Phibes himself seems to have no idea how life will be restored to his beloved Victoria when they get to Egypt since he says, "The waters of the Nile and the tides of the sea will somehow meet and life will flow within your veins and love within our hearts."

After a capsule retelling by narrator Gary Owens of what went before, the film begins three years later with "...the moon coming into proper conjunction with the eternal planets shown upon the golden moon of the crypt, pulsing with a fantastic life of its own." As the embalming process is reversed and blood is pumped back into Phibes, he rises again and stretches his neck which gives off a creak. In a nice touch, he dusts off his organ bench, cracks his fingers and tells his lifeless Victoria that he is taking her to Egypt to resurrect her. Unfortunately, his house is in ruins and the safe has been opened. For some reason, Phibes seems to know that archeologist Darius Beiderbeck (Robert Quarry) has stolen the sacred map with directions to the River of Life, since he and his adversary are the only ones seeking the secret of eternal life.

Beiderbeck, his fiancée Diana (Fiona Lewis) and their anthropologist companion Ambrose (Hugh Griffith) leave their mansion for dinner. Beidecker's manservant (Milton Reid) takes advantage of their absence by playing pool in the game room. As he taps the balls into the table's pockets, he hears a hissing. Looking underneath the table he is shocked to see a boa constrictor slithering toward him. After crushing the snake's head with his cue, he hears clicking, and sees a second boa sliding toward him. He smashes this one with his cue, only to discover the bludgeoned boa is mechanical with a small motor concealed inside. When a third snake with a clicking motor on its back slithers onto the pool table, the servant laughs and picks it up. The "toy" turns out to be lethal, not mechanical, and it bites him. He grabs a knife and cuts his arm to suck out the venom (totally unnecessary since boas are nonpoisonous). The servant rushes to a wall phone to call for help, but as he presses the instrument to his ear and dials, a spike shoots out through the receiver and impales his head. This is probably the most contrived of all of Phibes' murders, and although very clever and funny, one later reflects how much could have gone wrong with the setup. Phibes, however, retrieves his map and he and Vulnavia embark for Egypt. (Vulnavia is now played by Miss Australia of 1970, Valli Kemp, since Virginia North was reportedly pregnant.) How she returns unscathed after having been bathed in acid in the first *Phibes* is a mystery, but as explained in *Cinefantastique* (p. 76), "...Fuest wrote the part as a different character, but AIP wanted name continuity." *Plot* continuity, apparently, was unimportant!

On board ship, Ambrose explores the hold to retrieve the model of a mountain for Beiderbeck. There he discovers Victoria encased in a calliope, the Clockwork Wizards (now called The Alexadrian Quartet) and a seven-foot bottle of Miller's gin. We are never certain about Ambrose's disappearance (although we hear a splash in the night) until he is reported washed up at a London dock inside the gin bottle. Phibes and

LAWRENCE FRENCH: Who wrote the third Phibes script?

VINCENT PRICE: The same people who wrote the other two. Bob would be wonderful doing this one, but they all get scared of doing similar things. They get frightened that they're going to be stuck in it. Yet Bob has never done anything that was nearly as good as the Dr. Phibes films.

LAWRENCE FRENCH: Yes, he even turned down directing *Theater of Blood*, because he felt he would be remaking what he had already done in the two Dr. Phibes films.

VINCENT PRICE: Bob sent me a script last year (1978) that was dreadful, absolutely dreadful. It didn't make a word of sense. It was just sort of a mish-mash. I mean, you will go along with a script if you think that the director is going to bring a lot to it, but it was not a question of that because there was nothing he could bring to it. It was just not a good script. I understand he had some money to make it in Italy, and then it all fell through.

LAWRENCE FRENCH: That was announced as *The Coming*, with Peter Cushing set to play the part that you had turned down.

VINCENT PRICE: Yes. Peter and I have done a lot together.

Love means never having to say you're ugly.

JAMES H. NICHOLSON and SAMUEL Z. ARKOFF present

VINCENT PRICE

JOSEPH COTTEN

the abominable

dr. phibes

also starring

HUGH GRIFFITH and **TERRY-THOMAS** presenting **VIRGINIA NORTH** as Vulnavia

JAMES WHITON and WILLIAM GOLDSTEIN · PRODUCED BY LOUIS M. HEYWARD and RONALD S. DUNAS
SAMUEL Z. ARKOFF and JAMES H. NICHOLSON · ORIGINAL MUSIC BY BASIL KIRCHIN · DIRECTED BY ROBERT FUEST

GP ALL AGES ADMITTED **COLOR** BY MOVIELAB An AMERICAN INTERNATIONAL Picture

Vulnavia celebrate by dining on fish, but the doctor gets a bone caught in his throat and must remove it through the socket in his neck. Sadly, Peter Cushing is wasted in a brief role as the ship's captain investigating the disappearance of Ambrose. The actor appeared worn out since he was taking on many film assignments to compensate for the death of his wife Helen earlier that year. In subtle British humor, Detective Trout tries to explain the murder of Beiderbeck's manservant to his supervisor Waverly (Peter Jeffrey and John Cater again) by saying the spike "went in one ear and out the other." Later they interview the shipping agent, Lombardo, as well as Ambrose's cousin (Terry-Thomas and Beryl Reid also as walk-ons), but the police function in this film as basically comedy relief with little care or concern in solving the mystery.

Dr. Phibes and Vulnavia set up residence in a temple under a mountain, while Biederbeck and Diana are joined in the desert by four fellow explorers: Hackett (Gerald Sim), Shavers (John Thaw), Stuart (Keith Buckley) and Baker (Lewis Flander), all, of course, destined to be the recipients of ghoulish deaths via Phibes. Shavers is the first to go, attacked by an eagle who shreds his face and plucks out his liver and eats it. When the bird returns to its perch inside Phibes' temple, the doctor asks, "Did you have a good dinner?" Oddly enough, in the newspaper ads for the film, the "See!" copy refers to "The Caress of the Man-eating Canary."

Stuart is next, and his death is a little more elaborate. Vulnavia entices the explorer into the mountain palace and positions him in such a way that his arms are within the claws of a giant golden scorpion. Phibes enters, turns a key, and the spiked claws clamp shut around Stuart's arms. He then places a replica of the RCA Victrola dog in front of Stuart and drops the key through a slot in the ceramic animal's back. After Phibes and Vulnavia leave, Stuart painfully lifts the statue and drops it. When it shatters on the ground, an army of real scorpions pour forth, covering his body and stinging him to death. Amidst Stuart's screams, Phibes and Vulnania feast again with the doctor reflecting, "If music be the food of love, play on," as he slips a grape into his assistant's mouth. The assault of the scorpions is rather graphic, with one crawling down the front of Stuart's pants and another scurrying around his eye in close-up. The latter must have caught the attention of the film's promoters since it was used as art for some of the posters and newspaper ads, only instead of a scorpion, a spider was substituted.

Consistently, after each shocking scene, a little humor is supplied. Trout and Waverly, on the trail of Phibes and the Beiderbeck expedition, study a map by their overheated Jeep in the desert. Waverly, never one to admit defeat, tells Trout who has asked him if he thinks he knows where he is, "I don't *think*! I *know*!" and Trout replies, "I don't think you know either." Meanwhile, Phibes has concealed Victoria's body in a secret compartment under a sarcophagus operated by a snake lever that ejects the all-important key that controls the flood gates to the River of Life. But Beiderbeck and his henchmen have stolen the sarcophagus. That night, after the arrival of Trout and Waverly, Beiderbeck tells Baker to sleep in the tent with the sarcophagus to guard it. When all have retired, Phibes creates a sandstorm with a gigantic wind machine (to drown out any screams, naturally). He then slips a large vise under Baker's cot and slowly turns a clamp that compresses the man (who has been reading *The Turn of the Screw*) into a solid square foot cube, with only his head protruding, and then steals the sarcophagus back. The next morning, when the party makes the grim discovery, Trout asks "Should we dispose of his body?" to which Waverly replies, "No, not his body. I think we should give his head a decent burial."

Beiderbeck, fearful for Diana after three murders, decides to send her home, and asks Hackett to drive her. As their Jeep plows through the desert sands, Hackett spots a British flag over the dunes and hears fusiliers playing Scottish bagpipes. Leaving Diana in the Jeep, he climbs the dune only to see that the waving banner and music comes from the Clockwork Wizards in kilts. In many ways, these musical mannequins—mechanical with a hint of human malevolence—are the most chilling aspects of the *Phibes* films, and their unexpected appearance in the middle of the desert is quite eerie. He rushes back to the Jeep to find Diana gone. When he turns on the ignition, he is sandblasted to the bare bone.

The finale is a confused mess. Phibes has encased Diana in wire mesh at the bottom of a pit in a mini-pyramid. As the waters fill the pit, a multitude of golden phallic snake heads, each projecting a sharply pointed forked tongue, descends upon the luckless woman. The gates to the River of Life are closed and locked, stopping Phibes and Victoria, in their quest for eternal life, from entering. Since Beiderbeck holds the golden key, Phibes reminds him that once the gates are unlocked, the waters from Diana's tomb will drain out and she will be free. Beiderbeck must choose between saving his fiancée or passing through the gates to replenish his elixir from the River of Life, for unbeknownst to Diana or anyone else, Beiderbeck is over 100 years old. In his first decent act of selflessness, Beiderbeck gives Phibes the key and rushes to release Diana as the water in the pit recedes and Phibes and Victoria sail off through the gates. With Diana safe, Beiderbeck tries to reach the gates, but they have closed and he reverts to his true age. In the theatrical release of *Rises Again*, Phibes sings "Over the Rainbow" as he and Victoria embark on their final adventure down the River of Life. But when a film is released to video, previously published music must be renegotiated, and this tongue-in-cheek interlude by Price was cut.

A second sequel was planned, but never came to fruition. Various titles such as *Dr. Phibes in the Holy Land*, *The Brides of Dr. Phibes* and *Phibes Resurrectus* appeared in trade papers and in monster magazines. Price said he would do a third only if Robert Fuest directed, but Fuest refused. Executive producer James H. Nicholson had left American International and his partner Samuel Z. Arkoff felt that black exploitation was the next wave. As Robert Quarry put it in

Cinefantastique (p. 79 and 80), "Jim was the artistic supervisor. Sam was money and promotion—though God knows he was clever. It's like everybody pulled the plug, and the ark sank—or the Arkoff sank, I should say." Recently, *Monsterscene* interviewed Caroline Munro (who had a great deal more "lifeless" screen time in *Rises Again*), and asked her if she had heard anything about another sequel. Her reply (p.12): "There was talk, and the talk that I'd heard, that seemed quite fascinating to me, was that she would actually come back... and she'd be far worse than he was!"

Robert Quarry as Darius Beiderbeck does a nice job as a man torn between his desperate greed for eternal youth and his love for Diana. Fresh from starring roles in *Count Yorga—Vampire* (1968) and *The Return of Count Yorga* (1971), Quarry apparently was being groomed by American International as a successor to Price, especially since Vincent earlier had a falling out with Arkoff. Quarry reiterates how difficult it was to keep from laughing at Price's antics on the set. In *Cinefantastique* (p. 77), he comments on Vincent's sadistic mischievousness that caused him to blow takes: "...Vincent's loving every minute of it, because he knows what he's doing to me—I thought, I'll just relate it to someone I really hate, in real life, and just look at his ear. Vincent said, 'You did better than Joe Cotten did.'"

I preferred Valli Kemp as Vulnavia in *Rises Again* to Virginia North. Kemp seemed warmer, more fragile, from her colorful entrance to when she is invited by Phibes to the Other Side, both occasions filmed kaleidoscopically. As a matter of fact, we almost feel sorry for her since she conveys a sense of sadness as "the other woman," as she dutifully helps Phibes in his plan of resurrecting Victoria. In *The Complete Films of Vincent Price* (p. 231), Kemp also refers to Price's creativity in one of the feast scenes and how difficult it was to keep from breaking up: "[Vincent] then gets another grape and shoves that in my mouth, so I have two grapes in my mouth and I daren't swallow them because if I did, I'd burst out laughing. Then he picks up a pineapple and goes to put that in my mouth as well, but then he shakes his head when he realizes it's too big... and he puts it down.... It's hysterical, as it is complete improvisation."

Although *Rises Again* is inferior to the first *Phibes* in plot and puns, Price surpasses himself in his characterization, albeit he is a bit too prissy. But isn't that what Vincent does so well? Consider his role in *Tales of Terror* (1962) as Fortunado in the famous wine-tasting scene, or as the magician Dr. Erasmus Craven in *The Raven* (1963): In these, as well as others, doesn't Price's flair for comedy tend toward the effeminate? There were times when I considered Vincent Price more sissy than sinister, but having seen him in *Leave Her to Heaven* (1945) as the relentless prosecuting attorney Russell Quinton or the cruel witchfinder Matthew Hopkins in *Conqueror Worm* (1968), I realize that this range of roles justifies Price as one of America's more distinguished character actors. Robert Quarry, once again in *Cinefantastique* (p. 77), comments on Vincent's talent to do horror films: "People think it isn't tough to act in horror films.... It's the toughest acting in the world. That's why I have nothing but admiration for all those years Vincent played those horror films. They're all peak emotions; they're all phony. And you have to create a characterization out of something that doesn't exist. There's a great difference between that and being able to play scenes with real situations where emotions come honestly."

It's unfortunate that a third *Phibes* wasn't made, if only to see how much further Price could have gone with the role. He created a character that was both terrifying and funny, majestic and sad, a character that audiences could identify with. It was a change of pace where Vincent could show how varied he could be with his talents. As Parish and Whitney sum up in *Vincent Price Unmasked* (p. 130), "For many viewers and critics *Phibes* personified the perfect Vincent Price film. It was wrapped in an art deco style; it had an insane, yet misunderstood, hero; it contained ingenious and bloody murder; and the whole package underscored a high camp atmosphere that constantly highlighted and reinforced the comedy elements. Moreover, it finally gave Price an originally devised screen character that could be totally associated with him. For a change, Price was not portraying a figure from Edgar Allan Poe literature, but fleshing out a characterization devised especially for him."

Even if a writer were to script a second sequel, and if Robert Fuest would agree to direct it, there could never be another Anton Phibes. For like Phibes, Vincent Price has passed through those mysterious gates and traveled down that River of Life. Phibes will be missed, but more importantly, we will miss the talented performances of the beloved versatile Vincent.

THE ABOMINABLE DR. PHIBES:
CREDITS: Executive Producers: James H. Nicholson and Samuel Z. Arkoff; Producers: Louis M. Heyward and Ronald S. Dunas; Director: Robert Fuest; Screenplay: James Whiton and William Goldstein; Production Manager: Richard Dalton; Production Designer: Brian Eatwell; Cinematography: Norman Warwick; Camera Operator: Godfrey Godar; Art Director: Bernard Reeves; Assistant Art Director: Christopher Burke; Assistant Director: Frank Ernst; Music: Basil Kirchin in Association with Jack Nathan; Editor: Tristram Cones; Sound Mixer: Dennis Whitlock; Sound Assistant: Ken Nightingale; Continuity: Gladys Goldsmith; Casting: Sally Nicholl; Production Secretary: Elizabeth Green; Wardrobe Supervisor: Elsa Fennell; Makeup: Trevor Crole-Rees; Hairdresser: Bernadette Ibbetson; Special Effects: George Blackwell; Dubbing Editor: Peter Gennard; Stills Cameraman: John Jay; Properties: Rex Hobbs; An American International Picture; Released May 1971 in color by Movielab; 90 minutes; Rating: GP

CAST: The Protagonists: Vincent Price (Dr. Anton Phibes); Joseph Cotten (Dr. Vesalius). The Girl: Virginia North (Vulnavia). The Victims: Terry-Thomas (Dr. Longstreet); Sean Bury (Lem Vesalius); Susan Travers (Nurse Allan); David Hucheson (Dr. Hedgepath); Edward Burnham (Dr. Dunwoody); Alex Scott (Dr. Hargreaves); Peter Gilmore (Dr. Kitaj); Maurice Kaufmann (Dr. Whitcombe). The Law: Peter Jeffrey (Detective Trout); Derek Godfrey (Crow); Norman Jones (Sergeant Schenley); John Cater (Waverley); Alan Zipson and Dallas Adams (Police Officials); James Grout (Sergeant); Alister Williamson, Thomas Heathcote, Ian Marter, and Julian Grant (Policemen). Interested Parties: Hugh Griffith (Rabbi); Aubrey Woods (Goldsmith); John Laurie (Darrow); Barbara Keogh (Mrs. Frawley); Charles Farrell (Chauffeur); John Franklyn (Graveyard Attendant); Walter Horsbrush (Ross, the Butler); Paul Frees (Singer of "Darktown Strutters Ball"); Scott Peters (Singer of "One for My Baby"); Caroline Munro (Victoria).

DR. PHIBES RISES AGAIN:
CREDITS: Executive Producers: James H. Nicholson and Samuel Z. Arkoff; Producer: Louis M. Heyward; Director: Robert Fuest; Screenplay: Robert Blees and Robert Fuest (Based on Characters created by James Whiton and William Goldstein); Production Manager: Richard Dalton; Production Designer: Brian Eatwell; Cinematography: Alex Thomson; Camera Operator: Colin Corby; Camera Assistant: John Golding; First Assistant Director: Jack Wright; Music: John Gale; Editor: Tristram Cones; Sound: Les Hammond and Dennis Whitlock; Dubbing Editor: Peter Lennard; Sound Assistant: Fred Tomlin; Continuity: Jane Buck; Casting: Sally Nicholl; Wardrobe: Ivy Baker; Vulnavia's Costumes Designed by Brian Cox; Hairdresser: Bernadette Ibbetson; Makeup: Trevor Crole-Rees; Construction Manager: Harry Phipps; Supervising Electrician: Roy Bond. An American International Picture released July 1972 in color by Movielab; 89 minutes; Rating PG

CAST: The Protagonists: Vincent Price (Dr. Anton Phibes); Robert Quarry (Darvius Biederbeck); The Girl: Valli Kemp (Vulnavia). The Victims: Hugh Griffith (Ambrose); Gerald Sim (Hackett); John Thaw (Shavers); Keith Buckley (Stuart); Lewis Flander (Baker); Milton Reid (Manservant). The Law: Peter Jeffrey (Inspector Trout); John Cater (Waverley). Interested Parties: Fiona Lewis (Diana); Peter Cushing (The Captain); Beryl Reid (Ms. Ambrose); Terry-Thomas (Lombardo); Caroline Munro (Victoria); Gary Owens (Narrator)

THEATER OF BLOOD (1973)
by John Stell

Here's where it all started, for me that is. One Saturday night (I think the year was 1976) *Theater of Blood* was featured as the "prime time movie." My dad had turned the film on, but retired early. I was entranced—there would be no early retirement for me. I don't remember laughing too much: I was too scared and mesmerized by this guy who never looked the same from one scene to the next. Then the finale came, and this horribly wonderful (or wonderfully horrible) man fell to his death in the burning theater. My reaction? A tear came to my eye (or maybe I actually cried and then chose to forget). And this was the magic of Vincent Price: He made you *love* the villain. With all due respect to the other horror icons, Vincent is the one closest to my heart. He was the first one I actually "got to know" in terms of being familiar with his work. *Theater of Blood* is, perhaps, his finest achievement, a role that required him to be funny and sad, scary and charming, witty and banal (some of those one-liners are real groaners). Often considered a black comedy, the film is actually quite horrific considering the very violent and graphic nature of the crimes (which are heavily edited for most TV showings). But it is, without question, immensely entertaining— the kind of film that leaves you with a grin from ear to ear, and, at the same time, a tear in your eye.

The plot can be viewed as a not-so-thinly-disguised slap at certain award establishments that, throughout film history, have denied the horror genre its due in terms of recognition and respect. (Sorry, the Oscar given to *The Silence of the Lambs* isn't enough.) Thus, in *Theater of Blood* we meet some of London's most well-known and respected theater critics, who are members of the revered (or reviled, take your pick) Critics Circle. They vote, each year, for the Best Actor of the Stage. Enter Edward Lionheart (Vincent Price), a "very vigorous" actor who has dedicated his 30-year stage career to presenting the works of William Shakespeare. He is not popular with said critics (although, one must assume he is popular with audiences since he's apparently gainfully employed throughout his career). Although Lionheart is supposed to be dead, he becomes the prime suspect when the critics are murdered in ways that resemble death scenes from Lionheart's final repertory season. Of course, Shakespeare must be updated for the 1970s, so Julius Caesar is stabbed by a pack of derelicts, Joan of Arc is burned by faulty hair curlers and the "queen" is fed his poodles, his babies you know, in two pies. Lionheart is alive, and "you thought me slain." Lionheart's ultimate goal, after "punishing" those who "betrayed" him, is to force the head of the Circle, Peregrine Devlin (Ian Hendry), to personally present Lionheart with the Best Actor award.

Is this screenwriters—story-conceivers Anthony Greville-Bell, Stanley Mann and John Kohn's revenge on behalf of Vincent and his ilk? Well, perhaps it is, given the obvious importance of the Critics Circle Award. The film certainly paints the critics as a self-obsessed, snobby group. But the film does *not* suggest that these people "deserved" it, merely that they went too far in persecuting a man who obviously loved what he did. And let's face it: Lionheart is a self-obsessed snob himself. (He calls the winner of the actor award a "twitching, mumbling boy... who could barely grunt his way through a performance.") But *he's* played by Vincent Price.

I suppose one could quibble about the extremely contrived plotting. I mean, in order for Lionheart's revenge plots to work, we must have drunkards, womanizers, a jealous husband, a "mother" of two, a guy named Hector, etc. Then we have to buy into the cliché of the incompetent police department, who continually screw up. Yet, the cast is so engaging and the murders so inventive that the mechanical nature of the script is soon forgotten. We don't pull out our copy of *Theater of Blood* and grade it based on "reality." We watch it again and again to watch Vincent Price kick ass.

Price, of course, in real life, had often been accused of turning in "hammy" performances, as if that were necessarily a bad thing. (Lionheart murmurs, "My reputation," after reading a review that calls him the center of an acting trio's "ham sandwich.") And *Theater of Blood* contains several references, whether intentional or not, to several of Price's earlier films. First, the structure of the film itself emulates the *Dr. Phibes* films, specifically the first one. In *The Abominable Dr. Phibes* Price plays the title character who murders the doctors who "let" his wife die on the operating table. The murders are fashioned after the fictitious "seven curses of the Pharaohs." In *Theater*, several critics "kill" Price himself and are offed in ways inspired by the Bard's work. Okay, this similarity is fairly obvious.

In 1939 Price found himself drowned in a vat of wine in Universal's *Tower of London*. When the film was remade by Roger Corman in 1962, Price took the role of Richard III, doing the drowning this time. And here, in *Theater of Blood*, we find Price once again donning a Richard costume as he gently hammers the lid on a critic who "slept like a drunken hog" through one his "finest performances," i.e., Richard III. Is it just a coincidence that the name of the wine shop where the crime takes place is called Clarence & Co.? I think not.

How about this one: In 1953's *House of Wax* the police learn the truth about Henry Jarrod (Price) by tempting a henchman of Jarrod's, who is a pathetic alcoholic, with a drink. In *Theater of Blood*, the police find out Lionheart's location—the deserted (haunted?) palace—by promising one of Lionheart's drunken compatriots some booze. And when said drunkard reaches his arm for the bottle, which is filmed against what looks like a projection screen, one is reminded of that shot in *The Tingler* when the frisky fiend crawled across the movie theater's screen.

Now let's really have some fun. In *Theater of Blood* Price creates a mask of himself for that drunkard-henchman to wear in order to create a diversion. Of course, Price fashioned many masks for himself to wear in *The Mad Magician*. And is it possible that the plot device of the "undead dead" (the person thought dead who is really alive) was inspired by 1944's *Laura*, which featured Price as a prime suspect? And then there's that surgeon's outfit he wears when beheading Horace Sprout—the same outfit (or so it appears) he dons in *Scream and Scream Again!* There's an exciting sword fight—a bow to the 1948 version of *The Three Musketeers*? When the horse was dragging Hector across the

LAWRENCE FRENCH: Of course, you got to play several Shakespearean roles when you did *Theater of Blood*.

VINCENT PRICE: Yes, I got to play eight Shakespearean parts in one picture, which very few actors get to do in their whole lifetime if they're American. It's one of my favorite pictures for a lot of reasons, one being the premise of it, which is really hysterically funny. You know, I'm the Shakespearean actor who thinks he should be given the critic's award, and instead they give it to someone who mumbles like Marlon Brando. So I set out to kill all the critics, and all the murders are done according to a Shakespearean play. The cast of critics were really extraordinary. They were all major actors in England: Jack Hawkins, Robert Morley, Arthur Lowe, who was a great comedian, the late Ian Hendry. God, a lot of them are late now. If we go on long enough we'll get rid of them all. It's getting so this is the way I explain most of the pictures I'm in, "so-and-so passed away a few years ago," and it won't be long until I can say that about myself. I think a lot of them had seen the Dr. Phibes films, which were very popular in London, and they all kind of wanted to be in one of these crazy pictures that I do. It was wonderful, except it was kind of embarrassing, because between them all, they had done every single play of Shakespeare's on the stage. Harry Andrews, for instance is probably the greatest supporting actor of Shakespearean plays. I've known Harry for a long time, ever since he played Laertes to John Gielgud's Hamlet, years and years ago.

field, I thought of the rustic setting of *Conqueror Worm*. Whether these moments are accident, fate or sly in-jokes (like Price being allowed to cook—a real-life passion of his—for Meredith Merridew) doesn't necessarily matter. The fact remains that *Theater of Blood* provides some fond Price memories—as well as creating new ones—that add to the enjoyment.

And Vincent Price is joy to behold in *Theater of Blood*. In the first murder scene, for instance, Vincent has several terrific moments. Dressed up like a constable, he adopts a slight accent and a polite manner while escorting George Maxwell (Michael Hordorn) to the squatters who

Vincent Price is a joy to behold in *Theater of Blood*.

have taken over a deserted building. During the attack, Maxwell turns to face the "constable," who stands there motionless, the shadows almost completely hiding his expressionless face (a creepy moment). Then, when the dying Maxwell staggers toward the officer, Price removes his hat, adopting a look of mock pity and concern, while quoting from the Bard's play. After Maxwell falls to the ground, he whimpers, "You… It's you. But you're dead," to which Price responds, with amusement in his voice, "No. No, another critical miscalculation on your part, dear boy. I am well. It is you who are dead." Price manages to sound both sinister and delighted. Cutting then to the theater Price and company have adopted, we find him delivering the "Friends, Romans, countrymen…" speech. When the derelicts prematurely burst into applause, Price whines, "I haven't finished yet." He calls for the stage manager, his daughter Edwina (Diana Rigg) in disguise, to bring about order.

Thus the first scene of carnage establishes the basic rhythm that the death sequences will take, with Price dressed up in appropriate costume, and the relevant lines (in addition to some witty one-liners) memorized. The victims, at first, don't realize who the strangely dressed fellow is. By the time they do, it is too late. The "punishments" are particularly brutal.

After Maxwell is punished, Hector Snipe (Dennis Price) is next on the list. Lionheart says he wants Snipe to write his life story. "It's a grave tale, Snipe," he tells him, "And difficult to write. But I'm sure you can rise to the occasion," at which point the stage floor Hector is standing on springs upward, sending Snipe into the arms of the derelicts. Lionheart then drives a spear through Hector's body, and ties him to a horse. The horse, with body in tow, rudely interrupts the funeral of George Maxwell. "But he's supposed to be one of the mourners," Devlin observes.

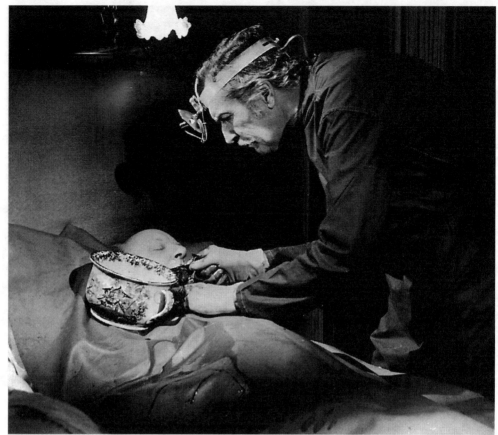

Edward Lionheart (Vincent Price) prepares to do a little surgery on critic Horace Sprout (Arthur Lowe).

Perhaps the most humorously gruesome murder is next. Father and daughter have themselves delivered in a large oak chest to the home of Horace Sprout (Arthur Lowe). Once the Sprouts are asleep, the deadly duo knock out the wife (a pre-Miss Marple Joan Hickson) with a hypodermic and prepare to cut off old Sprouty's head. Edward gives his daughter a mildly annoyed glance when she none-too-gently gives him the heavy medical sheet. As he saws off the head, blood squirts everywhere, and Lionheart calls for the basin. Mrs. Sprout tells her husband to stop snoring. The following morning, the maid enters the bedroom, screams and faints, which causes Mrs. Sprout to awaken. She shakes her husband's body, which causes the head to fall to the floor. When the maid regains consciousness, she finds herself eye to eye with Sprout's head and screams again. The head then winds up serving as the lid for Devlin's morning milk jars.

Even though the police, by now, have figured out they must protect the remaining critics, they just miss Trevor Dickman (Harry Andrews), who is asked to play the role of Antonio in "The Merchant of Venice." Edwina warns him they've made some, "slight alterations in the text. And one rather large… cut." When Dickman panics, Lionheart scolds him: "You're hardly worth the trouble and expense of this special performance." More gruesomeness ensues as Price removes the heart from Dickman's body and shaves enough off so that it measures exactly one pound. The heart is sent to Devlin ("Sorry to have missed the meeting but my heart is with you.") who observes, "It's Lionheart all right. Only he would have temerity to rewrite Shakespeare."

While the next two punishments are rather tame by comparison (one critic is drowned in wine and another is tricked into killing his own wife), the death of Miss Moon (Coral Browne) is decidedly a howl. The film's funniest sight gag has to be Price donning that bright orange afro: "Hi. I'm Butch." Impersonating a hairdresser, Price recommends the color "flame, with ash highlights." Miss Moon then gets "a bit of a shock" when she's electrocuted to the point where her face burns.

But that's child's play compared to the fate that awaits Meredith Merridew (Robert Morley) and his "babies." The elaborate "This Is Your Dish" prank, whereby Merridew thinks he's appearing on his favorite television program, is really a set-up for the robust critic to be fed his children. When Meredith insists his dogs be found, Lionheart calls, "Props!" as the TV "crew" members whistle in unison. "Two dogs, two pies," Lionheart tells him, pointing to a pair of pies topped off with whipped cream molded to look like poodles. For the first time in his life, Merridew is speechless. After force feeding Merridew his children, Lionheart observes, "He didn't have the stomach for it." Again, one senses the sick fun Morley and Price are having during this scene. Since we're sure what's in store for Merridew, one can't help but relish the moment the critic tastes the prepared meal, his face registering absolute joy.

One of the possible stumbling blocks in a film that pretty much repeats itself throughout the running time (i.e., a critic being isolated, then viciously murdered) is that the actors involved may appear to be bored, or that the film itself becomes boring. Luckily this doesn't happen in *Theater of Blood*. Certainly the screenplay is inventive and features witty and droll dialogue. But clearly this is a film that works because it features a beloved horror hero, striking a blow against those who would damn a particular genre or star. Shakespeare is basically substituting for horror. Price essentially plays himself in the sense that he's an unappreciated genius. I mean, not everyone could have approached each death scene with the enthusiasm Price clearly has. In short, the film never feels redundant.

It is interesting to note that during the 1980s many "slasher" films featured "creative" deaths too. The *Friday the 13th* films had an arsenal of tools at their disposal, while the *A Nightmare on Elm Street* films attempted to present various horrific nightmare sequences. But these films were frequently skewered themselves by critics, while many critics look upon *Theater of Blood* with a twinkle in their eyes. Why? There are many reasons— the film's obvious style and high-class production values, for instance—but the main reason is the sense of fun Price and his fellow cast members bring to the screen. Yes, the crimes are bru-

LAWRENCE FRENCH: You also got to co-star with Coral Browne, who became your (third) wife.

VINCENT PRICE: Yes, I met her on this picture. It was funny, because one night I was having dinner with Diana Rigg, who I happen to adore. I had never met Diana, but I had seen *The Avengers* and loved her in it. So she said, "I hear you're going to meet Coral Browne tomorrow." And I said, "Yes, I am, and I'm quite anxious about it, because I hear she's a woman with a tongue like a lash!" So Diana said, "Well you be sure and say hello to her for me, and take down everything she says, because she's supposed to be so funny." The next day when I was introduced to her I said, "Hello Miss Browne, Diana Rigg told me to take down everything you say, because you're so witty," whereupon she shut her mouth and never opened it again! (laughter). After *Theater of Blood* we did a Jean Anouilh play, *Ardele* in London, but the English hate Anouilh and it was not a success. Coral is really brilliant at that drawing room type of comedy. She had also done Anouilh's *Waltz of the Toreadors*, among others. We did a commercial together, which is really very funny. Everyone thinks it's for a fly-trap, but it's for a bank. Same thing (the commercial was for Citibank). When I was doing *Diversions and Delights* in San Francisco, Coral was there with me and she kept saying to me, "Oh I love it here, I don't want to go back to California." (laughter) I said to her, "Coral, San Francisco is in California. She said, "Not to me it isn't."

tal (Leonard Maltin criticizes the film for the "incredibly gory killings"). But the focus is always on the players, not the murders. (The 1980s films focused, instead, on the graphic nature of the crimes themselves.) When Price is off murdering, he's always quoting Shakespeare, so our attention is on him. Each actor gets to give his/her own variation on the "panic scene," that moment they realize Lionheart has them where he wants them. We can hear Robert Coote's "gulp" when he recognizes Lionheart. We can hear the fear in Merridew's voice when he asks, "Where are my dogs?" We see the terror in Hector Snipe's eyes when, after trying to put the blame on Devlin with respect to the Critics Circle Award, Lionheart tells him, "Do you think you can hide your guilt behind his? Maxwell thought so, too." We have a top notch cast here, and they make perfect foils for Price, here again playing the elegant villain.

As Edward Lionheart, Price brings a dignity to this role that is truly necessary for *Theater of Blood* to work. Lionheart has been wronged and humiliated by the critical establishment. They delight in his embarrassment at having lost the award. Still, it is a wonderful moment when they realize that Lionheart is going to jump, the smiles leaving their now-concerned-looking and horrified faces. Lionheart gives them a "last" contemptuous look over his shoulder before he jumps to his death. Thus, Lionheart sees his revenge as very serious work, dressing himself and his compatriots in appropriate costumes, rehearsing the "scenes," and, in the end, being impressed with his original and imaginative "performances" of what turns out to be his final "season."

Director Douglas Hickox reinforces the "theatrical" nature of the story with several clever visual ideas. The first murder—the stabbing death of George Maxwell—is seen through a plastic "curtain" which Maxwell runs into. The critics "draw back the curtains" to see Lionheart's soliloquy from *Hamlet*, just before he jumps to his death. And there's the marvelously choreographed sword fight in the gym, involving trampolines, recalling the days of swashbucklers. Such theatricality was obviously intended by the screenwriters too, as they have Dickman state, "Good heavens, dar-

Edward and daughter Edwina (Diana Rigg) cook up a little treat for Robert Morley.

ling. What an entrance, what suspense," when Rosemary (Madeline Smith) tells the critics she has grave news concerning George Maxwell. After Lionheart falls to his death, Devlin remarks, "…you must admit he knew how to make an exit."

Not that *Theater of Blood* ever becomes or feels stagy. Hickox also has some very "cinematic" visuals up his sleeve. The opening titles feature reenactments from various Shakespeare plays which are shot in black and white, immediately giving the film a "classic" feel. A worried Mrs. Maxwell, sighing heavily as the thunder booms, watches her husband leave, and the screen "dissolves" over the windshield of Maxwell's car, giving the impression that Mrs. Maxwell is praying over her husband. As Price's body hits the water, we cut to the splash created by an ice cube that has been dropped into some liquor. As the critics gather around the open grave of George Maxwell to pay their last respects, a point of view shot from the perspective of the corpse is utilized, as Mrs. Maxwell tosses a handful of dirt onto the camera lens. When Edwina, in disguise, seduces Trevor Dickman, we get close-ups of various features of her lovely face: her full, red lips, her come-hither eyes, etc. There's an amusing sight gag which shows Price's "young man" associate (Edwina in drag) sitting calmly, reading a magazine while Miss Moon fries nearby. The death of Sergeant Dogge (Eric Sykes) is "heard" over a homing device, as he reports, hidden in a trunk, the events leading up to his death (the car stopping, the approaching sound of a siren): He's actually giving a play-by-play of his own murder.

Complementing the fine visual touches and clever script ideas are a gorgeous production design by Michael Seymour and a tragic, moving score by Michael J. Lewis. The deserted theater that Lionheart and company call home is an impressive sight, providing an appropriate "stage" for Price's performances/punishments. Even better is the passionate music composed

Vincent Price is Edward Lionheart.

by Lewis (which has been isolated on the analog track of the most recent laser disc release). The piano-driven, at times operatic, score is quite gentle and sad, which, as it plays over the opening titles, has one expecting a Shakespearean tragedy (which, I suppose, this film is). But the music is incredibly invigorating during the duel scene, or appropriately intense during Miss Moon's torching. *Theater of Blood*'s finale, set inside the massive auditorium, certainly feels operatic, with father losing daughter, and being betrayed by those he trusted. In fact, it's suggested that the revenge may have been Edwina's idea, since Edward tells his dying daughter, "You did me wrong to take me out of the grave." Is he merely quoting more Shakespeare, or is there real truth in these lines?

Diana Rigg, playing the way-too-devoted offspring of Edward Lionheart, must have enjoyed her rare turn as a villain. Rigg, in fact, does have background in Shakespeare, although she is perhaps best known for her role as that sexy *Avenger* Emma Peel. Like Price, she would eventually host PBS' *Mystery* series. Rigg spends most of her time in *Theater of Blood* under a wig of curly, red hair, wearing dark sunglasses and a red mustache. If we were meant to be surprised by the real identity of the "young man" (as Snipe calls "him"), this doesn't quite come off. In several scenes we can hear "him" talking even though "he" isn't on screen, and damn if it doesn't sound like Rigg. Plus, there's the trick played on Dickman to lure him to the theater, which requires Edwina to dress as a woman. In other words, there's only so much a wig can do this time around. Still, this is in no way harmful to the film. Rigg even gets to deliver one of the film's best lines when she refers to Devlin as, "Wielder of the brutal aphorism, master of the killing phrase."

While *Theater of Blood* contains no hero per se, Ian Hendry is quite good as the only critic to escape Lionheart's wrath. (His escape from being blinded by some hot pokers is pure luck, as the sandbag controlling the descending blades gets caught on a statue long enough for the police to arrive and free Devlin.) A veteran of *Children of the Damned* (1964), *Repulsion* (1965), *Tales From the Crypt* (1972) and *Captain Kronos: Vampire Hunter* (1972), Hendry was well cast as Peregrine Devlin. Although at times Devlin appears to be amused by what's going on, Hendry delivers the dramatic goods during those moments he's supposed to be scared (as the hot blades approach), defiant (he tells Lionheart to "get it over with" during the duel scene) or concerned (he frets over the safety of Edwina).

As good as Hendry is, however, he is no match for Price. The proof? During the finale we're less concerned about Devlin's rescue than we are about Lionheart's suffering brought on by the death of his daughter. Their final scene together is quite moving, with Price cradling

Rigg, gently stroking her hair, as she, with her last words, expresses no regrets over helping her father. And after she passes away, our eyes are still on Lionheart/Price, as he tries to escape the burning flames and falling timbers of the theater. Devlin and Inspector Boote (Milo O'Shea) may not be particularly upset at Lionheart's demise, but we sure are.

If the rumors are to be believed, Vincent Price considered *Theater of Blood* his favorite film. Of course this may have to do with the fact that Price met his future wife, Coral Browne (who plays Miss Moon), while making the film. Or it could have to do with his working with a stellar supporting cast (Rigg, Hendry, Morley, O'Shea, etc.) Perhaps he was pleased with the fact that, in contrast to Edward Lionheart, Price received some of the best reviews of his career for his work in this *Theater*. (He certainly deserved them.) But the most likely explanation is that it was "all of the above."

It is quite impossible to imagine this film being the joy it is without Price's presence, the proof of which can be found in the reactions to proposed remake (which probably will never happen). A few years ago director Christopher Columbus (*Home Alone*) announced his intention to remake the film for no particular reason. Maybe he would be able to gather an interesting supporting cast. But it is doubtful that he could have cast a lead as significant as Price since the days of the "horror star" are long gone. Price brought a rich history and built-in, adoring fan base to *Theater of Blood* that no one else (at least no one I can think of) working today could possibly duplicate. It's not that there aren't talented people out there. It's just that none of the people working today have the background or "horror importance" that Price had. Unfortunately for those growing up today, the days of the "horror star" are over.

Lionheart turned out to be Price's last "great" horror role. His next released film, *Madhouse*, is certainly enjoyable, once again casting Vincent as an actor (this time named Paul Toombes). But this time out the character is a brooding, depressed one. Price isn't allowed to have as much fun. And certainly no one would line up to defend *The Monster Club*, *The House of the Long Shadows* or *Dead Heat* as being Price classics. Instead Price found memorable roles in non-horror films like *The Whales of August* and *Edward Scissorhands*. He even had fun spoofing his image in commercials for Tilex stain remover, or providing the voice for Ratigan, the villain of Disney's *The Great Mouse Detective*. But if you want to see Price doing first class work in a first-rate horror production, *Theater of Blood* is the fitting finale to Price's horror film career.

Theater of Blood holds up very well today, and gets high marks in video guides and other similar publications. It's funny and scary, sad and touching. And it gave Price, who was just over 60, yet another wonderful role to call his own. Edward Lionheart is immortal all right, but that's because the person who immortalized him is Vincent Price.

CREDITS: Producers: John Kohn and Stanley Mann; Director: Douglas Hickox; Executive Producers: Gustave Berne and Sam Jaffe; Screenplay: Anthony Greville-Bell (Based on an Idea by Stanley Mann and John Kohn); Cinematography: Wolfgang Suschitzky; Production Designer: Michael Seymour; Editor: Malcolm Cooke; Costume Designer: Michael Baldwin; Music: Michael J. Lewis; Camera Operator: Ronnie Taylor; A Sam Jaffe & Harbor Productions, Inc. Presentation; Released by United Artists April 1973, 104 minutes

CAST: Vincent Price (Edward Lionheart); Diana Rigg (Edwina Lionheart); Ian Hendry (Peregrine Devlin); Harry Andrews (Trevor Dickman); Coral Browne (Miss Moon); Robert Coote (Oliver Larding); Jack Hawkins (Psaltery); Michael Hordern (George Maxwell); Arthur Lowe (Horace Sprout); Robert Morley (Meredith Merridew); Dennis Price (Hector Snipe); Milo O'Shea (Inspector Boot); Eric Sykes (Sergeant Dogge); Madeline Smith (Rosemary); Diana Dors (Mrs. Psaltery); Joan Hickson (Mrs. Sprout); Renee Asherson (Mrs. Maxwell); Bunny Reed and Peter Thornton (Policemen); Charles Sinnickson (Vicar); Brigid Erin Bates (Maid); Tony Calvin (Police Photographer); and Tutte Lemkow, Stanley Bates; Eric Francis; Sally Gilmore; John Gilpin; Joyce Graeme; Jack Maquire; Declan Mulholland (Meth Drinkers)

MADHOUSE (1974)
by Mark Clark

Madhouse haunts me, but not the way a horror film should. It haunts me the way Angie Underwood haunts me. Angie was a bodacious high school classmate I never worked up the nerve to ask out. Ten years later at my high school reunion, long after we were both married, Angie revealed she had held a secret crush on me all those years ago. Life is riddled with missed opportunities. So is *Madhouse*.

The picture remains notable not so much for what it is, but for what it isn't. Boasting a fine cast and a fertile premise, *Madhouse* could have, and maybe even should have, provided the kind of showcase for star Vincent Price that *Targets* offered Boris Karloff six years earlier. The similarities between the two movies are striking: Both Karloff and Price play over-the-hill horror stars; in both plots, the actor crosses paths with a real-life murderer; both stories involve a behind-the-scenes wrangling between actor and producer; in both films, the stars pontificate about the nature of horror cinema; both were produced on modest budgets and incorporate a great deal of stock footage from old American-International releases.

Unfortunately that's where the comparisons end. *Targets*, an intelligent, provocative thriller helmed by gifted critic-turned-director Peter Bogdanovich, could serve as a blueprint for the production of a powerful, low-budget thriller. Its supporting performances are excellent and Karloff contributes one of the most spectacular portrayals of his lifetime. At once chillingly believable and disarmingly sentimental, the picture wrote a beautiful coda for Karloff's career.

Madhouse, on the other hand, succumbs to cliché at every opportunity. No amount of money could have rescued a project as badly botched as this dog from hack director Jim Clark. Not even the two greatest horror stars of their generation (Price and co-star Peter Cushing) could save this muddled mess. Its performances, even those from Price and Cushing, are perfunctory at best. Maddeningly predictable and agonizingly dull, *Madhouse* ranks among the most profound disappointments of Price's career.

As our story opens, horror star Paul Toombes (Price) revels in his fortune and fame. Paul and a few dozen of his closest friends gather to celebrate the release of the fifth movie featuring his character Dr. Death. After screening a short clip (Price in Dr. Death makeup intercut with sequences from his own 1963 feature *The Haunted Palace*), Paul makes a brief speech. He praises his screenwriter and longtime collaborator Herbert (Cushing) then stuns his guests by announcing he has agreed to marry his busty, brainless co-star, Ellen (Julie Crosthwait).

Faye (Adrienne Corri), an old flame of Paul's, snipes bitterly about the prospective bride. Slimy producer Quayle (Robert Quarry) reveals that the star's beloved is a former porn actress. Stung by this revelation, Paul lashes out at Ellen, who retreats to her dressing room. Moments later, someone dons the Dr. Death costume (which looks suspiciously like Price's creeper get-up from *House of Wax*) and sneaks into Ellen's room. When Paul arrives some time later to make amends with his bride-to-be, he discovers Ellen—beheaded.

Before seeing *Madhouse*, I would have wagered it was impossible for any actor to overplay the shock of discovering your lover's head has been lopped off. Somehow Price manages this dubious feat of histrionics, howling and corkscrewing his face with so much *faux* anguish that he looks positively comical. Clark and photographer Ray Parslow only make matters worse. They record Price's reaction with a low-angle close-up, shot through a fisheye lens. The result borders on the surreal, falling somewhere on the weird-o-meter between the Salvador Dali dream sequence from *Spellbound* and Jim Carrey talking out of his ass in *Ace Ventura: Pet Detective*.

It may seem like nit-picking to single out one shot for scorn, but this brief sequence sets the tone for the rest of the film: Price, as he often did when dealt subpar material, chews the scenery

Paul Toombes (Vincent Price) is haunted by his horror film past in *Madhouse*.

shamelessly. Clark, meanwhile, works in as many silly stylistic flourishes as he can, often to the detriment of fundamental storytelling.

Back to the alleged plot. Psychologically shattered by this experience, Paul retreats from filmmaking and spends the next five years in and out of sanitariums. He's cleared of any involvement in his fiancée's death, yet still wonders if he may somehow be at fault. He becomes obsessed with his Dr. Death persona. At last he's coaxed out of retirement by old buddy Herbert, who has struck a deal with producer Quayle to revive the Dr. Death character for a television series. Reluctantly, Paul sails to London to discuss the idea with his friend. As soon as Paul arrives, his acquaintances begin dropping dead.

The film devotes the balance of its running time to unraveling the "secret" of who killed Ellen and a handful of subsequent victims. As a mystery, however, *Madhouse* flounders laughably. Anyone who's seen an episode of *Columbo* can identify the killer in about five minutes.

The scenario supplies only four suspects: Paul himself (too obvious a choice even for this picture); Faye (but then we see the killer's hands are male, so she's out); Quayle (but he has no motive, since Paul's star power is important to the success of the TV series and thus the producer's paycheck) and Herbert (who doesn't have an apparent motive, either, but doesn't need one because, for Chrissakes, he's Peter Cushing). Guess who the murderer turns out to be? Suffice to say the Hardy Boys would have wrapped up this case by page 12.

There's a reasonably well-written sequence between Paul and Herbert when the star arrives in London. Paul despairs: "Everyone thinks I'm dead—and so do I." Herbert replies: "I made you come here to bring you back to life." But Paul counters: "But you're not bringing me back to life, you're bringing Dr. Death back to life and he terrifies me."

This small exchange stands as *Madhouse*'s most believably scripted and straightforwardly played scene, but again Clark undercuts the sequence. Price delivers his final lines staring into a beveled mirror. His reflection is splintered, so we can't see Price's face as he delivers his lines.

Horror show host Paul Toombes is adored by his fans.

In a bizarre and pointless subplot, Paul discovers that Faye has gone wacko and now lives in Herbert's basement, among dusty Dr. Death mementos and hundreds, perhaps thousands, of spiders. In still more wasted footage, a detective screens old Dr. Death flicks to dig up clues about Paul, who the cop thinks killed a young girl who idolized the star (the first of "Dr. Death's London victims"). This detective mucks around for three or four scenes, then vanishes and is not involved at all in the film's resolution.

It stands to reason that Scotland Yard would suspect Paul, especially when the actor's co-star and his director get bumped off. But why devote so much screen time to the police if they don't solve the crime? Clark and screenwriters Greg Morrison and Ken Levison clutter this project with a heap of irrelevant debris. Another superfluous subplot involves the foster parents of Paul's murdered groupie, who attempt to blackmail the star when they find his watch on the girl's body. After pestering Paul a couple of times, they turn up dead, too.

The film's most disappointing scene is Paul's chat with real-life TV interviewer Michael Parkinson. Parkinson asks Paul why horror films remain popular. This scene recalls Karloff's heart-to-heart with Bogdanovich about the changing nature of horror cinema in *Targets*. In that film, Karloff offered insightful criticism that seemed to flow straight from his heart.

In *Madhouse*, however, Price replies in trite psychobabble. Fright flicks remain popular, he says, "because they're not about the ordinary, the everyday world around us. They're about a world that's deep inside of us, a world of impulses and instincts we're taught to repress." These were not Price's true feelings about his life's work, and it shows. At least this scene features some decent stock footage (clips from *The Fall of the House of Usher* and *Pit and the Pendulum*).

All this builds to what's supposed to be a heart-stopping climax when Paul discovers his publicist has been killed, under circumstances almost identical to Ellen's murder. Paul wigs out and burns down the TV studio and himself along with it. He even films his demise for posterity.

Herbert Flay (Peter Cushing) tries to kill Paul in the finale of *Madhouse*.

Naturally, however, he's not really dead. Paul returns to thwart the true killer in the final reel. The real killer is, of course, Herbert. A failed actor, Herbert wanted to bump off Paul so he could take over the Dr. Death role from his longtime collaborator. In a curious and awkward denouement, Paul kills Herbert, then disguises himself as the star and goes to live with Faye in her spider-filled cellar. This dark comedic finale might have worked for a picture like *The Abominable Dr. Phibes* but seems jarring for *Madhouse*, which is for the most part played as straight (though inept) drama.

There's little to recommend here among the cast or crew, although Quarry isn't bad as the conniving Quayle. Most of the time Cushing simply appears bored. He invests the role with none of the radiant intensity he generated as Victor Frankenstein and Van Helsing and Sherlock Holmes and Grand Moff Tarkin.

Certainly the most surprising names in the film's cast list belong to Basil Rathbone and Boris Karloff, who receive screen credit even though both actors were long dead! Rathbone passed away seven years prior, and Karloff had been deceased for three years, yet both stars are credited with "special participation" in *Madhouse*. This participation is limited to stock footage—Rathbone appears in a clip from the "The Case of M. Valdemar" segment from *Tales of Terror*, Karloff in a scene from *The Raven* (1963). Nevertheless *Madhouse* may be the final film to list either star in its opening credits.

It's difficult to blame Price for his subpar work here. The actor loved to ham it up, and he surely realized that no matter kind of performance he gave, *Madhouse* was going to suck like an Electrolux. Why shouldn't Price at least enjoy himself?

Perhaps because of pictures like *Madhouse*, however, Price began choosing his projects more carefully. In the decade preceding *Madhouse*, 24 Vincent Price films were released. Price would not appear in that many more films the rest of his career, let alone during any 10-year span.

Advancing age and changing cinematic fashion lessened demand for Price's services, but the star also showed greater wisdom about which projects to accept. Providing voice-over narration for the title track from Michael Jackson's megahit *Thriller* album in 1984 was just one savvy move. In 1990, he made a touching appearance in director Tim Burton's offbeat parable *Edward Scissorhands*.

As his career wound to a close, Price could look back on an enviable body of work both in film and on stage (not to mention a lifetime of service to the fine arts, a sizable personal fortune and other personal achievements). While he scored successes outside the genre, he remained in the minds of the public the Prince of Horror, a title he never bemoaned. His contribution to horror cinema is unsurpassed by any actor not named Karloff or Lugosi.

Ultimately, his performances themselves stand as testament to Price's brilliance. Although he was prone to overact, especially when handed banal dialogue, the star gave only a handful of truly bad performances in a career which included nearly 100 films. Too often, Price was terrific when the picture around him was not. Alas, neither *Madhouse* nor Price's work in it measure up to the star's usual standard.

The sad part isn't that *Madhouse* is a lousy movie. Price made plenty of those, and in them he was often quite fun to watch. The sad part is that *Madhouse* might have been so much better.

Upon further reflection, I've decided "haunts" is probably too strong a word to describe my feelings about either *Madhouse* or Angie Underwood. I never really think about Angie except when I dig out my old high school yearbooks, or when the radio plays a certain Jackson Browne song. Likewise, I seldom watch *Madhouse* and don't even think about it very often. But sometimes I see the video sitting on my bookshelf (between my copies of *The Mad Ghoul* and *The Mad Magician*), and I can't help wondering What If.

What if a director like Bogdanovich had been in charge of *Madhouse*, someone more concerned with storytelling than style points? What if the screenwriters had eschewed their trite mystery formula in favor of a more character-driven story? Surely this would have elicited a better performance from Price, and perhaps Price's enthusiasm would have restored Cushing's verve. What caliber of film might the project might have blossomed into?

Perhaps *Madhouse* could have become the movie Price so richly deserved.

CREDITS: Executive Producer: Samuel Z. Arkoff; Producers: Max J. Rosenberg and Milton Subotsky; Director: Jim Clark; Screenplay: Greg Morrison and Ken Levison; From the Novel *Devilday* by Angus Hall; Associate Producer: John Dark; Cinematography: Ray Parslow; Camera Operator: Ken Coles; Assistant Director: Allan James; Editor: Clive Smith; Art Director: Tony Curtis; Assistant Art Director: John Siddall; Set Decorator: Keith Wilson; Construction Manager: Bill Waldron; Casting Director: Rose Tobias Shaw; Continuity: Lorna Selwyn; Sound Editor: Peter Horrocks; Sound Recording: Danny Daniel and Gerry Humphreys; Makeup: George Blackler; Hairdresser: Helen Lennox; Wardrobe: Dulae Midwinter; Music: Douglas Gamley; Song by Gordon Clyde. An American-International-Amicus Production filmed at Tuckingham Studios, London, England. Released by American International Pictures in 1974 in color; Running Time: 92 minutes

CAST: Vincent Price (Paul Toombes); Peter Cushing (Herbert Flay); Robert Quarry (Oliver Quayle); Adrienne Cori (Faye); Natasha Pyne (Julia); Michael Parkinson (himself); Linda Hayden (Elizabeth Peters); Barry Denner (Gerry Blount); Ellis Dole (Alfred Peters); John Garrie (Harper); Ian Thompson (Bradshaw); Julie Crosthwait (Ellen); Peter Halliday (Psychiatrist); "With special participation by Boris Karloff and Basil Rathbone"

Christopher Lee, Vincent Price, John Carradine and Peter Cushing teamed up for *House of the Long Shadows*.

HOUSE OF THE LONG SHADOWS (1983)

by John Stell

Pete Walker's *House of the Long Shadows* is a black and white film shot in color. Or, to put it another way, it's a 1930s/1940s old-dark-house mystery made in 1982. If it can be viewed this way, then the film offers some fun, not the least of which is seeing the teaming of four horror greats: Vincent Price, Peter Cushing, Christopher Lee and John Carradine. If, on the other hand, one looks at it as a strictly 1980s film, then *House of the Long Shadows* is a bit of a bore, with little new to offer in terms of mysterious-manor thrillers. While many people would probably disagree with me, I find *House of the Long Shadows* eminently watchable, however, because of its cast. Granted, that's the only reason, really. But, no matter. The four principals' performances are perfectly suited to the material, giving them a final chance to work together on screen. (Price, Cushing and Lee had appeared in *Scream and Scream Again!*, but had no scenes together as a trio.) If you can make it through the first half hour or so (which predominantly features an in-over-his-head Desi Arnaz, Jr.), then the rest of the film is an enjoyably familiar outing.

Top billing goes to Vincent Price, which is a bit of a surprise given the film was made in England and features *the* top British horror stars: Lee and Cushing. Thus *House of the Long Shadows* offers further proof of Price's international appeal. But there is no snobbery to be found among this ghoulish gathering, for there is great chemistry between the stars. As a result, it's hard to see *House of the Long Shadows* as a total failure.

Famous author Kenneth Magee (Desi Arnaz, Jr.) makes a bet with his publisher Sam Allyson (Richard Todd): For $20,000, Magee can knock out a Gothic thriller in a mere 24 hours just to prove how easy it is. He arranges to stay in the supposedly deserted Baldpate Manor in Wales to write his novel. Of course, things are particularly busy this same evening, as members of the Grisbane family gather to release their imprisoned brother. Then people start getting murdered.

Given this is the sixth screen version of George M. Cohan's adaptation of Earl Derr Biggers' *Seven Keys to Baldpate*, it's not surprising that *House of the Long Shadows* is fairly predictable. The climax offers three supposed "surprise" twists: 1.) Corrigan (Christopher Lee), the soon-to-be new owner of the property, turns out to be the homicidal brother Roderick; 2.) the carnage is just a scam arranged by the publisher to win the bet; and 3.) the entire film is really the novel Magee is writing, hence nothing has actually happened. All of these devices have been used before, and certainly will be again.

Thus it's up to the cast, playing parts that were tailor-made for them, to pull this thing off, which they almost do. The only really misfire here is Arnaz, Jr., obviously cast to bring in the young people. But the Magee character is poorly written. He's too cynical and too sarcastic for much of the film, rendering him an unsympathetic bore. It would be true to say that this was intentional, since the whole point of the film seems to be Magee's realizing that there's more to writing than just money. (After winning the bet, he admits to caring about his characters for the first time, and then tears up the check.) But Arnaz doesn't make this guy even remotely likable. We don't really care whether he's learned anything or not. The hero is decidedly unheroic.

As a result *House of the Long Shadows* relies solely on the veterans for its appeal. And, for my money, they make the film worth seeing, at least once. Judging by the "entrances" the stars make, Vincent Price seems to be the big fish here. As Arnaz and Julie Peasgood (a lukewarm *femme fatale*) investigate Vincent's arrival, they are facing the stairway when the door behind

LAWRENCE FRENCH: You got to act with Christopher Lee and Peter Cushing much more extensively in *The House of the Long Shadows* (1983), although it could have been a much better film. Christopher Lee told me that he felt the film worked fairly well.

VINCENT PRICE: I did too, we all thought it was good, until this woman took an ax to it! It has to be re-cut. I really don't know what she was doing. She called me up and said, "Will you go out and promote the film," and I said, "If you show the film that we shot," because it's just not the same film. She cut out all of the comedy payoffs to everything. As you know, we were all hired actors to scare Desi Arnaz, Jr. out of the house, people who just came in to do a job. After everything that happens in the house, Chris (Lee) getting killed, and all the other things, suddenly we all come out and take a bow, and it is revealed to Desi that we are all actors. We had these marvelous comments on all the things that happened, and that was all cut out. They tried to turn it into a horror picture and destroyed it.

LAWRENCE FRENCH: When I saw it, the bows you all take at the end are still in the film. It reminded me of the Fritz Lang film, *The Woman in the Window.*

VINCENT PRICE: That's the way it should have been done, so maybe they've put it back together. But I think there was way too much of Desi Arnaz in the beginning, and it does take too long to get into the story, so I don't quite understand it. I don't know if it was Golan and Globus (the producers) who wanted it to be a horror picture, or what. If they did, then why did they shoot a comedy?

LAWRENCE FRENCH: Is it true that you were watching Christopher Lee's death scene, and said, "I just love to see Chris bleed."

VINCENT PRICE: (laughing) Yes! We're great friends you know. We both find each other hysterically funny. Before we met, I heard he was very pompous, and I was really worried about meeting him. It was on *The Oblong Box*, the first film we did together. Well, we took one look at each other and started laughing. We spend our lives screaming and laughing at each other, and having a wonderful time. I'm really devoted to him. I think he's really one of my few very good friends in the business.

them suddenly opens and a sinister shadow is cast on the wall. They turn to face Price—clad in cape and red-feathered fedora. As the music swells he announces, "I have returned." The sound of thunder is then heard. Barely pausing for proper introductions ("Who might you be?"), he begins a pompous speech ("Decay... Nothing but the stench of decay. Time has such little respect for man's vanity, such little regard for his possessions."), delivered by Price in typical Price fashion. When Arnaz attempts to get a word in, Price scolds him saying, "Please don't interrupt me whilst I am soliloquizing." While it at first seems Price is being deliberately hammy, it turns out his character, Lionel Grisbane, is an immodest actor who has a tendency toward the melodramatic. For instance, with respect to his family he comments, "...All of us, locked in the past forever. A doomed family to whom destiny has denied a future." When Magee wants to release the imprisoned brother from his room Lionel states, "What you are about to unleash is evil, unspeakable evil." These gloom-and-doom lines certainly make Lionel sound like a tortured soul. But subtle, they ain't.

For his role as Lionel Grisbane, Vincent Price seems to be playing a character from the Roger Corman-Edgar Allan Poe films he did for AIP. Since Lionel is tortured by past events, he has much in common with Roderick Usher (afraid of the family curse) from *The Fall of the House of Usher*, Nicholas Medina (afraid he buried his wife alive) from *Pit and the Pendulum*, and Verden Fell (afraid his wife has returned from the dead)

Desi Arnaz, Jr. appeared with Vincent Price in *House of the Long Shadows*.

from *Tomb of Ligeia*. "[Y]ou must remember that this is my ancestral home," Lionel tells Magee when questioned why he has arrived at Baldpate Manor. "My heritage, what I am lies within these walls." This is certainly a Poe-esque line, considering it has both figurative (he grew up here) and literal (he imprisoned his brother in the manor) meaning. As it turns out, it was Lionel who committed the crime (killing a girl pregnant with his child) for which brother Roderick was blamed. Thus Lionel's worry and guilt seem very understandable. When brother Sebastian (Peter Cushing) asks him if he knows the meaning of suffering, Lionel quietly responds, "Oh I do, dear brother. I do."

As expected, Price is his reliable self here. Despite a few clunky one-liners ("He must have heard her singing," is Lionel's reaction to finding his sister strangled with piano wire), Price's Lionel Grisbane is essentially a serious character. Lionel doesn't smile much, not that he has reason to. Constantly being interrogated by Magee and Corrigan about his family's "right" to be at Baldpate, Lionel finally loses his temper. "Right? Three hundred years is our right. For three hundred years, the Grisbanes have dominated and held sway here!" Later, in defending what his family did to Roderick, he says, "For centuries the Grisbanes have been their own law. What were we to do, expose our shame to the entire world?" Price is able to bring out Lionel's pride and dignity (and arrogance). More importantly, he manages to convince us that he cares for his family, such as when he smiles sweetly as his sister (Sheila Keith), following tradition, sings after dinner. Price also gets away with lines like, "Can't you feel it? It's as though he were watching us this very moment," and, in response to finding yet another body, "Is there no end to it?" Somehow he makes us take Lionel seriously. But this is because of Price's firm place in horror history. If it were anyone else delivering this dialogue, the results would not have been the same.

Ironically, one the flaws of *House of the Long Shadows* is that characters, including Price's, keep repeating themselves, or say the same thing another character just got finished saying. They go on and on about what they did and why they did it and what they should do now. How many times do we need to hear that the imprisonment took place 40 years ago? How many times do we have to listen to the same discussions about fate and destiny? The answer to both questions: too many. Lucky for the filmmakers, they gave the right people the right parts.

Peter Cushing does quite well as the most guilt-ridden member of the Grisbane family. Speaking with an endearing lisp, Sebastian feels nothing but remorse about locking up brother Roderick. He gets drunk at dinner and tells the strangers the real reason for the Grisbane gathering. (They came to free him.) Cushing comes off as a lovable puppy dog. Christopher Lee, meanwhile, gives a no-nonsense performance as Roderick aka Corrigan. While the film's plotting may give away Corrigan's real identity early on, Lee's acting does not. He plays the role straight-faced, without "winking" at the audience, such as when he urges the young ones to leave even though he already (secretly) slashed their tires. Unfortunately, John Carradine isn't given much to do except to act paternal (he's supposed to be Price, Lee and Cushing's dad?), but he does it well. While none of the roles are deeply written, the actors manage to bring some dimensions to their parts. Or perhaps, they have already won us over, because of who they are, even before the movie begins. (The magic of the VCR is that you can fast-forward through the first half hour or so, which is when the first of the horror quartet appears.)

Nevertheless, one of the frequent criticisms lodged against *House of the Long Shadows* is that it didn't live up to its "promise" in bringing Price, Cushing, Lee and Carradine together. I don't quite agree with this. It would have been very difficult to concoct a scenario whereby each of the four gets to play a villain. One need only look back at films which featured multiple horror stars (e.g., *You'll Find Out*, *Scream and Scream Again!*) to see this is no easy feat. Perhaps this is a film which is best viewed a second time, after the initial disappointment has passed, so that one can see there is fun to be had with respect to the film's classic cast. How could you not bust a gut when, during the "cast party" after the scam has been uncovered, Price's character says to Lee's, "Bitch."

LAWRENCE FRENCH: I imagine that's one reason why you wanted to do the picture, even if it wasn't first rate material, because you got to work with Christopher Lee, Peter Cushing and John Carradine.

VINCENT PRICE: Oh yes, absolutely. It was like a marvelous class reunion. John is an adorable character, who I've known for about 40 years now. Peter is unfortunately, a little gloomy, because of his wife's death, but he's still a sweet man.

LAWRENCE FRENCH: It's too bad about Peter Cushing, because Christopher Lee was telling me how's he's really just waiting to join his wife, Helen.

VINCENT PRICE: I know, it's like, "Are you kidding?" It's very sad. He's just waiting to die, but he's going to have to wait a long time. He's going to live to be 100 years old. (Peter Cushing died August 11, 1994, at age 81.)

character says to Lee's, "Bitch."

Director Pete Walker (*Frightmare, Schizo, The Comeback*) throws in plenty of reliable atmospherics, or clichés, if you prefer. There's a thunderstorm, a mysterious dark-cloaked woman in a train station, a secret passageway in the Grisbane home, at least two fake scares involving a black cat and plenty of shadows cast on the nearest walls. While there are certainly attempts to give the film an old-fashioned feel, *House of the Long Shadows* isn't particularly stylish or inventive. Still, the direction is competent enough.

The true problem with *House of the Long Shadows* is its script. The movie seems to want to be a horror-comedy. But writer Michael Armstrong gives most of the "jokes" to Arnaz, who doesn't have the right timing or attitude to make them funny. Worse, they give Price an incongruous bit of dialogue: He makes a cold wisecrack upon finding his sister's body, just moments after he appeared pleased to hear her sing again. If the whole plot is a set-up by the boss, then, when Arnaz isn't present, there shouldn't be any "scenes" where the "actors" perform because the only member of the "audience" isn't around. And how is it that no family member recognized

Corrigan as Roderick, but it only takes Magee seconds after seeing the portrait of Roderick? After all, the portrait couldn't show a boy older than 14 since Roderick was locked up at that age. No, the story of *House of the Long Shadows* is not well thought out, and maybe we weren't supposed to take it seriously at all.

Still, *House of the Long Shadows* looks pretty good when you realize it was released between *The Monster Club*, a boring anthology hosted by Price and John Carradine, and *Bloodbath in the House of Death*, a none-too-humorous and vulgar haunted house spoof. (If you want to hear Price say the "s word," then this is the film for you.) Compared to these films, *House of the Long Shadows* is a minor classic.

Although one would be hard-pressed to call *House of the Long Shadows* a quality film, it nonetheless is an enjoyable enough throwback to the days when haunted house mysteries were a dime a dozen. The polished and classic cast, which brings along a vast amount of horror history, do their best with the material they have been given. And while certainly not Vincent Price's finest hour, *House of the Long Shadows* proved that Price still had what it takes to keep your eyes glued to the screen, even if *what* was actually on the screen would have been unwatchable otherwise.

CREDITS: Producers: Menahem Golan and Yoram Globus; Director: Pete Walker; Associate Producer: Jenny Craven; Screenplay: Michael Armstrong (Suggested by the Novel *Seven Keys to Baldpate* by Earl Derr Biggers and the Dramatization by George M. Cohan); Cinematography: Norman Langley; Editor: Robert Dearberg, G.B.F.E.; Music: Richard Harvey; Released 1983 by The Cannon Group, Inc.; 102 minutes; Rated PG

CAST: Vincent Price (Lionel Grisbane); Christopher Lee (Corrigan); Peter Cushing (Sebastian); Desi Arnaz, Jr. (Kenneth Magee); John Carradine (Lord Grisbane); Sheila Keith (Victoria); Julie Peasgood (Mary Norton); Richard Todd (Sam Allyson); Louise English (Diana); Richard Hunter (Andrew); Norman Rossington (Station Master)

The Great Mouse Detective © Walt Disney Productions

THE GREAT MOUSE DETECTIVE (1986)

by John Stell

There are many reasons why the great horror stars (Karloff, Lugosi, Lorre, etc.) can lay claim to their status. Yes, their ability as actors has a lot to do with it. But it's more than that. They have a certain look, or style or attitude that comes through in their best performances. We sense that they enjoy what they're doing: being evil, trying to scare us or some similar feat. But there is another element that always seems to be present: the voice. Think about it. If someone came across a "lost" horror film that no one, until now, knew existed, and you heard only the soundtrack, I bet you could identify whether Boris or Bela, Peter or Basil were in the cast.

What's the point to all of this talk? Well, not surprisingly, Vincent Price falls into the horror-star-with-great-voice category. And, like Boris "the Grinch" Karloff, Price had the opportunity to lend his talents to the world of animation. In Disney's *The Great Mouse Detective*, there is never any doubt about who is the voice of Professor Ratigan, the most evil, nasty, despicable, loathsome, horrible mouse (well, he's really a rat but don't let on you know) in all of mousedom, more wicked than *Willard*, more baneful than *Ben*. It is, vocally speaking of course, a *tour de force* performance for Price. And considering that Price, the villain, gets top billing, it's obvious that Disney knew what a coup they scored in casting the priceless Vincent.

The Great Mouse Detective is an animated tribute, based on the *Basil of Baker Street* books, to Sir Arthur Conan Doyle's greatest creation, Sherlock Holmes. Price's Professor Ratigan is the rodent equivalent of Holmes' greatest nemesis, Professor Moriarty. Instead of Dr. Watson, we have Dr. Dawson. And Mrs. Judson takes the place of Mrs. Hudson. The great detective himself is Basil of Baker Street, perhaps named for Basil Rathbone, the actor who is most often identified with the Holmes role. (In fact, Rathbone has a voice cameo as the tenant who lives above Basil.) As in the Doyle novels, the caper at hand is narrated by the detective's doctor friend.

Set in 1897 London, chock full of fog enshrouded streets, horse-drawn carriages and seedy dives, *The Great Mouse Detective* features plenty of knowing winks to Holmes and company. Basil immediately knows Dawson is a doctor, and he relays to the audience the clues which lead him to his conclusion. Like Holmes, he plays the violin. Like Holmes, he is confident, arrogant and aloof ("Young lady, this is a most inopportune time."). He uses such Holmesian expressions as, "The game is afoot," and "Actually, it's elementary, my dear Dawson." When Olivia asks Mrs. Judson if this is the home of Basil, Judson replies, "I'm afraid it is." And it doesn't hurt matters that he lives at the same 221 B Baker street which houses Sherlock himself. In fact, Basil likes to borrow Holmes' bloodhound, Toby.

The case at hand: Professor Ratigan (Vincent Price) has kidnapped toymaker Flaversham (Alan Young). The missing mouse's daughter Olivia (Susanne Pollatschek), in turn, seeks out Basil of Baker Street (Barrie Ingham), whom she finds with the help of Dr. Dawson (Val Bettin). When Olivia tells the seemingly distracted dick of a peg-legged bat who committed the crime, Basil realizes this accomplice is none other than Fidget (Candy Candido), right hand, er, man to Ratigan, "The Napoleon of crime!" Basil thus agrees to aid the young lady in finding her lost Pop, as well as learn what Ratigan is really up to.

The best detective stories are usually those which feature a villain who is every bit as fascinating as the detective. And *The Great Mouse Detective* features a joyously evil brute. "Oh, I love it when I'm nasty!" Ratigan exclaims after threatening the poor toymaker. But the words really come alive thanks to Price's delightfully over-the-top vocalization. Take Ratigan's very first lines of dialogue, for example: "Quite an ingenious scheme, 'ey Flaversham. And aren't you proud to be a part of it?" The first sentence is said with a hearty laugh, in a tone that demonstrates how pleased Ratigan is with himself. Then, for the second line, Price immediately switches to a patronizing voice, knowing full well how Flaversham really feels.

The rapidity of the tone shifts in this first, seemingly simple exchange sets the pace for Ratigan's dialogue as delivered by Price. Ratigan, in but a few lines, will go from being amused, to being happy, sad, empathetic, evil, shocked, concerned or all of the above. As the plot of *The Great Mouse Detective* thickens, Olivia is kidnapped to persuade the hesitant Flaversham to continue his work, which is to make an electronic Queen which Ratigan will substitute for the live one. (He will then have the robot declare him the ruler of all mousedom.) Needless to say, Ratigan takes pleasure in making Flaversham all the more miserable. "Ah, Mr. Flaversham. Allow me to present your charming daughter," he laughingly announces. (Again, Price's joy of being evil shines through.) Ratigan then switches tone again, this time to mock-sympathy, dabbing his eyes with a hankie as daddy and daughter hug. "Oh, how sweet. Oh, I just love tearful re-unions," he says, nearly crying. The animators must keep up with Ratigan's/Price's sudden shifts, which means the animated rat is constantly changing facial expressions to match the verbiage's velocity.

Ratigan is one of those villains who is aware of his own villainy. "My friends," he tells his followers, "we are about to embark on the most odious, the most evil, the most diabolical scheme of my illustrious career. A crime to top all crimes, a crime that will live in infamy!" In response to Ratigan's pledge of evil, the crowd bursts into applause. As you can tell, there is no pretense of nobility, no bone or emotional scar to pick with society. He is bad because he enjoys it, pure and simple. There will be no conversion from the dark side of The Force.

Despite his arrogance and seemingly Teflon-coated exterior, however, Ratigan does have a weak spot. Ratigan, despite his claims, is not a mouse. He is a rat. A big, slimy, icky rat. But if anyone happens to mention this, whether they mean to or not, they are cat bait. "I'm not a RAT!...You know what happens when someone upsets me," Ratigan tells poor Bartholomew, a well-meaning drunkard who lets the word "rat" slip out during some merriment. In

VINCENT PRICE: I just recorded a song a few weeks ago with Henry Mancini, who is doing the score to a full-length animated feature being done by Disney, called *Basil of Baker Street* (Disney subsequently re-titled the film *The Great Mouse Detective*). He wrote two songs for me. One of them is called "The World's Greatest Criminal Mind." It's done like a big Busby Berkeley production number. It's about Sherlock Holmes, who is a mouse called Basil. I play... naturally... the rat, who is Moriarty, but he's called Ratigan. Strangely enough I seem to be overrun with Sherlock Holmes, because every week I introduce the new episode of Sherlock Holmes on *Mystery*

LAWRENCE FRENCH: This is the first time you've worked for Disney, isn't it?

VINCENT PRICE: Yes, but I've always been visually minded and a big fan of animation, so when they asked me to do it, I was thrilled! The thing was, they wanted me to audition! If anyone but the Disney people had asked, I would have been offended. I was really in a state of terror, because I didn't know what they wanted. It turned out to be a very enjoyable experience, because the animators wanted my interpretation of the character. They showed me hundreds of character sketches that they had already done, and then gave me the freedom to expand on that. So Ratigan's personality was based, in part, from my readings of the dialogue, and also from my gestures in the recording booth. Ratigan is really a larger than life villain, so I did the part by exaggerating it.

Ratigan is one of those villains who is aware of his own villainy. © Walt Disney Productions

this instance, the punishment is being fed to Felicia, Ratigan's cat. "Did daddy's little honey bunny enjoy her tasty treat?" he asks in a sickeningly sweet tone after Bartholomew is devoured.

Like many villains, Ratigan has an evil henchman, a loyal rube who does anything his master wishes, even if it means taking the master's abuse. In this case, said compatriot is a crippled bat named Fidget, who actually does the dirty work: He kidnaps father and, eventually, daughter, as well as gathers the raw materials Ratigan needs for his plan. Fidget also lures Basil and Dawson into a trap. But Ratigan, upon learning that the bat allowed Basil to get hold of an incriminating list, has no problem almost feeding the faithful Fidget to Felicia. Lucky for Fidget, Ratigan gets a brainstorm and has a change of heart. ("Fidget, you delightful little maniac.")

Unlike many villains, on the other hand, Ratigan gets his own theme song: "To Ratigan! To Ratigan! The world's greatest criminal mind!" his admirers sing as Ratigan dances about his secret hideaway. Thus Ratigan gets to brag about his past crimes (in a marvelously animated segment) and we, the fans, get to hear Price belt out a tune with his typical, infectious enthusiasm. Later, he gets to croon another ditty, recorded especially for Basil's demise: "Good-bye, so soon…"

Ah yes, Basil, the hero… almost forgot about him. It is, of course, the battle between mouse and rat that is at the crux of *The Great Mouse Detective*. Basil is a thorn in Ratigan's side and vice versa. "I haven't had a moment's peace of mind," Ratigan complains to his cronies, who respond with a group, "Awwww…" Later Ratigan whines, "How dare that idiot Basil poke his stupid nose into my wonderful scheme and foul everything up." Price's hilarious rapid-fire reading of this line sounds as if he were being directed by Howard Hawks.

Eventually, Ratigan gets the better of Basil, luring him into a trap which could spell the end of the great detective. He immediately chides the great Basil for being 15 minutes later than expected. Ratigan can't even get the line "The greatest detective in all mousedom" out without breaking into fits of laughter. Having been unable to decide how to off Basil, Ratigan devises a contraption which incorporates mousetrap, gun, arrow, hatchet and anvil. "Oh this is wicked, so delightfully wicked," Ratigan giggles. Of course, Basil eventually outfoxes the rat: He escapes

Directors Burny Mattinson and John Musker confer with Vincent Price during work on *The Great Mouse Detective*. © Walt Disney Productions

from the trap, spoils Ratigan's potential takeover of the mouse kingdom and causes the evil rodent to fall to his death from Big Ben.

Ratigan, believe it or not, may very well be one of the most evil characters Price ever portrayed. In many of his horror outings, Price's characters were sympathetic and/or tortured souls who were driven to madness by others. In *House of Wax*, a crooked business partner tried to kill Price's kindly Dr. Jerrod and drove him insane. In *The Mad Magician*, a fellow wizard double-crossed Price's Galico the Great, who then turns to murder. Most of the Corman-Poe films featured a tortured (*The Fall of the House of Usher*) or haunted (*Pit and the Pendulum*, *The Tomb of Ligeia*) character for Vincent to portray. And even the latter day efforts such as the Dr. Phibes films and *Theater of Blood* had Price exacting revenge on those who wronged him. Sure, *Shock*, *The Masque of the Red Death* and *Witchfinder General* offered Price the opportunity to portray unapologetic villains. But for a man whose reputation is built largely around his genre efforts, in reality, few of his horror films show a truly evil character. In the case of Ratigan, however, there is no sympathy to be had.

And Price must have realized this, because Vincent's voice work here is unlike anything he's ever done. He doesn't approach Ratigan as just another bad guy. Price's performance, instead, is a comedic one, despite Ratigan's viciousness. (It reminds one of his excellent work as Mr. Trumble in *The Comedy of Terrors*, although Trumble never really bragged about being no good.) Thus, there's nothing subtle or mysterious about Ratigan. You know exactly what he's thinking and feeling. He's either extremely excited and happy about his nefarious schemes,

284

or he's exceptionally ticked off about the interference of do-gooders like Basil. Price's line readings are, therefore, full of emotion and verve. Every syllable of every word of every line is jam-packed with enthusiasm. You can "see" Price smiling or scowling as he says the dialogue. And you can't help but smile at the thought of him having so much fun, and winning over unknowing new fans (probably younger than seven) who just wanted to see a great cartoon.

Looking over Price's '80s output, Ratigan rates as his most memorable film effort next to his dramatic turn in *The Whales of August*. Such horrors as *The Monster Club*, *House of the Long Shadows*, *The Offspring* and *Dead Heat* couldn't do justice to one of horror's greatest stars. (Luckily, Price had another chance to make movie magic when he teamed with Tim Burton for 1990's *Edward Scissorhands*.) In fact, the 1980s seemed to be a decade where Price was continually flexing his vocal muscles. He narrated Tim Burton's tribute to the actor, a stop-motion animated short feature called simply *Vincent*. Price teamed with Hanna-Barbera for *The 13 Ghosts of Scooby Doo*, in which an animated Price helped Scooby and company track down 13 escaped demons. And then there's, perhaps, his most famous contribution: his memorably creepy "poem" incorporated into Michael Jackson's hit single "Thriller," a song which ends with Price laughing most heartily. Of course, I had no choice but to give in and buy the album.

As with most of my own teenage film-going experiences during the 1980s, I can vividly recall seeing *The Great Mouse Detective*. I went with a group of four or five friends to the now-defunct Liberty cinemas. As we walked into the theater, the parents stared at this motley, teen-age crew of adolescents and started groaning, cursing beneath their breaths. Obviously they thought—quite incorrectly—we were there to cause trouble. As the film unspooled, we found our child-like hearts soaring. We laughed, we gasped, we applauded. I swear we were having more fun in that theater than anyone else, kids included. I knew why I was having such a good time: I was there because of Vincent Price. And I was not disappointed.

After all his villainous turns, Vincent Price proved with *The Great Mouse Detective* that nobody did it better. The magic, if you will, was still there. Ironically, at a time when box office horror was pretty much saying good-bye to the horror star, Price was being heard by kids and teenagers, and most likely building a new fan base. And with respect to Price's turn as Ratigan, I can do no better than to quote the rat himself: "Bravo! Bravo! A marvelous performance!"

CREDITS: Producer: Burny Mattinson; Directors: John Musker, Ron Clements, Dave Michener, Burny Mattinson; Screenplay: Pete Young, Steve Hulett, John Musker, Matthew O'Callaghan, Dave Michener, Vance Gerry, Ron Clements, Bruce M. Morris, Burny Mattinson, and Melvin Shaw (Based upon the *Basil of Baker Street* Book Series by Eve Titus and Paul Galdone); Music: Henry Mancini; Supervising Animators: Mark Henn, Glen Keane, Robert Minkoff, Hendel Butoy; Animation Consultant: Eric Larson; Art Director: Guy Vasilovich; Editors: Roy M. Brewer, James Melton; Produced in association with Silver Screen Partners II; Released July 2, 1986 and re-released February 1992 as *The Adventures of the Great Mouse Detective* by Walt Disney Pictures, 74 minutes, Rated G

VOICE TALENTS: Vincent Price (Ratigan); Barrie Ingham (Basil); Val Bettin (Dawson); Susanne Pollatschek (Olivia); Candy Candido (Fidget); Diana Chesney (Mrs. Judson); Eve Brenner (The Mouse Queen); Alan Young (Flaversham); Basil Rathbone (Sherlock Holmes); Laurie Main (Watson); Shani Wallis (Lady Mouse); Ellen Fitzhugh (Bar Maid); Walker Edmiston (Citizen); Barrie Ingham (Bartholomew)

Vincent Price, Ann Sothern, Bette Davis and Lillian Gish starred in *The Whales of August*.

THE OFFSPRING (1987)
and
THE WHALES OF AUGUST (1987)

by Michael H. Price

"I sometimes feel that I'm impersonating the dark unconscious of the whole human race!" a Hollywood publicist quoted Vincent Price in the press notes for the actor's least favorite film of a distinguished career. "This may sound sick, but I love it!"

The film is novice director Jeff Burr's *From a Whisper to a Scream*, released in America as *The Offspring*. By whatever name, the picture contributed generously toward making 1986 "a terrible time, I'm afraid I must admit," as Price himself put it without the assistance of any exclamation-happy publicity flacks. It helped matters considerably that Price found a welcome escape from typecasting that same year in Lindsay Anderson's *The Whales of August*—"a delightful picture to make, though I must say terribly uncomfortable in the shooting"—but Price's love/hate relationship with horror movies continued apace despite the respite and the modest valedictory that *Whales* afforded him.

He was appalled, for example, to see his fondly remembered starring picture of 1958, Kurt Neumann's *The Fly*, remade in '86 as "one of those dreadful 'splatter' movies" (Price's words). Never mind that David Cronenberg's provocative remake went beyond its own superficial—and Oscar-anointed—shock value to deliver a thoughtful elaboration on the historic original film's tale of a disastrous scientific experiment. And never mind that Cronenberg and his chief producer, Mel Brooks, had approached the project with an affectionate regard for the source-film.

No, Price had by now begun to exercise the prerogative of cranky impatience that comes with advancing age. "You'd think *we* hadn't done *The Fly* right to begin with," he fumed while visiting my newspaper office during a tour of North Texas' art museums. "At least, they could've exhibited the good grace to give *their* version some other title."

But the mood faded soon enough—Price remained genial and expansive, even when complaining—and his disappointments with A.D. 1986 assumed a lighter tone.

"Well, I've some effrontery, I suppose, to dismiss Mr. Cronenberg's *Fly* as a 'splatter' movie," Price said, "for I fear that this—this *thing* I've been snookered into doing, this *Whisper to a Scream* picture, is about as 'splattery' as they come.

"I believe it's about time I swore off the 'horror' pictures, at any rate," he added. "That sort of film has become meaner, more vile and destructive, than the pictures we used to call 'horror'—and how I despise *that* term—when I was really turning 'em out. Now, today, when rarely I participate anymore, I always come away feeling that they've gone too far this time.

"They promised me otherwise on *Whisper*, you know," Price said. "I should've known better."

Jeff Burr, *Whisper*'s director and co-writer, offered in 1987 a sugar-coated version of how he enlisted Price:

> Determined that no true horror-thriller would be complete without the master himself, Vincent Price, Jeff relied on a celebrity mail service to get the actor's Hollywood address. With script in hand, Jeff went up and knocked on the

door. "He opened the door, and I said that I wanted him to be in my film. It worked!"[1]

"Actually," Price explained, "I had told Mr. Burr and his partner [producer Darin Scott] that the script seemed promising but that I was trying my damnedest to get away from this sort of story. I hope I was sufficiently polite. This was in the summer of 1985. They persisted—could they drop back by? Could they show me some footage they had completed? Could they think of any ways to annoy me into accepting the part?—and finally, I relented.

"Foolish, on my part, y'know, because I really wanted nothing to do with their little picture," said Price. "Would my presence elevate their production, or would their production diminish me? I suspect we *know* the answer to that one, eh?

"But although I've had my lecture tours going all along, these past several years, and although I don't fear becoming 'forgotten' or any such thing, still I *do* fear the risks of not keeping a hand in. De Maupassant said that 'solitude is a dangerous thing for the vigorous mind,' and I've never cared to find out what he meant by that. And so I accepted *From a Whisper to a Scream* over misgivings that I should have heeded."

Burr had screened for Price the least grotesque, relatively speaking, of the episodes that make up *Whisper*—a short yarn about a hoodlum (played by stage and television veteran Terry Kiser) who covets the secrets of a Voodoo priest (jazz artist-turned-actor Harry Caesar). Once Price had come aboard as the framing-segment host/narrator of this anthology picture, he would find himself attached to a set of stories touching on perversions from necrophilia to wartime atrocities. His character, apart from a jarring finale, has little more to do than relate the hideous local history ("written in blood on pages of human skin") that supposedly ties the short episodes together.

"I was allowed a fairly free rein, in throwing out what of my role struck me as inane and tedious, and the fellows treated me like visiting royalty in what little time I was with them to shoot my scenes." Price said. "But still, I feel it was a case of bait-and-switch, plain and simple—not all that uncommon a practice when some low-rent producer is trying to latch onto a recognizable 'name,' like mine, whose heyday has come and gone in Hollywood."

A couple of years down the line, Price and Burl Ives, a fellow veteran of better days at classier studios, would compare notes over similar experiences: Zalman King convinced Ives to play a Southern lawman in the steamy melodrama *Two Moon Junction* (1988) by providing the actor with a proxy script containing none of the erotic business that is predominant in the finished picture.

Ives took his brush with trickery somewhat more philosophically, however: "Old fellows like Vincent and me, we're more fortunate than we often let on, just to have these youngsters admire our work so much that they want us to lend something of ourselves to their pictures. It's all honest work, so long as we approach it as something more than a walk-through.

"And besides," added Ives, "the occasional screen assignment helps keep us visible without intruding on the labors of love that both Vincent and I have found to occupy our interests. Better to take the little disappointments as a joke, says I, and concentrate on the elements of your work that are within your control."

Ives' "labors of love" reference involved the traveling solo productions that represented the final productive surges of both himself and Vincent Price. Ives' late-in-life *magnum opus* was an impersonation of the poet Walt Whitman, performed internationally well past the actor's 80th year. Price, meanwhile, divided his energies between a portrayal of the flamboyant playwright, poet and novelist Oscar Wilde and a constantly evolving lecture/performance called *And the Villains Still Pursue Me*.

It was during a *Villains* tour that Price and I had met, ascertained by comparing ancestors that our shared surname bespoke a *bona fide* blood kinship, and forged a cordial acquaintance that would keep us in touch until his death in 1993. Fellow newspaperman George E. Turner and I first visited with Price on his arrival in 1974 at the Amarillo, Texas, airport, a few hours before

Vincent Price appeared as Julian White in *The Offspring*. (Photofest)

he was to lecture at West Texas State University. George and I wound up unashamedly hogging a press conference; the session was otherwise attended by local television personalities whose idea of interviewing Vincent Price consisted of questions like: "How does it feel, being the scariest guy in the movies?" and "Don't you ever wish you could make a serious picture?"

Price preferred conversation over Q&A—"especially," he said, "when the same questions are asked of me, time and time again, as though there were some guidebook circulating among the news media on 'How to Interview Vincent Price.'"

"Don't you people have anything better to do," he asked one television reporter in a seethingly mellow voice, "than to waste my time with this fatuous drivel?"

Evidently not, for any number of interviews with Price during his last two decades seem to have provoked him to such indignant outbursts. Still, he traveled frequently and made North Texas a regular stop. "I'd rather deal with the public than with the news media—present company excepted, you understand," he told me while holding forth at a home-and-garden trade exposition at Dallas' Market Hall. "The public puts me in a larger context—for my interests in the arts, in cooking, in literature, *and*, by the way, in the movies—whereas the movie critics and the news people tend to see me only as this Hollywood bogeyman who has this quirk of appreciating a good painting."

By 1980, I had joined the newsroom of the *Star-Telegram* at Fort Worth, Texas, where Price was a frequent visitor on account of his fondness for the city's wealth of art museums: The Modern, he said, spoke to his fondness for the 20th-century *avant-garde*, while the Kimbell suited his Old World sensibilities and the Amon Carter indulged his affinity for the great artists of the American frontier.

Price's 1986 visit, in the midst of a frustrating year for his motion picture ambitions, also included a presentation of the *Villains* lecture at Texas Christian University. As grumpy as he could become on thinking of *From a Whisper to a Scream* or the then-current remake of *The Fly*, Price was just as ready to turn on the charm.

Which he did, in volume, that night in the college's concert hall. *And the Villains Still Pursue Me* is a sweeping historical document fashioned as an intimate monologue, predicated on Price's five decades as a working actor but surveying the history of dramatic villainy as a class.

A version very close to the lecture Price gave that night appears as the closing chapter in George Turner's and my 1996 book, *Human Monsters: The Bizarre Psychology of Movie Villains* (Kitchen Sink Press). Price had long intended to write a preface for one of George's and my volumes of movie history, but such circumstances as his waning health and the death of his wife, the actress Coral Browne, kept intruding. We arranged shortly after the actor's death to publish the essential text of his lecture for the first time, combining an early draft filed for copyright protection with a later typewritten and annotated variation.

But what cold print fails to convey is the very glee, the energetic immediacy and the whip-lash comic timing that made Price's *Villains* piece such a favorite on the lecture circuit. That night at Texas Christian University, before a packed house of (mostly) students scarcely old enough to have grown up on his movies, Price filled the stage like a one-man ensemble cast, by turns joking and ranting and waxing eloquent on his favorite bad guys (Richard III and His Satanic Majesty), his favorite actors (Ronald Colman, Basil Rathbone and Clifton Webb), and even his favorite names ("Gustav von Seyffertitz—roll it over on your tongues—every villainous actor should have a name like Gustav von Seyffertitz!").

Two hours passed like so many minutes, and Price—though sweating profusely at the finale—seemed merely to be getting warmed up. His program had run its course, however, and he made a brisk exit. The audience cheered him back on, and he replied with a recitation of Poe's "The Raven." Another attempted exit, another massed cry for an encore, and Price re-emerged: "*This* should shut you up," he grinned, and proceeded to recite the rap he had performed on Michael Jackson's 1983 recording of "Thriller." Later, backstage in the Green Room, Price seemed fatigued but still eager to give his show the appropriate finishing touches by visiting with his admirers.

From a Whisper to a Scream was finally issued during the fall and winter of 1987, given a spotty U.S. release as *The Offspring* by a doomed little distribution company called The Movie Store Entertainment Group. *The Whales of August* arrived at about the same time from a cine-snob company called Alive Films, with a strategic "platform" release pattern that started in October of 1987 in New York and Los Angeles and spread gradually. *Whales* and *Whisper* scarcely could have attracted the same audience—apart from the core of Vincent Price's enthusiastic fans—but if considered together, they offer a fascinating look at how the actor let professionalism and generous inventiveness unify his work, whether he believed in an assignment or found it distasteful.

It is easy to see what attracted Price to *The Whales of August*: Not only did the film pose his first opportunity in many years to tackle an ordinarily human dramatic role, without psychological kinks or dark motives; it also afforded him the good company of Bette Davis, Lillian Gish, an Oscar-nominated Ann Sothern and Harry Carey, Jr. The role, a courtly fellow named Mr. Maranov, had first been assigned to Sir John Gielgud, an early-day stage hero of Price's, and Price landed it (along with the subsequent pleasure of the studio's attempt to secure for him an Oscar nomination) after a conflict arose in Gielgud's schedule. The tradepapers and many main-

Price's Mr. Maranov, a Russian émigré, has little to offer besides fresh-caught fish and a genteel, somehow sad, manner in *The Whales of August*.

stream critics remarked it unusual that Price should tackle such a role, but his performance received favorable reviews. Some of the more wide-awake reviewers likened the portrayal to Price's utterly mannered impersonation of Prince Albert opposite Helen Hayes in *Victoria Regina* on the legit stage during the 1930s.

"The *Whales* assignment seemed perfectly natural to me," Price said. "It's this 'horror' typecasting that I find unnatural. I mean, Red Skelton used to say I was one of the funniest *comedians* he'd ever worked with."

The Whales of August, adapted by David Berry from his stage play, finds Davis and Gish as sisters at odds with one another. Having spent countless summers in their island homestead, they are now considering sacrificing their independence in the name of comfort and security. Davis is cantankerous about the prospect, however, while Gish is more accepting. Price's Mr. Maranov, a Russian émigré who has little to offer besides fresh-caught fish and a genteel, somehow sad, manner, passes gracefully through the sisters' combative orbits.

"The role could have been bigger and I wouldn't have complained," Price said, "but then perhaps I have a tendency to mentally 'over-write' a role beyond what exists on the typewritten page. I saw Maranov the way I once saw my brother, Mortimer—a most charming fellow whose charm is practically all he has to offer.

"It was delightful, filming the thing—and I say this, despite the terrible discomfort we all endured with the cold of autumn off coastal Maine and our desolate island location—because of

291

the exquisite simplicity of the story, the sense of community we had amongst our little cast and the spectacle of watching these two astonishing actresses playing so intensely off one another."

By the time *The Whales of August* and *The Offspring/From a Whisper to a Scream* had arrived in the theaters, Price had once again lapsed in his intention to quit horror pictures and accepted a small but showy role in Mark Goldblatt's cops-and-zombies thriller *Dead Heat* (1988). Here, he plays a wealthy man who intends to cheat death at a dire cost. Joe Piscopo, who shares star billing with Treat Williams, called *Dead Heat* "a disappointment, I guess you could say—except for the pleasure of working with Vincent Price. We seem to have been uncertain whether to make a police thriller, a comedy, or a horror movie. Mr. Price, now—he kept things serious and honest while he was on the picture."

Price graced his friend and fellow art collector Dennis Hopper's ill-fated crime melodrama *Backtrack* (1991), shooting a few scenes as a soft-spoken mob capo in 1988 and "essentially, just playing myself," as Price put it, "with a hint of a threatening tone." He was served more elegantly by Tim Burton's *Edward Scissorhands* (1990), which gave him the tailor-made role of a kind-hearted inventor who brings to life a humanoid creature (played by Johnny Depp). Price regarded Burton as "a peculiar talent—but so respectful of his origins and inspirations, and a very good storyteller."

The Disney group helped keep Price before the mass audience in 1992 with its reissue of *The Great Mouse Detective* (aka *The Adventures of the Great Mouse Detective*; 1986), a cartoon homage to Sherlock Holmes. Price supplied the voice of the Moriarty-like Professor Ratigan.

Price's final motion-picture appearance, filmed in 1991 for director Bruno Barreto, occurred in *The Heart of Justice*, which finally surfaced as a Turner Network Television premiere in 1993. Here, Price plays an enigmatic aesthete who seems to have been the last person to see a notorious author (played by Dennis Hopper) alive.

Price had once again lapsed in his intention to quit horror pictures and accepted a small but showy role in *Dead Heat*.

The posthumous release of Richard Williams' animated fantasy *Arabian Knight* (aka *The Thief and the Cobbler*; 1995) employs a Price vocal performance, as a villainous member of a royal court, that had been recorded 22 years earlier.

Not to sell *Edward Scissorhands* short or to trivialize Tim Burton's admiration of Price, but not one film in this final handful comes anywhere near being the farewell vehicle that so fine an actor deserves. Though *The Whales of August* is an ensemble piece, even where Davis and Gish are concerned, it comes closer than anything else to being Vincent Price's valedictory. And even *From a Whisper to a Scream* bespeaks a generous professionalism under duress.

"I suppose I must have absorbed some of Karloff's attitude," Price said in 1990. "He *had* his formal valedictory—in [Peter] Bogdanovich's picture, *Targets* [1968], you know—and still he kept working in throwaway pictures, quite to his own detriment, at least in terms of his failing health. But he said it often, even when we had worked together some years before: 'I intend to die in harness,' Boris would say. Just like that: 'Die in harness.'

"And there are worse fates than dying in harness. I call it the dignity of honest work, and it beats waiting around for the perfect assignment to come your way."

FROM A WHISPER TO A SCREAM
AKA: *THE OFFSPRING*
CREDITS: A Conquest Entertainment Production; Executive Producer: Bubba Truckadaro; Producers: Darin Scott and William Burr; Director: Jeff Burr; Screenplay: C. Courtney Joyner, Darin Scott and Jeff Burr; Cinematography: Craig Greene; Film Editor: W.O. Garrett; Production Designers: Cynthia K. Charette and C. Allen Posten; Musical Score: Jim Manzie; Special Makeup and Effects: Rob Burman; Costume Designer: Cindy Charette; Running Time: 101 minutes; U.S. Release: September-October 1987 as *The Offspring* by The Movie Store Entertainment Group

CAST: Vincent Price (Julian White); Clu Gulager (Stanley Burnside); Terry Kiser (Jesse Hardwick); Harry Caesar (Felder Evans); Rosalind Cash (Snake Woman); Cameron [mis-billed as "Cammeron"] Mitchell (Gallen); Angelo Rossitto (Tinker); Ron Brooks (Steven Arden); Susan Tyrrell (Beth Chandler); Martine Beswicke (Katherine White); Lawrence Tierney (Warden)

THE WHALES OF AUGUST
CREDITS: An Alive Films/Circle Associates, Ltd. Production; Executive Producer: Shep Gordon; Producers: Mike Kaplan and Carolyn Pfeiffer; Director: Lindsay Anderson; Screenplay: David Berry (Based upon his Play); Cinematography: Mike Fash; Production Designer: Jocelyn Herbert; Art Directors: K.C. Fox and Bob Fox; Set Decorator: Sosie Hublitz; Musical Score: Alan Price; Musical Score Arranged & Conducted by: Derek Wadsworth; Film Editor: Nicholas Gaster; Costume Designer: Rudy Dillon; Makeup Artist: Julie Hewett; Hair Stylist: Peg Schierholz; Location Scout: Roger Berle; Produced in Association with Nelson Entertainment; Running Time: 90 Minutes; Released October 1987

CAST: Bette Davis (Libby Strong); Lillian Gish (Sarah Webber); Vincent Price (Mr. Maranov); Ann Sothern (Tisha Doughty); Harry Carey, Jr. (Joshy Brackett); Frank Grimes (Mr. Beckwith); Frank Pitkin (Old Randall); Mike Bush (Young Randall); Margaret Ladd (Young Libby); Tisha Sterling (Young Tisha); Mary Steenburgen (Young Sarah)

[1] From press materials for *The Offspring*; The Movie Store/Cassidy-Watson Associates, 1987

Vincent © **Walt Disney Productions**

VINCENT PRICE AND TIM BURTON ON *VINCENT*

by Lawrence French

Long before Tim Burton became known for films like *Batman* and *Mars Attacks!,* Vincent Price provided him with the inspiration to make his first film short, *Vincent.* Like many kids growing up in the 1960s Burton was intrigued by the Price persona on display in such seminal Edgar Allan Poe films as *The Fall of the House of Usher* and *Pit and the Pendulum.* "Vincent was like my psychologist when I was growing up," recalled Burton. "He helped me get through the abstractions of my early years. For some reason I was always likening the Poe movies to my own life. The characters Vincent played would always go through some grand dark catharsis. They were usually plagued by some sort of abstract demons. I found I could relate to those characters in a very meaningful way."

It was while Burton was toiling away on his weird drawings at the Disney animation department that he first dreamed the idea of a children's book that would pay homage to Vincent Price in verse. Then, with his producing partner Rick Heinrichs, Burton managed to convince Tom Whilite, then the head of production at Disney, to invest a small amount of money for a short film that would enable Burton to bring his poem to life, via stop-motion animation.

Around the end of 1981, Price got a phone call from someone at Disney. "They asked me to come down and meet Tim and Rick Heinrichs," says Price. "So I went down and they showed me the drawings and mock-ups they had planned for this short film, as a sort of tribute to me. Tim recited the poem for me and asked me to narrate it. I was really struck by his charm and enthusiasm, so I said, 'yes.' Tim is really in love with film and is a wonderful kind of mad fellow. I thought it was marvelous of Disney to give these two kids a chance to make the film. They were only about 20 when they did it, and the two of them have really gone on to do great things. Then, when it was finished, it went out to film festivals all around the country, because we don't really show short subjects much anymore, and it won a lot of awards. I was really very proud to be a part of it."

Indeed, Tim Burton's career might have taken quite a different path if Price had not been such a gracious and enthusiastic supporter of his talent. But Price has always gone out of his way to support artists who are unrecognized. In the '50's he was among the first art buyers to champion the works of abstract artists like Jackson Pollack, Richard Diebenkorn and Mark Rothko. And long before Marlon Brando or Robert Redford, Vincent Price was supporting the work of the American Indians, who Price says, "could have been the most creative people on the face of the planet, until we shut them off."

After Tim Burton became a director with clout, following the huge success of *Beetlejuice* and *Batman*, he went out of his way to acknowledge Price's early encouragement and influence. "Vincent Price was always a great inspiration to me," exclaimed Burton. "It would have been devastating to me if he hadn't been so responsive. He really shaped my life when I was starting out and gave me hope to grow. He's a really wonderful person, just incredible."

Interestingly enough, Price had a similar patron when he got his first big break as a young actor. He had been chosen to play Prince Albert opposite Helen Hayes as Queen Victoria in the Broadway production of *Victoria Regina.* "When I did that I was only 23," says Price. "Helen could have made it very tough for me. Here I was, an inexperienced young man coming in and doing my first play on Broadway, with the biggest star of the day. Helen was 35 then, and had already been on the stage for 25 years, since the age of 10! Well, I had the most wonderful

experience with her. She was so marvelous to me. She is one of the kindest people I've ever met. I really owe so much to Helen."

Shortly before Price's death in 1993, Tim Burton visited the actor's home and was able to show him about 30 minutes of footage from *The Nightmare Before Christmas*. Burton had earlier asked Price to voice Santa Claus in the movie. Unfortunately, Price's declining health made it impossible for him to accept the part. Price's final appearance on the big screen came a few years earlier, when Burton called on Price to play the kindly inventor in *Edward Scissorhands*. "I was enormously touched when Tim asked me to be in the movie," says Price. "I was only in three scenes, but Tim is really my idea of a good filmmaker."

For Burton, it was sheer pleasure to be working with Price once more. "It was very thrilling to have Vincent play the inventor," enthused Burton. "He gave it an emotional weight that made it very strong for me."

Reflecting on the nature of fame over his long career, Price notes that, "Fame is an extraordinary thing. When I played Oscar Wilde in *Diversions and Delights*, I had to shave off my mustache, because Oscar Wilde didn't have a mustache. Then one day, a woman came up to me, looked at me very closely and said, 'Weren't you Vincent Price?' Well that is a kind of fame. Real fame, though, is being identified with something very popular, like being in a comic strip, or having Disney do a movie named after you, like *Vincent*. Now that's what I call real fame."

Vincent
by Tim Burton and Rick Heinrichs

Vincent Malloy is seven years old
He's always polite and does what he's told

For a boy his age he's considerate and nice
But he wants to be just like Vincent Price

He doesn't mind living with his sister, dog and cats
Though he'd rather share a home with spiders and bats

There he could reflect on the horrors he's invented
And wander dark hallways alone and tormented

Vincent is nice when his Aunt comes to see him
But imagines dipping her in wax, for his wax museum

BACKTRACK (1991)
EDWARD SCISSORHANDS (1990)
THE HEART OF JUSTICE (1993)
by Don G. Smith

Given that everyone dies, film fans naturally hope that their favorite actor's final film is one in which the performer could take pride—a dignified and memorable last bow, so to speak. John Wayne was fortunate in that *The Shootist* provided him a memorable and moving final curtain. The same could be said of Judy Garland's *I Could Go on Singing*. On the other hand, *The Black Sleep* was hardly what we would have wished for Bela Lugosi, and *Flesh Feast* was certainly not a fitting final curtain for Veronica Lake. Sometimes an actor makes what would be the perfect final film, only to complete one or more inconsequential efforts before passing on. A case in point is Boris Karloff's *Targets*, a fine film that paid homage to the actor and provided him with a memorable part. The fairytale ending was not to be, however, as Boris quickly went on to make five forgettable pictures before his last bow. While we are glad that Boris died with his boots on, how fitting it would have been if *Targets* could be remembered as his last picture—instead of the inferior *Macabre Serenade* .

Vincent Price made his final three films in the 1990s. The 1980s had been a spotty decade for the actor. First, he co-starred with horror film peer John Carradine in the omnibus misfire *The Monster Club* (1981). He followed up with the disappointing *House of the Long Shadows* (1983, co-starring Carradine, Peter Cushing and Christopher Lee). Next came the forgettable parody *Bloodbath at the House of Death* (1984). One high spot of the decade was his work in the animated Disney feature *The Great Mouse Detective* (1986). Unfortunately, he followed up with *The Offspring* (1987), a tasteless gore anthology featuring Price as on-screen narrator. Then came the second high spot of the decade, the bittersweet *The Whales of August* (1987, co-starring Bette Davis and Lillian Gish) for which Vincent should have received an Academy Award nomination for best supporting actor. He closed out the decade with the offbeat *Dead Heat* (1988)—which brings us to the 1990s and the main subjects of this chapter.

Examining Vincent Price's final three films, it becomes clear that sandwiched between two lesser vehicles, the marvelous *Edward Scissorhands* is to Price what *Targets* was to Boris Karloff. So let's take a look at the last three films of Vincent Price, the renaissance man who became one of Hollywood's greatest "bogeymen" as well as one of its most durable performers.

Backtrack, filmed in 1988, premiered on the Showtime television channel on December 14, 1991. The film concerns Milo (Dennis Hopper), a hitman sent to kill conceptual artist Anne Benton (Jodie Foster), who has witnessed a mob killing. Financing Milo is Lino Avoca (Vincent Price), an art-collecting mafia don. When Milo and Anne fall in love, they are pursued by both Avoca's henchmen and the law.

Director/star Dennis Hopper specifically wanted Vincent Price in the Avoca role because the two had for 35 years shared an enthusiasm for art and art collecting. In Lucy Chase Williams' *The Complete Films of Vincent Price* (1995), Hopper explains his debt to Price:

> When I was 18 and under contract to Warner Bros., I spent a lot of time at Vincent and Mary's. I used their kiln, and I fired tiles there ... I saw my first abstract paintings at Vincent's house in 1954; my first Jackson Pollock, Richard Diebenkorn, Franz Kline... At one point, Vincent gave me a painting and

JOHNNY DEPP   WINONA RYDER

edward
SCISSORHANDS

said, 'Keep this, because one day I think you'll probably collect art.' Vincent
was the one who gave me the idea, the courage and intensity, to be able to say,
"yeah I *like* this stuff, and I'm gonna stand by this stuff," and not to be disturbed by the fact that other people might not understand my preference. As
far as art is concerned, my whole life would be enormously diminished without having met Vincent Price...

The role of Avoca was not very demanding. In all, Vincent appears in only seven scenes, three
of which run for only a second, and none of which run for over 90 seconds. In his best scene, he
sits before an elegant breakfast setting as three thugs inform him of Milo's betrayal. Surrounded
by book-lined walls, antiques and lovely statues, he takes the news in stride, dismisses his thugs,
momentarily ponders a red rose and taps into his egg benedict.

The film itself experienced problems. The original title, *Time to Die*, was changed to *Backtrack*. It was then re-titled *Catchfire* and severely edited against Hopper's will for European screenings, and then released in its restored version to American cable television and home video with the alternate title *Do It the Hard Way* . Though the film features a fine cast and a Bob Dylan cameo, it is not Hopper's best work. Still, it is entertaining. Hopper's saxophone-playing, hard-edged hitman is the kind of character the actor plays best, and Jodie Foster's Anne is experimental enough in her philosophy and art to make her eventual attraction for Hopper believable. The chemistry between the two characters is ultimately what saves the film. Vincent Price took the part of Avoca as a favor to Hopper and delivered all that was expected.

In June 1990, Vincent shot his three scenes in what would be one of the finest genre films of the decade, *Edward Scissorhands*. Crack cinematography, a unique approach to an old theme, a fine cast and a beautifully evocative musical score all combine to make the film a hit. The scenario concerns "an innocent boy-creature," (Johnny Depp) constructed by an elderly eccentric billed only as "the inventor" (Price). In a line evocative of *The Wizard of Oz*, we are told that the inventor "gave [the boy] insides, a heart, a brain. Everything. Well, almost everything." Unfortunately, the inventor dies before substituting real hands for the scissors attached to Edward's wrists. The boy remains alone in the inventor's mansion on the hill until he is "adopted" by a suburban Avon lady (Dianne Wiest) and her family. The boy-creature, however, is a misfit in materialistic, pastel suburbia, and despite winning the heart of Wiest's daughter Kim (Winona Ryder), he is finally forced back to the lonely mansion on the hill by a mob reminiscent of those in the Universal Frankenstein films. This parabolic tale, though beautiful, touching and humorous, raises disturbing, unpleasant questions about contemporary American life and the general tendency of people to fear, ridicule or exploit those who are different.

Director Tim Burton, who had grown up admiring Price's work in the American International Poe series, conceived the basic scenario and knew exactly who he wanted to play the inventor. Before tackling *Edward Scissorhands*, Burton had directed *Pee-Wee's Big Adventure* (1985), *Beetlejuice* (1988) and *Batman* (1989). Television star Johnny Depp beat out Tom Cruise and Tom Hanks for the role of Edward, and Winona Ryder, who had worked with Burton in *Beetlejuice*, landed the role of Edward's heartthrob. In 1994, Burton would choose Johnny Depp for the lead role in *Ed Wood*, the story of the man who directed Bela Lugosi's last films.

Let us now examine Price's three scenes, all of them flashbacks. In the first, we see the inventor pleasurably supervising his quirky laboratory inventions. When a series of wildly constructed machines produces a heart-shaped cookie, the inventor sadly offers it to one of his lifeless inventions. The old man lives a life "incomplete and all alone," but the gesture with the cookie has given him an idea. Price's frailty is clear in this scene as he moves about with a cane, his thin face deeply wrinkled by the years.

In the second scene, we see that the inventor, like old Geppetto in *Pinocchio*, has built himself a "son." With fatherly devotion, the inventor teaches Edward etiquette and introduces him to laughter by reading a limerick.

In the third scene, the inventor presents Edward with a pair of hands he has constructed. Price beams and smiles expansively as Edward touches the hands with his scissors-fingers. Suddenly, however, the old man's smile fades into an expression of distress, and he crumples to the floor dead. Uncomprehending, Edward bows down and moves a scissors finger across the face of his fallen "father," accidentally leaving a mark.

It may sound corny, but whenever I watch that scene, I feel a bit like Edward must have felt as he bent over his fallen creator. I know Vincent Price is gone, but I want him back. I miss not being able to anticipate his next film, and, like Edward, I reach out to touch the man who gave me so many hours of pleasure. To be specific, my thoughts return to my childhood when we neighborhood children were taken to see *House on Haunted Hill* and *The Fly*. With gratitude I remember that day when, as a 10-year-old boy in 1960, I received a response from my fan letter to Vincent Price. I flash back to my parents taking me to see most of Price's Corman/Poe films, as well as *Master of the World*, *War-Gods of the Deep* and *Diary of a Madman*. I relive double-dating at the drive-in and watching *The Conqueror Worm* between popcorn and kisses. I thank Price again for enriching my experience by introducing me to the world of art. And last, but not least, I remember the times I saw Price live on stage in *Oliver*, *Damn Yankees* and *Diversions and Delights*. Fortunately, we all can still reach out and touch Price, for in ways that matter most, he still lives. Like the inventor, he left a legacy. The films are still out there, and as long as there are film fans, the name of Vincent Price will live forever through television re-runs and video store rentals. Though most of his books are out of print, those who seek can still find. I particularly recommend his *Vincent Price Treasury of American Art* (1972). Price also lives in the stories told by those who knew him, in the many articles and interviews devoted to him in genre magazines, and in the continuing work of The Vincent Price Gallery in Monterey Park, California.

Yes, in some ways Vincent Price was like the inventor. And like the inventor, he died leaving much more to do.

Ah, if we could only end this chapter here! But we cannot, for life often doesn't play like a well-crafted screenplay. Price appeared in one more film after *Edward Scissorhands*, a made-for-cable movie called *The Heart of Justice* . Filmed in Los Angeles in the fall of 1991, it aired on February 20, 1993 as part of TNT's "Screenworks" series. While the film maintains interest, it is not in a class with *Edward Scissorhands*. The plot concerns the murder of trash novelist Austin Blair (Dennis Hopper) by Elliot Burgess (Dermot Mulroney), a young member of a prominent family. After shooting Blair in front of a private club where the author has had lunch, Burgess turns the gun on himself and commits suicide. Award-winning journalist David Leader (Eric Stolz) enlists the aid of Elliot's sister (Jennifer Connelly) in an attempt to discover the murderer's motivation. Before walking out of the club to his death, Blair lunches with his friend Reggie Shaw (Price), an elderly, wealthy homosexual. Here is some of their conversation:

> Price: I was sitting in a lecture Auden gave at Harvard about *Don Quixote* in which he admitted he never managed to read the novel through to the end, and he doubted whether anyone in the audience could finish the damn thing either... Afterwards, I hung around and invited Auden for tea or sherry or opium, and he accepted.
> Hopper: And did he seduce you, you old catermite?
> Price: No, he fell asleep... You know, this poached salmon was a little off today. How was your veal?

Price picks up the check, and moments later Hopper is shot.

Later, Stolz interviews Price at the private club. They chat briefly about Austin Blair and the unpredictability of life. Then Vincent Price delivers his final screen dialogue:

> Price: The thing I have learned about people who join clubs like this—they like quiet, and they're willing to pay for it. I don't suppose you have a price?
> Stolz: Everybody's got a price.
> Price: What's yours, young man?
> Stolz: A good lunch in a fancy private club.
> Price: (raising his martini, eyes sparkling) With a charming old fart like me.

Of the two scenes, Lucy Chase Williams writes that "Price's voice is mellifluous as ever, his timing understated, his smile as warm." Though the voice isn't as strong as it once was, I could not agree more. Still, after *Edward Scissorhands*, Price's last film is anti-climactic.

One Price film was released after *The Heart of Justice*, but it was not one of Price's last three films. *Arabian Knight*, an animated feature to which Price lent his voice, was made in 1968 but not released until August 25, 1995. By that time Vincent Price was gone, having passed away from lung cancer and Parkinson's disease on Monday, October 25, 1993—just six days before Halloween.

BACKTRACK

CREDITS: Executive Producers: Steve Reuther and Mitchell Cannold; Producers: Dick Clark and Dan Paulson; Co-producer: Lisa Demberg; Director: Dennis Hopper; Screenplay: Rachel Kronstadt Mann and Ann Louise Bardach; Story: Rachel Kronstadt Mann; Cinematography: Ed Lachman; Production Designer: Ron Foreman; Music: Michel Colombier; Editor: Wende Phifer Maye

CAST: Dennis Hopper (Milo); Jodie Foster (Anne Benton); Dean Stockwell (John Luponi); Vincent Price (Lino Avoca); John Turturro (Pinella; Fred Ward (Pauling); Charlie Sheen (Bob); C. Anthony Sirico (Greek); Julie Adams (Martha); Sy Richardson (Captain Walker); Frank Gio (Frankie); Helena Kallianiotes (Grace Carelli); Bob Dylan (artist); Joe Pesci [unbilled] (Leo Carelli)

EDWARD SCISSORHANDS

CREDITS: Executive Producer: Richard Hashimoto; Producers: Denise Di Novi and Tim Burton; Associate Producer: Caroline Thompson; Director: Tim Burton; Screenplay: Caroline Thompson; Cinematography: Stefan Czapsky; Production Designer: Bo Welch; Art Director: Tom Duffield; Set Decorator: Cheryl Carasik; Set Designers: Rick Heinrichs, Paul Sonski, and Ann Harris; Music: Danny Elfman

Cast: Johnny Depp (Edward Scissorhands); Winona Ryder (Kim); Dianne Wiest (Peg); Anthony Michael Hall (Jim); Kathy Baker (Joyce); Robert Oliveri (Kevin); Conchata Ferrell (Helen); Caroline Aaron (Marge); Dick Anthony Williams (Officer Allen); O-Lan Jones (Esmeralda; Vincent Price (The Inventor); Alan Arkin (Bill); Susan J. Blommaert (Tinka); Linda Perry (Cissy); John Davidson (TV Host); Bill Yaeger (George); Marti Greenberg (Suzanne); Bryan Larkin (Max); John McMahon (Denny); Victoria Price (TV Newswoman)

THE HEART OF JUSTICE

CREDITS: Executive Producer: Michael Brandman; Co-executive Producer: Barbara Corday; Producer: Donald P. Borchers; Associate Producer: Sarah Bowman; Director: Bruno Barreto; Screenplay: Keith Reddin; Cinematography: Declan Quinn; Production Designer: Peter Cannon; Costume Designer: Betty Madden; Makeup Supervisor: Belinda Bryant

CAST: Eric Stolz (David Leader); Jennifer Connelly (Emma Burgess); Dermot Mulroney (Eliot Burgess); Dennis Hopper (Austin Blair); Vincent Price (Reggie Shaw); Keith Reddin (Simon); Paul Teschke (Alex); Arthur Eckdahl (George); Ross Leon (Officer McCrane); Harris Yulin (Keneally); John Capodice (Harte); Katherine Lanasa (Hannah); William H. Macy (Booth); Bradford Dillman (Mr. Burgess); Gail Neely (Jean)

VINCENT PRICE—HIS RADIO APPEARANCES

by Martin Grams, Jr.

"Radio is not an old medium. It's a very present medium."
—Vincent Price, 1991

Whenever I hear a recording of Vincent Price's voice, I think about his radio appearances on *Suspense, Escape* and *The Price of Fear*. If he wanted to, Price could ham up a performance. With a crooked voice, he could inject goosebumps down into the marrow of my bones. He had that kind of voice—like Karloff's. Rough and chilling, but grandfather-like.

My initial intention was to compile a list of Price's radio credits with a brief synopsis of each broadcast, but such an undertaking would fill half of this book. So instead—with my apologies to the purists at heart—I am going to give a brief, abbreviated summary of Price's radio career, covering a wide variety of radio programs ranging from comedies to horror.

Price's first radio appearance is not officially known, but certainly one of his earliest appearances was on *The Royal Gelatin Hour*, broadcast over NBC on April 14, 1938. *The Royal Gelatin Hour* was hosted by Rudy Vallee. Price starred in a drama entitled "Ever After." Vallee introduced many unknown wanna-be performers to radio: Eddie Cantor, Alice Faye, Milton Berle, Bob Burns, Mary Martin and Edgar Bergen.

On February 26, 1939, Price co-starred with Ruth Gordon in an adaptation of Henrik Ibsen's "A Doll's House," on *Great Plays*, a popular anthology series.

On June 22, 1941, Price guested on what was the final broadcast of *The Helen Hayes Theatre*, playing the male lead in "Victoria and Albert." Helen Hayes played the female lead. Hayes not only performed the principal roles in this series, but she also supervised the productions, selections of stories and casting... including asking for Price via a hand-signed letter. Hayes had performed with Price before on another drama, "Victoria Regina," broadcast on the *Hayes Theatre* in 1937.

Heirs of Liberty was a program presenting stories of memorable incidents in the life of our founding fathers,and featured various guests from Hollywood and Broadway. The series was originally entitled *Speaking of Liberty*, but the title changed on August 28, 1941. Vincent Price starred in the broadcast of January 15, 1942, and was heard over NBC, Thursday evening from 6:30 to 6:45 p.m., EST. Sadly, no recordings of this show exist.

The Lux Radio Theatre was probably one of the most popular—if not the most popular—Hollywood programs on the air. Price starred in a handful, among the most notable: "The Letter" (broadcast on March 6, 1944), co-starring Bette Davis and Herbert Marshall. Davis and Marshall reprised their Somerset Maugham–created characters from the film of the same name. Davis attempted to plead innocent hoping to get away with murder. The radio script, based on the 1940 screenplay, was adapted for *Lux* by Howard Koch, known for having scripted the famed *War of the Worlds* panic broadcast script, and the 1942 screenplay to *Casablanca*. "Laura" (broadcast February 5, 1945) featured Lionel Barrymore as guest producer and host. The regular host, Cecil B. DeMille, had lost his position on *Lux* (which paid him a salary of $100,000) when he failed to pay a one dollar fee to the AFRA. Hollywood stars such as Barrymore filled in after DeMille was banned from radio.

In 1980 Vincent Price took time from his schedule to pose with Easter Seal Child Jessica Beigbeder to promote an Easter Seals Halloween campaign.

Vincent Price starred in two *Radio Reader's Digest* broadcasts. The first was "Flight of the Chetniks," broadcast on September 27, 1942. Henry Hull co-starred. The second was broadcast on November 29, 1942, entitled "The Love Story of Mark Twain." Price played the role of Samuel Clemens, writer, wit, and lovemaker in a biography about Mark Twain.

Columbia Presents Corwin, a short-run series of dramas scripted by radio playwright Norman Corwin, was one of Vincent Price's more humorous radio appearances. The drama was entitled "The Undecided Molecule." The premise concerned a trial—to decide the fate of a single rebellious molecule, who almost upset the universe by refusing to combine with other elements. Co-starring with Price was Robert Benchley, who served as the interpreter for the molecule, Groucho Marx as the judge, Sylvia Sidney as "Anima" speaker of the animal kingdom, Norman Lloyd,

Elliott Lewis and Keenan Wynn (who played four different roles). Price had the featured role of the vile prosecutor. This witty and poetic verse was dramatized on July 17, 1945.

On the theatrical side, Vincent Price reprised his stage role from Patrick Hamilton's "Angel Street," for *Theater of Romance*, on October 9, 1945, co-starring Anne Baxter and Sir Cedric Hardwicke. Almost 10 years later, on June 22, 1952, *Best Plays* presented "Angel Street" with Price in the same role. Elizabeth Eustis, Judith Evelyn and Melville Cooper joined the cast. *Best Plays* was hosted by John Chapman and broadcast over NBC. Two years later, on April 4, 1954, a recording of the 1952 *Best Plays* drama was rebroadcast over *NBC Star Playhouse*. Same drama, with the exception of a new opening and closing theme. On January 10, 1956, *Your Radio Theatre* reprised the format, using recordings of the same dramas, again with a new opening and closing theme. Herbert Marshall was the host when *Your Radio Theatre* premiered in October of 1955, Price took over the hosting duties during November and December, and in January, Marshall returned.

Horror, of course, is what comes to everyone's mind when they hear of Vincent Price. *Suspense*, one of the most popular horror programs on radio during the 1940s and 1950s, broadcast many Price offerings. "Fugue in C-Minor" (broadcast June 1, 1944) was scripted by Lucille Fletcher, author of "Sorry, Wrong Number." In this drama, Price starred as Theodore Evans, a widower with a passion for pipe organs, who actually had one built in his house. One day Theodore met Miss Peabody (played by Ida Lupino), and the two fell in love. After the marriage, he brought her home where she met his knee-high children, who secretly inform Miss Peabody that "Father is mad. Mother is not dead. She's alive within the walls of this house." Miss Peabody soon learns that the children are correct regarding their father's madness.

Another *Suspense*-ful drama was "Hunting Trip," broadcast on September 12, 1946. Price co-starred with Lloyd Nolan in a two-man radio play, performing the roles of Eric and Stan, who go up to the mountains for a quiet hunting trip. Both loved a woman named Karen—Eric loved Karen but Stan married her. Now that Karen was dead, the two men decide to settle their differences with real loaded guns in what became a *Most Dangerous Game* plot.

On the *Philip Morris Playhouse*, Vincent Price starred in a chilling tale about a theater critic who was being blackmailed by a vaudeville mindreader. Entitled "Leona's Room," this program was broadcast on February 25, 1949. Price co-starred with Donna Reed in an adaptation of Charlotte Bronte's "Jane Eyre" on *The Family Theater*, broadcast on October 26, 1950.

On the lighter side, Price loved humor, and starred in (almost) as many comedies as he did horror. *The Lucky Strike Program*, starring Jack Benny, was one of two appearances Price made on the program. On the February 6, 1949 broadcast, Benny tried to get Vincent Price's part on a *Ford Theater* broadcast. Price had, in fact, made a guest appearance on *The Ford Theater* two days before in a drama entitled "No Time for Love," with Claudette Colbert and Glenn Ford.

As an artist, Price collected, drew and painted. His love of art was known throughout Hollywood, and on more than one occasion, Price was offered radio roles playing artists and art collectors. On the *Philip Morris Playhouse* (May 6, 1950) Price co-starred with William Conrad in the drama "Murder Needs an Artist." Price played a writer who discovered a famous artist with amnesia, living in a Bowery flop house. After getting the artist to start painting again, the facts of the case come to the surface, and the writer protects his investment with murder. On *Suspense* (April 11, 1946), Price guested as an artist who sheltered a murderer, on the condition that he could use the killer as a model for his present-day painting. After he finished his masterpiece, Price stole the money from the murderer, and then tried to turn him in to the police. On April 29, 1947, Vincent Price was invited to appear in a panel discussion entitled *A Conversation on the Art of Collecting*.

Hollywood Star Time was an anthology series featuring adaptations of popular and not-so-popular films. Vincent Price participated in many of these broadcasts, always in the starring role. Linda Darnell and Fay Marlowe co-starred in "Hangover Square" (April 7, 1946). Price reprised his film role in "Shock," (February 3, 1946), co-starring Michael Dunn and Lynn Bari. Price even starred as Jack the Ripper in "The Lodger," (May 19, 1946). Ida Lupino was originally scheduled to appear in the later drama, but she was struck with laryngitis and could not appear. Cathy Lewis subbed. Price's appearance in "The Lodger" was a pitch for *Dragonwyck*, which was in the theaters at the time. Vanessa Brown and Lee J. Cobb co-starred with Price in "The Song of Bernadette," broadcast on April 21, 1946.

In 1947, RKO pictures released *The Long Night*, starring Henry Fonda, Barbara Bel Geddes, Ann Dvorak and Vincent Price. In an attempt to publicize the film, RKO hired their screenwriting staff to adapt the movie for radio, in seven 15-minute adaptations. Fonda, Bel Geddes, Dvorak and Price all reprised their film roles for the radio series, which was syndicated and released the same year. The mini-serial was broadcast on various radio stations at various times.

One of the many characters Price portrayed over radio—and one of his most prominent portrayals—was that of Simon Templar, alias "The Saint": A wealthy gentleman-like figure, a modern-day crook and a patron of the arts. The radio series, based on the fictional character created by Leslie Charteris, began in January 1945 with Edgar Barrier in the title role. That format ran for three months. From June to September of 1945, a summer series (replacing *The Jack Carson Show* for the summer) featured Brian Aherne in the lead. Almost two years later, on July 9, 1947, a third series began broadcasting on the West Coast, with Price as the lead. On July 10, 1949, the series went National over the Don-Lee Mutual Network, consisting of repeats from the West Coast productions. On January 15, 1950, *The Saint* began featuring new adventures. Price stayed on until May 20, 1951, after which Tom Conway took over beginning May 27.

On November 26, 1947, the Committee for the First Amendment sponsored a network radio broadcast attacking the House Un-American Activities Committee hearings and sent a chartered plane from Hollywood to Washington carrying numerous stars. The threat of Communism was in the air, and Hollywood stars were already feeling the heat. Bogart, Bacall, Boyer, Garland, Kelly, Holden, Loy, Ball, March, Wilde, Douglas, Conte, Keyes, Lancaster, Henried, Lorre, Havoc, Kaye, Hunt, Wanger, Shaw, Garfield and Cotten were among the many who appeared on the program to protest the McCarthy hearings—Price among them.

On March 13, 1950, Price joined other Hollywood stars for a radio broadcast entitled the *Parade of Stars*, sponsored by the American Red Cross. The broadcast reminded listeners how important the Red Cross was and how their services were required when disasters hit across the nation. The guests, including Price, pleaded with the listening audience for donations of food and money to their local Red Cross.

Another charitable cause came from Price in December 1955 when *Army of Stars* featured Christmas music, and a performance of Price reading the editorial, "Yes, Virginia There is a Santa Claus." As a salute to the Salvation Army, Price starred in the Christmas episodes of *Army of Stars* in December 1957 and 1959.

To help entertain the troops overseas, Price was guest on *Command Performance* in 1948, performing a West Coast version of *Naked City* called the "Sunset Strip." Joan Davis and Kay Starr performed, while Price was master of ceremonies. This episode was not broadcast in the United States, but overseas for the troops.

The Constant Invader was a series of specials produced and sponsored by the National Tuberculosis Association, which Price narrated. Each broadcast ran 15 minutes, and ran for a total of 13 broadcasts during the 1950s.

On July 3, 1949, Price starred in a Fourth of July special, entitled *Author of Liberty*. Shortly after this patriotic performance, Price visited a sound studio in California where he recorded a pilot entitled *The Croupier*. This was an audition program for a proposed psychological/supernatural series. The audition was entitled "The Roman," and broadcast on September 21, 1949. A week or two later, the series premiered, broadcast from October 5 to November 16 1949. It was probably Price's name attached to the pilot that prompted a regular series. "The Roman" concerned a rediscovery of the Malediction scroll on a deserted aircraft carrier, becoming a weird story of an ancient roman gladiator roaming the seas as a modern flying Dutchman. Milton Geiger wrote and directed, Dan O'Herlihy co-starred.

Another attempt at an original series was presented on May 10, 1942. *The Columbia Workshop* was a CBS program that presented experimental dramas such as "Alice in Wonderland" with music substituting sound effects, and "Beauty and the Beast" in operatic style. For this broadcast, *Columbia* presented an idea for a new program entitled *Chapter One*, a series that would dramatize only the first chapter of famous books, so that listeners would be urged to go out, purchase a copy and read the conclusion. Vincent Price starred in "Flight to Aris," a well-done story about World War II. An interesting idea that did not go anywhere.

On April 23, 1949, *The Thirteenth Juror* premiered, an NBC Saturday-evening series that featured different murder and mystery cases. Price co-starred with Hans Conried in the premiere broadcast, entitled "What Ever Happened to John Wilkes Booth?"

On June 9, 1957, Price co-starred with Ben Wright on *Suspense* in an adaptation of Philip MacDonald's 1949 short story "The Green-and-Gold String." Price played Dr. Alcazar, a mystic in the realm of the future, who used common sense and his sharp, keen observations to con his customers out of a few bucks with a fortune telling performance. When he read of an obituary in the papers, Price remembered that the woman had been a client of his only days before, and set out with his assistant to offer his services to the grieving kin, in an attempt to solve what turned out to be a murder case. This broadcast was actually a pilot for a series based on the Dr. Alcazar character. This was another broadcast pilot that never went anywhere.

Price guested on *The Dean Martin and Jerry Lewis Show* on July 19, 1949. Price appeared on other comedy radio programs such as *The Lucky Strike Program* starring Jack Benny in February 1948. Price joined Art Linkletter on *People Are Funny* on January 3, 1950. In January 1951, Price paid a visit to *Duffy's Tavern*, where Ed Gardner was attempting to bring culture to the tavern by changing it into an actors' studio. (A similar plot was used previously when Charles Laughton guested years before.) Price guested as a hillbilly on *The Sealtest Village Store* on March 20, 1947.

Back to drama: On May 17, 1947, Price co-starred with Kim Hunter and David Niven on *This is Hollywood*, hosted by Hedda Hopper. The drama presented was an adaptation of "Stairway to Heaven." Hunter and Niven reprised their film roles. Price took the place of an ill Raymond Massey, who was originally scheduled to star. "The big radio shows carried tremendous publicity value, and the movie producers were delighted when their stars were offered the exposure." Niven recalled years later. "Some shows were popular with the top film producers, others if possible, they avoided like the plague, but Louella Parsons had a blackmailing show called *Hollywood Hotel*, and a few years later Hedda Hopper, the other all-powerful columnist, came up with her own con game—*Hedda Hopper's Hollywood*. The big stars, goaded by their studios, performed on these programs at great inconvenience and for no salary because the chicken-hearted producers believed that refusal to "lend" their stars would bring swift retribution in the shape of bad publicity and poor reviews." Price may have substituted for Massey, but by no means did he volunteer.

One series showing an interesting side of Price was *Favorite Story*, a Ziv syndication hosted by Ronald Colman. Each week, a different Hollywood star was asked "What is your favorite story?" The novel, short story, or stage play the star or stars selected would be broadcast. Fred Allen actually said *Frankenstein* was his favorite! When Vincent Price was asked, he chose "Mr. Shakespeare," the 30th episode of the series, broadcast on April 10, 1948 and January 14, 1947 (East Coast and West Coast).

Vincent Price in a Western? You bet! *Stars Over Hollywood* presented "Continental Cowboy," the tale of Sagebrush Sam, Hollywood cowboy who tried to escape his hordes of fans in Paris. One of Price's hamiest roles, this episode was transcribed, directed and co-hosted by Hans Conried. Broadcast on December 30, 1950.

On the educational side, Price co-starred with Richard Whorf on *The Cavalcade of America*. The two starred as Frederick Grant Banting and Charles H. Best, who together discovered insulin. Walter Huston was the host of the broadcast entitled "A Race for Lennie," heard over NBC on January 29, 1945.

Back to the horror programs: On December 2, 1948, *Suspense* presented an adaptation of Thomas Burke's "The Hands of Mr. Ottermole." Sydney Greenstreet was originally scheduled to star in this broadcast, but for reasons unknown, Greenstreet bowed out. The sponsors hired two actors to fill in for Greenstreet (no joke intended), Claude Rains and Vincent Price. The classic story of a reporter attempting to up-stage the inspector of Scotland Yard by appearing at the crime scenes first. Only the reporter had no idea that the Inspector and the killer-on-the-loose had very much in common.

After the success of *Suspense*, CBS officials decided to create another anthology series featuring adaptations of suspenseful tales, stories ranging from Poe to Doyle. Vincent Price appeared on three episodes—one was "Blood Bath," broadcast on June 30, 1950. On March 17, 1950, Price starred in an adaptation of George Toudouze's "Three Skeleton Key." This terrifying tale involved three men tending to a lighthouse on the sea coast who watched their impending doom as a huge ship drifted toward land. Through binoculars, they were able to preview the crew and cargo, which consisted of thousands and thousands of rats. Soon the rats surrounded the light house and the three men attempted everything physically possible to prevent the rats from invading their shelter... with no way to escape.

Bill James, sound effects man for that particular job, recalled how technically challenging it was. "The rats were a challenge itself. [Tom] Hanley and I must have went through hundreds of records of bird calls to create the illusion for [Daphne DuMaurier's] 'The Birds.' We couldn't find rats or mice on record, so we had to use our fingertips on what I think was a wood board to make the footsteps and scratching against the lighthouse walls. The squeaking—I can't exactly remember what we used—but was a combination of sounds of animals other than rats."

On January 31, 1950, Price starred in "Present Tense," another *Escape* drama, written exclusively for *Escape* by CBS staff writer James Poe. Price starred as a condemned man enroute via train to the death house, for the murder of his wife and her lover. A twist of fate caused the train to crash, allowing Price to switch identities with his armed escort, and flee the scene. After arriving home, however, he discovered his wife and her lover alive and well, and were laughing over their successful plot to fake their own murders. Filled with rage, Price took a knife from the kitchen and sliced their throats. The police caught him, and as before, Price found himself enroute to the death house... on the very same train with the very same armed escort!

Knowing something was wrong, and sensing *deja vu*, Price faked an internal injury, causing the train to stop so a trip in an ambulance would be provided. Another means for Price to escape, and again he made for his home, this time to pack and make for the border. And once again, as before, he found his wife and her lover laughing about his predicament. Somehow—some way—Price was caught in a time-warp revisiting the same butchering over and over and over and over and over ...

William N. Robson, the director, commented: "It is a principle of law that a man cannot be charged, convicted and sentenced twice for the same crime. But there is no law in the book that says a man cannot murder his wife over and over again in his fantasy. For a man with sufficient imagination repetitive luxuricide can indeed become a pleasant way of bringing time to a stop as Vincent Price accomplished it in 'Present Tense.'"

Price reprised his *Escape* roles "Three Skeleton Key" and "Present Tense" for *Suspense* during the late 1950s. The *Escape* production of "Three Skeleton Key" was much more emotionally stimulating than the *Suspense* version (October 19, 1958), but in relation to "Present Tense," the *Suspense* production (March 3, 1957) was rich with sound effects, fast-paced background music and acting talents. I heartily recommend the 1957 version performed on *Suspense* if you want to hear one of Vincent Price's best radio performances ever.

While we are on the topic of *Suspense*, Price starred in "Rave Notice" (June 1, 1958), as an actor who shot the director of his stage play, and then had to use his acting abilities to play insane, in order to get away with murder. (Price played the role Milton Berle had enacted back in 1950.) An interesting footnote: A few years before Price acted in Roger Corman's *Pit and the*

Pendulum, Price starred in an adaptation, scripted by John Dickson Carr, for *Suspense* on November 10, 1957, with John Hoyt and Ben Wright.

In the mid-1950s, CBS reprised their previous *Columbia Workshop* series under a new title, *The CBS Radio Workshop*. Again, using experimental dramas utilizing the most talented men and women in the profession, and using guests on occasion—Price among them. On April 6, 1956, "Speaking of Cinderella," subtitled "If the Shoe Fits," was presented on *Workshop*, a well done look at the old story told in the conventional way, and then a modern "Madison Avenue" style version. Cool daddy! Price co-starred with Jeanette Nolan (Norman Bates' mother's voice in *Psycho*) and Vic Perrin (the control voice on the original *Outer Limits*).

During the 1960s, horror stars were hired by the Armed Forces Radio Service to host recordings of previous broadcasts. The hosting jobs were recorded in a sound studio, merely as openings and closings. Peter Lorre, for example, was host of an AFRS series entitled *Mystery Theater*, which featured recordings of various programs from *The Adventures of Ellery Queen*, *The Whistler*, *Inner Sanctum* and *Mr. and Mrs. North*. Price was also hired for a short-run AFRS series entitled *The Globe Theater*, which presented adaptations to numerous Hollywood films, the majority originating from *The Lady Esther Screen Guild Theater*.

From January 2, 1977 to February 6, 1977, Vincent Price co-starred with Peter Cushing in a six-episode mini-series entitled *Aliens in the Mind*. Broadcast over the BBC, this science-fiction serial dealt with mind-controlling genetic mutants, the next step in human evolution, and the efforts to remain concealed and/or conquer the world. [1/2/77 "Island Genesis"; 1/9/77 "Hurried Exodus"; 1/16/77 "Unexpected Visitations"; 1/23/77 "Official Intervention"; 1/30/77 "Genetic Revelations"; and 2/6/77 "Final Tribulations"].

From February 5, 1979 to August 3, 1979, Vincent Price hosted the *Sears Radio Theater*, sponsored by—what else?—Sears. This 60-minute anthology series was heard over CBS, Price narrated a total of 133 broadcasts!

Sometime during the late 1970s and early 1980s, Vincent was invited by Himan Brown to guest on a broadcast of *The CBS Radio Mystery Theater*, which was hosted by E.G. Marshall. Price declined the invitation from Brown, who asked that the next time Price was in New York, to stop by the studio and they would make a position available. "The only thing I have against the E.G. Marshall ones was that they were a little old-fashioned," Price recalled years later. "They were sort of consciously old-fashioned, as if, 'here we are: we're listening to an old medium.'"

One of Vincent Price's last radio appearances—certainly the last radio program to feature Price as a regular, was *The Price of Fear*, a BBC presentation. In this series, Price starred as himself, relating fictitious murder mysteries that he had a hand in as he toured the world pursuing his hobbies and movie career. "I do a series in London called *The Price of Fear* for World Service on BBC, and the listening audience is a hundred million people, which ain't bad!" Price laughed. "These stories are written by the very best writers in England, and all the top actors of England do these stories. And I've been the host, the connection between them." Dramas on this series included variations of Sir Arthur Conan Doyle's "Lot 132" and A.M. Burrage's "The Waxwork."

The Price of Fear had three broadcast runs. The first began on September 1, 1973 and ended October 13, 1973. The second broadcast run began a few months later, from April 6, 1974 and lasting until May 11, 1974. Almost 10 years later, the BBC revived the series again from May 30, 1983 to August 15, 1983.

A total of 25 broadcasts were recorded.

Those are some of Vincent Price's radio credits. It is quite surprising to see how many different programs, from straight drama to comedy, he starred in. From charity causes to pilot programs, Westerns to mysteries, Price did it all. Narrator, host and star. The next time I hear Vincent Price's voice, whether it originates from a music video or television commercial, his radio dramatizations will always come to mind. He had that kind of voice.

Vincent Price as Oscar Wilde. (Photofest)

ONE MAN SHOW—
VINCENT PRICE
AS OSCAR WILDE

by Tom Johnson

"The only thing worse than being talked about is not being talked about."—Oscar Wilde

Today's taboo-breaking celebrities could learn a thing or two from Oscar Wilde, the Victorian era's "bad boy." He was possibly the most discussed man in England, if not the world. And, up to a point, that suited him just fine; there was little chance of his not being talked about.

Wilde was a successful poet, playwright, novelist, trendsetter, flashy dresser, peerless conversationalist and devastating wit. He was also gay, and as reticent about it as he was about declaring his genius. Homosexuals, in Victorian England, were accepted on the same level as arsonists. It was punishable by hard time in prison... as Wilde was to discover first hand.

"Those who go beneath the surface do so at their peril."—Oscar Wilde

Oscar Wilde was born in Dublin, Ireland, on October 16, 1854. Following a precocious childhood, he graduated from Magdalen College at Oxford, finding success as a poet and personality, and failure in his pursuit of Florence Balcombe, who later married Bram Stoker.

After graduating, Wilde settled in London in 1878. Realizing that one path to fame is to be seen with the famous, Wilde made sure that he was seen courting Ellen Terry and Lily Langtry (two of the period's most famous actresses), while outrageously dressed and, more often than not, clutching a sunflower. He toured America—to a mixture of incredulity and dismissal—but was at this point a curiosity, carried more by his appearance and wit than by any concrete achievements.

When he returned to London, Wilde's world was an odd mixture of the gay and straight. He lived, for a time, with Frank Miles, a notoriously camp "artist" who was interested in very young girls and was an "in" to London society. When Miles failed to open enough doors, Wilde married Constance Lloyd in 1884, with whom he had two sons. Wilde was now famous for being famous... in fact, he was a minor drama critic for a minor women's magazine, living a dangerous double life.

"Like all children, he failed to recognize the moment at which the grownups would stop laughing."—Wilde biographer, Sheridan Morley

Oscar Wilde hit both his stride and the skids during the next decade. In 1890 he published his only novel (and most famous work), *The Picture of Dorian Gray*. Awash with witty epigrams, chilling horror and thinly veiled homosexual activity, the famous story of the portrait-that-ages would, in five years, help put its author in prison. Between 1892 and 1895, Wilde had four smash hits on the London stage: *Lady Windemere's Fan, A Woman of Importance, The Importance of Being Ernest* and *An Ideal Husband*, with the last two playing simultaneously in the West End. But...

Wilde had been sexually involved with Lord Alfred Douglas, the estranged son of the Marquis of Queensbury, and on February 18, 1895, the outraged father (no saint himself) left a note at Wilde's club accusing him of sodomy. Wilde could have ignored the note (the charge, after all, *was* true), but, spurred on by his lover, Wilde sued for slander. He seriously overestimated both society's freedom from convention and its embrace of those who disregard those conventions.

With "purple passages" from *Dorian Gray* and several "rent boys" thrown in his face, Wilde found *himself* in the dock and on May 25, 1895, was sentenced to two years hard labor at Pentonville and Reading prisons.

> "We sewed the sacks, we broke the stones,
> We turned the dusty drill:
> We banged the tins and bawled the hymns,
> And sweated on the mill...
> —*The Ballad of Reading Goal*, Oscar Wilde

Oscar Wilde was released on May 17, 1897. While a prisoner at Reading, he wrote his greatest poem; he would write no more. Broken by his prison experiences—including a serious ear injury that would eventually kill him—Wilde was often stoned and lived a pointless existence on the Continent, sponging off his few remaining friends. He died in Paris on November 30, 1900, at 46 years of age. "It's the wallpaper or me," he said of his death-room. "One of us has got to go."

> "I believe my role as Oscar Wilde was my greatest achievement as an actor."—Vincent Price, 1992

By the mid-1970s, Vincent Price—star of stage (*Angel Street*), screen (take your pick), and television (mostly sending himself up) had done it all. Now, in his mid-sixties, what was left? The answer came from Mrs. Price (Coral Browne): "Go stick your neck out." He did... in the most dangerous venture an actor can choose: a one-man show.

"Oscar Wilde is irresistible," said author John Gay (*New York Post*, April 12, 1978). "He doesn't go out of style." Gay was seldom out of style himself, having written screenplays (the Oscar-nominated *Separate Tables*, 1958), teleplays (*The Red Badge of Courage*, 1974), and plain old plays (*Christophe*, 1977). While on "vacation" during a strike by the Writers Guild of America, Gay used the time to tackle the subject that had long fascinated him. "Wilde still has a lot of relevance for people today," Gay said, "not just because of gay liberation, but on matters of art, politics and economics."

Gay's resultant play imagined Wilde, on November 28, 1899, ruined in reputation and health, lecturing on his life to anyone who would listen, in a shabby hall, on Paris' *Rue de la Repinier*. Suffering from humiliation as well as the ear infection that would kill him the following year, Wilde sustains himself with a bottle of absinthe (which is doing more harm than his assorted maladies).

The play would require only one character; the question was, who could play Wilde with the right combination of arrogance, wit, self-pity and horror?

Joseph Hardy was no stranger to the theater, having directed *Child's Play* (Tony winner), *Play It Again, Sam* (Tony nomination), and *You're a Good Man Charlie Brown*. When Gay's finished play, titled *Diversions and Delights*, was being cast in Los Angeles, the producers, recalled Hardy (*Esquire*, April 25, 1978) "kept coming up with all sorts of Hollywood-type actors, and I said, 'Look: Vincent Price!' Everyone looked blank... then said they were sorry they hadn't thought of it first!"

Eager to produce *Diversions and Delights* were Roger Berlind, Franklin R. Levy and Mike Wise.

Berlind began his theatrical career at Princeton University, directing and acting in Theatre Intime productions. He became a founding partner in a brokerage firm, but later returned to the theater, producing the Richard Rodgers–Sheldon Harnick musical *Rex*, then entered film production with *Aaron Loves Angela* (1975).

Levy was a theatrical agent for SCM before becoming a producer for 20th Century-Fox, packaging *Great Expectations* (1974–directed by Joseph Hardy) and *Voyage of the Damned* (1976).

Wise, like Levy, had been associated with SCM, then became head of development and production for Norman Rosemont Enterprises. He made his Broadway debut producing *I Have a Dream* (1977) which starred Billy Dee Williams as Dr. Martin Luther King, Jr.

Hardy felt that, while on the surface Price and Wilde had nothing in common, both men had a "take it or leave it" attitude about their work. When asked by *Esquire* about his horror films, Price commented, "They have a message even a pigeon wouldn't carry." Wilde could have easily said the same. "When Vincent comes on," said Hardy, "he's thinking... 'they're not throwing things... fine... they're lucky to have me.'"

Joseph Hardy described Price's special ability to play Wilde convincingly as being "because of the space he fills—his size, his age, everything about him—is perfect to fill Oscar's. It's a *dignified* space."

John Gay agreed (*New York Post*): "Vincent Price was a marvelous choice. You just felt it *was* Oscar Wilde up there."

"Up there" was a tacky proscenium held by two Grecian columns, leather

LAWRENCE FRENCH: How did you come to do *Diversions and Delights*?

VINCENT PRICE: The director, Joseph Hardy, asked me to read the play, which was written by a very good writer, John Gay. Hardy felt I would be right as Oscar Wilde and I found it was something I really wanted to do. It has really been the most critically acclaimed play I've ever done. It's great fun to be able to lose myself in the character. Wilde probably had the greatest command of the English language, as far as wit is concerned, of any man who ever lived.

LAWRENCE FRENCH: I've seen it three times already.

VINCENT PRICE: Have You?

LAWRENCE FRENCH: Yes, and I found I appreciated it even more, after seeing it the second time.

VINCENT PRICE: I guess you need to see it more than once. We had one woman in San Francisco who saw it 33 times. I couldn't believe it. Every time I came out, she'd be there, and I would just about faint. My God, she could have played it herself. She probably would be very good as Oscar Wilde (laughter).

armchair in about the same shape as its occupant, a table and a lectern. And, of course, Vincent Price: velvet jacket, green tie, tweed trousers and several tons of makeup.

Diversions and Delights, presented by the American Conservatory Theater, opened on July 11, 1977 in San Francisco's Marine Memorial Theatre. Over the next five years, Price would play Wilde more than 800 times in over 300 cities, ranging from New York to Hong Kong... and most of the college campuses in between.

Most critics found the shows both diverting and delightful... Bernard Walker (*San Francisco Chronicle*, July 12, 1977): "Price slides easily into the style, affecting a slight lisp and effete manner with just the right inflection, look, and gesture. Gay has done his homework... much is fascinating, even if one doesn't know all the facts."; Herb (*Variety*, June 12): "Vincent Price takes this Gay gavotte and Wilde waltz and runs with it... smug, snobbish, arrogant. Joseph Hardy's direction, just as the setting and lighting of H.R. Poindexter, is simple, straightforward. Hardy moves Price around very little. No need to; Price takes care of everything."

Diversions' success eventually led it to Broadway which, while an honor, was probably not the play's best venue, being better suited to smaller stages and audiences. Still, Broadway is Broadway.

The New York Times (March 3, 1978) announced, somewhat smugly, "Long before Mr. Price made some of those celebrated clinkers, he was on stage opposite Helen Hayes in *Victoria*

Price applys makeup before *Diversions and Delights*. (Photofest)

Regina. On April 12, he will open at the Eugene O'Neill. Mr. Price was last here in *Darling of the Day* in 1968."

Price's return to Broadway after the 10 year absence was not quite the triumph everyone would have liked it to be; *Diversions and Delights* barely lasted a month. Critics again praised Price's performance, although dissenters found it to be "mannered"; others faulted Gay for allowing Wilde to wallow in self-pity. These, however, were a distinct minority. As Wilde once said, "I am told drama critics can be bought; judging from their appearance, they can't be very expensive."

Undaunted, Price and Hardy diverted from Broadway and delighted audiences on the road for the next four years.

Up to a point, one's enjoyment of *Diversions and Delights* depended upon one's interest in Oscar Wilde or Vincent Price. This is not *The Phantom of the Opera* or *Miss Saigon*, it's a one-man (or, if you will, two-man) show. At its most basic level, the play involves a man sitting in a chair or standing by it, talking. There was nothing else... not a falling chandelier in sight.

Price plays Wilde as what he almost certainly was—a proud, broken, bitter man who still had his wit—but little else. Wilde wins our sympathy not by begging for it, but by flaying himself wide open for our approval or disapproval. His honest appraisal of his ruined life—and how easily it could have been avoided—is heartbreaking. Wilde realizes that his downfall was mostly his own doing, yet reminds us that Victorian hypocrisy also played a major role.

Vincent Price revealed his thoughts on Wilde in the play's souvenir booklet:

> There are few famous men or women whose character, humanity, humor or even tragedy can survive the scrutiny of a 'one-man show'... by that I mean author, actor and audience scrutiny.
>
> Oscar Wilde is the ideal personage to be examined by this all-revealing kind of theatre presentation. The fame of his wit is enough justification, but underneath the brilliant facade is a very human being, vulnerable to his own fame, his own strengths and weaknesses, and a being who inspires a kind of very real and identifiable audience admiration and appreciation.
>
> For the actor, the assumption of such a volatile personality is not only challenging but thrilling by the very nature of this audience identification. Wilde, and through his genius, the actor seems to have something to say to everyone. He becomes almost lovable in his self-conscious avoidance of love-ability. He is admirable for his ability to admire his own talent and to make it so especially his own. He is unique and that one-of-a-kindness quality, perhaps more than anything else, make him qualify for this form of theatrical revelation.
>
> Wilde is a joy to play. For his personal tragedy is as universally appealing as his private-public wit is individually enchanting.

I'm embarrassed to admit that my memory of *Diversions and Delights* isn't what it should be. I was more caught up in actually seeing VINCENT PRICE than I was in seeing the play.

The second time I saw it, I'd made arrangements to meet Mr. Price after the show; you can imagine what it was like waiting for the play to end. Still, 20 years later, I regret my impatience.

Fortunately, others were more astute.

> "It is through Art and through Art only that we can realize our perfection...
> and shield ourselves from the social perils of actual existence."—Oscar Wilde

Author/editor Bob Madison (*Dracula: The First Hundred Years*) had the kind of break at 16 that all fans dream of but, presumably, only he got. In the fall of 1979, *Diversions and Delights* moved into New York's Roundabout Theatre and young Bob was there... often. The manager (a Price fan?) offered Bob a job as an usher since he was there practically every night anyway.

"I got to see Vincent Price a great deal over the next few weeks," Madison recalls, "going backstage for a party he hosted, trading jokes and general theater horseplay. Just before the show closed, I asked for an interview..."

Do you mind the way your career turned out?
Turned out pretty good! Still working!
No, I mean would you rather have been doing other *things?*
Well, I do. *Diversions and Delights* is entirely different from anything I've ever done and it's the biggest success I've ever had. Seriously. A couple of critics said they had seen me do so many horror pictures that they were amazed to see me do this.
Do you admire wit and think it's a sign of intelligence?
Oh, yes. The ultimate sign. Wit... not funniness. Take the Wilde thing... there isn't a single double meaning, there isn't even a vaguely dirty word and yet it's funnier than 90 percent of the stand-up comics. Because it's real wit.
When you play Wilde, you alter your speech pattern. Why?
Well, number one, I'm trying as hard as I can to be as close to Wilde as I can. Wilde had a very peculiar speech pattern... an "Irish Protestant accent." A kind of meticulous pronunciation of every single syllable. I also raise my voice to a different pitch... I'm terribly well known for my voice and I don't want to have that voice... because I'd still be Vincent Price.
How much research did you do?
When I created the part, I found it very difficult to know too much. You should enter a part with a kind of innocence... I *did* the research at the time... and since... a lot during rehearsals and after we started trying it out.

"What were my first impressions?" Bob asks. "That at 68, he was a man of enormous energy, vitality, and enthusiasm. I believe I first saw the October 11 performance, and I saw most of them up to November 4. It was fascinating. Every night he would throw Wilde's yellow rose out to a female member of the audience. His stagecraft was incredible. He could work an audience and, amazingly, there was little variation in his performance. I saw the show from the first row, the stairwell, the side hall... every place but the roof.

"It's one of the great tragedies that *Diversions and Delights* was never recorded. Even on audio tape, it was a performance that demanded some kind of permanence. I thought, at the time, it was the best thing he ever did. I think I still believe that."

My own experience with Mr. Price was shorter but equally memorable. I saw the show at the Roundabout (was I shown to my seat by Bob Madison?) with Randy Vest, who has since become a reporter for *People*. It's a shame he wasn't *then*! We sent a rather rude—but hopefully funny, card backstage to Mr. Price, asking to meet him after the show. The card was returned with the message, "How dare you treat a star of my magnitude in this way? I'm forced to meet with you after the show to discuss this." We hoped he was being funny and would actually come out and talk to us.

He was, and he did.

AN INTERVIEW WITH VINCENT PRICE

by Lawrence French
(Conducted in Westport, Connecticut, 1979 and
San Francisco, California, 1985)

LAWRENCE FRENCH: Would you like to do some Shakespeare on the stage?

VINCENT PRICE: I would love to do some. I'd like to do Prospero (in *The Tempest*), Shylock (in *The Merchant of Venice*) and *King Lear*. I'm old enough now, to do Lear. You know, I don't think we do Shakespeare as well as the English do. We just don't. It's their language. I saw John Gielgud's *Hamlet* 14 times! It was extraordinary. They attack a Shakespearean part, like a piece of music. If you listen to John Gielgud's *Seven Ages of Man*, it is an incredible display of vocal and mental acumen. They understand Shakespeare. He wrote for them. We just borrow it. We understand Eugene O'Neill and Tennessee Williams better. We also do the musical theater better, much better, than the English.

LAWRENCE FRENCH: English actors have more training in the classic parts than Americans, don't they?

VINCENT PRICE: Yes, it's a tiny little country. It isn't nearly as big as California. It's got one major city, which is the major city in the world, London. Everything is done there, and the actors work for very little. There's a theater in London, the Royal Court, which is only dedicated to new playwrights. Alec Guinness, Gielgud, Ralph Richardson, all of them go there and work for 50 pounds a week to do a play by a new playwright. In America it wouldn't happen, because we're all so money conscious. On *Theater of Blood* the picture was worked around the schedule of the actors playing the critics, because a lot of them were doing plays in the West End. That's the type of thing they do over there.

LAWRENCE FRENCH: Didn't Katherine Hepburn once ask you to play Prospero in *The Tempest*, and you turned her down?

VINCENT PRICE: Yes, because I couldn't afford it. It was at that Shakespearean theater in Stratford, (Connecticut) and you were supposed to go and give up the whole summer. You only played for three weeks and the rest of the time you were laid off. Now it was a very different situation with Miss Hepburn, because she's a very rich lady. So it was a different kettle of fish on that score.

LAWRENCE FRENCH: The great Shakespearean actor, Morris Carnovsky, ended up playing Prospero, which got him some wonderful acclaim.

VINCENT PRICE: Yes, I know it. Morris is from my hometown of St. Louis, too. He was a marvelous actor. I saw him in *Golden Boy* when he did it with the Group Theater. I once played the same part Morris played in *Golden Boy*. Morris was wonderful in it, and I was terrible.

LAWRENCE FRENCH: At the Group Theater, Morris was working with directors like Lee Strasberg and Elia Kazan, who later founded The Actor's Studio that gave rise to 'Method acting' made famous by people like Marlon Brando and James Dean, but which you never really utilized.

VINCENT PRICE: Yes, but Morris came from the Yiddish theater as well, which had a great discipline. I'm sure he said (playwright) Clifford Odets' lines. You know, he didn't fool around with mumbling them, although he did bring a mood to them. He was a wonderful actor. That was a very exciting time in the theater, because there was the Group Theater, and then there was Orson Welles' Mercury Theater, which I was part of. We were doing the classics, and The Group was doing the modern plays. It was a time when New York was just filled with exciting theater. It was a really wonderful time.

LAWRENCE FRENCH: How did you like working with Orson Welles?

VINCENT PRICE: Welles was a marvelous director. I did two plays with him, *The Shoemaker's Holiday* and *Heartbreak House*. He was a really brilliant director, although I never thought he was a very good actor. I mean he's too Orson Welles. There's absolutely no characterization at all. More he did when he was young, then he does now, because he really is a caricature of himself now. I mean, that fat!

LAWRENCE FRENCH: Was Welles as undisciplined as some people have claimed?

VINCENT PRICE: He was completely undisciplined. You see, he had the theater like that! (holds up his hand in a fist). I would have loved to have worked with him again, but everybody in the Mercury Theater had a bit of a falling out with Orson. There were two plays we were supposed to do, Oscar Wilde's *The Importance of Being Ernest*, and John Webster's *The Duchess of Malfi* (intriguingly described by a Mercury press release as, "one of the great horror plays of all time"). My then wife, Edith Barrett, was going to be in *The Duchess of Malfi* as well. Orson was going to direct both of them, and the actors had contracts to do them. Then, when we went to rehearse them, Orson never showed up. He didn't show up for either show. He just decided he didn't want to do them, but he didn't bother to tell the actors.

LAWRENCE FRENCH: One book on Welles claims he had a fear of completion.

VINCENT PRICE: I think so. Like Michelangelo. I think he could have been the greatest director of the American theater and of the cinema, but there was something missing there.

LAWRENCE FRENCH: It's sad, because when Welles directs, his films are so brilliant. I think his *Chimes at Midnight* (*Falstaff*) is one of the greatest films ever made.

VINCENT PRICE: And *Citizen Kane*. *The Magnificent Ambersons* I saw the other day, and it falls apart completely at the end.

LAWRENCE FRENCH: But the ending of *Ambersons* was re-edited by the studio.

VINCENT PRICE: Yes, I know it.

LAWRENCE FRENCH: Was there ever any talk of you acting at RKO when you first went out to Hollywood, perhaps working with Orson Welles, or with Val Lewton's horror unit?

VINCENT PRICE: No. I first went to Hollywood under contract to Universal, and then was with 20th Century-Fox for seven years. However, at that time, my first wife (Edith Barrett) made two films with Val Lewton: *I Walked with a Zombie* and *The Ghost Ship*, although I never worked with Val Lewton. Later on, I did *The Comedy of Terrors* with Jacques Tourneur, who had worked a great deal with Val Lewton.

LAWRENCE FRENCH: You finally got to RKO in the '50s, when Howard Hughes was in charge.

VINCENT PRICE: Well, working for Howard Hughes was like working for the Invisible Man! (laughter). He used to call me up from Las Vegas on the telephone. That's as close as I ever got to meeting him. For some reason or other he liked me, so he would call me up because he wanted to know if there were any dirty jokes told on the set during the day (laughter). So I'd make little notes on all the dirty jokes that he loved to hear. I had to scream into the phone, because he was half-deaf.

LAWRENCE FRENCH: Was this on *Son of Sinbad*?

VINCENT PRICE: Yes. We had 250 girls in that, so there was a lot to report to him. *Son of Sinbad* was hilarious. They sent me the script, and said "What do you think of it?" I said, "I think it's the worst script I've ever read in my life!" So they said, "It is, isn't it?" (laughter). I said, "Certainly you're going to improve it," and they said, "No!" I asked them why they were going to make it then, and they told me there is a federal law, that if you offer a prize, and the prize is a part in a picture, then you have to pay it off. Howard Hughes had 250 girls who had all won a prize to be in a movie, so to pay off all these girls he made *Son of Sinbad*. Dale Robertson who was Sinbad, would knock on the gate and say, "Open sesame," and the gate would open, and inside were not the 40 thieves, but the daughters of the 40 thieves. That way they got rid of

Vincent Price and Judith Evelyn in *Angel Street*. (Photofest)

40 of Howard Hughes' girls. Every girl you ever knew in your life was in it, and some of them became very big stars... who shall remain nameless. (Kim Novak was one of the girls.)

LAWRENCE FRENCH: I read that they recently discovered your screen-test for *Gone With the Wind*.

VINCENT PRICE: Yes, I was doing *Victoria Regina* with Helen Hayes on Broadway, and they thought I'd be right for Ashley Wilkes (played in the film by Leslie Howard). I was playing a

German Prince in *Victoria Regina*, with an accent, and George Cukor (the first director of *Gone with the Wind*) had just seen the play and came backstage to see me. I said to him (Price does a southern accent), "Hello Mr. Cukor, how are you?" Now, I'm from Missouri, and I natively have, not a southern accent, but an accent of that area, but Cukor thought I was putting it on! (laughter). I didn't get the part, of course. I wish I had. I think I would have been better than Leslie Howard, because I never thought he was anything but English. He was just wrong. Everyone else was perfect; Gable, Olivia de Havilland and Vivien Leigh. It would have been fun.

LAWRENCE FRENCH: Later on George Cukor directed *Gaslight*, the film version of the play you did on Broadway, *Angel Street*. Was there ever any talk of you repeating your stage role for the movie?

VINCENT PRICE: The story I heard later on was that they wanted to hire the whole original cast of *Angel Street* for the film, because it was an enormous success. It was one of the greatest hits on Broadway, ever! The reviews, and everything were tremendous, and it ran for five years. The studio wanted to buy it with us to do it, but the guy who directed it, Shepard Traube, insisted that if they did it with us, he had to direct it, and he wasn't a movie director, and they needed a big name movie director. Then Cukor, as I understand it, wanted to do it with all of us: myself, Judith Evelyn and Leo G. Carroll. It would have been marvelous, because the thing that was wrong with the movie, even though it won Ingrid Bergman the Academy Award, was that Charles Boyer (in the part Price played on-stage), was not sinister. He was too charming. You know he's the most charming man that ever lived. I knew him terribly well, and adored him. Later, we did a play together, *Don Juan in Hell*, in which I played the devil and Charles played Don Juan. But also, in the film Joseph Cotten became a romantic interest for the woman, where Leo G. Carroll, who did the play, was never that. He was always a peculiar, eccentric little old man, who came into their lives and disrupted them. I think it would have been a really great film with the original cast. Joe even felt that he was mis-cast. He was really upset about it, because he had seen the play, and he felt he was wrong for it. It should have been an eccentric man, and Joe is not an eccentric man. He is a real romantic leading man.

LAWRENCE FRENCH: That role was your first villain, and I heard that you studied Krafft-Ebing to prepare for the part.

VINCENT PRICE: Yes, you know I'm not a psychopathic killer (laughter). I had to do a lot of research, so I read all of Krafft-Ebing's *Psychopathia Sexualis*, which dealt with case histories of psychotic murderers, and all that type of thing, because I had no idea what this kind of really determined, evil man would do. It was fascinating to study, but it scared the hell out of me.

LAWRENCE FRENCH: Did that help you later on when you played such evil characters as Prince Prospero or Matthew Hopkins?

VINCENT PRICE: Well Prospero was a fictitious character, but Matthew Hopkins was a really evil person, and it was a true story. He wasn't just a sadist though! If he were I wouldn't have wanted to play him.

LAWRENCE FRENCH: One of things Christopher Lee fervently believes in, is the reality of evil and the dark forces. You've played several very evil characters, from the Satan-worshipping Prince Prospero, to Satan himself.

VINCENT PRICE: Satan is the ultimate hero.

LAWRENCE FRENCH: But do you believe in evil or the occult?

VINCENT PRICE: I don't believe in the occult, but I do believe there is a power of evil. How do you read the Bible? It is divided equally between good and evil. You can't have good without evil, because there's no conflict. One of the lectures I do is basically that: trying to explain that the role of the villain has a definite part in the history of drama. He is the fellow who creates the suspense and the conflict. You can't have drama without suspense.

LAWRENCE FRENCH: That goes back to the Greeks, and Aristotle.

VINCENT PRICE: Sure, to the Greeks and long before that even.

LAWRENCE FRENCH: Another great director you worked for, and very few people know about it, is Alfred Hitchcock.

VINCENT PRICE: Yes, I did one of his TV shows, *The Perfect Crime*. You know, he's a character. Everybody knows about him, but he's a fellow who plays as much of a role as the director, as the actors do who are on the screen. It was just Jim Gregory and myself. We were the only two actors in it, actually. There were a couple of bit parts, but Hitch's whole direction to us was speed. It was two men talking about a murder, with Jim Gregory accusing me of doing it. There was one point where we looked over at Hitchcock in one of the run-throughs, and he was sound asleep, or else he was pretending to be sound asleep (laughter). He did that all the time. He did it with Cary Grant, he did it with everybody. It was part of his routine, or his image.

LAWRENCE FRENCH: That's a great story, because you hear about people visiting the set and seeing Hitchcock reading a newspaper while everyone's busy shooting the most important scene in the picture. He claimed to have planned everything so precisely, that he didn't have to see what was happening.

VINCENT PRICE: I know it. He only directed about a dozen of those TV shows himself, so when Jim and I were going to do it, we were both terribly excited. I don't think Hitchcock had ever done anything in four days in his life before this.

LAWRENCE FRENCH: You are both regarded as the leading exponents of screen terror, so it's nice that you worked together, although you never did a picture with Hitchcock.

VINCENT PRICE: No, but I liked him a lot. I met him many times, but I don't really know him very well.

LAWRENCE FRENCH: Did you read that controversial biography about Hitchcock, *The Dark Side of Genius*?

VINCENT PRICE: Yes, and apparently it was mostly true. I don't think that came as a surprise to a lot of people. From the people I know, who knew Hitchcock well, there was always this very mysterious area of his life. I must say though, I'm glad I worked with him, in the same way I'm glad I worked with DeMille.

LAWRENCE FRENCH: And you worked for DeMille on his 1956 version of *The Ten Commandments?*

VINCENT PRICE: Yes. He was a wonderful movie director. He was primarily interested in the visual aspects of the story. In *The Ten Commandments* I played Baka, the architect of Egypt, who is building this great city for the Pharaoh Sethi, played by Cedric Hardwicke. Charlton Heston was Moses, and we had a scene where I say, "Behold, it is the city of Sethi's glory," but what we were looking at was just an empty screen, because it was a special effects shot that was going to be added later on. DeMille said to me, "You don't say that line with very much conviction." I said, "That's because I don't know what in God's name I'm supposed to be looking at." So DeMille took us all down to the projection room to see this shot. It was 2,000 people carrying an obelisk towards the gateway of the city. A really unbelievable shot, the kind of thing that DeMille was so good at— you know, those spectacular

crowd scenes. (Apparently DeMille was never pleased with Price's reading of the line, because in the finished film, it is Charlton Heston who says to Cedric Hardwicke, "It shall be the city of Sethi's glory." Price looks on from the background, but has no dialogue.)

LAWRENCE FRENCH: Would you like to work with George Lucas or Steven Spielberg, on one of the *Indiana Jones* or *Star Wars* movies?

VINCENT PRICE: Oh yes. I would have loved to have been in *Star Wars*. Peter Cushing was really marvelous in that. Of course, when you talk about Spielberg and Lucas, you're talking about really popular pictures. The whole thing of science-fiction, which they do, are really at their peak today. There are things they know now about the technique of those pictures, which they never could have done years before. When I was in Paris at a retrospective of my films, I was so amazed that the French people really have a different view of this kind of picture. They take them very seriously, because the original films done were science fiction. You know, Melies and *A Trip to the Moon*. Then later on there was *Nosferatu*, which was really in the Gothic tradition. They last and they

go on and on. It's really amazing to me that some of these pictures, like the Poe films, which are over 20 years old, really hold up.

If you look at the history of fright, it is partly a catharsis of a kind. The fairy tales that Grimm wrote and are the first thing we read to our children, are much more frightening than anything I ever made, or that anybody has ever made! They were done as a kind of catharsis for children. They take the onus off of the parent. I've done a lot of research about this. The child suddenly thinks of the villain as the villain, not of the parent as the villain. That's why almost any child psychologist will tell you that this kind of fairy tale is, in a way, very good for a child. I think that some of the films I made were fairy tales in a way.

LAWRENCE FRENCH: That's interesting, because you never really played the classic monsters, like Karloff or Christopher Lee.

VINCENT PRICE: No, not really. The only one I did where I played a monster was *Dr. Phibes*, but that was kind of ridiculous (laughs).

LAWRENCE FRENCH: You played the Invisible Man.

VINCENT PRICE: The Invisible Man wasn't a monster, he was just a fellow who was lucky!

LAWRENCE FRENCH: You did *The Monster Club* for producer Milton Subotsky, although it never got shown in American theaters.

VINCENT PRICE: No, it didn't get much play, but I thought it had possibilities. The stories were very good, and the thing with John (Carradine) and myself, the whole description of the monsters was funny, but the thing that went wrong with *The Monster Club*, was that Milton Subotsky had found some man, who was a milkman, that had a hobby of making masks. Well he hired this fellow, and thought they would look great, but they're terrible, just terrible! It looks like amateur night. They really should have been wonderful, elaborate masks, that look real, but these look like some kid made them.

LAWRENCE FRENCH: I guess he had a low budget.

VINCENT PRICE: Well you can have a low budget, but that doesn't mean that! You can still go out and rent them. The other thing was the rock 'n' roll music was no good. There were no good names. The stories were excellent though. You know, we were the bridge between the three stories.

LAWRENCE FRENCH: I had to laugh at the ending, when you and John Carradine start dancing with the monsters. You're quite obviously enjoying it.

VINCENT PRICE: Oh yes! We just had fun, but we were so shocked at the rock 'n' roll music. I have great admiration for rock 'n' roll, but not when it's done badly. My God!

LAWRENCE FRENCH: Actually, you've been involved in a number of projects with rock stars, like Alice Cooper, Ringo Starr, and Michael Jackson.

VINCENT PRICE: You know, I have a theory about how I get selected for these things. I think they've based a lot of their stuff on my movies. They go out and do the rock 'n' roll, and they're all high, and making the noise and flying around, and then they go back to their hotel room, turn on the TV, and there I am! (laughter). Alice and I met a couple of times, and I liked him, then he asked me to do *Welcome to My Nightmare*. Then one time I got a call and they said would you

Vincent Price and Patricia Routledge record the cast recording of *Darling of the Day*. (Photofest)

come and do a recording with Michael Jackson, called *Thriller*. I said, "Sure, I'll do anything." (laughter). So I went and did it, and I didn't think anything would happen with it. Then it came out and sold 40 million copies! I didn't do it for the money, because I didn't have a percentage of it. It was just fun to do. You know to be identified with the most popular record ever made is not just chopped liver! It has really done me a lot of good, because it has given me a new audience.

LAWRENCE FRENCH: I see you get to do some singing in *Ruddigore* (or *The Witches Curse*), which was made for British television and shown in American on PBS.

VINCENT PRICE: That was great fun. I was in England and they decided to do all of the Gilbert and Sullivan operas and they asked me to play in *Ruddigore*. It was really a challenge,

Vincent Price personally selected art for the Fort Worth Sears. He is shown with the manager of the Sears store, Clay Ross.

because the English know how to do it better than anybody. After all, they wrote it. I love music and I started out as a singer. I was with the glee club at Yale and I took singing lessons in Vienna, but I stopped singing because I always had this terrible fear that the orchestra would win out, and they always did. I think studying singing is enormously important in the theater, because it is an interpretive art, as much as it is a musical art. Doing *Ruddigore*, the marvelous thing about it was that it was prerecorded, so there was no chance of the orchestra winning while I was there. They had already won, before I got there. I've done a lot of musical-comedy, although I'm not really a singer, I just fake it. On the stage I've done *Oliver* (as Fagin), *Peter Pan* (as Captain Hook) and I sang in *Victoria Regina*. I did a musical on Broadway, which was a very good show written by Jules Styne, called *Darling of the Day*. It got very good notices, but it was at a time (1968) when *Grease* and *Hair* and all those shows were really popular and this was just a nice old-fashioned musical-comedy, and the public didn't go for it.

LAWRENCE FRENCH: Perhaps we could end with a little bit about your interest in art. How did you become an art collector?

VINCENT PRICE: I'm not really interested in buying anything else. I was once voted one of the 10 worst dressed men in Hollywood, because I don't really care about clothes. I'm not interested in that particular aspect, like a lot of other people are. Or jewelry, or something like that. I have always bought art. I've never had a lot of money, so I don't own a lot of expensive art, but I do love American Indian Art and I do work for the American Indians. I worked for 15 years with the Department of the Interior. I have an enormous respect for the American Indian. I think we shut them off, at a period when they might have become the most creative people on the face of the earth. But we killed them off. How man creates is what always concerns me. What he does to really display his talent. You know, I have a theory that art is everything that man creates. I think that in America we tend to departmentalize the arts. We say that theater is an art, movies are an art, if we admit they are an art at all, and we say that art is hand-painted oil on canvas. Then we forget about architecture and poetry and music. I'm really interested in all of the arts, and I find a lot of people limit themselves. But people who are in the theater should remember that the theater is the mother of the arts. It cannot exist without sets, without music, without acting and particularly without writing.

LAWRENCE FRENCH: That applies to movies as well, only more so.

VINCENT PRICE: Yes, I have a great admiration for the motion picture as a profession. I think it's a great art form. It's something that is more identifiable with America, probably than anywhere else. Other countries make magnificent pictures, too, but it is a very American thing, movies. This is what people think about us. I really love movies. I was always very much in the way on the set, because I was so fascinated with the technical side of filmmaking and I was always behind the camera, when I should have been in front of it. I love the whole thing about moviemaking, but, I also found that as an actor, it wasn't very satisfying. You need the theater, you need to do both. I also found that radio was a great place to learn my craft. Television is probably the least exciting of all the mediums. There's a kind of impersonality about television, although I think it has great potential. I think if I had it to do all over again, I would have stayed in the theater. I would have gone back to the theater much sooner than I did, because I quit movies to go back to the theater.

LAWRENCE FRENCH: During the time you stopped doing movies to do your stage show, *Diversions and Delights* (from 1977 to 1982), there was a mini-revival in horror films. Were you ever offered anything that interested you?

VINCENT PRICE: I was offered a couple, but I didn't like them, so I didn't do them.

LAWRENCE FRENCH: I would have thought you would have been in the forefront of that new interest.

VINCENT PRICE: I don't know. I mean, really and truly, about five years ago everyone said, "Well, that's the end of that (horror films)." Now, of course, they're back, but they never really left.

LAWRENCE FRENCH: Did you ever want to direct a movie?

VINCENT PRICE: No, I never thought of doing my own film, although I have worked with some of the great cameramen, and have known them very well. *Leave Her to Heaven* was shot by Leon Shamroy. Artie Miller did *Dragonwyck*. Joe LaShelle won an Academy Award for

Laura. *The Baron of Arizona* was shot by James Wong Howe, who was one of the best camera-men in the business. On *Baron of Arizona* we had a 19-day schedule, because it was (director) Sammy Fuller's first picture. Nobody wondered if the actors could do it, or if anybody else could do it. They all wondered if James Wong Howe could do it, because he was a perfectionist. It's just like the television directors today, who've had to adjust to doing a picture in two weeks. It ain't easy! I used to adore trying to find out how some of the technical and special effects people did things, like John Fulton on *The Invisible Man Returns*. They were all really brilliant, but I never thought about directing a movie of my own.

LAWRENCE FRENCH: What do you think of the old studio system, compared to the way movies are made today?

VINCENT PRICE: Well, I was with Fox for about seven years, and with RKO for about four years—when Howard Hughes was in charge. I found that the studio system was a kind of team effort, that made it fun. Some of those old pictures were very lavishly produced, with a great deal of care. I think today, there's a kind of impersonality, which didn't exist in the old days. At Fox, you went on the set of a picture like *Dragonwyck* or *Leave Her to Heaven*, and you already knew everyone. You knew the technicians and you knew the other actors, so it was like a little stock company, just as Ingmar Bergman had so brilliantly in Sweden. You knew all the people, so you could work better with them and it was fun. Nowadays I think some of the fun has gone out of moviemaking.

LAWRENCE FRENCH: There was a time when Hollywood was making a series of biographi-cal films on great artists. Jose Ferrer played Toulouse Lautrec for John Huston in *Moulin Rouge* and Kirk Douglas did Van Gogh in Vincente Minnelli's *Lust for Life*.

VINCENT PRICE: And Charlton Heston played Michelangelo (in Carol Reed's *The Agony and the Ecstasy*), which was just ridiculous, because Michelangelo was this tiny little man! The only person who ever really played a great painter, and played it correctly, was Kirk Douglas as Van Gogh. He was marvelous in that. John Houseman (the producer of *Lust for Life*) told me he used the letters of Van Gogh in the film, after he had heard about a program I do, called 'Dear Theo.' It's a reading of the letters of Van Gogh to his brother Theo. *Lust for Life* was really wonderful, everything was just wonderful. There was that marvelous score (by Miklos Rozsa), and Kirk was brilliant. The only thing that was really wrong with it was Anthony Quinn as Gauguin. I didn't believe him for a minute. I would have been better than Tony Quinn as Gauguin, I can tell you that.

LAWRENCE FRENCH: Are there any painters you would like to play in a movie?

VINCENT PRICE: No, not really, because a painter has to have a dramatic life, it's not enough to just be a painter. If you're going to play Rubens, or somebody like that, you have to have a dramatic story. Actually, somebody like Ben Gazzara should have played Michelangelo. It would have been wonderful if they had portrayed Michelangelo with that broken face of his. You know, he had a broken nose. Another movie that wasn't really right was Charles Laughton as *Rembrandt* (1936). It was too much Laughton, and too little Rembrandt. Leonardo da Vinci, I would love to do, but I don't think you can, because it would have to be the world's biggest production.

LAWRENCE FRENCH: You worked with Charles Laughton in a movie at MGM, *The Bribe*, and later on he directed you in a play, *Don Juan in Hell*.

Vincent Price starred with Charles Laughton in *The Bribe*.

VINCENT PRICE: Yes, I was here in San Francisco, doing a play, Christopher Fry's *The Lady's Not for Burning* and Laughton wanted to get out of *Don Juan in Hell*. He was playing the part of the Devil, and he asked me if I would take over the role from him. The play was taken from George Bernard Shaw's *Man and Superman* and it was an extraordinary experience. I worked with Laughton for about three weeks, every night after the show, and I learned the part without a single rehearsal. That's not an easy thing to do with three people who've already been playing in it for two months (Charles Boyer, Cedric Hardwicke and Agnes Moorehead). Laughton was a brilliant man. Eccentric, peculiar, nasty, nice, funny, disgusting—but an extraordinary man. I got to know him probably as intimately, in that theater way, as anybody ever did, working with him every night on the play.

LAWRENCE FRENCH: What do you think of about these tell-all autobiographies by actors and actresses?

VINCENT PRICE: I really find the revelation of people's personal life, unless it has to do with their art, to be boring. Like Shelley Winters. For that you just get a large bed (laughter). When they have to do with people's art, then they're interesting. Some of those biographies are wonderful pictures of a period that is past. That's what history is.

LAWRENCE FRENCH: Unlike many actors, you don't seem to shy away from being in the public eye.

Vincent Price studio portrait (Photofest)

VINCENT PRICE: No, I'm really not the kind of actor who hides away. I think I've had a wonderful and very public life. It doesn't bother me at all to be recognized when I go out. The only people I can spot, like a bird-dog, are drunks. I see a drunk and I disappear, because they come up and ask you, "Who do you think you are?" Now that's a hard question to answer! (laughter) I was out one night with Robert Mitchum, we're great friends you know, and somebody came up to him and said, "Who do you think you are?" He went, (punches the air) "Bamm!" and they found out who he was (laughter). I think people feel in me a friend. I've done about 5,000 radio and television shows, some of which were very popular. These are things that are very personal to people, because you're coming into their homes. If you do a *Lucy Show*, people come up to you the next day and say, "I saw you on *The Lucy Show*." They don't do that with a movie. I've kept in the public eye all of my life, very definitely on purpose. I feel I have been closer to the public than most actors. I love my work and I love being associated with the public.

LAWRENCE FRENCH: And the public certainly enjoys your work. Thanks again for all your time.

On May 29th, 1991, two days after Vincent Price's 80th birthday, his beloved wife, Coral Browne, succumbed to a long battle with breast cancer. That fall, a memorial service was held at London's Farmers Church, with many of Miss Browne's friends from the theater and cinema in attendance, including actors Alan Bates and Alec Guinness, as well as director John Schlesinger (Schlesinger guided Coral Browne through her brilliant, award winning role in *An Englishman Abroad*). At the service, Schlesinger read a moving letter from Vincent Price, whose own frail health made it impossible for him to attend the memorial in person. Following is the text of Price's letter:

Coral Browne and Vincent Price (Photofest)

Dear John:

When I was courting Coral, the first gift she gave me was a photo of herself simply signed: "Remember Coral"—not really a challenge as the problem was: How could you forget her? I've come to believe remembering someone is not the highest compliment—it is missing them. I find I miss every hour of Coral's life—I miss her morning cloudiness, noon mellowness, evening brightness. I miss her in every corner of our house, every crevice of my life. In missing her, I feel I'm missing much of life itself. Over her long illness, as I held her hand or stroked her brow, or just lay still beside her, it was not the affectionate contact we'd known as we wandered down the glamorous paths we'd been privileged to share in our few years together; we were marching towards the end of our time and we both knew it. But, in our looks, our smiles, the private, few, soft-spoken words, there was hope of other places, other ways, perhaps, to meet again.

One fact of Coral I'll always miss: her many, many devoted friends—many here, today, in this beautiful church, celebrating her life more than mourning her death, and missing the liveliness of her wit, her personal beauty, her outgoing self. I love them all for loving her. Many of you have shared more of her life than I have, but that very private and intense passion for her is mine alone.

She survived that last long year on the love of her friends, their caring and concern—and very especially yours, dear John. I miss you all, and though we may not meet as often, nor in the great good company of my wife, you are in my memory locked.

All my love,
Vincent

TELEVISION CREDITS

As a regular:

Pantomime Quiz (CBS, 1950-1951, NBC, 1952)
A program based on the game of charades. Two teams composed of four competed against each others. Besides Vincent Price other regulars included such stars as Hans Conried, Adele Jergens and Jackie Coogan.
ESP (ABC, 1958)
The Hilarious House of Frightenstine (syndication, 1975)
Time Express (CBS, 1979)
Passengers aboard a train found themselves going back in time to pivotal points in their life. Vincent Price and his wife Coral Browne co-starred as a mysterious couple, Jason and Margaret, who escort the passengers. The show was on Thursday nights from 8:00 p.m. until 9:00 p.m.
Mystery (PBS, 1982-1989)
Vincent Price was host of the long running public television series from 1982 until 1989. The show brought classic mystery stories to television.

As a guest star:

Lux Video Theatre "The Promise" (CBS, 1951)
Lights Out "The Third Door" (NBC, 1951)
Lux Video Theatre "The Game of Chess" (CBS, 1952)
Summer Theatre "Dream Job" (ABC, 1953)
Schlitz Playhouse of Stars "Sheila" (CBS, 1952)
Philip Morris Playhouse "Bullet for a Stranger" (CBS, 1953)
Climax! "Night of Execution" (CBS, 1955)
Alcoa Hour "Sister" (NBC, 1956)
Science Fiction Theatre "One Thousand Eyes" (NBC, 1956)
The $64,000 Question (CBS, 1956)
Playhouse 90 "Forbidden Area" (CBS, 1956)
Crossroads "God's Healing" (ABC, 1956)
Washington Square (NBC, 1956)
Shower of Stars (CBS, 1957)
The Red Skelton Show (CBS, 1957)
The $64,000 Challenge (CBS, 1957)
Schlitz Playhouse of the Stars "The Blue Hotel" (CBS, 1957)
Odyssey: Revolution of the Eye (CBS, 1957)
Playhouse 90 "Lone Woman" (CBS, 1957)
G.E. Theatre "Angel in the Air" (CBS, 1958)
Schlitz Playhouse of Stars "The Kind Mr. Smith" (CBS, 1958)
The Jack Benny Program (CBS, 1958)
Matinee Theatre "Angel Street" (NBC, 1958)
The Jack Parr Show (NBC, 1958)
Person to Person (CBS, 1958)
Have Gun, Will Travel "The Moor's Revenge" (CBS, 1959)
The Jack Benny Program (CBS, 1959)
The Red Skelton Show (CBS, 1959)
The Red Skelton Show (CBS, 1960)
Startime "Tennessee Ernie Meets King Arthur" (NBC, 1960)
Chevy Mystery Show "Run-Around" (NBC, 1960)

Vincent Price puts his cooking talent to good use on *Dinah's Place*.

Here's Hollywood (NBC, 1960)
Family Classics "The Three Musketeers" (CBS, 1960)
U.S. Steel Hour "Shame the Devil" (CBS, 1960)
Tell It to Groucho (CBS, 1962)
Stump the Stars (CBS, 1963)
The Red Skelton Hour (CBS, 1964)
The Danny Kaye Show (CBS, 1965)
The Red Skelton Hour (CBS, 1965)
The Man from U.N.C.L.E. "The Foxes and the Hounds Affair" (NBC, 1965)
Batman "An Egg Grows in Gotham/The Yegg Foes in Gotham" (ABC, 1966)
F Troop "V is for Vampire" (ABC, 1967)
Voyage to the Bottom of the Sea "The Deadly Dolls" (ABC, 1967)
Batman "The Ogg and I/How to Hatch a Dinosaur" (ABC, 1967)
Batman "The Ogg Couple" (ABC, 1967)
The Mike Douglas Show (syndication, 1968)
Get Smart "Is This Trip Necessary" (CBS, 1969)
The Red Skelton Hour (CBS, 1970)
Love American Style "Love and the Haunted House" (ABC, 1970)
Here's Lucy "Lucy Cuts Vincent's Price" (CBS, 1970)
The Mod Squad "A Time for Hyacinths" (ABC, 1970)
Night Gallery "The Class of '99" (NBC, 1971)
Here Comes Peter Cottontail (ABC, 1972)
Night Gallery "The Return of the Sorcerer" (NBC, 1972)
The Carol Burnett Show (CBS, 1974)
The Brady Bunch "The Tiki Caves" (ABC, 1972)
Columbo "Lovely But Lethal" (NBC, 1973)

The Carol Burnett show (CBS, 1974)
The Snoop Sisters "A Black Day for Bluebeard" (NBC, 1974)
Hollywood Squares (syndication, 1975)
The Merv Griffin Show (syndication, 1975)
Joys (NBC, 1976)
Hollywood Squares (NBC, 1977)
The Captain and Tennille (ABC, 1977)
The Love Boat "Ship of Ghouls" (ABC, 1978)
Freddy the Freeloader's Christmas Dinner (HBO, 1981)
Blacke's Magic "Wax Poetic" (NBC, 1986)

Television movies and miniseries:
What's a Nice Girl Like You...? (ABC, 1971)

Mr. Price was also a frequent talk show guest, even demonstrating his cooking skills on *Dinah's Place*.

Patrica Morison and Vincent Price in *Have Gun Will Travel*. (Photofest)

In July of 1998, Greg Mank met Patricia Morison, foxy villainess of such 1940s melodramas as *Calling Dr. Death* and *Dressed to Kill* and the legendary star of Broadway's *Kiss Me Kate*. Ms. Morison had been Helen Hayes' understudy in Broadway's *Victoria Regina* (1935/1936), in which Vincent Price had played Prince Albert. Naturally Ms. Morison watched every performance, and knew Price's death scene (which he delivered partly in German!) by heart.

In 1958 Patricia Morison and Vincent Price were reunited for "The Moor's Revenge," an episode of TV's *Have Gun Will Travel*. She amazed Vincent by reciting for him his entire *Victoria Regina* death scene!

P.S. Patricia Morison can still recite it!

FILMOGRAPHY

Service De Luxe
Director: Rowland V. Lee; Universal, 1938
Cast: Constance Bennett, Vincent Price (Robert Wade); Charlie Ruggles, Helen Broderick, Halliwell Hobbes
Vincent Price stars as an inventor who romances Constance Bennett in this comedy.

The Private Lives of Elizabeth and Essex
Director: Michael Curtiz; Warner Bros.; 1939
Cast: Bette Davis, Errol Flynn, Olivia de Havilland, Vincent Price (Sir Walter Raleigh); Henry Daniell
The romance of Queen Elizabeth and the Earl of Essex is given the Hollywood treatment.

Tower of London (see chapter)

The Invisible Man Returns (see chapter)

Green Hell
Director: James Whale; Universal; 1940
Cast: Douglas Fairbanks, Jr.; Joan Bennett; George Sanders, Alan Hale, Vincent Price (David Richardson)
Price portrays a man in love with two different women and so joins an expedition to the Amazon. While chasing natives, he is shot with a poison arrow and dies. Many critics said he should consider himself lucky for exiting the film so early while the other actors had to endure the entire script.

The House of the Seven Gables (see chapter)

Brigham Young
Director: Henry Hathaway; 20th Century-Fox; 1940
Cast: Tyrone Power, Linda Darnell, Dean Jagger, Brain Donlevy, Jane Darwell, John Carradine, Mary Astor, Vincent Price (Joseph Smith)
Vincent Price portrays Morman founder Joseph Smith who is assassinated in this all-star biopic of Brigham Young.

Hudson's Bay
Director: Irving Pichel; 20th Century-Fox; 1941
Cast: Paul Muni, Gene Tierney, Laird Cregar, John Sutton, Vincent Price (King Charles II)
The first film for Price with soon-to-be frequent co-stars Gene Tierney and John Sutton. The story concerns French-Canadian explorer Pierre Esprit Radisson.

The Song of Bernadette (see chapter)

The Eve of St. Mark
Director: John M. Stahl; 20th Century-Fox; 1944
Cast: Anne Baxter, William Eythe, Vincent Price (Pvt. Francis Marion), Henry Morgan
A change of pace for Vincent Price as he portrayed a soldier fighting in the trenches. Many critics consider this his finest role.

Wilson

Director: Henry King; 20th Century-Fox; 1944

Cast: Alexander Knox, Charles Coburn, Thomas Mitchell, Sir Cedric Hardwicke, Vincent Price (William Gibbs McAdoo)

Wilson was the baby of producer Darryl F. Zanuck and although the film won several Academy Awards it was a disaster financially. Price portrayed the secretary of the treasury and the son-in-law of President Wilson. Dwight Frye was thrilled to receive a part in the film, but died before he could begin filming.

Laura (see chapter)

The Keys of the Kingdom

Director: John M. Stahl; 20th Century-Fox; 1944

Cast: Gregory Peck, Thomas Mitchell, Vincent Price (Dr. Willie Tulloch), Roddy McDowall

Vincent Price portrays the boyhood friend of Father Francis Chisholm (Peck) who gave up everything to do missionary work in China.

A Royal Scandal

Director: Otto Preminger; 20th Century-Fox; 1945

Cast: Tallulah Bankhead, Charles Coburn, Anne Baxter, William Eythe, Vincent Price (Marquis de Fleury)

Otto Preminger would again direct Vincent Price, this time in the fictionalized biopic of Catherine the Great. Price portrays the French ambassador.

Leave Her to Heaven (see chapter)

Shock

Director: Alfred Werker; 20th Century-Fox; 1946

Cast: Vincent Price (Dr. Dick Cross), Lynn Bari, Frank Latimore, Anabel Shaw

Price plays a murderer who tries to convince a witness she is going mad.

Dragonwyck (see chapter)

The Web

Director: Michael Gordon; Universal-International; 1947

Cast: Ella Raines, Edmond O'Brien, William Bendix, Vincent Price (Andrew Colby), Fritz Leiber

Price is once again cast as a villain in this thriller. He appears as a wealthy businessman who frames his partner and resorts to murder.

Moss Rose

Director: Gregory Ratoff; 20th Century-Fox; 1947

Cast: Peggy Cummings, Victor Mature, Ethel Barrymore, Vincent Price (Inspector Clinner); George Zucco

This time Price is on the right side of the law as he portrays a police detective investigating a murder.

The Long Night

Director: Anatole Litvak; RKO; 1947

Cast: Henry Fonda, Barbara Bel Geddes, Vincent Price (Maximilian), Ann Dvorak

Price stars as a magician whose influence over Bel Geddes is upsetting to her lover Henry Fonda. Price is killed by Fonda.

Mary Grant (Price's wife whom he met on this film), Vincent Price and Deanna Durbin relax during filming of *Up in Central Park*.

Up in Central Park

Director: William A. Seiter; Universal-International; 1948

Cast: Deanna Durbin, Dick Haymes, Vincent Price (Boss Tweed); Thurston Hall

America's sweetheart, Deanna Durbin, starred with Price is this fictionalized story of Boss Tweed and his wooing of a young girl (Durbin). Price met his future wife Mary on this film.

Abbott and Costello Meet Frankenstein

Director: Charles T. Barton; Universal-International; 1948

Cast: Bela Lugosi, Glen Strange, Bud Abbott, Lou Costello, Vincent Price (the Invisible Man)

Price's well-known voice is put to use in the finale of the film when he spooks Abbott and Costello.

Rogues' Regiment

Director: Robert Florey; Universal-International; 1948

Cast: Dick Powell, Marta Toren, Vincent Price (Mark Van Ratten)

Price stars as another scoundrel, this time as a German gunrunner.

The Three Musketeers (see chapter)

The Bribe

Director: Robert Z. Leonard; MGM; 1949

Cast: Robert Taylor, Ava Gardner, Charles Laughton, Vincent Price (Carwood), John Hodiak

Price appears as a black marketeer in the Caribbean.

Vincent Price and Bob Hope in *Casanova's Big Night*.

Bagdad (see chapter)

Champagne for Caesar (see chapter)

The Baron of Arizona (see chapter)

Curtain Call at Cactus Creek
Director: Charles Lamont; Universal-International, 1950
Cast: Donald O'Connor, Gale Storm, Walter Brennan, Vincent Price (Tracy Holland)
     Price appears as the leader of a traveling theatrical troupe who are joined by outlaw Brennan hoping to evade the law.

His Kind of Woman (see chapter)

Adventures of Captain Fabian
Director: William Marshall; Republic, 1951
Cast: Errol Flynn, Micheline Prelle, Vincent Price (George Brissac); Agnes Moorehead
     Price vies with Errol Flynn for the love of Prelle.

The Las Vegas Story
Director: Robert Stevenson; RKO; 1952
Cast: Jane Russell, Victor Mature; Vincent Price (Lloyd Rollins), Hoagy Carmichael
     Price again stars with Jane Russell. He portrays another cad, an embezzler who is falsely accused of murder.

House of Wax (see chapter)

Dangerous Mission
Director: Louis King; RKO; 1954
Cast: Victor Mature, Piper Laurie, William Bendix, Vincent Price (Paul Adams)
     Price is a hitman sent after Piper Laurie in this thriller.

Casanova's Big Night
Director: Norman Z. McLeod; Paramount, 1954
Cast: Bob Hope, Joan Fontaine, Audrey Dalton, Basil Rathbone, John Carradine, Vincent Price
(Casanova)
 Price appears in the beginning of this Hope comedy as the real Casanova who is forced to
flee Parma. When Casanova is offered a high reward for seducing Dalton, his servant (Rathbone)
with the help of Fontaine and Hope, tries to pass off Hope as Casanova.

The Mad Magician
Director: John Brahm; Columbia; 1954
Cast: Vincent Price (Don Gallico), Mary Murphy, Eva Gabor, John Emry
 Price stars as a magician whose tricks are stolen by another magician. He goes off the deep
end and resorts to a vengeful killing spree.

Son of Sinbad
Director: Ted Tetzlaff; RKO; 1955
Cast: Dale Robertson, Sally Forrest, Lili St. Cyr, Vincent Price (Omar Khayyam)
 Price portrays best pal of Sinbad (Robertson).

Serenade
Director: Anthony Mann; Warner Bros.; 1956
Cast: Mario Lanza, Joan Fontaine, Vincent Price (Charles Winthrop)
 Price portrays a concert manager. Lanza is a working-class opera singer seduced by Fontaine.

While the City Sleeps (see chapter)

The Ten Commandments
Director: Cecil B. DeMille; Paramount, 1956
Cast: Charlton Heston, Yul Brynner, Anne Baxter, Edward G. Robinson, Yvonne De Carlo, Debra
Paget, Vincent Price (Baka), John Carradine
 Price is a murder victim for a change as he portrays the carpenter to the pharaoh.

The Story of Mankind
Director: Irwin Allen; Warner Bros., 1957
Cast: Ronald Colman, Hedy Lamarr, the Marx Brothers, Virginia Mayo, Agnes Moorehead,
Peter Lorre, Vincent Price (Mr. Scratch)
 Price is the devil who argues his case against Ronald Colman in this all-star extravaganza.

The Fly (see chapter)

House on Haunted Hill (see chapter)

The Big Circus
Director: Joseph M. Newman; Allied Artists; 1959
Cast: Victor Mature, Red Buttons, Rhonda Fleming, Vincent Price (Hans Hagenfeld), Peter Lorre
 Price is ringmaster in a down-on-its-luck circus.

Return of the Fly (see chapter)

The Tingler (see chapter)

Vincent Price stars in *The Bat*.

The Bat
Director: Crane Wilbur; Allied Artists; 1959
Cast: Vincent Price (Dr. Malcolm Wells), Agnes Moorehead, Gavin Gordon, John Sutton
    Price would work again with Agnes Moorehead as well as John Sutton in this mystery-comedy. Once again, he is a murderer.

The Fall of the House of Usher (see chapter)

Master of the World (see chapter)

Pit and the Pendulum (see chapter)

Convicts 4
Director: Millard Kaufman; Allied Artists; 1963
Cast: Ben Gazzara, Stuart Whitman, Ray Walston, Vincent Price (Carl Carmer)
    In true-to-life casting, Price portrays an art critic who discovers a new talent who is serving time in prison.

Tales of Terror
Director: Roger Corman; AIP; 1962
Cast: Vincent Price, Peter Lorre, Basil Rathbone, Debra Paget
    Price appears in three different horror stories based on the work of Edgar Allan Poe. "Morella," "The Black Cat" and "The Case of Mr. Valdemar" all feature Price. (See chapter for a more in-depth look at "Morella.")

Confessions of an Opium Eater
Director: Albert Zugsmith; Allied Artists; 1962
Cast: Vincent Price (Gil de Quincey), Linda Ho, Philip Ahn, Richard Loo
    Price headlines as an adventurer who infiltrates the Tongs in San Francisco and rescues slave girls.

Tower of London (see chapter)

The Raven (see chapter)

Diary of a Madman
Director: Reginald LeBorg; United Artists; 1963
Cast: Vincent Price (Simon Cordier), Nancy Kovack, Chris Warfield
    Price is a French magistrate who is possessed by a man he killed in self-defense. He must kill himself to destroy the spirit.

Rage of the Buccaneers
Director: Mario Costa; Colorama Features; 1963
Cast: Ricardo Montalban, Vincent Price (Romero) Guilia Rubini
    Price is leader of a slave trade who overthrows the governor only to be defeated by ex-slave Montalban.

The Haunted Palace
Director: Roger Corman; AIP; 1963
Cast: Vincent Price (Charles Dexter Ward/Joseph Curwen), Debra Paget, Lon Chaney, Elisha Cook
    Price stars as a warlock who is burned at the stake, but not before proclaiming he will return to have his revenge. Many years later, his great-great grandson (Price) returns to the town and slowly becomes possessed by his ancestor's spirit. He goes on a killing spree and is about to sacrifice his wife when the castle is burned and the possession is broken.

Twice-Told Tales
Director: Sidney Salkow, United Artists; 1963
Cast: Vincent Price, Sebastian Cabot, Beverly Garland, Richard Denning
    Price again stars in a trilogy of horror tales, this time they are based on Nathaniel Hawthorne stories: "Dr. Heidegger's Experiment," "Rappaccini's Daughter" and "The House of the Seven Gables."

The Comedy of Terrors
(see chapter)

Queen of the Nile
Director: Fernando Cerchio; Max; 1964
Cast: Jeanne Crain, Vincent Price (Benakon), Edmund Purdom
    Price portrays a power-hungry Egyptian who forces his daughter to marry the unbalanced ruler of the country. Price kills a priest which drives the ruler to suicide. His daughter takes over and Price is done in by a Gypsy girl.

Vincent Price and Lon Chaney in *The Haunted Palace*.

Vincent Price in *Dr. Goldfoot and the Girl Bombs*.

The Last Man on Earth (see chapter)

The Masque of the Red Death (see chapter)

The Tomb of Ligeia (see chapter)

War-Gods of the Deep
Director: Jacques Tourneur; AIP; 1965
Cast: Vincent Price (Sir Hugh Tregathion), Tab Hunter, Susan Hart
    Last film helmed by Lewton alumnus Tourneur finds Price as the ruler of an undersea kingdom who sends henchmen to kidnap the above-water Hart who resembles his dead wife.

Dr. Goldfoot and the Bikini Machine
Director: Norman Taurog; AIP; 1965
Cast: Vincent Price (Dr. Goldfoot), Frankie Avalon, Dwayne Hickman, Susan Hart
    AIP cashed in on the popularity of Bond films with this spoof that has Price manufacturing girl robots to seduce the world's most rich and powerful men.

Dr. Goldfoot and the Girl Bombs
Director: Mario Bava; AIP; 1966
Cast: Vincent Price (Dr. Goldfoot), Fabian, Ciccio Ingrassi, Franco Franchi
    Goldfoot is at it again, but this time his female robots explode when they seduce leaders of NATO.

The Jackals
Director: Robert D. Webb; 20th Century-Fox; 1967
Cast: Vincent Price (Oupa), Diana Ivarson, Robert Gunner
 Price portrays a South African gold miner who is terrorized by outlaws.

House of a Thousand Dolls
Director: Jeremy Summers; AIP; 1967
Cast: Vincent Price (Felix Manderville), Martha Hyer, George Nader
 Price is once again a magician but this time he kidnaps girls for a slave ring.

Witchfinder General (see chapter)

More Dead Than Alive
Director: Robert Sparr; United Artists; 1968
Cast: Clint Walker, Vincent Price (Dan Ruffalo), Anne Francis
 Price stars as the owner of a Wild West show who is killed by his sharpshooter.

The Trouble With Girls
Director: Peter Tewksbury; MGM; 1969
Cast: Elvis Presley, Marlyn Mason, Sheree North, Anissa Jones, Vincent Price (Mr. Morality), John Carradine
 Price appears as Mr. Morality in a traveling Chautauqua. His lecture on morality causes North to rethink her relationship with a married man. This leads to his murder and her confession on stage. Presley is only given a few songs to sing but really gets to cut loose on "Swing Low, Sweet Chariot." This number makes us long for more musical interludes and less emoting from the actors. Price is only on-screen a short time, but as always is fun to watch.

The Oblong Box
Director: Gordon Hessler; AIP; 1969
Cast: Vincent Price (Julian Markham), Christopher Lee, Alister Williamson, Rupert Davies
 Williamson, who has been mutilated by African natives and has gone mad, urges his brother (Price) to lock him up. Williamson manages to arrange his escape and sets about terrorizing the surrounding area.

Scream and Scream Again (see chapter)

Cry of the Banshee (see chapter)

The Abominable Dr. Phibes (see chapter)

Dr. Phibes Rises Again (see chapter)

Theater of Blood (see chapter)

Madhouse (see chapter)

It's Not the Size That Counts
Director: Ralph Thomas; EMI; 1974
Cast: Leigh Lawson, Elke Sommer, Denholm Elliott, Judy Geeson, Vincent Price (Stavros Mammonian)
 Price appears as the richest man in the world who kidnaps Percy (Lawson). Because of a chemical in the water, Lawson is the only man alive who is not impotent in this British comedy.

Journey Into Fear
Director: Daniel Mann; Stirling Gold; 1975
Cast: Sam Waterston, Zero Mostel, Yvette Mimieux, Shelley Winters, Vincent Price (Dervos)
   Price appears as a mercenary who hires a hit man to bump off Waterston.

Scavenger Hunt
Director: Michael Schultz; 20th Century-Fox; 1979
Cast: Richard Benjamin, James Coco, Scatman Crothers, Ruth Gordon, Roddy McDowall, Vincent Price (Milton Parker)
   Price is in the film a few short minutes. He portrays board game tycoon Milton Parker (a combination of Parker Brothers and Milton Bradley) who devises a scavenger hunt for his fortune-seeking relatives to participate in after his death.

The Monster Club
Director: Roy Ward Baker; ITC; 1981
Cast: Vincent Price (Eramus), Donald Pleasence, John Carradine
   Price plays a vampire who takes horror writer Carradine to a club where monsters hang out. Price relates three stories to Carradine, none in which he appears.

House of the Long Shadows (see chapter)

Bloodbath at the House of Death
Director: Ray Cameron; Goldfarb; 1984
Cast: Kenny Everett, Pamela Stephenson, Vincent Price (Sinister Man)
   Price appears as a Satanic cult leader in this convoluted horror/comedy film.

The Great Mouse Detective (see chapter)

The Offspring (see chapter)

The Whales of August (see chapter)

Dead Heat
Director: Mark Goldblatt; New World; 1988
Cast: Treat Williams, Joe Piscopo, Darren McGavin, Vincent Price (Arthur P. Loudermilk)
   Horror/comedy that fails to deliver as either a comedy or a horror film. Price portrays a dying millionaire who is seeking eternal life.

Backtrack (see chapter)

Edward Scissorhands (see chapter)

The Heart of Justice (see chapter)

Arabian Knight
Director: Richard Williams; Miramax; 1995
Cast (voices): Vincent Price (Zigzag), Jennifer Beals, Matthew Broderick, Jonathan Winters
   Although Price recorded the vocal track for this film in 1973, it was not released until 1995. Price voices the villain Zigzag, advisor to King Nod.

SELECTED BIBLIOGRAPHY

Arkoff, Samuel: *Flying Through Hollywood by the Seat of My Pants*, Birch Lane Press, New York, NY, 1992

Bartel, Pauline: *Reel Elvis*, Taylor Publishing Company, Dallas, TX, 1994

Brooks, Tim; Marsh, Earle: *The Complete Directory to Prime Time Network TV Shows*, Ballentine Books, New York, NY, 1988

Brunas, John; Brunas, Michael; Weaver, Tom: *Universal Horrors*, McFarland and Company, Jefferson, NC, 1990

Inman, David: *The TV Encyclopedia*, Perigee Books, New York, NY, 1991

Parish, James Robert; Steve Whitney: *Vincent Price Unmasked*, Drake Publishers, New York, NY, 1974

Roy, Sue; Taylor, Al: *Making a Monster*, Crown Publishers, Inc., New York, NY 1980

Silverman, Kenneth: *Edgar A. Poe: Mournful and Never-ending Remembrance*, HarperCollins, 1991

Stanley, John: *Creature Feature Movie Guide Strikes Again*, Creatures at Large, 1994

Thomas, Tony: *The Films of Gene Kelly*, Citadel Press, Secaucus, NJ, 1974

Weaver, Tom: *SF and Fantasy Film Flashbacks*, McFarland and Company, Jefferson, NC

Weaver, Tom: *Attack of the Monster Movie Makers*, McFarland and Company, Jefferson, NC, 1994

Williams, Lucy Chase: *The Complete Films of Vincent Price*, Citadel Press, Secaucus, NJ, 1995

If you enjoyed this book you will also enjoy the following books in the Midnight Marquee Actors Series.

For more information or to place an order call 410-665-1198
or write:
Midnight Marquee Press, Inc.
9721 Britinay Lane
Baltimore, MD 21234

AUTHORS

Marty Baumann is the award-winning designer/editor of the webzine *The Astounding B Monster*: http://www.bmonster.com and a contributor to *Midnight Marquee* magazine.

Paul Castiglia works for Archie Comic Publications, Inc. as well as being a freelance comic writer. He is currently working on a screenplay.

Mark Clark is a contributor to *Midnight Marquee* magazine and is working on his first book on horror films.

Bruce Dettman is a San Francisco-based writer whose film-related articles have appeared in *Filmfax, The Monster Times, Fangoria*, and *Good Old Days*. He is also co-author of *The Horror Factory*.

Lawrence French is a film author/historian who has written for *Filmfax* and *Cinefantastique*.

Martin Grams, Jr. is the author of *Suspense: Twenty Years of Thrills and Chills* and co-author of McFarland's *The CBS Radio Mystery Theater: An Episode Guide and Handbook to Nine Years of Broadcasting, 1974—1982*.

Dennis Fischer is the author of *Horror Film Directors* (McFarland) and contributes to *Midnight Marquee, Filmfax* and *Cinefantastique*.

David J. Hogan is the author of *Who's Who of the Horrors and Other Fantasy Films, Dark Romance: Sexuality in the Horror Film* and *Your Movie Guide to Drama Video Tapes and Discs*. He contributes to *Cinefantastique, Filmfax* and *Moviegoer*.

Tom Johnson is co-author of *Peter Cushing: The Gentle Man of Horror* and is working on a book on the films of Christopher Lee. He would like to thank Bob Madison, Mark Miller, Louis Paul (Lincoln Center Library for the Performing Arts), Randy Vest, Tom Weaver, Carol Werner, and Lucy Chase Williams (*The Films of Vincent Price*).

Jonathan Malcolm Lampley is a frequent contributor to *Midnight Marquee* and has written for *Movie Club*.

Mark A. Miller dedicates his chapter to the memory of Andrew Starinchak. "I trust, Andrew, that even now you are teaching the angels a thing or two about Rugby. You are missed here." He would like to thank Paul M. Jensen. Thanks also to Brett Miller, the late Lucille Miller (who introduced him to Poe), Ron and Sherry Miller, Teresa Miller, Frederick C. Peerenboom (Fritz the Nite Owl), Patty Musgrove, David Walker and those wonderful librarians of Gahanna Lincoln High School (OH).

Scott Allen Nollen is the author of *Robert Louis Stevenson: Life, Literature and the Silver Screen* and *Sir Arthur Conan Doyle at the Cinema*. He has spent more than two decades researching the life and career of Boris Karloff, a quest that resulted in two books: *Boris Karloff: A Critical Account of His Screen, Stage, Radio, Television and Recording Work* (for McFarland) and *Boris Karloff: A Gentleman's Life*, the definitive authorized biography, for Midnight Marquee Press. He recently finished another book for McFarland, *Robin Hood: A Cinematic History of the English Outlaw and His Scottish Counterparts, William Wallace and Rob Roy MacGregor*, and currently is writing *The Cinema of Sinatra* for Midnight Marquee. Meeting Vincent Price in 1980 remains one of the most memorable events of his life.

John E. Parnum has been a contributor to nearly a dozen Midnight Marquee books. He has been writing articles for magazines as far back as *Photon* and *The Monster Times*. Of major importance to him in his research is his collection of over 75 scrapbooks that contain reviews of horror, fantasy, and science-fiction films, which he has been adding to since the early 1950s. He resides in a nightmare museum in Wayne, PA, with his wife Edie and a python named Monty. Acknowledgments: Many thanks to Laura Parnum for her editing of my two chapters in this book.

Michael H. Price is a veteran crime journalist, newspaper editor, and film and music critic, recently turned to the movie-theater business. His books include *Jazz Guitars* (with James Sallis; University of Nebraska Press); *Human Monsters: The Bizarre Psychology of Movie Villains* (with George E. Turner; Kitchen Sink Press); and a newly issued anthology called *Southern-Fried Homicide* (Cremo Studios/Shel-Tone Publications). Price and George Turner also are responsible for *Forgotten Horrors*, the definitive history of the Depression Years' wealth of low-budget horror films—due presently in a revised and expanded edition from Midnight Marquee Press.

Bryan Senn is the co-author of *Fantastic Cinema Subject Guide* and author of *Golden Horrors* and *Drums of Terror: Voodoo in the Cinema*.

David H. Smith has contributed to *Midnight Marquee Actors Series': Boris Karloff, Lon Chaney, Jr.* and *Bela Lugosi*. He would like to say special thanks to Lucy Chase Williams for her gracious correspondence while researching this chapter.

Don G. Smith is the author of *Lon Chaney, Jr.* (McFarland) and *The Cinema of Edgar Allan Poe*. He also contributes to *Midnight Marquee* magazine.

John Stell is the author of *Psychos, Sickos and Sequels: Horror Films of the 1980s*. He also contributes to *Monsters from the Vault* and *Midnight Marquee*.

Gary J. Svehla has contributed to *Midnight Marquee Actors Series': Boris Karloff, Bela Lugosi* and *Lon Chaney, Jr.* as well as contributing to many other MidMar titles and editing Midnight Marquee magazine.

Susan Svehla is co-editor of *Midnight Marquee* magazine and has contributed to *Guilty Pleasures* and *It's Christmas Time at the Movies*.

Nathalie Yafet lives in New Jersey with her husband Steven. She is originally from Wisconsin where she saw Vincent Price on stage in *Charley's Aunt*, as Oscar Wilde in *Diversions and Delights* and in *The Villain Still Pursues Me*. Nathalie reviewed the last two shows and had the privilege of meeting the very kind and gracious Mr. Price, a memory she will always cherish.

INDEX